SCHAUM'S OUTLINE OF

THEORY AND PROBLEMS

OF

Introduction to
COMPUTER SCIENCE

•

BY

FRANCIS SCHEID

Professor of Mathematics
Boston University

•

SCHAUM'S OUTLINE SERIES

McGRAW-HILL BOOK COMPANY

New York, St. Louis, San Francisco, Düsseldorf, Johannesburg, Kuala Lumpur, London, Mexico,
Montreal, New Delhi, Panama, Rio de Janeiro, Singapore, Sydney, and Toronto

07-055195-2

14 15 SH SH 8 7 6 5 4 3

Preface

Today even first graders know that computers can do fantastic things, that for certain purposes at least computers are truly superhuman, one computer being more than a match for a million human rivals. The fundamental question facing any beginner in computer science asks just how it is that electricity can be trained to such a spectacular level of performance. The answer can be compressed into two words, *hardware* and *software*. Computer hardware involves circuits, memory units, reading and writing devices. An elementary description of these things, requiring no background in electricity or engineering, is presented in Chapters 1 to 4. No effort is made to tell the whole story, only to suggest the underlying ideas. Computer software means programming, and this aspect of the subject is treated in Chapters 5 to 14. The book thus divides into two parts which are almost entirely independent of each other. This means that it may be used in several different ways.

1. *A short study of programming* may be based on Chapters 7 and 8, with further examples drawn from later chapters as desired.

2. *A longer study of programming* may include most of the material in Chapters 7 to 14. Not all of the longer programming examples need be taken in detail. A few in particular, such as the scheduling program of Chapter 11 and the checkers program of Chapter 14, may be omitted entirely without losing continuity. It would be a shame not to find time for the quite different Chapter 5.

3. *A general introduction to computer science* is available by undertaking the entire book. Here again there is the option of omitting some of the longer programming examples, with the further option of abbreviating the hardware presentation as well. This could be done, for example, by selecting just a few samples from Chapter 3 and taking Chapter 4 only up to Problem 4.22 or perhaps 4.36. The main purpose, of seeing how electricity can be trained, will still have been achieved. For those who want to deepen their study of the subject a bibliography is appended.

All the Fortran programs in this book were tested on the IBM 7090/7094 at the Ecole Polytechnique of the University of Lausanne, Switzerland, where it has been a genuine pleasure to spend my sabbatical leave. I am very grateful to Professor Blanc, director of the computing center, for this opportunity and have expressed a liquid merci with an offering of vin blanc Vaudois. Unless copying errors have been made, all programs should work. A few in later chapters, notably those in which random numbers are generated, include statements designed particularly to be used on the Lausanne machine. The changes needed to adapt such programs to other machines are minor and local experts will be happy to demonstrate their talents in making them. It is also possible that some of the programs can be improved and suggestions will be welcomed.

To better mutual understanding between man and machine,

FRANCIS SCHEID

CONTENTS

Chapter 1

Information Processing

Computer science involves the development and use of devices for processing information. Information in one form is presented to the device and information in another, presumably more useful, form is required from it. The former is called the input information; it is the raw material of the process. The latter is the output information, the finished product. (Fig. 1-1.)

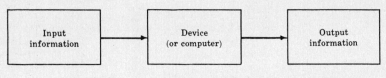

Fig. 1-1

Information is not an easy word to define with precision. It is related somehow to ideas and meaning, and can be communicated between intelligent sources as well as processed or converted into different forms. Part of the difficulty is that information may be presented in a variety of languages. Unless one understands the language the information may be meaningless or "uninformative". Several languages will be used as we proceed, some of which were designed specifically to be understood by electrical machines, or computers. Such machines do exhibit certain aspects of intelligence. At least, they are capable of receiving and processing information. The extent of machine intelligence, whether the processing they perform can be called "thinking", the potential capability of machines of the future and their relationship with the human population of this planet, such issues suggest the more exotic levels of our subject. Most of our time and energy will be devoted to the simpler aspects of computer science today, but at times it will be interesting to speculate about its future.

Example 1.1.

What is the product 12×43? This question serves as the input information for the present example. Elementary school students soon learn a routine for discovering the answer to the question and thus they serve as the device which processes this input information, perhaps as follows.

$$
\begin{array}{r}
12 \\
43 \\
\hline
36 \\
48 \\
\hline
516
\end{array}
$$

The output information is the number 516. There are of course many other ways of finding the same result, and this is typical of computer science. Here, for example, one could always arrange twelve 43's in a column and obtain the same 516 by addition. There is also the method of continually doubling one factor while halving the other, ignoring remainders until a 1 is produced.

12	43	√	12	43
6	86	√	24	21
3	172 √		48	10
1	344 √	√	96	5
			192	2
		√	384	1

1

Where remainders occur, the doubled factors (shown checked) are then added together. The sum will be 516. By any of these methods the human computer may process the input information (12×43) and generate the output information (516) as summarized in Fig. 1-2. It is worth noting that someone unfamiliar with decimal symbols for numbers or with decimal procedures of computation would find no meaning in any of the information involved in this example.

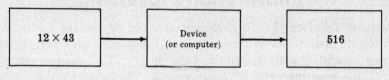

Fig. 1-2

Example 1.2.

Arrange the names JOHN, JOAN, JILL, JACK, FRED in alphabetical order. These five names, together with the instruction to alphabetize them, are a form of information, the input information of the present example. For anyone, or any device, familiar with the particular alphabet (or language) involved it is no severe challenge to process this information and achieve the output shown in Fig. 1-3.

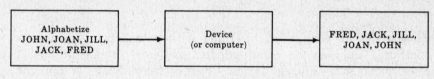

Fig. 1-3

Example 1.3.

Find the largest number in the set consisting of 43, 12, 47, 31, 44, 25, 46, 39. The eye will quickly pick out the number 47, a few visual comparisons being enough to identify it. In a set including several thousand numbers it is conceivable that the eye might be outperformed by some other device, but here it is clearly adequate. Here again a human computer familiar with decimal language and with the meaning of largest number can perform the required information processing. Fig. 1-4 summarizes the flow of information.

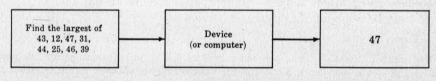

Fig. 1-4

A computer, for our purposes, will be an electrical device, or machine, which processes information. No knowledge of electricity will be needed except for a few very primitive ideas, such as that a wire may at one time be carrying a current and at another time may not. These two states of the wire will be called hot and cold, respectively. It is this basic fact, that two easily identifiable electrical states exist, which has been exploited to represent information in forms "understandable" by electrical machines. Our purpose in the first part of this book will be to examine some of the details of this exploitation, to see *how it is that human beings and electrical machines can both understand the same information processing efforts,* or to put it loosely, to watch the machines think. We will look only for the general view, the precise electrical details being left to the engineers.

The language for an electrical machine, or computer, will thus be based on hot and cold values, rather than on decimal symbols or alphabets. For example, if alternate hot and cold values are introduced to a wire by turning the current on and off, the wire's experiences may be recorded as

1 0 1 0 1 0 1

where for our own human understanding 1 means hot and 0 means cold. The wire itself will understand, so to speak, the actual current pulses and has no need for our symbols. The sequence

$$0\ 0\ 0\ 0\ 0\ 1\ 1$$

means similarly that five cold values are followed by two hots. In such sequences we have the beginning of a language that can be understood by both man and machine.

An OR circuit is a very simple but very useful electrical device. As shown in Fig. 1-5 it receives input information at two contacts and presents output information at one contact. Its function may be described by saying that the output is cold only when both inputs are cold. This is also shown by the four-value sequences appearing in the diagram. The input

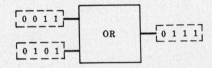

Fig. 1-5

values are received in pairs and only the 0, 0 pair produces a 0 output. It is important to notice that these two input sequences have been carefully selected so that all possible input combinations are included; both contacts may be cold (0 and 0), both hot (1 and 1), or one hot and the other cold (1 and 0, or 0 and 1). There are no other possible input combinations. There is also here a first suggestion that timing is important. Each input pair must be received simultaneously, and the OR circuit must have time to produce the correct output before the next input pair appears. The OR circuit may be viewed as our first electrical device for information processing, our first computer. As already noted it is a very simple one.

Example 1.4.

An OR circuit processes the two seven-value sequences presented a moment ago as shown in Fig. 1-6. The output sequence is 1010111. Comparing with Fig. 1-1 one sees that the pattern is the same; information is being processed. Both we and the electrical device agree that simultaneous cold values occur in only two positions.

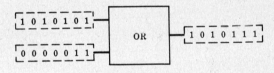

Fig. 1-6

Example 1.5.

An old-fashioned but easily understood OR circuit is shown in Fig. 1-7. A power source is trying to move current to the indicated output contact, through either of the two switches which are shown in the open position. Either switch may be closed by energizing the companion magnet (shown as a coil) and this is done by making the appropriate input contact hot. Only when both input contacts are cold will current fail to flow, since then both switches remain in the open position. More modern OR circuits use vacuum tubes, transistors or other devices.

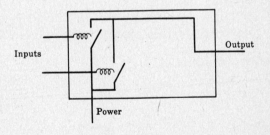

Fig. 1-7. An OR circuit.

An AND circuit is another simple but useful electrical device, or computer. Like the OR circuit it receives input information at two contacts and presents output information at one. Its function may be described by saying that the output will be hot only when both inputs are hot. This is also shown by the sequences appearing in Fig. 1-8, which once again include

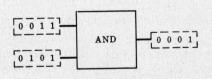

Fig. 1-8

the only possible input combinations. Only the 1, 1 combination produces a hot output. The AND circuit is our second electrical information processor.

Example 1.6.

An AND circuit processes the two sequences of Example 1.4 as shown in Fig. 1-9. The output information is the sequence 0000001. Both we and the machine arrive at this same result; simultaneous hot inputs occur only in the last position.

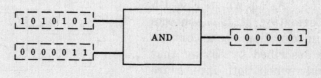

Fig. 1-9

Example 1.7.

An old-fashioned AND circuit is shown in Fig. 1-10. As with the OR circuit a power source is trying to move current to the output contact, but here it is clear that both switches must be closed if this is to occur. Closing these switches is achieved by making the input contacts hot, so only when both are hot simultaneously will current flow and produce a hot output.

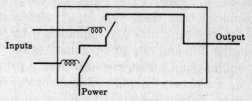

Fig. 1-10. An AND circuit.

The names OR and AND which are traditionally applied to the two circuits just introduced were originally suggested by the fact that for the first a hot output will occur if either one *or* the other (or both) of the input contacts is made hot, while for the second a hot output occurs only when both one input *and* the other are hot simultaneously. These circuits have important logical applications which will be mentioned in Chapter 3. They also prove to be fundamental in the design of more complex machines for handling arithmetical and other types of problems.

A NOT circuit has one input contact and one output. The two contacts always have opposite values. Fig. 1-11 expresses this same fact by showing that the sequence 01, which includes the only two input values possible, is processed into 10. The name NOT is obviously inspired by the fact that the output is hot precisely when the input is *not*, and vice versa. This circuit is heavily involved with OR and AND in the design of more complex devices.

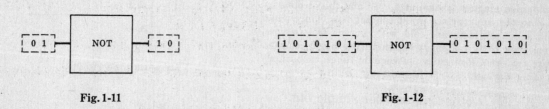

Fig. 1-11   Fig. 1-12

Example 1.8.

A NOT circuit processes the alternating sequence of Example 6 as shown in Fig. 1-12. Though this is information processing at a rather primitive level, the point is that the electrical circuit does "understand" what it is doing. The language involved is the one language which such a device can handle. Moreover, once again we and the machine agree on the result; we both understand the nature of the information processing involved. Achieving higher and higher levels of understanding between man and machine is one of the larger tasks of computer science.

Example 1.9.

An old-fashioned NOT circuit is shown in Fig. 1-13. Here the switch will be assumed to be naturally closed, rather than naturally open as in Figs. 1-7 and 1-10. A hot input will energize the magnet (again represented as a coil) and pull the switch open. Since this stops the flow of current the output contact will be cold. The two contacts thus have opposite values at all times, exactly what is wanted. Crude models of OR, AND and NOT circuits have now been presented. Modern versions use transistors or other electrical components, but it is not our purpose to plunge deeply into these engineering affairs.

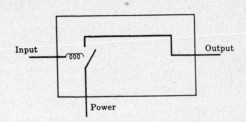

Fig. 1-13. A NOT circuit.

Solved Problems

1.1. Given the input information "Find the remainder when 144 is divided by 17", what is the correct output information?

Ordinary division soon leads to the remainder 8. Note that in addition to a knowledge of decimal symbols and the division process one must also understand the *words* used in the input information or he cannot proceed.

1.2. Given the input information "How many prime numbers are between 10 and 50", what is the correct output information?

Eleven. Here again both the number and word *languages* must be understood by the device (human being) which is to do the information processing.

1.3. The input information consists of "Arrange in increasing order the numbers represented by II, VII, XI, IV, VI". What is the correct output information?

After recognizing the Roman numerals one easily manages II, IV, VI, VII, XI.

1.4. The input information is "Changing one letter at a time convert CAT into TIN in three steps, each step producing an English word". What is the correct output information?

CAN, TAN, TIN is one suitable output. Here a memory of English words is needed to determine acceptable steps. For example, is TAT, TIT, TIN acceptable, or CIT, CIN, TIN? Problems like this one are not difficult for human beings but can be somewhat substantial hurdles for electrical machines.

1.5. The input information is "Rhyme the word BOWL from the set of words FOWL, SCOWL, HOWL, POLL". What is the correct output?

POLL. This is also easy for a human computer but could be severe for an electrical one.

1.6. What output information would be provided by an OR circuit given the following sequence pairs as inputs?

(*a*) 00001111   (*b*) 01010   (*c*) 0011
00111100   10101   0101

Recalling that a cold (0) output only comes from a pair of simultaneous cold inputs, we can answer as follows.

(*a*) 00111111   (*b*) 11111   (*c*) 0111

The computation is easy enough, but the important point is that we and the OR circuit are on common ground here. We do the same information processing.

1.7. What output information would be provided by an AND circuit given the sequence pairs of the preceding problem as inputs?

> Recalling that a hot (1) output only comes from a pair of simultaneous hot inputs, we can answer as follows.
>
> <div align="center">(<i>a</i>) 00001100   (<i>b</i>) 00000   (<i>c</i>) 0001</div>

Again the computation is trivial, but again the important thing is that we have established rapport between man and machine. Though the level of rapport is meager at the moment, at least we have made a start.

1.8. What output information would be provided by a NOT circuit given the three outputs of the preceding problem as successive inputs?

> Recalling the reversal of values, we can forecast the machine's answers.
>
> <div align="center">(<i>a</i>) 11110011   (<i>b</i>) 11111   (<i>c</i>) 1110</div>

1.9. Fig. 1-14 shows an electrical circuit (or machine, or computer) which combines an AND circuit with a NOT circuit. The original input sequences are called simply A and B. The output sequence of the AND circuit has been labeled C, and this sequence also serves as input to the NOT. The final output sequence has been called D. What will C and D become if this machine is offered the sequence pair 00001111 and 00111100 as A and B?

> C will be 00001100 as in Problem 1.7 and D will be 11110011 as in Problem 1.8. This machine essentially combines the circuits of Problems 1.7 and 1.8, and is known as a NAND circuit.

1.10. What will the C and D of the preceding problem become if A is the sequence 01010 and B is 10101?

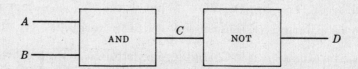

Fig. 1-14.   NAND circuit.

> C will be 00000 as in Problem 1.7 and D will be 11111 as in Problem 1.8.

1.11. What will be the output D of the NAND circuit in Fig. 1-14 if A is the sequence 0011 and B is 0101?

> 1110, as Problems 1.7 and 1.8 show. This pair of input sequences is particularly important since, as mentioned in connection with the OR and AND circuits of Figs. 1-5 and 1-8, it presents the only four input combinations possible. The operation of a NAND circuit may therefore be completely described by giving its output for this pair. (See Fig. 1-15.)

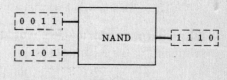

Fig. 1-15

1.12. The machine of Fig. 1-16 below is known as a NOR circuit. What will be the output sequence of this machine if the inputs A and B are 0011 and 0101? Notice once again that these four-value sequences offer the machine all four possible input combinations.

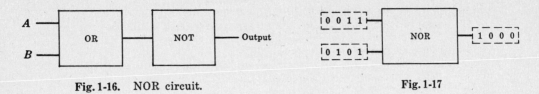

Fig. 1-16.   NOR circuit.   Fig. 1-17

The output of the OR circuit is 0111 as in Problem 1.6. The final output is therefore 1000 and this is exhibited in Fig. 1-17.

1.13. The machine of Fig. 1-18 combines two NOT and one OR circuits. What is its output sequence if A is 0011 and B is 0101?

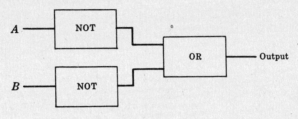

Fig. 1-18

The outputs of the two NOT circuits are 1100 and 1010. The final output is therefore 1110. But this is exactly the same output given by the NAND circuit of Fig. 1-14, as Problem 1.11 shows! And because the A and B being used include the only possible input combinations to either circuit, we have shown that the two machines will always produce the same output information if given the same inputs. Such machines will be called equivalent machines.

1.14. Show that the circuit of Fig. 1-19 will produce the same output information as a NOR circuit if given the same inputs A and B.

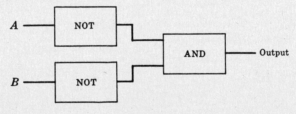

Fig. 1-19

It will be sufficient to compare their outputs when A is 0011 and B is 0101, since this includes all possible input combinations. In this case the two NOT circuits output 1100 and 1010, after which the AND manages 1000. This agrees with the output of a NOR circuit as summarized in Fig. 1-17.

1.15. Describe the output of the circuit in Fig. 1-20.

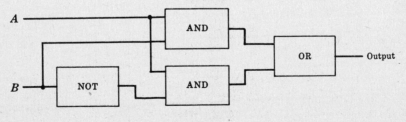

Fig. 1-20

Here a word of explanation may be helpful. In diagrams of this sort, wherever wires are joined with a heavy spot, contact is to be assumed, so that both wires carry the same 0 or 1 value. Where wires appear to touch but there is no heavy spot, no contact is assumed. This agreement is helpful in the representation of circuits. As usual we now choose 0011 for A and 0101 for B. Then the NOT circuit outputs 1010. The two ANDS then manage 0001 and 0010. Since these two sequences are the inputs to the OR circuit, the final output will be 0011. But this is identical with the sequence A itself! In other words, no information processing of any real significance has been achieved by this machine. Its output information will always be one of the original input sequences. Wasted labor is not uncommon but it makes sense to try to recognize and eliminate it where possible, and we shall try to avoid such machines as the one in Fig. 1-20.

1.16. Describe the output of the circuit in Fig. 1-21.

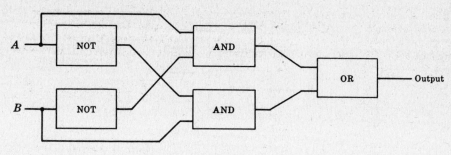

Fig. 1-21

Although this machine has a superficial resemblance to the useless circuit of the preceding problem it will prove to have important applications. Let A be 0011 and B be 0101 as usual, to cover all possible input combinations. Then the two NOT circuits produce 1100 and 1010. The ANDS then manage 0010 and 0100, after which the OR gives the final output of 0110. Notice that this output is hot (1) whenever the two inputs disagree and cold (0) when the inputs do agree. It therefore indicates with a hot output value the times when either one or the other, but *not both*, of the two input values is hot. It is sometimes called a comparator circuit, since it essentially compares the two input values and tells whether they agree or not. Fig. 1-22 summarizes the operation of such a comparator.

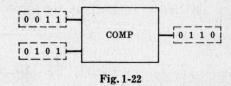

Fig. 1-22

Supplementary Problems

1.17. Given the input information "$(10 + 3)(5 + 7)$", what is the correct output information?

1.18. Given the input information "Find the largest number which divides evenly into 1365, not counting 1365 itself", what is the correct output information?

1.19. A journey from position A to position B in Fig. 1-23 will be six blocks long, if only eastward or northward travel is allowed (to minimize the length of the journey). There are several different paths by which this six-block journey can be completed. How many? Consider the foregoing as input information. What is the correct output information?

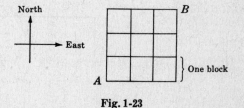

Fig. 1-23

1.20.   Given the input information "Alphabetize the six possible arrangements of the letters CAT", what is the correct output information?

1.21.   What output information would be provided by an AND circuit given the following pairs of sequences as inputs?

            (a) 010101   (b) 01110   (c) 0011

               110011   11011   1100

1.22.   What output information would be provided by an OR circuit given the pairs of sequences of the preceding problem as inputs?

1.23.   What would be the output information from a NOT circuit, given the output sequences of the preceding problem as inputs?

1.24.   Fig. 1-24 shows four simple combinations of AND and NOT circuits. For one of them the response to the standard A and B inputs (0011 and 0101) is indicated, the output information being 0100. Fill in the remaining outputs in the boxes provided, showing that each machine provides a hot output value for only one of the four possible input combinations, but that between them all four cases are covered.

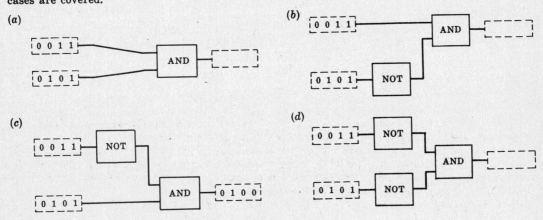

Fig. 1-24

1.25.   The comparator of Fig. 1-21 uses two of the circuits of the preceding problem, channeling their output information into an OR circuit. Which two are used?

1.26.   The circuit of Fig. 1-25 also uses two of the circuits of Problem 1.24. What will be its final output information if the usual 0011 and 0101 sequences are used as inputs?

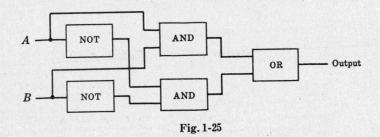

Fig. 1-25

1.27.   The circuit of Fig. 1-26 does no useful information processing. Explain.

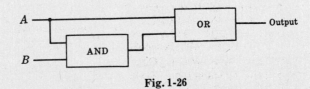

Fig. 1-26

1.28. Show that the circuit of Fig. 1-27 always gives the same output information as the comparator of Fig. 1-21, by finding the performance of each machine with the usual input sequences, 0011 for A and 0101 for B.

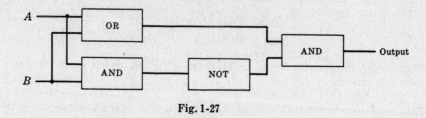

Fig. 1-27

1.29. Show that the circuit of Fig. 1-28 also gives the same output information as the comparator.

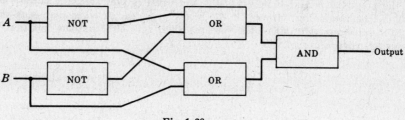

Fig. 1-28

1.30. Why are the two circuits of (a) Fig. 1-29 and (b) Fig. 1-30 not useful information processors?

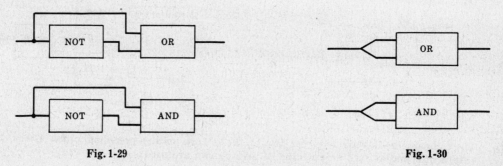

Fig. 1-29   Fig. 1-30

Chapter 2

Boolean Algebra

Boolean algebra has been found to be very useful in systematically combining the simple AND, OR, NOT circuits of the preceding chapter into more complex circuits designed for information processing. This chapter presents a brief introduction to this important modern mathematical structure, in the form most suited to our needs. It is not an algebra of numbers but, for our purposes at least, of sequences of zeros and ones. There are three operations. Two sequences A and B may be *added* by treating them exactly as an OR circuit would do. The result will be called $A + B$. Thus for our two basic sequences the computation runs as follows.

$$
\begin{array}{ll}
A & 0\ 0\ 1\ 1 \\
B & \underline{0\ 1\ 0\ 1} \\
A + B & 0\ 1\ 1\ 1
\end{array}
$$

The sum is the sequence 0111. As the example suggests, each column (each pair of input values) is added separately, making

$$0 + 0 = 0, \quad 0 + 1 = 1, \quad 1 + 0 = 1, \quad 1 + 1 = 1$$

These are the basic addition facts of Boolean algebra. The OR circuit implements this Boolean addition operation electrically, and we shall use the symbols OR and + more or less interchangeably.

In the second Boolean operation two sequences are *multiplied*, by treating them exactly as an AND circuit would do. The result will be called AB. For our two basic sequences the computation runs as follows.

$$
\begin{array}{ll}
A & 0\ 0\ 1\ 1 \\
B & \underline{0\ 1\ 0\ 1} \\
AB & 0\ 0\ 0\ 1
\end{array}
$$

The product is the sequence 0001. As the example suggests, each column (each pair of input values) is multiplied separately, making

$$0 \times 0 = 0, \quad 0 \times 1 = 0, \quad 1 \times 0 = 0, \quad 1 \times 1 = 1$$

Here the $\times$ denotes multiplication. These are the basic multiplication facts of Boolean algebra. The AND circuit implements this Boolean multiplication process electrically, and we shall use the symbols $\times$ and AND interchangeably.

The third and last operation is inversion. Any sequence may be *inverted* by replacing zeros by ones and vice versa, that is, by treating it exactly as a NOT circuit would do. The inverse of a sequence A will be denoted $\bar{A}$. The operation is summarized by the two basic inversion facts

$$\bar{0} = 1, \quad \bar{1} = 0$$

one of which is applied to each value of the sequence to be inverted. These three operations form the foundation of a Boolean algebra.

Example 2.1.

Given the sequences $\qquad A = 1010101 \qquad B = 0000011$

compute $A + B$, AB and $\bar{A}$. Actually, this has already been done in the preceding chapter. Thus

$$A + B = 1010111$$

the zeros coming from $0 + 0$. Similarly

$$AB = 0000001 \quad \text{and} \quad \bar{A} = 0101010$$

For the rest of this chapter the equality symbol will mean "is exactly the same sequence as", just as it does in this example.

The theory of Boolean algebra is fairly extensive, but only a limited selection will be needed here. To begin at the simplest level, several important theorems announce properties which any single sequence will have. For instance, let $\emptyset$ (read OH) denote a sequence containing only zeros. Similarly I will be a sequence containing only ones.

$$\emptyset \quad \text{all zeros}$$
$$I \quad \text{all ones}$$

It seems clear that if any sequence at all is multiplied by $\emptyset$ the product will be the sequence $\emptyset$. If we choose $A = 01$ the computation

$$
\begin{array}{cc}
A & 0\ 1 \\
\emptyset & 0\ 0 \\
\hline
A \times \emptyset & 0\ 0
\end{array}
$$

quickly confirms this suspected result, at least for the particular A selected. But, and here we come to a very important point, with any other A sequence, though the computation may become longer it will just duplicate the two columns we already have over and over again. These two columns are sufficient to tell the whole story. Since $A\emptyset = \emptyset$ in this special case, it always will for any A sequence at all. This method of proving a theorem by examining a well chosen special case is entirely satisfactory here because, when properly selected, the special case will include all the possibilities which can arise.

Proof by testing all the possibilities, as the method just used is often called, is particularly effective in developing the theory of Boolean algebra. It will be exploited fully in the solved problems. Some of the results to be obtained will be listed here for ready reference.

Theorem 2.1.	$A\emptyset = \emptyset$	**Theorem 2.6.**	$AA = A$
Theorem 2.2.	$A + I = I$	**Theorem 2.7.**	$\bar{\emptyset} = I,\ \bar{I} = \emptyset$
Theorem 2.3.	$A + \emptyset = A$	**Theorem 2.8.**	$\bar{\bar{A}} = A$
Theorem 2.4.	$AI = A$	**Theorem 2.9.**	$A + \bar{A} = I$
Theorem 2.5.	$A + A = A$	**Theorem 2.10.**	$A\bar{A} = \emptyset$

Slightly more complex are various theorems which state properties of any pair of sequences. For example, with $A = 0011$ and $B = 0101$ the two sequences $\overline{A + B}$ and $\bar{A}\bar{B}$ are computed as follows.

$$
\begin{array}{cc}
A & 0\ 0\ 1\ 1 \\
B & 0\ 1\ 0\ 1 \\
A + B & 0\ 1\ 1\ 1 \\
\overline{A + B} & 1\ 0\ 0\ 0 \\
\bar{A} & 1\ 1\ 0\ 0 \\
\bar{B} & 1\ 0\ 1\ 0 \\
\bar{A}\bar{B} & 1\ 0\ 0\ 0
\end{array}
$$

For these A and B we have found that

$$\overline{A + B} = \bar{A}\bar{B}$$

both sequences being 1000. But as already noted in Chapter 1, these particular A and B present all possible input combinations. To say it differently, any other choice of A and B might involve more computation but each column of that computation would duplicate one of the four we have above. These four columns already tell the whole story. Because $\overline{A+B}$ and $\bar{A}\bar{B}$ are the same for this A and B, it follows that they will be the same for any A and B whatsoever. This is again a proof by the method of testing all the possibilities. In the solved problems the following results will be proved.

Theorem 2.11. $\overline{A+B} = \bar{A}\bar{B}$ 　　　　　**Theorem 2.17.** $A+B = A + \bar{A}B$

Theorem 2.12. $\overline{AB} = \bar{A} + \bar{B}$ 　　　　　**Theorem 2.18.** $A+B = AB + A\bar{B} + \bar{A}B$

Theorem 2.13. $A+B = B+A$ 　　　　　　**Theorem 2.19.** $\bar{A}B + \bar{A}\bar{B} = \bar{A}$

Theorem 2.14. $AB = BA$ 　　　　　　　　**Theorem 2.20.** $AB + A\bar{B} + \bar{A}B + \bar{A}\bar{B} = I$

Theorem 2.15. $AB + A\bar{B} = A$ 　　　　　**Theorem 2.21.** $(A+B)(\bar{A}+\bar{B}) = A\bar{B} + \bar{A}B$

Theorem 2.16. $A + AB = A$ 　　　　　　**Theorem 2.22.** $(A+B)\overline{AB} = A\bar{B} + \bar{A}B$

A small selection of still more complex theorems will also be developed including the following four which are true for any three sequences A, B, C whatsoever.

Theorem 2.23. $A(B+C) = AB + AC$ 　　　**Theorem 2.25.** $A + (B+C) = (A+B) + C$

Theorem 2.24. $A + BC = (A+B)(A+C)$ 　**Theorem 2.26.** $A(BC) = (AB)C$

These various theorems have been listed here merely for ready reference. They will become familiar as they are put to use in the problems.

Solved Problems

2.1.　Prove Theorems 2.1 to 2.10.

As suggested, it is enough to verify them for the sequence $A = 01$. The computations

A	0 1			A	0 1			A	0 1	
$\emptyset$	0 0			I	1 1			A	0 1	
$A\emptyset$	0 0	$(=\emptyset)$		$A+I$	1 1	$(=I)$		AA	0 1	$(=A)$
$A+\emptyset$	0 1	$(=A)$		AI	0 1	$(=A)$		$A+A$	0 1	$(=A)$

already prove the first six. Theorem 2.7 is immediate upon exchanging zeros and ones. For the final three we compute

A	0 1	
$\bar{A}$	1 0	
$\bar{\bar{A}}$	0 1	$(=A)$
$A + \bar{A}$	1 1	$(=I)$
$A\bar{A}$	0 0	$(=\emptyset)$

where $\bar{\bar{A}}$ means the inverse of $\bar{A}$.

2.2.   Prove the companion Theorems 2.11 and 2.12, page 13.

As suggested, theorems involving any two sequences A and B may be proved by verifying them with $A = 0011$ and $B = 0101$. Accordingly we compute as follows.

A 0 0 1 1		$\bar{A}$ 1 1 0 0
B 0 1 0 1		$\bar{B}$ 1 0 1 0
$A + B$ 0 1 1 1		AB 0 0 0 1
$\overline{A + B}$ 1 0 0 0		$\overline{AB}$ 1 1 1 0
$\bar{A}\bar{B}$ 1 0 0 0		$\bar{A} + \bar{B}$ 1 1 1 0

Both theorems are verified. The first of this pair is usually translated as, "The inverse of a sum is the product of the separate inverses". The companion translates similarly into, "The inverse of a product is the sum of the separate inverses". Note the alternate appearances of sums and products.

In general, $\overline{A + B} \neq \bar{A} + \bar{B}$ and $\overline{AB} \neq \bar{A}\bar{B}$.

2.3.   Prove Theorems 2.13 and 2.14, page 13.

This pair of companion theorems has a very unexciting content but is very important nonetheless. The computations

A 0 0 1 1		B 0 1 0 1
B 0 1 0 1		A 0 0 1 1
$A + B$ 0 1 1 1		$B + A$ 0 1 1 1
AB 0 0 0 1		BA 0 0 0 1

quickly confirm them. Basically these theorems are true because $0 + 1$ and $1 + 0$ are both 1, while 0×1 and 1×0 are both 0.

2.4.   Prove Theorems 2.15 to 2.20, page 13.

These involve the four products AB, $A\bar{B}$, $\bar{A}B$, $\bar{A}\bar{B}$ which will be computed first.

A 0 0 1 1		AB 0 0 0 1
B 0 1 0 1		$A\bar{B}$ 0 0 1 0
$\bar{A}$ 1 1 0 0		$\bar{A}B$ 0 1 0 0
$\bar{B}$ 1 0 1 0		$\bar{A}\bar{B}$ 1 0 0 0

Adding the first two of these four products produces 0011, agreeing with A itself and confirming Theorem 2.15. Adding the first three produces 0111 which agrees with $A + B$ and confirms Theorem 2.18. Adding all four manages 1111 which is the content of Theorem 2.20. Next $A + AB$ is 0011, agreeing with A and verifying Theorem 2.16. The remaining two theorems easily follow by similar computations which are gentle enough to be done mentally.

2.5.   In Problem 1.13 we found that the two circuits reproduced in Fig. 2-1 always give the same output if offered identical inputs. Which of the theorems of Boolean algebra agrees?

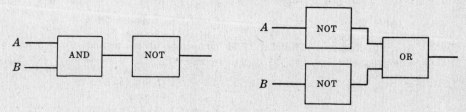

Fig. 2-1

Since OR, AND, NOT correspond to $+$, $\times$, $-$ the two outputs are $\overline{AB}$ and $\bar{A} + \bar{B}$. Theorem 2.12 guarantees their equality. Both machines are essentially NAND circuits.

2.6. In Problem 1.14 we showed that the two circuits of Fig. 2-2 always produce the same output if given the same inputs. Which of the theorems of Boolean algebra agrees?

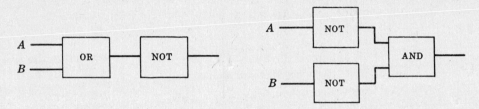

Fig. 2-2

The two outputs correspond to $\overline{A+B}$ and $\bar{A}\bar{B}$ which are equal by Theorem 2.11.

2.7. The circuit in Fig. 2-3 was found in Problem 1.15 to be useless for information processing. Express its output in terms of the inputs and apply one of our theorems to draw the same conclusion.

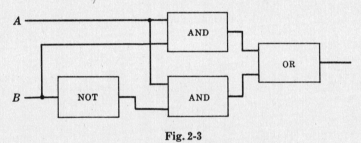

Fig. 2-3

The two AND circuits will produce AB and $A\bar{B}$. The final output is therefore $AB + A\bar{B}$. Theorem 2.15 indicates that this will be identical with input A.

2.8. In Problem 1.24 four simple circuits were presented. These correspond to the four simple products AB, $A\bar{B}$, $\bar{A}B$ and $\bar{A}\bar{B}$. Which is which?

Circuits (a), (b), (c) and (d) of that problem output AB, $A\bar{B}$, $\bar{A}B$ and $\bar{A}\bar{B}$ in that order.

2.9. The circuit of Problem 1.27 is useless for information processing. Which theorem of Boolean algebra agrees?

Its output is easily found to be $A + AB$, which Theorem 2.16 indicates is the same as the input A.

2.10. Which theorems are illustrated by the circuits of Fig. 1-29?

Theorems 2.9 and 2.10, page 12.

2.11. Prove Theorems 2.21 and 2.22, page 13.

Referring back to Problem 2.4 to avoid duplicating the computations made there, we now find

$$
\begin{array}{lcccc}
A+B & 0 & 1 & 1 & 1 \\
\bar{A}+\bar{B} & 1 & 1 & 1 & 0 \\
(A+B)(\bar{A}+\bar{B}) & 0 & 1 & 1 & 0 \\
A\bar{B}+\bar{A}B & 0 & 1 & 1 & 0
\end{array}
$$

proving Theorem 2.21. Replacing $\bar{A}+\bar{B}$ by $\overline{AB}$, which Theorem 2.12 guarantees to be the same, converts Theorem 2.21 into 2.22.

2.12. Represent the output of the comparator circuit of Problem 1.16 in terms of A and B.

The two AND circuits compute the products $A\bar{B}$ and $\bar{A}B$ after which the OR yields the final output information $A\bar{B} + \bar{A}B$. This is the same result achieved in Problem 1.16, since with $A = 0011$ and $B = 0101$ as was the case, it follows that $A\bar{B} + \bar{A}B = 0110$.

2.13. The circuits of Problems 1.28 and 1.29 were found to duplicate the output of the comparator circuit. Represent their outputs in terms of A and B. Which of the theorems of Boolean algebra confirm that these outputs are the same as that of the comparator?

The first circuit computes both the sum $A + B$ and the product AB. It then inverts the product and finishes up with the output $(A + B)\overline{AB}$. The second circuit inverts both A and B, then computes the two sums $A + B$ and $\bar{A} + \bar{B}$, and finishes with the product $(A + B)(\bar{A} + \bar{B})$. By Theorems 2.21 and 2.22 both of these equal the comparator output $A\bar{B} + \bar{A}B$ just discovered in the preceding problem.

2.14. Prove Theorem 2.23, page 13.

Here we are faced with three arbitrary sequences A, B and C. The method of testing all possible cases can still be used but we must be sure to include them all. A brief examination will show that the selection

$$A \quad 0\ 0\ 0\ 0\ 1\ 1\ 1\ 1$$
$$B \quad 0\ 0\ 1\ 1\ 0\ 0\ 1\ 1$$
$$C \quad 0\ 1\ 0\ 1\ 0\ 1\ 0\ 1$$

does actually exhaust the possible input combinations. There are eight of them in all, and each column presents one of the eight. Once convinced that no other combinations are possible, the rest of the proof is straightforward. First we find

$$B + C \quad 0\ 1\ 1\ 1\ 0\ 1\ 1\ 1$$
$$A(B + C) \quad 0\ 0\ 0\ 0\ 0\ 1\ 1\ 1$$

and then

$$AB \quad 0\ 0\ 0\ 0\ 0\ 0\ 1\ 1$$
$$AC \quad 0\ 0\ 0\ 0\ 0\ 1\ 0\ 1$$
$$AB + AC \quad 0\ 0\ 0\ 0\ 0\ 1\ 1\ 1$$

so that for this **particular choice** of A, B, C the theorem is secure. But any other choice, and this is the main point of the proof, would lead to no new kind of column, only to duplicates of the eight that we now have. For this reason our theorem is secure for any A, B, C whatever.

2.15. Fig. 2-4 shows two circuits. Express both outputs in terms of A, B and C and show that they are equal. Which machine is the simpler of the two?

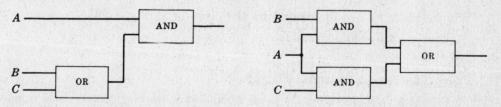

Fig. 2-4

The first circuit computes the sum $B + C$ and then outputs the product $A(B + C)$. The second computes the two products AB and AC and then outputs their sum $AB + AC$. By Theorem 2.23 these outputs are equal. Of the two the first circuit is the simpler, by one AND. Boolean algebra has found good use in the simplification of electrical circuits, the present example being a simple but appropriate first illustration.

2.16. Prove Theorem 2.24, page 13.

Using the special A, B, C sequences of Problem 2.14, the computation runs as follows.

$$
\begin{array}{rcccccccc}
A & 0 & 0 & 0 & 0 & 1 & 1 & 1 & 1 \\
B & 0 & 0 & 1 & 1 & 0 & 0 & 1 & 1 \\
C & 0 & 1 & 0 & 1 & 0 & 1 & 0 & 1 \\
BC & 0 & 0 & 0 & 1 & 0 & 0 & 0 & 1 \\
A + BC & 0 & 0 & 0 & 1 & 1 & 1 & 1 & 1 \\
A + B & 0 & 0 & 1 & 1 & 1 & 1 & 1 & 1 \\
A + C & 0 & 1 & 0 & 1 & 1 & 1 & 1 & 1 \\
(A + B)(A + C) & 0 & 0 & 0 & 1 & 1 & 1 & 1 & 1 \\
\end{array}
$$

For this selection of A, B, C it does happen that $A + BC = (A + B)(A + C)$, so by the argument of Problem 2.14, that no different kinds of column can occur, this will be true for any A, B, C whatever and the theorem is proved.

2.17. Prove Theorems 2.25 and 2.26, page 13, and then generalize them.

The procedure is now familiar. Borrowing the A, B, C of the preceding problem, we compute

$$
\begin{array}{rcccccccc}
B + C & 0 & 1 & 1 & 1 & 0 & 1 & 1 & 1 \\
A + (B + C) & 0 & 1 & 1 & 1 & 1 & 1 & 1 & 1 \\
A + B & 0 & 0 & 1 & 1 & 1 & 1 & 1 & 1 \\
(A + B) + C & 0 & 1 & 1 & 1 & 1 & 1 & 1 & 1 \\
\end{array}
$$

and it comes as no great surprise that $A + (B + C)$ does in fact equal $(A + B) + C$. This theorem is the first step in proving that the order in which any set of sequences is added is entirely immaterial, all orders of computation leading to the same final result. For example, it now follows that

$$A + (B + C) = A + (C + B) = (A + C) + B$$

where first Theorem 2.13 is used and then Theorem 2.25, the latter being known as the "shift parentheses" theorem. Looking back over these results we now see that any pair may be added first, $A + B$ or $A + C$ or $B + C$, and the third sequence accommodated afterward. With three sequences the order of addition is therefore completely immaterial.

This result can now be stretched. With four sequences A, B, C, D we might, for example, decide to sum A and B first.

$$(A + B) + C + D$$

But then only three sequences remain, $(A + B)$, C and D, so the order of addition now becomes immaterial. Choosing C as the next candidate brings the overall computation to

$$[(A + B) + C] + D$$

But a shift of the round parentheses converts this to

$$[A + (B + C)] + D$$

so that $B + C$, rather than $A + B$, could have been the first sum computed. By continuing in this way we could produce any order of computation desired, the results being always the same. This would show that four sequences may be added in any order whatever. Similar stretching would then further extend this result to five, six, and more sequences. The details are hardly fascinating and will be omitted. Similar arguments prove and generalize Theorem 2.26, in which products replace sums. These theorems have already been implied in our statement and proof of Theorems 2.18 and 2.20, where double and triple sums were involved and no order of computation was specified. Results of this sort are definitely not exciting but they are fundamental. The present pair will be stated as follows.

Theorem 2.27. Double, triple and longer sums such as $A + B + C$, $A + B + C + D$ and so on, may be computed in any order.

Theorem 2.28. Double, triple and longer products such as ABC, $ABCD$ and so on, may be computed in any order.

2.18. Generalize Theorem 2.23.

Consider first the expression $A(B + C + D)$ and temporarily use X to replace $B + C$. Applying Theorem 2.23 twice we find that

$$A(B + C + D) = A(X + D) = AX + AD = A(B + C) + AD = AB + AC + AD$$

Notice that Theorem 2.27 on the order of double sums is used here almost unobserved. Clearly the sum inside the parentheses can now be further stretched to obtain

$$A(B + C + D + E) = AB + AC + AD + AE$$

by a repetition of the same argument. Stretching to any required length is only a matter of patience. We can also stretch the first factor. For example,

$$(A + B)(C + D) = (A + B)X = X(A + B) = XA + XB = AX + BX$$
$$= A(C + D) + B(C + D) = AC + AD + BC + BD$$

Other similar results are recorded in the following pair of theorems.

Theorem 2.29. For any sequences, A, B, C, D, E, etc.,

$$A(B + C + D) = AB + AC + AD$$

$$A(B + C + D + E) = AB + AC + AD + AE$$

and so on.

Theorem 2.30. For any sequences A, B, C, D, E, etc.,

$$(A + B)(C + D) = AC + AD + BC + BD$$

$$(A + B + C)(D + E + F) = AD + AE + AF + BD + BE + BF + CD + CE + CF$$

and so on.

2.19. Illustrate how combinations of two sequences A and B may be developed into sums involving the products AB, $A\bar{B}$, $\bar{A}B$ and $\bar{A}\bar{B}$.

As a first example take $\bar{A}$. We find

$$\bar{A} = \bar{A}I = \bar{A}(B + \bar{B}) = \bar{A}B + \bar{A}\bar{B}$$

which incidentally proves Theorem 2.19, page 13. As a second example,

$$A + B = AI + IB = A(B + \bar{B}) + (A + \bar{A})B = AB + A\bar{B} + AB + \bar{A}B$$

But here the order of addition can be changed and Theorem 2.5 applied to affect a simplification. Thus

$$A + B = (AB + AB) + A\bar{B} + \bar{A}B = AB + A\bar{B} + \bar{A}B$$

again proving Theorem 2.18. In the same way

$$A + \bar{A}B = AI + \bar{A}B = A(B + \bar{B}) + \bar{A}B = AB + A\bar{B} + \bar{A}B$$

Since this agrees with our development of $A + B$, we have proved Theorem 2.17. Developing Boolean combinations into sums of such products provides a routine procedure by which the combinations may be compared.

2.20. Apply the development method of the preceding problem to reprove Theorems 2.20 and 2.21.

Applying Theorems 2.30, 2.10, 2.3 and 2.14 in that order, we find

$$(A + B)(\bar{A} + \bar{B}) = A\bar{A} + A\bar{B} + B\bar{A} + B\bar{B} = \emptyset + A\bar{B} + B\bar{A} + \emptyset = A\bar{B} + \bar{A}B$$

which is Theorem 2.21. The freedom to change the order within a triple sum is also involved in this computation. Similarly

$$I = II = (A + \bar{A})(B + \bar{B}) = AB + A\bar{B} + \bar{A}B + \bar{A}\bar{B}$$

brings us once again to Theorem 2.20.

2.21. Compute the values of the eight basic products ABC, $AB\bar{C}$, $A\bar{B}C$, $A\bar{B}\bar{C}$, $\bar{A}BC$, $\bar{A}B\bar{C}$, $\bar{A}\bar{B}C$, $\bar{A}\bar{B}\bar{C}$ for the standard input sequences A, B, C already introduced in Problem 2.14.

The following results are easily computed.

$$
\begin{array}{llllllllll}
A   & 0 & 0 & 0 & 0 & 1 & 1 & 1 & 1 \\
B   & 0 & 0 & 1 & 1 & 0 & 0 & 1 & 1 \\
C   & 0 & 1 & 0 & 1 & 0 & 1 & 0 & 1 \\
\bar{A} & 1 & 1 & 1 & 1 & 0 & 0 & 0 & 0 \\
\bar{B} & 1 & 1 & 0 & 0 & 1 & 1 & 0 & 0 \\
\bar{C} & \underline{1 \ \ 0 \ \ 1 \ \ 0 \ \ 1 \ \ 0 \ \ 1 \ \ 0} \\
ABC   & 0 & 0 & 0 & 0 & 0 & 0 & 0 & 1 \\
AB\bar{C}   & 0 & 0 & 0 & 0 & 0 & 0 & 1 & 0 \\
A\bar{B}C   & 0 & 0 & 0 & 0 & 0 & 1 & 0 & 0 \\
A\bar{B}\bar{C} & 0 & 0 & 0 & 0 & 1 & 0 & 0 & 0 \\
\bar{A}BC   & 0 & 0 & 0 & 1 & 0 & 0 & 0 & 0 \\
\bar{A}B\bar{C} & 0 & 0 & 1 & 0 & 0 & 0 & 0 & 0 \\
\bar{A}\bar{B}C & 0 & 1 & 0 & 0 & 0 & 0 & 0 & 0 \\
\bar{A}\bar{B}\bar{C} & 1 & 0 & 0 & 0 & 0 & 0 & 0 & 0 \\
\end{array}
$$

Listed in this particular order, the products offer a simple pattern of retreating ones. This pattern explains the usefulness of these products in the study and application of Boolean combinations of three sequences A, B and C.

2.22. Develop $A(B + C)$ in terms of the basic products just listed.

For this Boolean combination, using our standard A, B, C sequences as listed again in the preceding problem, we have already computed (see Problem 2.14) the following result.

$$A(B+C) \quad 0 \ \ 0 \ \ 0 \ \ 0 \ \ 0 \ \ 1 \ \ 1 \ \ 1$$

The ones in the last three positions may also be obtained in a different way, by adding together the first three of the eight basic products. A glance at the table in Problem 2.21 will quickly confirm this. This amounts to the proof of a new theorem.

Theorem 2.31. $A(B + C) = ABC + AB\bar{C} + A\bar{B}C$

This could also have been proved by the development method, the computation running like this.

$$A(B+C) = AB + AC = ABI + AIC = AB(C + \bar{C}) + A(B + \bar{B})C$$

$$= ABC + AB\bar{C} + ABC + A\bar{B}C = ABC + AB\bar{C} + A\bar{B}C$$

In the last step Theorem 2.5 has been used, in the form $ABC + ABC = ABC$.

2.23. Develop $AB + AC + BC$ in terms of the basic products.

For the same A, B, C just used, we compute

$$
\begin{array}{llllllllll}
AB   & 0 & 0 & 0 & 0 & 0 & 0 & 1 & 1 \\
AC   & 0 & 0 & 0 & 0 & 0 & 1 & 0 & 1 \\
BC   & 0 & 0 & 0 & 1 & 0 & 0 & 0 & 1 \\
AB + AC + BC & 0 & 0 & 0 & 1 & 0 & 1 & 1 & 1 \\
\end{array}
$$

This same exact pattern of ones, in columns four, six, seven and eight, can be generated by adding together the first three basic products and the fifth. This proves

Theorem 2.32. $AB + AC + BC = ABC + AB\bar{C} + A\bar{B}C + \bar{A}BC$

2.24. Show that $AB + (A+B)\overline{ABC}$ is equal to $AB + AC + BC$.

We compute, again using the familiar A, B, C

$$
\begin{array}{lllllllll}
AB & 0 & 0 & 0 & 0 & 0 & 0 & 1 & 1 \\
\overline{AB} & 1 & 1 & 1 & 1 & 1 & 1 & 0 & 0 \\
A+B & 0 & 0 & 1 & 1 & 1 & 1 & 1 & 1 \\
C & 0 & 1 & 0 & 1 & 0 & 1 & 0 & 1 \\
(A+B)\overline{ABC} & 0 & 0 & 0 & 1 & 0 & 1 & 0 & 0 \\
AB+(A+B)\overline{ABC} & 0 & 0 & 0 & 1 & 0 & 1 & 1 & 1
\end{array}
$$

and discover the same pattern as in the preceding problem, thus proving

Theorem 2.33. $AB + AC + BC = AB + (A+B)\overline{ABC}$.

2.25. Prove the following pair of theorems.

Theorem 2.34. $A\bar{B} + B\bar{C} + C\bar{A} = \bar{A}B + \bar{B}C + \bar{C}A$

Theorem 2.35. $A\bar{B} + B\bar{C} + C\bar{A} = \bar{A}BC + A\bar{B}C + AB\bar{C} + \bar{A}\bar{B}C + \bar{A}B\bar{C} + A\bar{B}\bar{C}$

Instead of proceeding with the familiar eight column computation, as in the preceding problem, we choose for the sake of variety the alternate method of developing these Boolean combinations algebraically.   First

$$
\begin{aligned}
A\bar{B} + B\bar{C} + C\bar{A} &= A\bar{B}I + IB\bar{C} + \bar{A}IC \\
&= A\bar{B}(C+\bar{C}) + (A+\bar{A})B\bar{C} + \bar{A}(B+\bar{B})C \\
&= A\bar{B}C + A\bar{B}\bar{C} + AB\bar{C} + \bar{A}B\bar{C} + \bar{A}BC + \bar{A}\bar{B}C
\end{aligned}
$$

which already disposes of Theorem 2.35.   Similarly

$$
\begin{aligned}
\bar{A}B + \bar{B}C + \bar{C}A &= \bar{A}BI + I\bar{B}C + AI\bar{C} \\
&= \bar{A}B(C+\bar{C}) + (A+\bar{A})\bar{B}C + A(B+\bar{B})\bar{C} \\
&= \bar{A}BC + \bar{A}B\bar{C} + A\bar{B}C + \bar{A}\bar{B}C + AB\bar{C} + A\bar{B}\bar{C}
\end{aligned}
$$

and we have exactly the same six products as before, simply in a different order.   This proves Theorem 2.34, which is a slightly surprising result in view of the positions of the inverse symbols on the two sides.   To the relatively casual observer these two Boolean combinations might appear to be inverses.   Instead they are equal.

2.26. Show that the two circuits of Fig. 2-5 produce exactly the same output information. Which seems to be simpler?

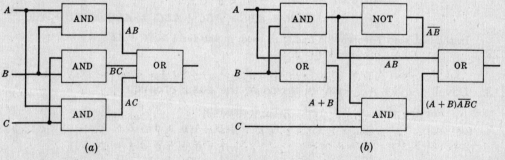

Fig. 2-5

Notice first that one OR circuit and one AND circuit are accepting three input sequences rather than two in these machines.   This involves a minor modification of these circuits from the form in which they were first presented, but the principle remains the same and it is no severe engineering challenge to provide OR and AND circuits which can accept several inputs.   In any case, an OR circuit provides a cold output only when all the inputs are cold; it thus executes

Boolean addition of all the inputs. Similarly an AND circuit provides a hot output only when all the inputs are hot, thus executing Boolean multiplication of all the inputs. With this observation behind us we now note that the circuit of Fig. 2.5a first computes the three products AB, BC and AC and then outputs their sum $AB + AC + BC$. The wires carrying the three product sequences have been appropriately labeled to help understand the action. The machine of Fig. 2-5b first computes the product AB and the sum $A + B$. It then inverts the product and multiplies the three factors $\overline{AB}$, $(A + B)$ and C. Finally the OR outputs the sum $AB + (A + B)\overline{ABC}$. Once again various wires have been labeled according to the sequence being carried, to expedite human understanding of the action. It now becomes evident, by Theorem 2.33, page 20, that the two circuits are producing identical output information. Of the two (a) seems slightly simpler.

2.27. Are the machines of Fig. 2-6 equivalent, that is, will they output the same sequence?

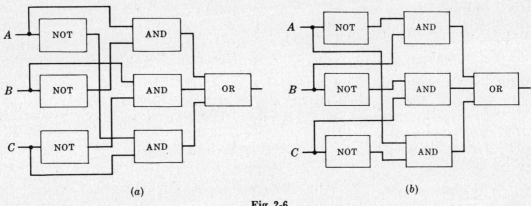

(a)   (b)

Fig. 2-6

In the circuit (a) we find the three AND circuits producing $A\bar{B}$, $B\bar{C}$ and $C\bar{A}$. The OR then outputs the sum of these three products, $A\bar{B} + B\bar{C} + C\bar{A}$. In the circuit ($b$) there are also three products, $\bar{A}B$, $\bar{B}C$ and $\bar{C}A$. Here the OR outputs $\bar{A}B + \bar{B}C + \bar{C}A$. Theorem 2.34 guarantees that these two outputs are identical.

2.28. Verify the following theorem.

   Theorem 2.36. The sum of all eight basic products is I.

   Referring back to the table in Problem 2.21 we note once again the retreating pattern of ones, each of the basic products having only a single 1 value, but these values being distributed one to each of the eight columns. Clearly the sum of all eight products will be

$$1\ 1\ 1\ 1\ 1\ 1\ 1\ 1$$

which is I.

2.29. Verify the following theorem.

   Theorem 2.37. The inverse of any sum is the product of the separate inverses. The inverse of any product is the sum of the separate inverses.

   For sums and products of just two sequences, this has long since been established in Theorems 2.11 and 2.12. Consider now the case of a double sum $A + B + C$. Since the order of computation does not matter, we may choose to compute $A + B$ first and call the result X. Then

$$\overline{A + B + C} = \overline{X + C} = \bar{X}\bar{C} = \overline{A + B}\,\bar{C} = \bar{A}\bar{B}\bar{C}$$

as required. The proof amounts to using Theorem 2.11 twice, thereby stretching that theorem to double length. This result for double sums can now be stretched further to cover triple sums.

$$\overline{A + B + C + D} = \overline{X + C + D} = \bar{X}\bar{C}\bar{D} = \text{etc.}$$

Clearly any amount of stretch can be applied. The corresponding result for products is proved in the same way.

2.30. Verify the following theorem.

Theorem 2.38. $(A + B + C)\overline{ABC} = A\bar{B} + B\bar{C} + C\bar{A}$

An algebraic proof might run as follows. First

$$(A + B + C)\overline{ABC} = (A + B + C)(\bar{A} + \bar{B} + \bar{C})$$
$$= A\bar{A} + A\bar{B} + A\bar{C} + B\bar{A} + B\bar{B} + B\bar{C} + C\bar{A} + C\bar{B} + C\bar{C}$$
$$= (A\bar{B} + B\bar{C} + C\bar{A}) + (\bar{A}B + \bar{B}C + \bar{C}A)$$

where the last step involves a substantial change in the order of addition. But now, according to Theorem 2.34, page 20, the two sums in parentheses are equal. Thus Theorem 2.5, which makes $A + A = A$ for any A, applies and either of the sums may be deleted. Deleting the second, we have the theorem.

A second proof takes us back to the eight columns of computation and the method of testing all possible cases. Again borrowing the results of Problem 2.21, we find

ABC	0 0 0 0 0 0 0 1	$A\bar{B}$	0 0 0 0 1 1 0 0
$\overline{ABC}$	1 1 1 1 1 1 1 0	$B\bar{C}$	0 0 1 0 0 0 1 0
$A + B + C$	0 1 1 1 1 1 1 1	$C\bar{A}$	0 1 0 1 0 0 0 0
$(A + B + C)\overline{ABC}$	0 1 1 1 1 1 1 0	$A\bar{B} + B\bar{C} + C\bar{A}$	0 1 1 1 1 1 1 0

so the two sequences involved in the theorem do agree. Actually, the two proofs just offered present precisely the same logic but in different disguises.

2.31. Prove this final pair of theorems (there is much more to the theory of Boolean algebra but we have already accumulated more than enough for our purposes).

Theorem 2.39. $ABC + (A + B + C)\overline{AB + AC + BC} = ABC + A\bar{B}\bar{C} + \bar{A}B\bar{C} + \bar{A}\bar{B}C$

Theorem 2.40. $[(A + B)\overline{AB} + C]\overline{(A + B)\overline{ABC}} = ABC + A\bar{B}\bar{C} + \bar{A}B\bar{C} + \bar{A}\bar{B}C$

Choosing the method of testing all the possibilities, we refer first to Problem 2.23 in which we found that for our standard A, B, C inputs

$$AB + AC + BC \quad 0 \ 0 \ 0 \ 1 \ 0 \ 1 \ 1 \ 1$$

and to Problem 2.30 which brought the following:

$$ABC \quad 0 \ 0 \ 0 \ 0 \ 0 \ 0 \ 0 \ 1$$
$$A + B + C \quad 0 \ 1 \ 1 \ 1 \ 1 \ 1 \ 1 \ 1$$

We can now compute the left side member of Theorem 2.39.

$\overline{AB + AC + BC}$	1 1 1 0 1 0 0 0
$(A + B + C)\overline{AB + AC + BC}$	0 1 1 0 1 0 0 0
$ABC + (A + B + C)\overline{AB + AC + BC}$	0 1 1 0 1 0 0 1

Checking back to the table of Problem 2.21 one finds that this same pattern, in the last row, ones in columns two, three, five and eight, may also be generated by adding together the basic products ABC, $A\bar{B}\bar{C}$, $\bar{A}B\bar{C}$ and $\bar{A}\bar{B}C$. This is precisely the right side of our theorem.

Turning to the final theorem we may again save some labor by referring back to previous computations, this time in Problem 2.24. From the ingredients available there we extract

$(A + B)\overline{AB}$	0 0 1 1 1 1 0 0
$[(A + B)\overline{AB} + C]$	0 1 1 1 1 1 0 1
$(A + B)\overline{ABC}$	0 0 0 1 0 1 0 0

and then compute these two additional sequences:

$\overline{(A + B)\overline{ABC}}$	1 1 1 0 1 0 1 1
$[(A + B)\overline{AB} + C]\overline{(A + B)\overline{ABC}}$	0 1 1 0 1 0 0 1

Since this is the same pattern obtained for Theorem 2.39, the same four basic products are again involved and Theorem 2.40 is proved. These two theorems do have a part to play in designing circuits which can compute sums of *numbers*, rather than of Boolean sequences.

Supplementary Problems

2.32. For the sequence $A = 01101$ compute $\bar{\bar{A}}$, $A + A$ and $A + \bar{A}$, noting the duplication of columns. Only the first two columns are distinct, as remarked in the introduction. Also see Theorems 2.5, 2.8 and 2.9.

2.33. For the sequences $A = 001101$, $B = 010111$ compute $\overline{A + B}$ and $\bar{A}\bar{B}$. They should be the same but notice especially the duplication of columns. Only the first four columns are distinct, as remarked in the introduction. Also see Theorem 2.11.

2.34. For the A and B of the preceding problem compute $A\bar{B} + \bar{A}B$ and $(A + B)\overline{AB}$. They should be the same, but notice the duplication of columns. Also see Theorem 2.22.

2.35. The circuits of Fig. 1-30 do no useful information processing. Which two of our theorems agree?

2.36. Represent the output of the circuit in Problem 1.26 in terms of A and B.

2.37. Compare $AB + \bar{A}B$ and $A\bar{B} + \bar{A}B$ using the standard $A = 0011$, $B = 0101$. Theorem 2.20, with the order of terms slightly altered, suggests the same result. What is the relationship between these two Boolean combinations?

2.38. Is the output of the circuit in Fig. 2-7 equal to $AB + \bar{A}\bar{B}$? See Theorem 2.22 and the preceding problem.

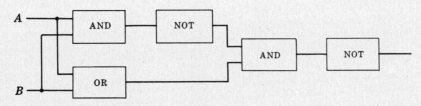

Fig. 2-7

2.39. Express the output of the machine in Fig. 2-8 in terms of A and B. One of our theorems shows that this circuit is equivalent to a simple OR circuit. Which theorem?

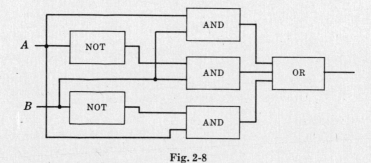

Fig. 2-8

2.40. Express the output information of the circuit in Fig. 2-9 in terms of A and B. One of our theorems shows that this circuit is equivalent to a simple NOT circuit. Which theorem?

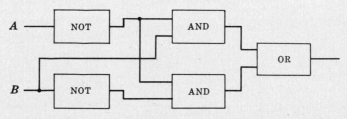

Fig. 2-9

2.41. Try to attach one more column to our standard selection

$$A \quad 0 \; 0 \; 0 \; 0 \; 1 \; 1 \; 1 \; 1$$
$$B \quad 0 \; 0 \; 1 \; 1 \; 0 \; 0 \; 1 \; 1$$
$$C \quad 0 \; 1 \; 0 \; 1 \; 0 \; 1 \; 0 \; 1$$

to confirm that no new type of column is possible. These eight combinations are the only possible A, B, C input combinations.

2.42. For the A, B, C of the preceding problem we have already computed

$$A\bar{B} + B\bar{C} + C\bar{A} \quad 0 \; 1 \; 1 \; 1 \; 1 \; 1 \; 1 \; 0$$

in Problem 2.30. Now compute $\bar{A}B + \bar{B}C + \bar{C}A$, verifying that it is the same. This once again proves Theorem 2.34, page 20.

2.43. Use the standard A, B, C input information of Problem 2.41 to compute $\overline{A + B + C}$, and $\bar{A}\bar{B}\bar{C}$, once again proving this part of Theorem 2.37, page 21.

2.44. Proceed as in the preceding problem to verify $\overline{ABC} = \bar{A} + \bar{B} + \bar{C}$.

2.45. Show that the two circuits of Fig. 2-10 produce identical output information. Which of our theorems is involved?

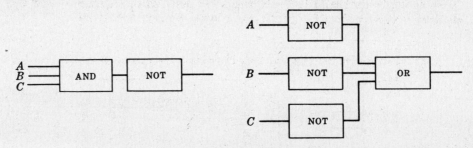

Fig. 2-10

2.46. Diagram circuits corresponding to both sides of Theorem 2.24, page 13. Which is simpler?

2.47. The circuit of Fig. 2-11 is equivalent to one of the three basic circuits OR, AND, NOT. Which one?

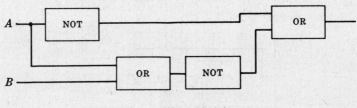

Fig. 2-11

2.48. Analyze the output information of the machine in Fig. 2-12 and then replace this machine by a single AND, OR, or NOT circuit.

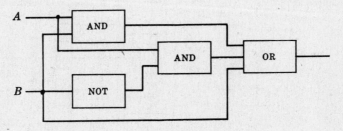

Fig. 2-12

2.49. Analyze the circuit of Fig. 2-13 and then replace it by one that uses only two AND, OR, NOT circuits altogether.

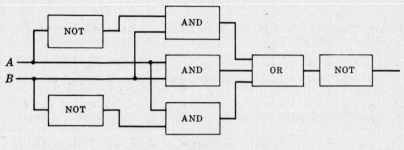

Fig. 2-13

2.50. In Fig. 2-6 we had two machines which produce the output

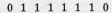

$$0\ \ 1\ \ 1\ \ 1\ \ 1\ \ 1\ \ 1\ \ 0$$

when offered the standard A, B, C inputs. Show how the four circuits displayed in Fig. 2-14 can be connected to create still another and simpler machine having this same output information.

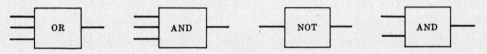

Fig. 2-14

Chapter 3

Special-purpose Boolean Machines

Boolean algebra was first applied to the logic of statements. George Boole in his "The Mathematical Analysis of Logic" in 1847 and "An Investigation of the Laws of Thought" in 1854 was the first to develop this algebra, and his motives are apparent from the titles. He was interested in the working methods of the human mind. It is thought-provoking to discover that Boolean algebra also proves to be applicable to the design of circuitry, that is, to electrical "minds" or computers. We have already begun this process of discovery in the preceding chapter and now continue it in this one, by observing how machines can be designed specifically for the solution of simple logical problems. The central issues in Boole's original application are:

(1) the idea of a *statement* as something which may be either true or false, one or the other, but not both at once;

(2) the combination of simpler statements into complex statements by use of the connectives *or, and, not*;

(3) determining the truth or falseness of the resulting statement, electrically or otherwise.

Example 3.1.

A statement such as "My dog has fleas" is clearly either true or false. However, it is quite possible that it will be true on some days and false on others, depending upon baths and other circumstances. Suppose that daily inspections for one week reveal the following results,

$$1\ 1\ 1\ 0\ 1\ 0\ 1$$

where 1 means true and 0 means false. The dog was flea-free only on Wednesday and Friday. The main point for the moment is, that since our interest in statements is to center on their truth or falseness, it is this sequence of zeros and ones rather than the original words which is important. Any other statement with the same sequence of true and false values would be equivalent, or equal, to this one for our purposes. To provide ingredients for more complex statements suppose that we have the following four statements altogether,

A: My aunt has fleas.
B: My brother has fleas.
C: My cat has fleas.
D: My dog has fleas.

with these accompanying sequences or "truth tables".

A 0 0 1 0 1 0 0
B 0 0 1 0 0 0 1
C 0 1 1 0 0 0 1
D 1 1 1 0 1 0 1

It will also be convenient to list two special statements,

$\emptyset$ 0 0 0 0 0 0 0
I 1 1 1 1 1 1 1

the first being always false and the second always true.

26

Example 3.2.

One simple combination of statements is "My aunt has fleas or my brother has fleas". Two of the statements of the preceding example have been connected by *or*. When will the resulting statement be true? Common usage suggests that it is true if either one of the two relatives, maybe even both, has fleas. The word *or* plays a double role in daily language. Sometimes it means "either or both" and sometimes "one or the other but not both". Here we choose the first meaning, so our statement will be false only when both parts are false. Referring back to Example 3.1 the complex statement then has this truth table:

$$A + B \quad 0\ 0\ 1\ 0\ 1\ 0\ 1$$

The appearance of the $+$ symbol may be justified as follows. Though this sequence was deduced by appealing to custom involving the use of *or*, it could also be computed by following the procedures of Boolean addition, in which a 0 can be obtained only from $0 + 0$. In other words, when two statements are connected by *or* the truth table of the resulting statement can be found by computation of a Boolean sum. In this sense the word *or* is equivalent to the Boolean $+$ and the resulting statement will be denoted $A + B$.

$A + B$:   My aunt has fleas or my brother has fleas.

Example 3.3.

A second way of combining statements is illustrated by "My aunt has fleas and my brother has fleas". Common usage tells us that this statement is true only when both parts are true. Referring back to Example 3.1 we may therefore deduce this truth table:

$$AB \quad 0\ 0\ 1\ 0\ 0\ 0\ 0$$

Only from matching ones do we get a one. But this is exactly what happens in Boolean multiplication, which explains our choice of the symbol AB for this sequence. It can actually be computed, rather than puzzled out from the meaning of *and*, and the computation needed is a Boolean multiplication. The same label will be applied to the statement itself.

AB: My aunt has fleas and my brother has fleas.

Example 3.4.

A third operation with statements is suggested by "My aunt does not have fleas". Referring back to the truth table for statement A, there is little doubt that for the present statement the correct table will be

$$\bar{A} \quad 1\ 1\ 0\ 1\ 0\ 1\ 1$$

and the symbol $\bar{A}$ obviously appears because Boolean inversion manages the same result. We shall also apply the same name to the statement itself:

$\bar{A}$:   My aunt does not have fleas.

The four examples just presented show that when statements are combined using *or*, *and*, *not* the truth or falseness of the resulting complex statement may be *computed* by Boolean operations rather than deduced by "logic". In this sense the Boolean operations are the operations of logic. Because this is true we may even use OR, AND, NOT circuits to perform the computations electrically, and this is the point which in a preliminary and lightweight way we are now bringing out. The theorems of Boolean algebra are also available for the simplification or design of statements, as will be illustrated in the problems.

Classification of sets into subsets is the second "logical" application of Boolean machines. Here the central issues are:

(1) representation of subsets by means of membership lists;

(2) the ideas of union, intersection and complement as arithmetic combinations of subsets;

(3) determination of the membership lists of such combinations, electrically or otherwise.

Example 3.5.

This is a miniature example but it does illustrate most of the main features of applications of this type. Suppose there are ten prisoners in a small jail. The following table suggests how prisoners may be classified into various subsets. The symbol 1 means that a particular prisoner does belong to the subset in question, while 0 means that he does not.

Prisoner number	1	2	3	4	5	6	7	8	9	10
A: Redheads	0	1	1	0	0	1	0	0	0	1
B: First-offenders	0	0	1	1	1	1	1	1	0	0
C: Six-footers	1	0	0	0	1	1	0	0	0	1
D: Females	0	0	0	1	0	1	1	0	0	0

Thus prisoners 2, 3, 6 and 10 are redheads, the others are not; prisoners 3 to 8 are first-offenders, and so on. Each row of this table is a membership list for the subset involved. Obviously each row is also a sequence of 0's and 1's. In the preceding application, sequences were truth tables; here they are membership lists. Two special "subsets" will also be helpful:

$$\emptyset \quad 0\ 0\ 0\ 0\ 0\ 0\ 0\ 0\ 0\ 0$$
$$I \quad 1\ 1\ 1\ 1\ 1\ 1\ 1\ 1\ 1\ 1$$

The first is the empty set; it has no members at all. The second is the universal set; it includes every member available.

Example 3.6.

The *union* of two subsets is obtained by combining their memberships. For instance, in the above jail the subset obtained by merging redheads with first-offenders would have this membership sequence:

$$A + B \quad 0\ 1\ 1\ 1\ 1\ 1\ 1\ 1\ 0\ 1$$

Only prisoners 1 and 9 fail to qualify. Putting it in another way, a zero can occur in this membership sequence only where matching zeros occur for the subsets being merged. Since exactly the same result can be *computed* by applying Boolean addition to the A and B sequences, the use of the $+$ symbol seems natural. $A + B$ will denote the union, or merger, of subsets A and B.

Example 3.7.

The *intersection* of two subsets is obtained by identifying the members common to both. For instance, prisoners who are both redheaded and first-offenders form the intersection of subsets A and B. It is easy enough to deduce the following membership list for this subset.

$$AB \quad 0\ 0\ 1\ 0\ 0\ 1\ 0\ 0\ 0\ 0$$

Only prisoners 3 and 6 qualify since they alone belong to both subset A and subset B. Putting it in another way, a one can occur in this membership sequence only where matching ones occur for the two subsets being intersected. Since exactly the same result can be *computed* by applying Boolean multiplication to the A and B sequences, the use of the symbol AB to denote this intersection seems natural. An intersection is sometimes called an overlap.

Example 3.8.

The *complement* of a subset consists of those members of the universal set I who are not in the subset. For instance, the membership sequence

$$\bar{A} \quad 1\ 0\ 0\ 1\ 1\ 0\ 1\ 1\ 1\ 0$$

describes the subset of "not redheads". Clearly the Boolean operation of inversion could be used to *compute* such a sequence from A itself, and so the use of the symbol $\bar{A}$ to denote a complement seems natural. Sometimes a complement is even called an inverse.

The four examples just presented show that membership lists for unions, intersections and complements of subsets may be computed by Boolean operations, rather than deduced by logic. This means that they can be produced by electrical circuits, or machines. The strong analogy between the two applications just outlined is the reason for calling the second a "logical" application, though this name was originally meant for the first.

Subset diagrams prove to be a convenient way of picturing and analyzing relationships between subsets when only a small number of subsets are involved. Because of the analogies just revealed they also prove useful in statement applications, as well as to OR, AND, NOT circuitry. In this way they have earned a place in computer science. Let the universal set I be represented by the inside of a square, as in Fig. 3-1. Also let the left half of the square represent subset A, as in Fig. 3-2. Then the right half, the part of I not included in A, will be $\bar{A}$. (Fig. 3-3.) Similarly let subset B be represented by the top half of the square and $\bar{B}$ by the bottom half. (Figs. 3-4 and 3-5.)

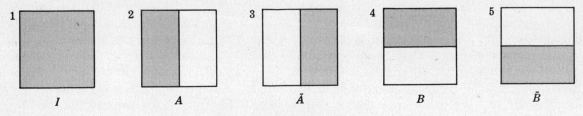

Figs. 3-1 to 3-5

These ingredients are already enough to afford pictures of the three basic subset operations. For example, where will the intersection of A with B be found? Clearly it must be in the upper left quarter, since this is where A and B overlap, or share a common part of I. (See Fig. 3-6.) Similarly, the intersections $A\bar{B}$, $\bar{A}B$ and $\bar{A}\bar{B}$ appear in Figs. 3-7 to 3-9. In this way the ideas of intersection and complement have already been made visible. As for unions, $A + B$ appears shaded in Fig. 3-10, in which the parts of I corresponding to A and B separately (see Figs. 3-2 and 3-4) have been merged. Similarly Fig. 3-11 shows $\bar{A} + \bar{B}$.

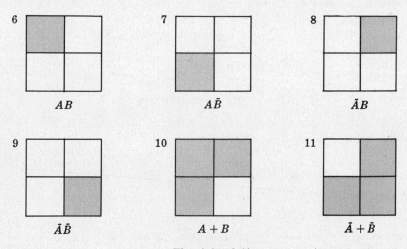

Figs. 3-6 to 3-11

If a third subset C is involved it may be represented as in Fig. 3-12 below, where it occupies the horizontal belt across the center. The complement $\bar{C}$ is then as shown in Fig. 3-13 below. Similarly a fourth subset D may be accommodated, together with its inverse, as in Figs. 3-14 and 3-15 below. With more than four subsets in action simultaneously, the picture becomes gradually less and less attractive but is used upon occasion. Because of the analogies mentioned above, subset diagrams can be used in statement applications, interpreting shaded areas as truth and unshaded as falseness. They may also be applied to electrical circuitry by thinking of shaded areas as hot and unshaded as cold.

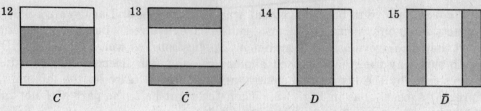

Figs. 3-12 to 3-15

Electrical machines can be designed for dealing with applications of logical character. This is already clear from the way in which truth tables and membership lists may be computed by the operations of Boolean algebra, as implemented by OR, AND, NOT circuits, and further clarification will result from a reading of the solved problems. This is our first suggestion that problems having some meaning to human beings can be processed by electrical circuits, or computers. In Chapter 1 we did observe some circuits in action, but the computations made there had no instant, impressive significance for human affairs. We have now taken a step toward bridging the gap between human and machine understanding. Many more such steps will be needed as we proceed. Two remarks may be appropriate even at this point.

1. There is a large gap between the languages being used by humans and our simple machines. Substantial preparation will be in order before a logical problem can be "understood" by a circuit.

2. Each machine we design in this chapter will be suitable for the particular problem involved and for no other; they are elementary examples of what are called special-purpose machines. Machines with greater flexibility, capable of solving a broad variety of problems if given proper instructions, will be discussed later. These are known as general-purpose machines and, needless to say, logical applications will be included in their repertoire. The machines of this chapter are not therefore intended as serious computing circuits but rather as first examples, as simple as we can find, of how "machine thinking" can help us. Besides, understanding very simple machines is the natural first step toward understanding more complex ones.

Solved Problems

3.1. Translate the following statements from English to Boolean and then compute their truth tables using the A, B, C, D statements and sequences given in Example 3.1, page 26.

1. My cat and dog both have fleas.
2. My cat has fleas but the dog does not.
3. Neither the cat nor the dog has fleas.

The first statement is an abbreviation of "My cat has fleas, and my dog has fleas" and so translates to CD. Similarly the second becomes $C\bar{D}$, the word but being equivalent to and. The third statement translates to $\bar{C}\bar{D}$. With the statements now in Boolean language the computation of truth tables is straightforward.

$$
\begin{array}{llllllll}
C & 0 & 1 & 1 & 0 & 0 & 0 & 1 \\
D & 1 & 1 & 1 & 0 & 1 & 0 & 1 \\
\bar{C} & 1 & 0 & 0 & 1 & 1 & 1 & 0 \\
\bar{D} & 0 & 0 & 0 & 1 & 0 & 1 & 0 \\
CD & 0 & 1 & 1 & 0 & 0 & 0 & 1 \\
C\bar{D} & 0 & 0 & 0 & 0 & 0 & 0 & 0 \\
\bar{C}\bar{D} & 0 & 0 & 0 & 1 & 0 & 1 & 0 \\
\end{array}
$$

In particular $C\bar{D} = \emptyset$, since whenever the cat has fleas the dog does also.

3.2. How could the truth tables of the preceding problem be computed electrically? Design an appropriate machine.

First of all, the C and D sequences which are the input information must be converted to electrical form. This could be done, and though the suggestion about to be made is much too primitive for serious present-day computing it at least has the proper spirit, by preparing two paper tapes with holes punched where 1's (hot values) are to occur, as in Fig. 3-16. If these tapes are then drawn simultaneously across the input terminals of the machine we are to design, then the holes will permit current to flow from the available hot wires (see figure) at precisely the right moments. Where no hole occurs current will not flow. The computing circuit itself is simple enough, requiring two NOT and three AND devices as shown. This part of the machine is very much like those already presented in the preceding chapters. Equipment for converting the electrical hots and colds at the output terminals into something more easily read by human beings is also needed, perhaps a hole-puncher which is triggered by a hot output value and produces paper tapes similar to the input tapes.

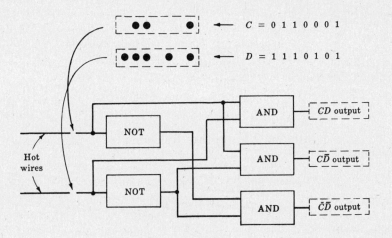

Fig. 3-16

Certain remarks made in the introduction are clearly illustrated by this problem. First, the proposed information system is admittedly primitive but it does point in the right direction. It shows, as this chapter is intended to show, that problems having some meaning to human beings can be converted into a form which is also meaningful to electrical circuits, and which can then be processed by such circuits. Second, the human task of converting the original problem into electrical form is an important part of the overall effort. Interpreting English prose is not what even the most sophisticated modern machines do best. And third, we have designed a special circuit, or machine, for the particular job in hand, as we shall do throughout this chapter except in Problems 3.3 and 3.13 which provide a brief and very fragmentary glimpse ahead.

3.3. As a first indication of how a general-purpose computer might handle a problem such as the preceding one, list the steps involved in the solution of Problem 3.1, assuming that the computations made there proceeded row by row.

The steps involved were these.

1. Read and save sequences C and D.
2. Compute and save $\bar{C}$.
3. Compute and save $\bar{D}$.
4. Compute and punch out (perhaps onto paper tape) CD.
5. Compute and punch out $C\bar{D}$.
6. Compute and punch out $\bar{C}\bar{D}$.

Note that only one NOT and one AND circuit are now needed, these being used repeatedly. Note also that a method of saving, or storing, intermediate results is required. But most of all, some-one or something must be in *control*, seeing that each instruction is understood and executed in its proper turn. Fig. 3-17 offers a rough, preliminary view of such a computer, or circuit. In Problem 3.1 the human solver provided the control, also serving as NOT and AND, while pencil and paper served as storage. The OR circuit appears in this diagram merely to round out this view of logical computing; it was not, of course, used in the present problem.

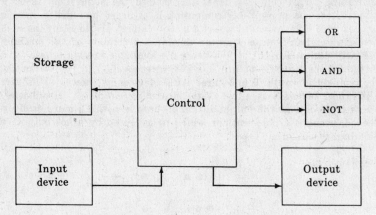

Fig. 3-17. A general-purpose computer.

3.4. Compute the truth tables of the following statements (refer to Example 3.1, page 26).

1. Either my aunt does not have fleas or else my brother does not.

2. It is not true that both of them have fleas.

The first translates into Boolean as $\bar{A} + \bar{B}$ while the second becomes $\overline{AB}$. From the theory of Boolean algebra we know these to be equal, so the two statements must have matching true-false values. We choose to compute $\overline{AB}$ since it requires only two operations.

$$A \quad 0\ 0\ 1\ 0\ 1\ 0\ 0$$
$$B \quad 0\ 0\ 1\ 0\ 0\ 0\ 1$$
$$AB \quad 0\ 0\ 1\ 0\ 0\ 0\ 0$$
$$\overline{AB} \quad 1\ 1\ 0\ 1\ 1\ 1\ 1$$

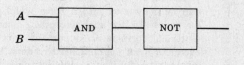

Both statements are true except on Tuesday. A trivial special-purpose machine for computing this result is shown in Fig. 3-18.

Fig. 3-18

3.5. Translate into Boolean and compute the truth table for "Only the dog has fleas". (See Example 3.1.)

Translation brings $\bar{A}\bar{B}\bar{C}D$ since we must state that the dog has fleas and that each of the others does not. This product will have the value one only when A, B, C, D equal $0, 0, 0, 1$ respectively. Referring back to the truth tables given in Example 3.1, we discover that this pattern occurs only on Sunday. The required truth table is as follows.

$$1\ 0\ 0\ 0\ 0\ 0\ 0$$

A special-purpose circuit for computing this same sequence is shown in Fig. 3-19.

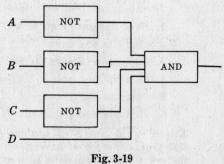

Fig. 3-19

3.6.   **Referring** to Example 3.1, compute the truth table for "At least one of the four has fleas".

Translation into Boolean brings $A + B + C + D$, after which it is only a matter of a few additions to obtain the sequence

$$1\ 1\ 1\ 0\ 1\ 0\ 1$$

and the job is already done. It is easy enough for a human being to come to this conclusion directly from the given data, the statements and sequences of Example 3.1. The statement in question is clearly false only on Wednesday and Friday. It is slightly harder to make the translation into Boolean language, realizing that the given statement is equivalent to "A or B or C or D". Translation is necessary, however, if machine help is to be involved. An electrical circuit is unlikely to know the meaning of "at least" unless a substantial engineering effort has gone into its design. The same remark applies to the word "only" in the preceding problem. As mentioned in Chapter 1, there is a formidable language problem in the design of sophisticated circuitry. For the present problem, however, and with adequate preliminary human effort, one OR circuit is all that is needed to compute the required truth table.

3.7.   Show that the following two statements are equivalent, that is, that their truth tables are the same (see Example 3.1).

1. My aunt has fleas but my brother does not, or else he does while the cat does not, or maybe the cat does but my aunt does not.

2. My aunt does not have fleas but my brother does, or else he does not while the cat does, or maybe the cat does not but my aunt does.

It is surely not clear from the English prose that these two statements say basically the same thing, but the first translates easily into Boolean language as

$$A\bar{B} + B\bar{C} + C\bar{A}$$

while the second becomes

$$\bar{A}B + \bar{B}C + \bar{C}A$$

Theorem 2.34, page 20, now guarantees the equality of these two Boolean combinations. It would also be possible for an electrical machine to prove this result, by computing both combinations for the standard inputs

$$
\begin{array}{llllllllll}
A & 0 & 0 & 0 & 0 & 1 & 1 & 1 & 1 \\
B & 0 & 0 & 1 & 1 & 0 & 0 & 1 & 1 \\
C & 0 & 1 & 0 & 1 & 0 & 1 & 0 & 1 \\
\end{array}
$$

as we ourselves did in the preceding chapter. Both outputs would of course be the same, just as they were back there. The two statements are thus equivalent for any A, B, C whatever, including those of Example 1 which present only five of the eight possible input combinations. Fig. 2-6, page 21, shows suitable circuits.

3.8.   Referring to Example 3.1, compare the following statements.

1. Either my aunt or brother has fleas, and so does either my cat or my dog.

2. My aunt and cat both have fleas, or else she and the dog do, or maybe it's my brother and cat, or perhaps my brother and dog.

Translating into Boolean language, the first becomes

$$(A + B)(C + D)$$

and the second

$$AC + AD + BC + BD$$

Theorem 2.30, page 18, guarantees the equality of these Boolean combinations. The two statements will thus have matching true-false values for any A, B, C, D. Of the two, the first seems preferable because it is simpler, even for human beings.

3.9. How could an electrical machine be designed to prove the result of the preceding problem?

It would have to compute both Boolean expressions for all possible input combinations. Since there are four input sequences A, B, C, D, a moment's thought will bring conviction that the following sixteen combinations are possible and no more.

$$A \quad 0\,0\,0\,0\,0\,0\,0\,0\,1\,1\,1\,1\,1\,1\,1\,1$$
$$B \quad 0\,0\,0\,0\,1\,1\,1\,1\,0\,0\,0\,0\,1\,1\,1\,1$$
$$C \quad 0\,0\,1\,1\,0\,0\,1\,1\,0\,0\,1\,1\,0\,0\,1\,1$$
$$D \quad 0\,1\,0\,1\,0\,1\,0\,1\,0\,1\,0\,1\,0\,1\,0\,1$$

Computation of $(A+B)(C+D)$ and $AC + AD + BC + BD$ for this selection of A, B, C, D will bring identical results, thus proving once again the equivalence of the statements in Problem 3.8. The A, B, C, D of Example 1, page 26, include only six of the sixteen possible input combinations.

3.10. Computing an output sequence from given input sequences could perhaps be described as an electrical machine's "thought process". At least, such machines can definitely perform this task. For comparison with human thought processes, consider the following problem. It is harder to imagine a machine capable of this sort of thought.

A captured warrior, the prince of his tribe, is given the following sporting chance by the chief of his captors. "You see these two doors. Behind that one is my daughter, behind the other a hungry tiger. I will have either door opened, whichever one you choose. And to help you, you may put one statement to one of your two guards. He will answer simply "true" or "false". However, I warn you that one of the guards never speaks the truth, whereas the other never lies". What statement should the warrior make?

At first glance the warrior's chances may seem about fifty-fifty, but most students of logic have discovered how they can be converted into a sure thing by a well-chosen statement. There are two basic statements with which our warrior must be concerned. Pointing to one of the two doors he can say

A: This is the lady's door.

Pointing to one of the two guards he can say

B: You tell the truth.

His problem is that he does not know whether these important statements are true or false. He is confronted with the usual four possibilities.

$$A \quad 0\,0\,1\,1$$
$$B \quad 0\,1\,0\,1$$

Put in another way, after choosing a door and a guard he does not know which of the four columns is involved. After some reflection it might occur to him that statement A is the most vital to him, and that it would therefore be very satisfactory if he could arrange for the guard's answer to be as follows:

Guard's answer 0 0 1 1

Here 0 means the word "false" while 1 means the word "true". If the warrior could formulate a statement which would provoke these answers, depending upon which door and which guard he has chosen, then his problem would be solved, because the answer "false" comes precisely *when statement A is false* and the answer "true" comes precisely *when A is true*. He could then *believe* the answer he gets, at least for distinguishing doors.

But what statement can achieve this very satisfactory result? Take the four columns one by one. In the first the guard's answer is to be "false". But in this column statement B also happens to be false, so it is the liar who is giving this answer. If the liar says "false" it must be because the warrior's statement is true. The truth table for this (still unknown) statement must therefore start with a 1 in the first column. In the second column the answer received is again "false". But here statement B is true, so it is the truth-teller speaking. If the truth-teller says that the guard's statement is false, then it must be false. This calls for a 0 in column two. The remaining columns respond to similar logic and the complete truth table for the warrior's statement is as follows:

Warrior's statement 1 0 0 1

Such a statement can easily be designed by using the basic products of the preceding chapter. In fact we have already found that for the above A, B sequences AB and $\bar{A}\bar{B}$ take these values:

$$AB \quad 0\ 0\ 0\ 1$$

$$\bar{A}\bar{B} \quad 1\ 0\ 0\ 0$$

A Boolean addition thus achieves $AB + \bar{A}\bar{B}$ $1\ 0\ 0\ 1$

so that in Boolean language a suitable statement is $AB + \bar{A}\bar{B}$. Translated into English prose this becomes

> "This is the lady's door and you tell the truth, or else
> it is not the lady's door and you lie."

If the guard fully understands this statement then our man is safe.

3.11. Referring back to the classification table of Example 3.5, compute membership lists, or sequences, and identify the following:

(1) a female redhead

(2) a short blond with a long criminal record.

In Boolean language these two subsets may be expressed as AD and $\bar{A}\bar{B}\bar{C}$. Computation then produces

$$AD \quad 0\ 0\ 0\ 0\ 0\ 1\ 0\ 0\ 0\ 0$$

$$\bar{A}\bar{B}\bar{C} \quad 0\ 0\ 0\ 0\ 0\ 0\ 0\ 0\ 1\ 0$$

identifying prisoner number 6 as the female redhead and prisoner 9 as the short blond.

3.12. Design a special-purpose machine for computing the results of the preceding problem.

The machine of Fig. 3-20 would serve.

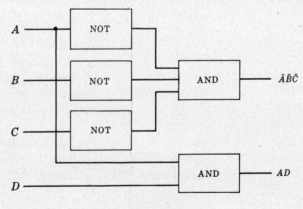

Fig. 3-20

3.13. To suggest in a preliminary way how a general-purpose computer might handle the preceding problem list the steps involved in the approach of Problem 3.11, assuming that the computations made there proceeded row by row.

The steps involved were as follows.

1. Read and save sequences A, B, C, D.
2. Compute and punch out AD.
3. Compute and save $\bar{A}$.
4. Compute and save $\bar{B}$.
5. Compute and save $\bar{C}$.
6. Compute and punch out $\bar{A}\bar{B}\bar{C}$.

The remarks made in the solution of Problem 3.3 are again appropriate, and Fig. 3-17 is again a suitable rough sketch of the computer since a general-purpose machine will surely be capable of handling that problem and this one too, and much more sophisticated problems as well.

3.14. How many of the prisoners of Example 3.5 are six feet tall, and also either female or redheaded?

> In Boolean language such prisoners form subset $C(A + D)$. Its membership sequence may be computed in the familiar way.
>
> $$A + D \quad 0\ 1\ 1\ 1\ 0\ 1\ 1\ 0\ 0\ 1$$
>
> $$C(A + D) \quad 0\ 0\ 0\ 0\ 0\ 1\ 0\ 0\ 0\ 1$$

Two prisoners qualify, numbers 6 and 10. For the very small jail involved here there would be no difficulty in solving this problem simply "by eye", a glance at the table of Example 3.5 being almost enough. For a jail with a thousand prisoners, however, it might be wise to have the records, such as the table of Example 3.5, on punched tape or something similar. The computations could then be made by Boolean machines, after adequate human preparations.

3.15. How many female, redheaded, hardened criminals are there in the jail of Example 3.5?

> This subset is described in Boolean language as $A\bar{B}D$. The separate factors have been used before and we need only compute their product, which is the sequence
>
> $$A\bar{B}D \quad 0\ 0\ 0\ 0\ 0\ 0\ 0\ 0\ 0\ 0$$

or $\emptyset$. There are no such prisoners.

This problem and the preceding few have illustrated how Boolean computations contribute to the solution of classification problems. For the small jail involved it has already been admitted that results are easily found without Boolean algebra, but on a larger scale it is convenient to exploit the availability of these methods, particularly the fact that Boolean computations can be done by OR, AND, NOT circuitry. We shall not stop to further emphasize this point by presenting further diagrams of special-purpose circuits, or machines, since the more flexible general-purpose computer is our ultimate goal anyway. The following problem offers still one more example of the availability of Boolean methods for logical applications of this type.

3.16. Twenty mice are introduced into a maze, one by one. If a mouse comes out at the correct exit he is rewarded with a piece of cheese; otherwise he gets nothing. Each mouse has three tries. With A, B and C representing the subsets that make successful first, second and third tries respectively, the results are as shown in Table 3.1. The membership sequence for each subset is packaged into two rows of ten values each. Thus four mice, numbers 2, 6, 12 and 19, are in subset A, having been successful on the very first try. Mouse number 1 is not in any of the three subsets; he is a slow learner, with no successful runs. Mouse number 11 did finally succeed, on the third and last try.

$$A \quad 0\ 1\ 0\ 0\ 0\ 1\ 0\ 0\ 0\ 0$$
$$0\ 1\ 0\ 0\ 0\ 0\ 0\ 0\ 1\ 0$$
$$B \quad 0\ 0\ 0\ 0\ 0\ 1\ 1\ 0\ 0\ 0$$
$$0\ 1\ 0\ 1\ 1\ 0\ 0\ 0\ 1\ 1$$
$$C \quad 0\ 1\ 1\ 0\ 1\ 1\ 1\ 1\ 0\ 0$$
$$1\ 1\ 0\ 1\ 0\ 0\ 0\ 0\ 1\ 1$$

Table 3.1

Use the data of this table to answer the following questions.

1. How many mice were successful every time?

2. How many were never successful?

3. How many succeeded only on the final try?

4. How many were successful the very first time?

5. How many were successful on the second try?

6. How many on the third try?

7. How many mice had at least one success?

8. How many had exactly one success?

9. How many had exactly two successes?

In Boolean language these nine questions ask that the memberships of subsets ABC, $\bar{A}\bar{B}\bar{C}$, $\bar{A}\bar{B}\bar{C}$, A, B, C, $A + B + C$, $A\bar{B}\bar{C} + \bar{A}B\bar{C} + \bar{A}\bar{B}C$, $AB\bar{C} + A\bar{B}C + \bar{A}BC$ be counted, taking them in the order listed. Computation of the membership sequences of these nine subsets proceeds in the usual way and produces Table 3.2.

ABC	0 0 0 0 0 1 0 0 0 0	$A + B + C$	0 1 1 0 1 1 1 1 0 0
	0 1 0 0 0 0 0 0 1 0		1 1 0 1 1 0 0 0 1 1
$\bar{A}\bar{B}\bar{C}$	1 0 0 1 0 0 0 0 1 1	$(A\bar{B}\bar{C} + \bar{A}B\bar{C} + \bar{A}\bar{B}C)$	0 0 1 0 1 0 0 1 0 0
	0 0 1 0 0 1 1 1 0 0		0 0 0 0 1 0 0 0 0 1
$\bar{A}\bar{B}C$	0 0 1 0 1 0 0 1 0 0	$(AB\bar{C} + A\bar{B}C + \bar{A}BC)$	0 1 0 0 0 0 1 0 0 0
	1 0 0 0 0 0 0 0 0 0		1 0 0 1 0 0 0 0 0 0

Table 3.2

The sequences for A, B and C themselves appear in Table 3.1. To answer the first question, three mice were successful every time, as the membership list for subset ABC shows, numbers 6, 12 and 19. As for question two, eight mice made no successful runs at all, their numbers being available if needed from the positions of the 1s in the membership sequence of subset $\bar{A}\bar{B}\bar{C}$. The answers to the remaining questions are found in the same way, by counting 1s in the membership sequences, and prove to be four, four, seven, eleven, twelve, five and four in that order.

Consider also these two extra questions.

10. How often was a success followed by a success?

11. How often was a success followed by a failure?

For the first of this pair of questions it is subset AB which is of interest, since mice in this subset followed a successful first run with a successful run; but in the same way subset BC must be considered, since its members followed a successful second run with a successful third. These are the two ways in which a success-success pattern can be produced. Similarly, for the remaining question it is subsets $A\bar{B}$ and $B\bar{C}$ which are involved. Computation of the corresponding membership sequences produces Table 3.3. Three 1s in AB and six more in BC combine to make nine success-success patterns, thus answering question 10. The single 1 in $A\bar{B}$ and the single 1 in $B\bar{C}$ combine to make two success-failure patterns, thus answering question 11.

AB	0 0 0 0 0 1 0 0 0 0	$A\bar{B}$	0 1 0 0 0 0 0 0 0 0
	0 1 0 0 0 0 0 0 1 0		0 0 0 0 0 0 0 0 0 0
BC	0 0 0 0 0 1 1 0 0 0	$B\bar{C}$	0 0 0 0 0 0 0 0 0 0
	0 1 0 1 0 0 0 0 1 1		0 0 0 0 1 0 0 0 0 0

Table 3.3

It is clear that record keeping of this sort requires space. For manual human labor it would be very easy to arrange a more compact notation which would make it unnecessary to write down all the zeros, a simple list of the successful competitors on each run probably being enough. For large scale experiments, however, it is usually desirable to take advantage of the fact that all the above computations can be carried out by Boolean machines. In this case the zeros and ones become electrical colds and hots and both must be recorded, as was done in the present example to simulate machine solution. The storage space needed is provided, in order to have the convenience of electrical information processing.

3.17. Prepare a subset diagram of $A\bar{B} + \bar{A}B$, the Boolean combination computed by the comparator circuit of Problem 2.12. Notice that it merely merges the shaded areas of Figs. 3-7 and 3-8, page 29.

The result appears as Fig. 3-21.

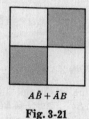

$A\bar{B} + \bar{A}B$

Fig. 3-21

3.18. Note that Figs. 3-6 and 3-11 display inverse Boolean combinations, since the shaded areas are complements of each other. These two diagrams offer a graphic view of Theorem 2.12, page 13, which states that $\overline{AB} = \bar{A} + \bar{B}$. Which two diagrams provide a similar view of the companion Theorem 2.11, page 13, which states that $\overline{A+B} = \bar{A}\bar{B}$?

Figs. 3-9 and 3-10, page 29.

3.19. Compare Figs. 3-10 and 3-11, observing in particular their intersection, or overlap. Which of the theorems in Chapter 2 does this illustrate?

Both diagrams are repeated as parts of Fig. 3-22, which also shows the intersection of the two subsets involved, $A + B$ and $\bar{A} + \bar{B}$. The result proves to be identical with Fig. 3-21, showing that

$$(A+B)(\bar{A}+\bar{B}) = A\bar{B} + \bar{A}B$$

By the preceding problem we may also replace $\bar{A} + \bar{B}$ by $\overline{AB}$, obtaining

$$(A+B)\overline{AB} = A\bar{B} + \bar{A}B$$

Both Theorems 2.21 and 2.22, page 13, have thus been deduced diagrammatically. This method of subset diagrams provides a simple, intuitive access to the theory of Boolean algebra, all of the theorems we have listed being provable in this graphic way.

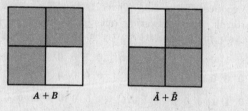
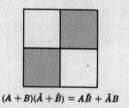

$A + B$ $\bar{A} + \bar{B}$ $(A+B)(\bar{A}+\bar{B}) = A\bar{B} + \bar{A}B$

Fig. 3-22

3.20. Diagram subsets A, $B + C$, $A(B+C)$, AB, AC and $AB + AC$, illustrating that $A(B+C) = AB + AC$ as Theorem 2.23, page 13, states. This may be considered a new proof of that theorem.

The subsets A, $B + C$ and their product, or intersection, $A(B+C)$ are covered by the top half of Fig. 3-23 below. Subsets AB, AC and their union $AB + AC$ appear in the bottom half of the figure. Clearly the results are the same.

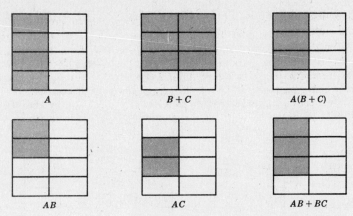

Fig. 3-23

3.21. Display the double product ABC on a subset diagram. It will be that part of the total square I which is common to A, B and C. In the same way display the other seven basic products $AB\bar{C}$, $A\bar{B}C$, etc.

   Instead of shading each of these regions on a separate diagram it is simpler to label each of the eight parts into which our square is divided by the basic layouts for A, B, C themselves. These basic layouts are repeated for convenience as a part of Fig. 3-24, the eight products then being shown in a magnified version. Notice that the part labeled ABC is in A, in B and in C. Similarly, the part labeled $AB\bar{C}$ is in A and in B, but not in C. Corresponding remarks apply to the other six regions of the square. Checking each one individually will confirm its label. Notice further that the four parts whose labels include A (rather than $\bar{A}$) make up the left half of the square, as they should since that part represents subset A. The four parts on the right include $\bar{A}$ in their labels. Similar remarks apply to B, $\bar{B}$ and to C, $\bar{C}$.

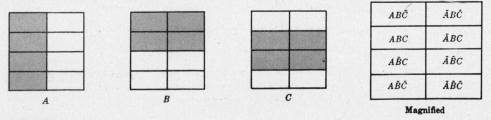

Fig. 3-24

   Stepping back for a moment to a simpler level, we could summarize Figs. 3-6 to 3-9 in the single diagram of Fig. 3-25, which displays the four basic products encountered in problems where only two subsets A and B appear.

AB	$\bar{A}B$
$A\bar{B}$	$\bar{A}\bar{B}$

Fig. 3-25

3.22. Which of the eight parts exhibited in the preceding problem combine to produce the $A(B + C)$ or $AB + AC$ area of Fig. 3-23?

   The top three of the left side. This provides a graphic proof of Theorem 2.31, page 19, namely, $A(B + C) = ABC + AB\bar{C} + A\bar{B}C$.

3.23. Prove by diagrams that $AB + (A + B)\overline{ABC} = AB + AC + BC$ as Theorem 2.33, page 20, claims.

The top half of Fig. 3-26 shows the development, from left to right, of $AB + (A + B)\overline{ABC}$. Here $(A + B)\overline{AB}$ is borrowed from Problem 3.19, intersected with C, and the result merged with AB. In the bottom half of the figure $AB + AC + BC$ is developed by obtaining the three products first and then merging them. The results at top and bottom are the same, again proving Theorem 2.33. What we have done also amounts to a direct verification by the use of subset diagrams that the two circuits of Problem 2.26 produce identical output information.

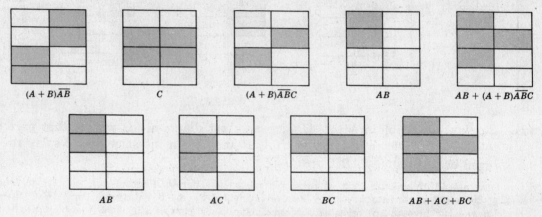

$(A + B)\overline{AB}$ $\qquad$ C $\qquad$ $(A + B)\overline{ABC}$ $\qquad$ AB $\qquad$ $AB + (A + B)\overline{ABC}$

AB $\qquad$ AC $\qquad$ BC $\qquad$ $AB + AC + BC$

Fig. 3-26

3.24. Show that $ABC + (A + B + C)\overline{AB + AC + BC}$ includes four of the eight basic products.

Borrowing $AB + AC + BC$ from the preceding problem, the development of the appropriate subset diagram is straightforward and appears as Fig. 3-27. The four parts shaded in the final result correspond to ABC, $A\bar{B}\bar{C}$, $\bar{A}B\bar{C}$ and $\bar{A}\bar{B}C$, which are the four basic products in question. This amounts to another proof of Theorem 2.39, page 22.

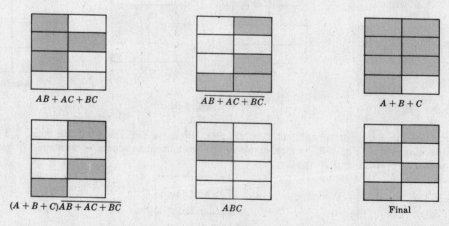

$AB + AC + BC$ $\qquad$ $\overline{AB + AC + BC}$ $\qquad$ $A + B + C$

$(A + B + C)\overline{AB + AC + BC}$ $\qquad$ ABC $\qquad$ Final

Fig. 3-27

3.25. Develop diagrams for $(A + B)(C + D)$ and $AC + AD + BC + BD$, thus verifying once again the first part of Theorem 2.30, page 18.

The top row of Fig. 3-28 below develops $(A + B)(C + D)$ by first exhibiting the two factors $A + B$ and $C + D$ and then their intersection. The bottom row then develops $AC + AD + BC + BD$ by first displaying the four products and then merging them. The final results in these two rows are the same. Note that the square has now been divided into sixteen basic parts, as will be the case whenever four subsets A, B, C, D are involved. These sixteen parts may be matched with the sixteen columns of Problem 3.9, following the procedure of Problem 3.21.

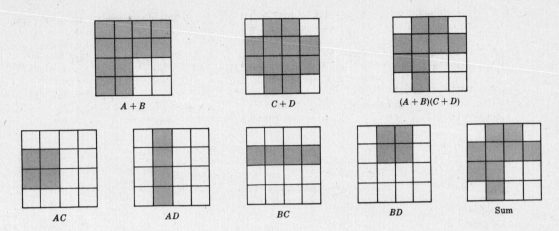

Fig. 3-28

3.26. Display the data of Problem 3.16, the mouse-maze problem, on a subset diagram.

Only three subsets A, B, C are involved, so an eight part diagram is once again adequate. The information of Table 3.1 can be duplicated by inserting the numbers of the various mice into the appropriate eight parts. Mouse number 1, for instance, is not in any of the subsets A, B, C, as Table 3.1 indicates with three 0's. Here this same fact is indicated by writing the number 1 in the $\bar{A}\bar{B}\bar{C}$ part of the diagram. Mouse number 2, however, is in subsets A and C but not B, so we write 2 in part $A\bar{B}C$. Continuing in this way we obtain Fig. 3-29, in which the number of each mouse appears in one of the eight parts. From this diagram all of the questions of Problem 3.16 may again be answered. Thus we find three mice in subset ABC, which answers question one, their numbers again being 6, 12 and 19. Similarly there are eight mice in subset $\bar{A}\bar{B}\bar{C}$, again answering question two, and so on. This diagram is fairly convenient for a human analyst of the mouse-maze problem, but the sequences of Table 3.1 are easily converted into electrical form and so are accessible to machine processing. As noted earlier this is an enormous convenience in large scale problems.

	15
6, 12, 19	7, 14, 20
2	3, 5, 8, 11
	1, 4, 9, 10, 13, 16, 17, 18

$AB\bar{C}$	$\bar{A}B\bar{C}$
ABC	$\bar{A}BC$
$A\bar{B}C$	$\bar{A}\bar{B}C$
$A\bar{B}\bar{C}$	$\bar{A}\bar{B}\bar{C}$

Fig. 3-29

3.27. Problems of deduction have not been prominent among the major applications of Boolean machines but the possibility of such exploitation does exist and is fascinating enough to warrant inclusion of the following miniature illustration. Assume these somewhat implausible facts to be true.

1. The murderer wore a tall silk hat.

2. All Irishmen are redheaded.

3. The butler's name is O'Brien.

4. Redheads never wear hats.

What can be deduced?

Any competent detective would be insulted if offered so pitiful an assignment, and an amateur can easily unravel the facts in no time at all with no more technique than a close scrutiny. Even so, it is interesting to see an analysis by Boolean diagrams, or equivalently by Boolean sequences, and to contemplate the possibility of machine aid in the similar analyses of larger scale problems. The following subsets of the set I of all possible suspects are used:

A   Irishmen

B   Redheads

C   Hatwearers

Figure 3-30 is our usual affair, but with some of the parts deleted. Thus all Irishmen being assumed redheaded, that part of subset A (the Irishmen) which is not also in subset B (the redheads) has been deleted. Similarly, redheads not being hatwearers, the intersection of subsets B and C has been deleted. Finally, the murderer has been placed in what is left of subset C, because he is a hatwearer, while the butler appears in what is left of subset A, it being assumed that all O'Briens are Irish. We can therefore deduce that the butler is not guilty, he and the murderer being in distinct parts of set I. We cannot identify the murderer from the given input information but can at least clear the butler.

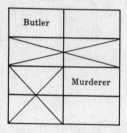

Fig. 3-30

The same exact output information is of course available from a sequence approach, which should not be surprising since subset diagrams and membership sequences represent exactly the same information in different forms. Table 3.4 presents the standard A, B, C sequences which still include the only eight distinct columns possible. Since no one may be a member of subset A without also belonging to B, however, columns 5 and 6 are not possible for this application. Accordingly they have been deleted. Similarly, since no one may be in subsets B and C simultaneously, columns 4 and 8 have also been deleted. It is worth pausing a moment to note that the four columns just deleted correspond to the four parts of Fig. 3-30 which were deleted a moment ago. Since the butler must be in subset A it now follows that he is classified in column 7, since this is the only active column in which A has a 1 value. Since the murderer must be in C, he is classified in column 2. Clearly the butler and murderer cannot be the same person. It is at least conceivable that a Boolean circuit could draw this very same conclusion, after adequate preliminary preparation of the original information.

$$A \quad 0 \ 0 \ 0 \ \cancel{0} \ \cancel{1} \ \cancel{1} \ 1 \ \cancel{1}$$

$$B \quad 0 \ 0 \ 1 \ \cancel{1} \ \cancel{0} \ \cancel{0} \ 1 \ \cancel{1}$$

$$C \quad 0 \ 1 \ 0 \ \cancel{1} \ \cancel{0} \ \cancel{1} \ 0 \ \cancel{1}$$

Table 3.4

Supplementary Problems

3.28. Translate into Boolean language, using the A, B, C, D statements of Example 3.1, page 26:

1. My dog has fleas but my cat does not.

2. It is not true that either the cat has fleas or else the dog does not.

Which of the theorems in Chapter 2 guarantees the equivalence of these two statements?

3.29. Compute the truth tables of the statements in the preceding problem, using the information in Example 3.1, page 26.

3.30. Referring to Example 3.1, group the English and Boolean statements below into equivalent pairs.

1. All four have fleas.   (a) $\overline{ABCD}$

2. None of them has fleas.   (b) $ABCD$

3. It is not true that they all have fleas.   (c) $\bar{A}\bar{B}\bar{C}\bar{D}$

3.31.   Fig. 3-31 shows a circuit which outputs truth tables corresponding to the three statements of the preceding problem. Label the outputs 1, 2 and 3 in suitable order, noting the application of Theorem 2.37, page 21.

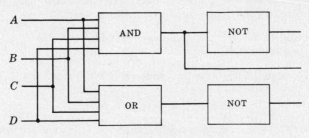

Fig. 3-31

3.32.   Compute the truth tables of the statements in the preceding two problems, using the sequences in Example 3.1.

3.33.   Group the English and Boolean statements below into equivalent pairs (see Example 3.1).

  1. Exactly one of the four has fleas.
  2. Exactly three of them have fleas.
      (a) $A\bar{B}\bar{C}\bar{D} + \bar{A}BC\bar{D} + \bar{A}\bar{B}C\bar{D} + \bar{A}\bar{B}\bar{C}D$
      (b) $ABC\bar{D} + AB\bar{C}D + A\bar{B}CD + \bar{A}BCD$

Translate into Boolean the statement, "Exactly two of them have fleas".

3.34.   Compute the truth tables of the statements in the preceding problem, using the data of Example 3.1.

3.35.   Translate into Boolean language and then simplify:

  1. My aunt has fleas or my aunt has fleas.
  2. My aunt has fleas and my aunt has fleas.
  3. It is not true that my aunt does not have fleas.
  4. My aunt and brother both have fleas, or else she does but he does not.
  5. Either my aunt has fleas or else she and my brother both do.

3.36.   Referring to Example 3.1, one of the following statements is always true, the other always false. Translate both into Boolean language. Which is which?

  1. Either my aunt does have fleas or else she does not.
  2. My aunt has fleas and she does not have fleas.

3.37.   Another very common way of combining statements A and B into a more complex statement is "A implies B", the symbol $A \to B$ being used to denote the result. Common usage dictates that if this statement $A \to B$ is true, then A being true forces B to be true also. This explains column four of the table below, and column three also. It also explains column one, since if $A \to B$ is true and B is false then A cannot be true. Try to convince yourself that $A \to B$ is also true, according to common usage, in column two, referring also to the following problem for comparison. Also show that $A \to B = \bar{A} + B$.

$$
\begin{array}{ll}
A & 0\ 0\ 1\ 1 \\
B & 0\ 1\ 0\ 1 \\
A \to B & 1\ 1\ 0\ 1
\end{array}
$$

3.38.   The statement "A implies B and B implies A" is given the symbol $A \leftrightarrow B$. If it is true, then the truth of either A or B forces the truth of the other also. This is according to common usage of the concept of implication. Convince yourself that the table below summarizes these facts correctly and then show that $A \leftrightarrow B = AB + \bar{A}\bar{B}$. The statement $A \to B$ of the preceding problem is also expressed in English as "If A then B". In the same way $A \leftrightarrow B$ becomes "A if and only if B".

$$
\begin{array}{ll}
A & 0\ 0\ 1\ 1 \\
B & 0\ 1\ 0\ 1 \\
A \leftrightarrow B & 1\ 0\ 0\ 1
\end{array}
$$

3.39. Using the information in Example 3.5 identify the redheaded, female, six-foot first-offender. How can this subset be described in Boolean language?

3.40. Which prisoners in Example 3.5 are either male redheads or else female blonds? Describe this subset in Boolean language.

3.41. One of the machines designed in Chapter 1 is suitable for computing the membership sequence of the subset in Problem 3.40 electrically. Which one?

3.42. Referring to Example 3.5 compute the membership sequences for the following subsets of prisoners. Also describe these subsets in English.

$$(A + B)(C + D), \quad \bar{A}\bar{B}$$

3.43. Show how the following circuits could be connected to output the membership sequences required in the preceding problem, applying Theorem 2.11, page 13, in the process. (Fig. 3-32.)

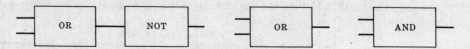

Fig. 3-32

3.44. In Example 3.5 a prisoner is identified as being in subset $B + \bar{D}$. Why is this information of no use?

3.45. By comparing the subset diagrams of AB and $A\bar{B}$ rediscover Theorem 2.15, page 13, which states that $AB + A\bar{B} = A$.

3.46. By comparing the diagrams of A and AB rediscover Theorem 2.16, page 13, which states that $A + AB = A$.

3.47. Verify Theorems 2.17 to 2.20, page 13, by means of subset diagrams.

3.48. Represent the outputs of the two machines in Fig. 3-33 in Boolean language and then use subset diagrams to determine whether or not these outputs are equivalent.

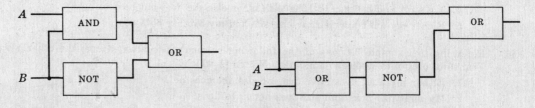

Fig. 3-33

3.49. Represent the output of the machine in Fig. 2-12, page 24, in Boolean language and then by a subset diagram. From the diagram deduce that just one AND, OR or NOT circuit can manage the same output. Which of the three is it?

3.50. Represent the output of the machine in Fig. 2-13, page 25, in Boolean language and then by a subset diagram. From the diagram deduce that a combination of only two AND, OR, NOT circuits can manage the same output. Which two?

3.51. Represent the outputs of the two machines in Fig. 3-34 in Boolean language and then by subset diagrams. From the diagrams determine whether or not the circuits are equivalent.

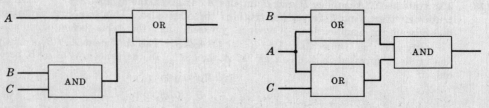

Fig. 3-34

3.52. Proceed as in the preceding problem with the two machines of Fig. 2-6, page 21. This will involve preparing and then merging subset diagrams of $A\bar{B}$, $B\bar{C}$ and $C\bar{A}$ and then similarly preparing and merging diagrams of $\bar{A}B$, $\bar{B}C$ and $\bar{C}A$. The two mergers should be the same. Which theorem does this again prove?

3.53. Represent the output of the machine in Fig. 3-35 in Boolean language and then by a subset diagram. Compare with the diagrams produced in the preceding problem. Note that the present machine seems far simpler than either of those in Fig. 2-6, page 21, on which the preceding problem was based. This is a miniature example of how diagrams have been used in the simplification of circuitry.

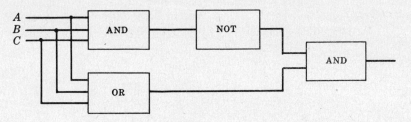

Fig. 3-35

3.54. Design a machine which computes the following output sequence.

$$A \quad 0\ 0\ 0\ 0\ 1\ 1\ 1\ 1$$
$$B \quad 0\ 0\ 1\ 1\ 0\ 0\ 1\ 1$$
$$C \quad 0\ 1\ 0\ 1\ 0\ 1\ 0\ 1$$
$$\text{output} \quad 0\ 0\ 0\ 1\ 0\ 1\ 1\ 1$$

Clearly this can be done by merging the four basic products $AB\bar{C}$, $A\bar{B}C$, $\bar{A}BC$ and ABC, but find a simpler machine. One way to do this is by observing that the subset diagram of this output can also be obtained from the merger of three simpler products, as study of Fig. 3-36 may suggest. The resulting machine may be viewed as a vote-analyzer, since the output will be hot when *a majority* of the inputs A, B, C are hot.

Fig. 3-36

3.55. Design as simple a machine as you can to output the following sequence.

$$A \quad 0\ 0\ 0\ 0\ 1\ 1\ 1\ 1$$
$$B \quad 0\ 0\ 1\ 1\ 0\ 0\ 1\ 1$$
$$C \quad 0\ 1\ 0\ 1\ 0\ 1\ 0\ 1$$
$$\text{output} \quad 0\ 1\ 1\ 1\ 1\ 1\ 1\ 0$$

3.56. A hall light is to be controlled by either of two switches, responding when either switch is changed. If it is to be off when both switches read "off", then it must come on when either switch is turned to read "on". Moreover, and this takes a moment's thought, it must also be off when *both* switches read "on". (See Fig. 3-37.) This situation is summarized in the following table, in which zero means off and one means on.

Fig. 3-37

$$\text{Switch } A \quad 0\ 0\ 1\ 1$$
$$\text{Switch } B \quad 0\ 1\ 0\ 1$$
$$\text{Hall light} \quad 0\ 1\ 1\ 0$$

Which circuit already presented in Chapter 1 computes this same output? Also compare with the result of Problem 3.10.

3.57. A hall light is to respond to each of three switches A, B and C. If it is to be off when all the switches read off, convince yourself that it will be on when either one or three switches read on, as the following table indicates.

Switch A	0 0 0 0 1 1 1 1
Switch B	0 0 1 1 0 0 1 1
Switch C	0 1 0 1 0 1 0 1
Hall light	0 1 1 0 1 0 0 1

This output could be achieved by generating the Boolean combination

$$ABC + A\bar{B}\bar{C} + \bar{A}B\bar{C} + \bar{A}\bar{B}C$$

but it is possible to economize somewhat. Show that the circuit of Fig. 3-38 produces an equivalent output, using a subset diagram or otherwise. Both this and the preceding problem should be viewed as mere exercises in the design of Boolean machines, since hall lights may be wired without appealing to Boolean algebra.

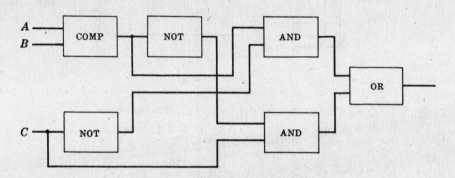

Fig. 3-38

3.58. When four subsets A, B, C, D are active in a problem, all may be represented simultaneously in a subset diagram as already shown in Figs. 3-2, 3-4, 3-12 and 3-14. This arrangement allows for all possible combinations to be displayed. In particular $A(B + C + D)$ can be developed as shown in the top row of Fig. 3-39. Shade in appropriate areas of the bottom row, developing a diagram for $AB + AC + AD$. The result should of course agree with that for $A(B + C + D)$, as Theorem 2.29, page 18, claims.

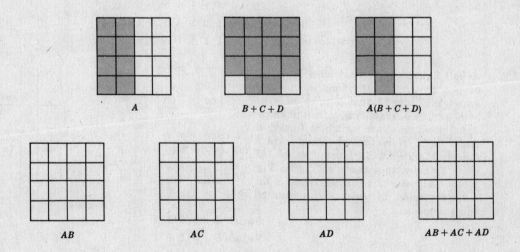

Fig. 3-39

3.59. The sixteen parts into which our square I is divided by the layouts for A, B, C, D correspond to sixteen basic products of the form $ABCD$, $ABC\bar{D}$, $AB\bar{C}D$, and so on. Some of these have been labeled accordingly in Fig. 3-40. Label those remaining.

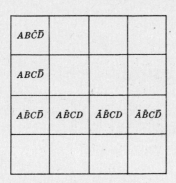

Fig. 3-40

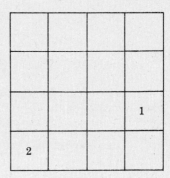

Fig. 3-41

3.60. Each of the prisoners of Example 3.5, page 28, may be classified in one of the sixteen parts of Fig. 3-40. In Fig. 3-41 the numbers of two prisoners have been entered in the appropriate parts. Enter the numbers of the remaining prisoners where they belong.

3.61. The following problem of deduction was created by Lewis Carroll, author of Alice in Wonderland. Assuming that

1. no one who is going to a party ever fails to brush his hair

2. no one looks fascinating if he is untidy

3. opium eaters have no self command

4. everyone who has brushed his hair looks fascinating

5. no one wears white kid gloves unless he is going to a party

6. a man is always untidy if he has no self command

what can be deduced? It is not too difficult to excavate the famous deduction which was Carroll's objective, simply by careful study of the six premises, but try also to make the deduction by means of subset diagrams or sequences as a computing circuit would have to do. These subsets will be involved.

> A party-goers
>
> B hair-brushers
>
> C those who look fascinating
>
> D those who are untidy
>
> E opium eaters
>
> F those with no self command
>
> G those who wear white kid gloves

For seven active subsets, a diagram with 128 parts can be drawn or sequences with 128 values are needed. Clearly a certain amount of preparation is in order.

Chapter 4

Computer Design

The arithmetic of numbers is one of the principal objectives in the design of serious computer circuits. As was the case with the simpler and more light-hearted circuitry of the preceding chapter, the core of the problem is once again the achievement of mutual understanding between man and machine. Somehow we must arrange for the result of a computation made by an electrical circuit according to the rules of Boolean algebra to be the particular result we need, perhaps the sum or product of two given numbers. The starting point for this particular effort at man-machine communication is usually the reinterpretation of sequences of zeros and ones as *binary symbols* for numbers. Though a sequence such as

$$10011$$

will continue, from the machine's point of view, to be a sequence of hot and cold values to be processed by a combination of OR, AND, NOT circuits, we shall unilaterally, for the purposes of number arithmetic, decide that each one in such a sequence is to have place value, much as in decimal symbolism. It is worth repeating, perhaps, that this is *a change in our own attitude* toward the sequence, the machine being asked to accept it and treat it on exactly the same terms as heretofore.

Binary symbols involve the doubling in value of the 1 symbol with each displacement toward the left, just as with decimal symbols such a displacement brings a tenfold increase. The key numbers thus turn out to be the following, decimal and binary symbols being paired to expedite recognition.

Binary	Decimal
1	1
10	2
100	4
1000	8
10000	16
100000	32

Other numbers may then be assigned binary symbols by building combinations of the key numbers above.

Example 4.1.

Express the numbers from one to ten in binary symbolism. To achieve this we first represent each such number as a sum of key numbers, using decimal symbols because they are so familiar.

$$3 = 2 + 1 \qquad 6 = 4 + 2 \qquad 9 = 8 + 1$$
$$5 = 4 + 1 \qquad 7 = 4 + 2 + 1 \qquad 10 = 8 + 2$$

The numbers 1, 2, 4 and 8 are of course themselves key numbers. The required binary symbols are

$$1 = 1 \qquad 3 = 11 \qquad 5 = 101 \qquad 7 = 111 \qquad 9 = 1001$$
$$2 = 10 \qquad 4 = 100 \qquad 6 = 110 \qquad 8 = 1000 \qquad 10 = 1010$$

the decimal equivalent appearing on the left of the equality sign.

Conversion between decimal and binary symbols for the same number can be carried out in various ways. For human computers it is probably most convenient to operate with decimal symbols while making the necessary calculations, since these are the more familiar. As will be seen later on, machines may prefer to use binary symbols during the conversion process. Either way, conversion routines are not hard to develop.

Example 4.2.

The binary symbol 10011 which was used as an example a moment ago can be converted to decimal by simply noting the place value of each 1. Thus

$$10011 = 16 + 2 + 1 = 19$$

all symbols except the original 10011 being decimal. Similarly

$$100110 = 32 + 4 + 2 = 38$$

each 1 having double its value in the preceding sequence. Again,

$$11111 = 16 + 8 + 4 + 2 + 1 = 31$$

These are typical binary to decimal conversions with decimal serving as the language for the intermediate computations.

Example 4.3.

To illustrate decimal to binary conversion take the number 52. The routine involves subtracting key numbers until nothing remains. Thus

$$52 - 32 = 20, \quad 20 - 16 = 4, \quad 4 - 4 = 0$$

so putting the pieces back together

$$52 = 32 + 16 + 4 = 110100$$

only the final symbol being binary. Similarly, to convert 43 we make the subtractions

$$43 - 32 = 11, \quad 11 - 8 = 3, \quad 3 - 2 = 1, \quad 1 - 1 = 0$$

and putting the pieces back together

$$43 = 32 + 8 + 2 + 1 = 101011$$

Electrical circuits for performing the basic operations of number arithmetic can be designed without serious difficulty once the decision to interpret a sequence of zeros and ones as a binary symbol has been made. It is then necessary to observe in detail how sums, differences, products and quotients can be obtained in binary language, and to duplicate the steps involved by the Boolean operations of AND, OR and NOT. This process will be followed in some detail in the solved problems, but the following two examples give the general idea.

Example 4.4.

The decimal result $9 + 3 = 12$ may be obtained using only binary symbols by a procedure very much like the familiar decimal addition routine.

$$
\begin{array}{r}
1001 \\
+ \ 0011 \\
\hline
1100
\end{array}
$$

Starting at the right we face $1 + 1$, which is definitely two, in number arithmetic if not in Boolean. But in binary language this two must be represented in the next column to the left, that is, it must be carried. The same computation is thus at hand in this second column, and produces another carry. The remaining steps are relatively obvious and the resulting sequence 1100 is binary for 12. Each step taken in obtaining this result may now be listed and a circuit designed to duplicate these steps. The addition circuit of Fig. 4-8 does precisely this, and in Problem 4.16 we follow the machine as it repeats our computation.

Our first adding machine is then complete and we may begin the search for refinements. For instance, if both positive and negative numbers occur, then the language must first be enlarged to indicate this. Attaching an extra leading value to our sequences, 0 for positive and 1 for negative, the problem

$$\begin{array}{ll} 10110 & -6 \\ +\ 00101 & +5 \end{array}$$

may be considered. Here the decimal form appears at the right for convenience. It may be recalled that this addition is actually effected by subtracting 5 from 6 and making the result negative. The sum is thus −1 or 10001, depending upon the language. A machine for making the appropriate computation appears in Fig. 4-15, and the above sum is developed in Problem 4.34. Further refinements of language and of the addition process, particularly the use of *floating point* symbols to avoid the problem of *overflow*, are also presented.

Example 4.5.

The decimal result $13 \times 6 = 78$ may be obtained using only binary symbols by a procedure very much like the familiar decimal multiplication routine.

$$\begin{array}{ll} 1101 & \text{First factor} \\ 0110 & \text{Second factor} \\ \hline 0000 \\ 1101 \\ 1101 \\ 0000 \\ \hline 1001110 & \text{The final product} \end{array}$$

The partial products

The partial products, the continual shifting to the left, and the final addition must all be reminiscent of early mathematical experiences. To begin, the rightmost digit of the second factor multiplies the first factor, forming the first partial product 0000. The other digits of the second factor then take their turns, one by one, as multiplier. Since only 0 and 1 occur as digits, only two types of partial product are possible, and these steadily shift toward the left because each multiplier value has double the value of the one before it. Adding up the partial products brings the binary equivalent of 78. Each step taken in generating this product may now be listed, and a circuit designed to take exactly the same steps. The multiplier of Fig. 4-25 does precisely this and in Problem 4.46 we follow it through the same computation just completed. The treatment of sign values, allowance for much larger numbers, and the operations of subtraction and division are all discussed in similar spirit.

General-purpose computers are designed by continuing in the direction set by the preceding examples. The *main purpose* of this chapter, to repeat briefly, is to show how the development of a suitable language can lead to the design of circuitry which will produce required results. Our goal is not to provide all the details but to answer with at least some detail the question of how it is possible to persuade electricity to serve our purpose. The resulting circuit, the general-purpose computer, is usually said to include four mutually supporting but somewhat distinct parts.

1. The arithmetic unit.
2. The control unit.
3. The memory or storage unit.
4. The input-output unit.

The significance of each part and their relationships to each other will become clearer as we proceed, but the examples already given provide some clues. For example, the addition and multiplication circuits are clearly in the arithmetic unit. But to add two given numbers one must first note their signs, then add if the signs are alike or subtract if they are unlike. This involves a *decision* process to set the course of action. And in multiplication one must note whether the next multiplier value is 0 or 1, since this determines whether the next partial product is to be 0000 or 1101, for instance. Such decisions are a form of control. Moreover, in multiplication the partial products must be saved, or totaled as they are produced and the running total saved. This requires a form of memory, or storage. Finally, the original numbers must be made available to the machine and the final result must be obtained from it. Clearly this is the function of the input-output unit. The standard eagle's eye view of the complete general-purpose computer, showing some measure of the inter-connectivity of its four parts, is provided in Fig. 4-1. This resembles very closely Fig. 3-17, and Problem 3.3, page 31, might very well be reread quickly at this time.

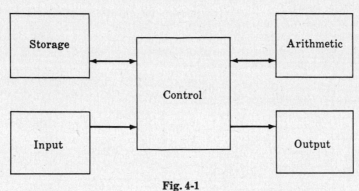

Fig. 4-1

Control circuitry holds the central position in Fig. 4-1 because it governs the action of all other units of the machine, determining when information is to be read in, where it is to be stored, when it must be retrieved from storage, sent to the arithmetic unit, and so on. One of the main functions of control will be held for the next chapter but certain simple though typical decision devices can be illustrated at once and appear in the circuits of this chapter.

Example 4.6.

Suppose the two numbers 10110 and 00101 (in decimal language −6 and +5) are to be added. Because the signs (represented by the leading values) are unlike, a subtraction must actually be made. A control circuit for recognizing this fact and taking proper action is shown in Fig. 4-2. The sign values are led to a comparator. If they are unlike the comparator output is hot and electrical energy flows through wire number one, ready to activate a subtraction unit. If the signs are like then the comparator output is cold, but now wire number two is active and triggers the addition unit. For the given numbers wire one is hot while wire two is cold, and the subtractor is called into use. The simple comparator thus serves as a decision or control device. Further details are given in Problem 4.33.

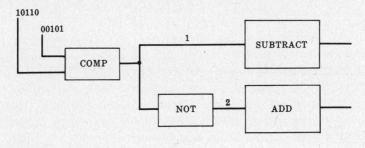

Fig. 4-2

Example 4.7.

Even simpler is the case in which the course of action to be taken depends upon the sign of a single number. As Fig. 4-3 suggests, a NOT circuit may then be enough to decide which wire will receive the hot output and trigger the next event. For the particular case shown the number in question is positive, so the NOT receives a cold input and the upper wire gets the nod.

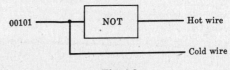

Fig. 4-3

Example 4.8.

The fact that there are eight possible combinations such as 000, 001, 010, and so on has already been put to use in various ways. It also means that eight possible lines of action may be identified by three input values. Fig. 4-4 shows, for example, what is called the tree method of making the selection. This control circuit resembles the plan of an elimination tournament, but the action is in the opposite direction. With $A_1A_2A_3$ denoting a combination, the A_1 value determines whether the right half or the left half of the circuit will contain the active line. The A_2 value then chooses the quarter, after which the A_3 value singles out the particular line. To be more specific, suppose that 011 is the incoming combination. Then the wires which have been labeled 1, for hot, show that the output terminal 011 will be hot. It is easy to verify that all the other output terminals will be cold, and further, that each one becomes hot for the input combination indicated. A control circuit such as this, which takes in a combination of hot and cold values and outputs a hot value on just one of several possible lines, is called *a decoder*. We will have more than one chance to use such a decision device.

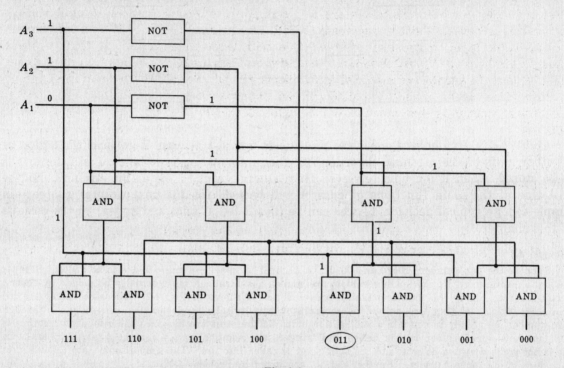

Fig. 4-4

The memory unit serves a number of purposes. To start we must provide any circuit with the information it will need to carry out its assignment, and it must "remember" this information long enough to finish. In a long computation many intermediate results must be saved at least temporarily. At a somewhat higher level, we will be asking the computer to assume many of the chores of translation between its language and ours. It will be necessary to teach it how to do this, and it will have to remember. Naturally, information will be stored in the form of sequences of zeros and ones, and it has proved convenient to keep all sequences at exactly the same length. In a serious computer this length may be thirty or forty values but for our purposes it will usually be much shorter. The circuitry required to store one sequence is called *a storage register*. The obvious basic requirements of such a register are:

1. It must be possible to "write" the desired sequence into it.

2. The sequence must stay there until deliberately changed.

3. It must be possible to "read" the sequence when it is needed, usually without destroying it, so that multiple use is possible.

Different ways of achieving these goals exist and several may be used in the same computer. All represent zeros and ones as electrical (or magnetic, which for our purposes may be taken to be the same thing) colds and hots. Although the details will not be presented here, two somewhat distinct types of storage may be mentioned.

1. Flip-flops.

2. Magnetic cores, films, drums, tapes, etc.

The first is a very flexible memory device and has very fast access, that is, values may be written into it or read from it at excellent speed. For these reasons it is used in the most active parts of the computer, such as the arithmetic unit. Some indication of how this kind of memory contributes to information processing is given among the solved problems (Problems 4.40 to 4.52). Flip-flops are also somewhat expensive and for general storage the various magnetic devices represent a sort of compromise between cost and speed. An important point to consider in connection with large-scale memory is that before a sequence can be read it must be found. Memory locations, or registers, must be identifiable. Some ideas on this point are provided in Problems 4.60 to 4.64. It is also possible of course to store information outside the machine, on punched-cards or similar means. Access to such information is then much slower, and the treatment of it involves the input-output unit.

The input-output unit reminds us once again of the language issue, which is central in computer science, since it is the means of communication between the computer and the human being who uses it. Instructions and necessary data must be supplied to the machine and results must be brought out. It might be convenient if one could simply tell a computer orally, "Add the following numbers, . . .", and someday it may be possible, but at present it is printed rather than spoken communication which prevails. Even with print the amount of preparation involved is formidable. For example, while a machine may be content to think in words such as

$$0\ 1\ 0\ 0\ 1\ 0\ 0\ 1\ 1$$

and in fact will probably insist upon doing so, human beings appear still to prefer

"Add the number in storage location 19 to the sum you have already accumulated."

The translation problem is very evident. Current practice for solving this translation problem involves two or three stages. First a sentence such as the above may be abbreviated to, for instance,

ADD 19

Next these five symbols are struck on the keyboard of a specially constructed typewriter-like device, which converts each into a pattern of holes on a paper card or paper tape. There are many codes which assign patterns to the various numbers and letters, as well as to special characters such as punctuation marks or business symbols. These are called *alphanumeric codes* and Fig. 4-5 shows the result of translating, by using the special typewriter, the phrase ADD 19 into one such code. Further details on this code and others are given in the solved problems. The punched tape or card is now introduced to a reading device which has contacts so placed as to sense the positions of holes, the spirit being the same as for the extremely primitive reading device of Problem 3.2. At last the instruction in question is inside the computer in electrical form, as the set of five sequences

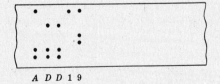

A D D 1 9

Fig. 4-5

$$1100001 \quad 1100100 \quad 1100100 \quad 0000001 \quad 0011001$$

which in this code stand for A D D 1 9. The final step of converting this electrical information into the machine's personal language to obtain perhaps the sequence

$$0 1 0 0 1 0 0 1 1$$

given a moment ago is itself a major task. Once a given machine has been fully designed, the "hardware" constructed, there remain certain substantial tasks such as the above, teaching the machine to change the electrical information from its input form to its working form. These are known as "software" problems. The sequence of steps just sketched, to summarize, allows the human user of a computer to write his instructions and data in something close to his familiar language, even with decimal symbols for numbers if he wishes, to type this information as written into a special punch, and then to patiently wait as the computer itself translates things into its own working language.

Output from a computer is available in several forms, and the choice depends in part upon the nature of the problem. It is possible for the circuit itself to guide a cutting tool which prepares metal parts of specified shapes, or to take a more prominent example, to steer a rocket during its ascent into orbit. It can also present charts on a television screen if so designed, or perhaps give a musical output via loudspeaker. As a general rule, however, it is the somewhat less exotic output devices which are most prominent. Certain warning lights on the operator's panel of a computer are usually included to allow the machine to signal malfunctions of one sort or another. Other lights may permit the operator to read out the contents of selected memory locations. By far the most common form of output, however, is the printed word, numbers and other useful symbols included. Here the translation problem faced at input appears in reverse, and once again the burden is placed in large part upon the computer itself, or more accurately upon the shoulders of those who prepare this part of the software, instructing the circuit so that it can handle the task. The final link is a printing device which accepts coded characters, in electrical form, such as 1100001 for *A*, and activates in each case the proper key.

Since high speed computation is one of the strong points of electrical circuits, strenuous efforts have been made to develop faster and faster methods of information input and output. Instead of mechanical contacts to sense the holes in a tape or card, a photocell may be placed beneath and a light source above each channel. Each hole in the tape or card permits light to reach the cell, which then produces an electrical pulse. The same principle is used for the automatic opening of doors in banks and department stores. Photoelectric reading devices can handle up to 1,000 characters each second, compared with 100 to 200 for mechanical readers. High speed printers have also been devised, some of which print an entire line at one time, others using a continuously revolving print wheel. Speeds of more than 1,000 lines each minute, with perhaps 160 characters to the line, have been reached. Even so the internal activity of the computer is faster and the search for better ways of communicating with the internal circuitry continues. As much as possible of the input-output detail is handled on "off-line" equipment, not in direct contact with the computer. The information on punched cards or tape may, for instance, be transferred to magnetic tape. Such tapes can be read at much higher speed by "on-line" equipment, that is, by readers having direct access to computer memory. In this way the computer's potential for rapid thinking is more fully exploited, though perhaps at the expense of greater human effort. The idea of time-sharing represents still another method of exploiting a computer's high internal speeds. Here many different users, each at his own electric typewriter known as a terminal, enjoy more or less simultaneous access to the machine. Each user types in his data and instructions and receives typed output, the response being so prompt that he may be tempted to believe he is the only one using the machine.

Solved Problems

4.1. For binary symbolism, what are the next five key numbers after 1, 2, 4, 8, 16 and 32, which were presented in the introduction?

The value of the 1 continues to double.

$$1000000 = 64$$
$$10000000 = 128$$
$$100000000 = 256$$
$$1000000000 = 512$$
$$10000000000 = 1024$$

4.2. Convert the following to decimal symbolism.

$$10010101 \quad 10101010 \quad 01110111$$

Giving each 1 its place value,

$$10010101 = 128 + 16 + 4 + 1 = 149$$
$$10101010 = 128 + 32 + 8 + 2 = 170$$
$$01110111 = 64 + 32 + 16 + 4 + 2 + 1 = 119$$

all except the original symbols being decimal. The lead-off zero in the last example is included just to keep the three sequences of uniform length, as they have been in the sequence computations of earlier chapters and as they will be whenever we are involved with sequence arithmetic.

4.3. Convert the following to binary symbolism.

$$200 \quad 144 \quad 225$$

Using the subtraction process,

$$200 - 128 = 72, \quad 72 - 64 = 8, \quad 8 - 8 = 0$$

so that, putting the pieces back together,

$$200 = 128 + 64 + 8 = 11001000$$

Similarly,
$$144 - 128 = 16, \quad 16 - 16 = 0$$

making
$$144 = 128 + 16 = 10010000$$

and
$$225 - 128 = 97, \quad 97 - 64 = 33, \quad 33 - 32 = 1, \quad 1 - 1 = 0$$

leading to
$$225 = 128 + 64 + 32 + 1 = 11100001$$

4.4. How are fractions represented in binary symbolism?

The principle remains the same. Decimal symbols for fractions are built from tenths, tenths of tenths, and so on. Binary symbols are built from halves, halves of halves, and so on. The key numbers are thus the following.

Binary	Decimal
.1	1/2 = .5
.01	1/4 = .25
.001	1/8 = .125
.0001	1/16 = .0625
.00001	1/32 = .03125

and so on. Other fractions are now represented as combinations of these key numbers. Thus

$$.11 = \tfrac{1}{2} + \tfrac{1}{4} = \tfrac{3}{4} \qquad .101 = \tfrac{1}{2} + \tfrac{1}{8} = \tfrac{5}{8}$$

and so on.

4.5. Convert .10101 from binary to decimal symbolism.

One method involves assigning each 1 its place value as in the preceding problem, obtaining

$$.10101 = \tfrac{1}{2} + \tfrac{1}{8} + \tfrac{1}{32} = \tfrac{21}{32} = .5 + .125 + .03125 = .65625$$

This is equivalent to ignoring the "binary point" momentarily and converting 10101 to decimal 21 by integer technique, then dividing by 32. In this connection see also the next problem.

4.6. Convert 110.011 from binary to decimal.

We can give each 1 its place value, obtaining

$$110.011 = 4 + 2 + \tfrac{1}{4} + \tfrac{1}{8} = 6 + .25 + .125 = 6.375$$

or equivalently, we can ignore the binary point momentarily to find

$$110011 = 32 + 16 + 2 + 1 = 51$$

and then divide by 8. The results are clearly the same.

4.7. Convert .421875 and .3333 from decimal to binary.

The subtraction routine used for integers again serves.

.421875	.3333
− .250000	− .2500
.171875	.0833
− .125000	− .0625
.046875	.0208
− .031250	− .0156
.015625	.0052
− .015625	− .0039

For the first decimal fraction the computation appears in the left column above. The subtraction of four key numbers leaves zero. Because these key numbers correspond to 1/4, 1/8, 1/32 and 1/64, the required result is

$$.421875 = .011011$$

exactly. The remaining decimal fraction .3333 leads to what is more typical, a non-terminating symbol. In the right column above key numbers have been subtracted, keeping four decimal places, up to a certain point. Noting which key numbers were involved leads to the conclusion that

$$.3333 = .01010101$$

approximately. As usual with fractional computations round-offs have been made and the accuracy of the final result is somewhat open to challenge. The result,

$$\tfrac{1}{3} = .010101010101\ldots$$

the binary symbol on the right being endless, is suggested by our present calculation and does prove to be correct. The fraction 1/3 thus has an endless representation in both decimal and binary.

4.8. Illustrate the remainder method of conversion by finding the binary equivalent of 137.

This routine involves continued division by 2, noting the remainders.

Division	Quotient	Remainder
137/2	68	1
68/2	34	0
34/2	17	0
17/2	8	1
8/2	4	0
4/2	2	0
2/2	1	0
1/2	0	1

The zero quotient indicates the end of the computation. The remainders are now read from the bottom to obtain 10001001 as the required binary symbol. Recalling the doubling in value of the 1 as it shifts leftward, it is not hard to convince oneself that the process is valid.

4.9. Illustrate the remainder method of conversion and also the use of binary symbols during the intermediate steps by finding the decimal equivalent of 10001001.

This problem is slightly premature at this point since we have not discussed computations using binary symbols for numbers. The details are not especially difficult, however, and it is important to bring out the point that the routine of conversion can be executed in binary language, because most conversions will be made in this way by machine rather than by man. The details are very similar to those in the preceding problem, but here we divide by ten, or 1010.

$$
\begin{array}{r}
1101 \\
1010\overline{\smash{\big)}10001001} \\
\underline{1010} \\
1110 \\
\underline{1010} \\
10001 \\
\underline{1010} \\
111 = \text{first remainder}
\end{array}
\qquad
\begin{array}{r}
1 \\
1010\overline{\smash{\big)}1101} \\
\underline{1010} \\
11 = \text{second remainder}
\end{array}
\qquad
\begin{array}{r}
0 \\
1010\overline{\smash{\big)}1} = \text{third remainder}
\end{array}
$$

Though the computation may not be completely clear note that it does continue until a zero quotient has been obtained, as in the preceding example. As there, the remainders are now reversed and give 137, it being assumed that the binary-decimal equivalents for zero through nine are known to both us and any machine which is to do such a conversion for us.

4.10. What are octal symbols and what is their role in computer science?

As with decimal and binary symbols, place value is again the basis for the octal system of representing numbers. Here the value of a digit is magnified eightfold with each displacement to the left, and only the digits 0, 1, 2, 3, 4, 5, 6, 7 are used. For purposes of comparison the first ten numbers are listed below in decimal, octal, and binary.

Decimal	1	2	3	4	5	6	7	8	9	10
Octal	1	2	3	4	5	6	7	10	11	12
Binary	1	10	11	100	101	110	111	1000	1001	1010

The role of octal symbols in computer science centers on the simple relationship between octal and binary symbols. To see this relationship clearly, examine the following equivalent symbols for some slightly larger integers.

Decimal	Octal	Binary
16	20	10 000
20	24	10 100
64	100	1 000 000
100	144	1 100 100
500	764	111 110 100

Each binary symbol has been split into groups of three values each, and it is to be observed that each group corresponds to the octal digit in similar position. As a further example, the binary 10001001 of a moment ago may be split into 10 001 001 and the octal equivalent is instantly available as 211, each octal digit corresponding to one of the groups. This may be verified by assigning each octal digit its place value,

$$211 = 2(64) + 1(8) + 1 = (137)$$

the symbols in parentheses being decimal.

The point is this. Decimal symbols provide the working language for human arithmetical computations; but sequences of zeros and ones (colds and hots) are the natural working language for machines. Mutual understanding is achieved by our interpretation of such sequences as binary symbols for numbers. But binary symbols tend to run rather long, the use of 10001001 in place of 137 being a typical example. Octal symbols prove convenient as abbreviations of binary symbols. Using them in place of the more familiar decimals amounts to a small sacrifice on the part of a human computer in the interest of narrowing the communications gap between man and machine.

The design of some machines, the IBM 360 for example, gives *hexadecimal* symbols a central role. See Problem 4.76 for a brief treatment.

4.11. Find the sum of the numbers having binary symbols 1001 and 0011, using only binary language.

Of course, these numbers are also represented by the decimal symbols 9 and 3 so the sum should prove to be 12, but the point is to observe the details of computation in binary language only. The calculation below is almost self-explanatory, proceeding column by column from right to left much like the corresponding decimal routine that one learns in the early years of school.

$$
\begin{array}{r}
1001 \\
+\ 0011 \\
\hline
1100
\end{array}
$$

In the rightmost column we face the sum $1 + 1$, which in binary language is 10. The zero is recorded on the lower level and the 1, since it actually represents two, is carried into the next column toward the left where in binary language it will represent two. In this second column we must first add 0 and 1, after which the carry must be included. The result is another zero recorded on the lower level and another carry toward the left. Continuing in this way the result 1100, binary for twelve, is obtained.

4.12. What basic addition facts must be learned before one can execute an addition in binary language?

Since the symbols 0 and 1 can occur in only the familiar four combinations there are only the following four basic addition results:

$$
\begin{array}{cccc}
0 & 0 & 1 & 1 \\
+0 & +1 & +0 & +1 \\
\hline
0 & 1 & 1 & 10
\end{array}
$$

It will be convenient to display this information in a slightly different way, indicating what is to be recorded in each case and what is to be carried.

	0	0	1	1
	+0	+1	+0	+1
Record	0	1	1	0
Carry	0	0	0	1

Thus there is a zero carry (or no carry as we would say informally) except in the case of $1 + 1$. In this case a zero is recorded, as was done in the rightmost column of the above example. The remaining entries for record and carry in the above table are relatively obvious.

4.13. How can the correct record and carry for addition using binary symbols be generated *by Boolean operations*?

This problem now illustrates the crucial step, since it asks how the results above may be achieved by operations which we already know can be carried out *by electrical circuits*. And the answer proves to be surprisingly easy. The 0110 pattern for record has occurred in a number of earlier problems. If the two digits to be added are called A and B, then $A\bar{B} + \bar{A}B$, the output of the comparator circuit of Chapter 1, is what is needed. Whatever input combination A, B is presented to a comparator, the output will be the correct record for that combination. The 0001 pattern for carry is still simpler. It corresponds to the Boolean multiplication AB, and is achieved by a single AND circuit. Whatever input combination A, B is presented to the AND circuit, its output will be the correct carry for that combination.

4.14. Design a circuit for computing the correct record and carry for given binary digits.

From the results of the preceding problem we see that it will be enough if we produce outputs $A\bar{B} + \bar{A}B$ and AB from given inputs A and B. The circuit of Fig. 4-6 will do this. In view of the Boolean theorem $A\bar{B} + \bar{A}B = (A + B)\overline{AB}$, the circuit of Fig. 4-7 will also serve and appears to be slightly simpler.

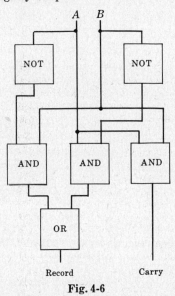

Fig. 4-6

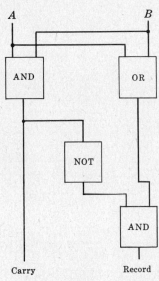

Fig. 4-7

4.15. The circuits of the preceding problem, and any equivalent circuits, are called *half-adders*. Such a circuit can accept only two input digits A and B at one time, but these two digits may be any combination of zeros and ones, and the correct output record and carry will be generated. How many individual steps of this kind were required in the computation of Problem 4.11? List these steps and establish the pattern for half-adder usage.

In the rightmost column only one step of this sort was needed, $1 + 1$ giving a record of 0 and a carry of 1. The second column is more typical, since a carry does enter this column from the right. Here two steps are involved. First $0 + 1$ produces what we might call a partial record of 1 and a partial carry of 0. The partial record is then combined with the incoming carry in the second step. Since this is again $1 + 1$, the final record is 0 and a second partial outgoing carry, this time 1, is produced. There is even a third step. The two possible outgoing carries must be combined. Since one of these is 0 and the other 1, it seems clear that the final outgoing carry will be 1. As we will see in just a moment, this last step does not require a half-adder, the simpler OR circuit being sufficient. For this second column then two half-adder steps are involved, the treatment of the outgoing carry being extra. The third and fourth columns are handled like the second, so that except for the somewhat special first column we must count two half-adder steps per column.

4.16. Design a circuit for computing the sum of two numbers which are represented by four-digit binary symbols as in Problem 4.11.

Following up on the comments of the preceding problem we are led fairly naturally to the circuit of Fig. 4-8. At first glance this may seem slightly complex but a brief scrutiny will show that the details are really rather simple.

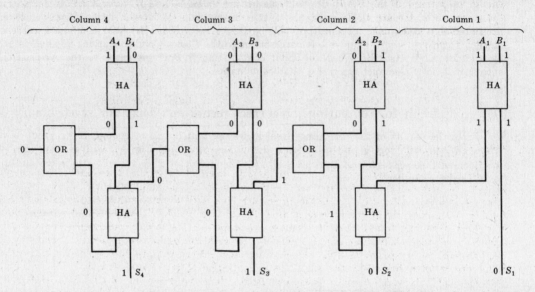

Fig. 4-8

The computation to be made is the following.

$$A_4 A_3 A_2 A_1$$
$$+ B_4 B_3 B_2 B_1$$
$$\overline{S_4 S_3 S_2 S_1}$$

Each A, B and S is either a zero or a one, since these are binary symbols. In Problem 4.11, for instance, we had

$$1001$$
$$+ 0011$$
$$\overline{1100}$$

from which the A, B and S digits may easily be identified. In Fig. 4-8 the two numbers to be added, the input information, enter at the top and the sum, the output information, comes out at the bottom. Each circuit labeled HA is a half-adder. The layout of the diagram preserves the column by column nature of the familiar addition routine, each column being handled by two half-adders and one OR circuit as suggested a moment ago, the simpler right hand column being the exception.

The best way to understand this addition circuit may be to actually follow it through a typical computation. For this purpose, and using the specific data of Problem 4.11, each wire in Fig. 4-8 has been labeled according to the value (hot or cold) which it carries. At the top are the input values $A_4 A_3 A_2 A_1 = 1001$ and $B_4 B_3 B_2 B_1 = 0011$. Other zeros and ones then indicate the repercussions within the circuit. Follow the action slowly from right to left just as though the computation were being done by hand. With record coming out at the lower right of each half-adder and carry coming out at the lower left, you will find that the circuit takes exactly the same steps that a human computer would take, and arrives at the same result. Beginning with the same $1 + 1$ step that we started with in Problem 4.11, which manages a zero record and a one carry over to column two, it generates the output information $S_4 S_3 S_2 S_1 = 1100$ which we may then interpret as the binary symbol for twelve. The use of an OR circuit instead of a third half-adder in each column, for combining the partial carries, will be explained in the next problem. The extra output at the left of the addition circuit, cold in the present example, will be discussed in Problem 4.18.

4.17.	Explain the treatment of partial carries in the addition circuit of the preceding problem.

> The thing to notice is that both partial carries cannot be hot at the same time. For, if the top half-adder in some column has produced a hot partial carry then that half-adder has processed a $1+1$ step, since only this kind of step produces a hot carry. But in this case the partial record sent to the lower half-adder will be cold, making it impossible for this second half-adder to produce a hot carry. There are thus only three, rather than the usual four, input combinations to the OR circuit, and it takes only a moment to discover that the OR circuit will output the correct final carry for each.

> First partial carry   0   0   1

> Second partial carry   0   1   0

> Output of OR circuit   0   1   1   =   Correct final carry

4.18.	What happens if the addition circuit of Fig. 4-3 is offered the problem $1100+0100$?

> We can answer very quickly by thinking in decimal language, translating the problem to $12+4$. Clearly the sum is the number 16, which in binary language is 10000. But the circuit of Fig. 4-8 is only a four digit computer, accepting four digit input sequences and generating a four digit output. For the present problem this output will be $S_4S_3S_2S_1 = 0000$, but there will be a hot carry from the fourth column. The extra output at the left of the circuit bears this carry. The point is that computing circuits must be designed to handle some specific number of digits, sequences of some specific length. In practice that length may be thirty or forty digits rather than our meager four, but for a particular machine it is a fixed length. If a computation produces a result which exceeds that fixed length, then some sort of action must be taken. The carry produced at the left of our circuit signals the occurrence of such an "overflow". If this wire is connected to a light bulb, for instance, then the light will go on, indicating that a very important value has just been lost. Conceivably some more constructive use of this overflow value can be arranged. It would probably be useful to follow the entire course of action through the computer, with the input data of this problem, watching the development of the zero sum and of the overflow.

4.19.	One typical column of an addition computation, of the sort considered in the preceding few problems, involves three input values, one A digit, one B digit, and the carry C from the column to the right. This means that the familiar eight A, B, C input combinations are possible. For each such combination there is a correct final record and a correct final carry, these being the two outputs from the column. A circuit which produces these outputs from the three given inputs is known as a *full-adder*. Represent the outputs in terms of the basic Boolean products.

> The eight input combinations are again

> A 0 0 0 0 1 1 1 1

> B 0 0 1 1 0 0 1 1

> C 0 1 0 1 0 1 0 1

and a moment's reflection will suggest that the corresponding output values are these:

> Record   0 1 1 0 1 0 0 1

> Carry   0 0 0 1 0 1 1 1

Noting the columns in which one values appear, and referring back to the table in Problem 2.21, we have at once

$$\text{Record} = ABC + A\bar{B}\bar{C} + \bar{A}B\bar{C} + \bar{A}\bar{B}C$$

$$\text{Carry} = ABC + AB\bar{C} + A\bar{B}C + \bar{A}BC$$

so that each output requires four of the eight basic products.

4.20. The addition circuit of Fig. 4-8 includes a full-adder for each column except the first, in which a half-adder is enough. Show that what such a full-adder actually computes are the outputs

$$\text{Record} = [(A+B)\overline{AB} + C]\overline{(A+B)\overline{AB}C}$$

$$\text{Carry} = AB + (A+B)\overline{AB}C$$

and that by the theorems of Boolean algebra these are the same as the record and carry prescribed by the analysis of the preceding problem.

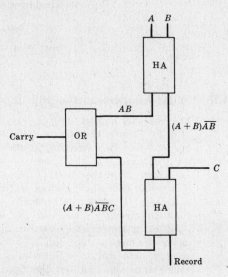

For convenience one such full-adder appears in Fig. 4-9. As before, the input digits A and B enter the top half-adder and the incoming carry goes direct to the lower one. Turning back to Fig. 4-7 to review the action of a half-adder, we see that its lower left output, the partial carry, is simply the Boolean product of the two inputs, while its lower right output, the partial record, is the sum of those inputs multiplied by the inverse of their product. It will be useful to have this verbal description of half-adder action. For the top half-adder in Fig. 4-9 the two outputs are thus AB and $(A+B)\overline{AB}$ as indicated. The lower half-adder does not, of course, have A and B as inputs but its action may easily be deduced from the verbal description just given. Its partial carry output, being the Boolean product of the inputs, must be $(A+B)\overline{AB}C$ and this wire has been so labeled. Its other output is really the final record for the column in question, the S digit, and being the sum of the input values multiplied by the inverse of their product, works out to

Fig. 4-9

$$\text{Record} = [(A+B)\overline{AB} + C]\overline{(A+B)\overline{AB}C}$$

as announced. Since carry is the output of an OR circuit, we finish easily with

$$\text{Carry} = AB + (A+B)\overline{AB}C$$

also as announced. The fact that the present record agrees with that of the preceding problem is guaranteed by Theorem 2.40, page 22. The equivalence of the two carrys is the content of Theorems 2.32, page 19, and 2.33, page 20.

4.21. Show that the circuit of Fig. 4-10 also computes the output information required of a full-adder.

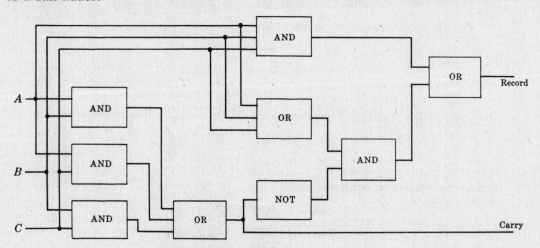

Fig. 4-10

The analysis of this machine is simple enough. The three AND circuits at the left compute AB, AC and BC. The OR sums these and produces one of the two outputs.

$$\text{Carry} = AB + AC + BC$$

Theorem 2.32, page 19, shows that this is the proper carry output for a full-adder. At top center of the diagram the product ABC and the sum $A + B + C$ are computed. The latter is then multiplied by $\overline{AB + AC + BC}$ and the result added to ABC, thus producing the other output

$$\text{Record} = ABC + (A + B + C)\overline{AB + AC + BC}$$

By Theorem 2.39, page 22, this is acceptable as the record output of a full-adder. Two designs for a full-adder are now available to us.

4.22. How must the circuit of Fig. 4-8 be changed to handle binary symbols of greater length?

One simply attaches more full-adders at the left until the required length has been achieved.

4.23. Find the difference of the numbers having binary symbols 1011 and 0101, using only binary language.

The computation is almost self-explanatory, much like the familiar decimal routine.

$$
\begin{array}{r}
1011 \\
-\ 0101 \\
\hline
0110
\end{array}
$$

Starting at the right, $1 - 1$ is clearly zero. In the second column $1 - 0$ clearly produces 1, binary place values making this column the equivalent of "two minus zero equals two". In column three we face a borrow. The 1 in column four must be brought over, and since this 1 has place value eight, an "eight minus four equals four" computation follows. The leftmost 1 in our answer represents this difference of four. Finally in column four we have $0 - 0$, the borrow having used up the 1. In decimal language the same subtraction would read $11 - 5 = 6$.

4.24. What basic subtraction facts must be learned before one can execute a subtraction in binary language?

The four possible 0,1 combinations have all occurred in the preceding problem. The action taken there may be summarized as follows.

	0	0	1	1
	$-\ 0$	$-\ 1$	$-\ 0$	$-\ 1$
Record	0	1	1	0
Borrow	0	1	0	0

Only the second combination requires a second glance. Here a borrow of 1 from the next column to the left, in whatever computation is underway, is needed. Moreover, a 1 will be recorded. In Problem 4.23 this happened in the third column, the 1 borrowed having value eight and the 1 recorded having value four.

4.25. How can the correct record and borrow for subtraction using binary symbols be generated by Boolean operations?

Once again this is a crucial step since the question asks, essentially, how subtraction may be achieved by electrical circuits. And once again the answer is surprisingly easy. The record pattern is exactly the same as for addition and may be computed as $A\bar{B} + \bar{A}B$, where A and B are the input digits. Borrow has a pattern similar to that of carry but with $\bar{A}B$ replacing AB.

4.26. Design a circuit for computing the correct record and borrow for given binary digits.

Using the result of the preceding problem one sees that the circuit of Fig. 4-11 will serve, its two outputs being $A\bar{B} + \bar{A}B$ and $\bar{A}B$.

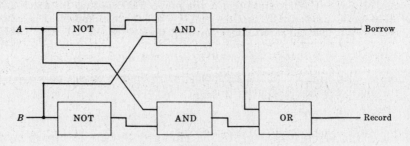

Fig. 4-11

4.27. The circuit of Fig. 4-11, and any equivalent circuit, is called a *half-subtractor*. Such a circuit can accept only two input digits A and B at one time, but these two digits may be any combination of zeros and ones and the correct output record and borrow will be generated. Design a circuit for computing the difference of two numbers represented by four-digit binary symbols. Do this by imitating our manual computation of Problem 4.23, using half-subtractors where needed.

Fig. 4-12 exhibits the required circuit. As with the binary adder of Fig. 4-8 it may appear somewhat complex at first glance but proves to be reasonably simple after a brief analysis. The computation to be made is

$$A_4 A_3 A_2 A_1$$
$$- B_4 B_3 B_2 B_1$$
$$\overline{D_4 D_3 D_2 D_1}$$

each A, B and D being either a zero or a one. The two numbers to be subtracted, the input information, enter at the top and the difference, the output information, comes out at the bottom. Each circuit labeled *HS* is a half-subtractor. The layout of the diagram preserves the column by column nature of the familiar subtraction routine, each column being handled by two half-subtractors and an OR circuit, except for the simpler first column.

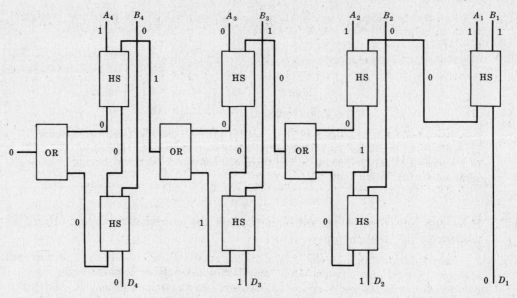

Fig. 4-12

To understand the circuit we follow it through a typical computation. For this purpose each wire has been labeled according to the value (hot or cold) that it would carry for the subtraction of Problem 4.23, in which $A_4A_3A_2A_1 = 1011$ and $B_4B_3B_2B_1 = 0101$. With record coming out at the lower right of each half-subtractor and borrow coming out at the lower left, the circuit duplicates the steps taken by hand in the solution of Problem 4.23. In column one the $1-1$ leaves a zero record and a zero borrow. This zero borrow is next subtracted from the A_2 digit, with B_2 then being subtracted from the result. The two partial borrows are then merged in an OR circuit (see the following problem) and we are on to the third column. Continuing in this way the output information $D_4D_3D_2D_1 = 0110$ is generated, and we choose to think of this as the binary symbol for six. The computer has processed the input sequences 1011 and 0101 and produced the output sequence 0110, strictly by Boolean operations, but we interpret the entire effort for our own purposes as the subtraction $11 - 5 = 6$.

4.28. Explain the merging of partial borrows in the circuit of Fig. 4-12.

The thing to notice is that both partial borrows in a given column cannot be hot at the same time. For, if the top half-subtractor has produced a hot borrow then that half-subtractor has processed a $0-1$ step, since only this combination requires a hot borrow. But in this case the partial record sent to the lower half-subtractor will be hot, making it unnecessary for this second half-subtractor to require a borrow. There are thus only three, rather than the usual four, possible input combinations to the OR circuit, and it takes only a moment to discover that the OR will output the correct final borrow for each.

First partial borrow	0	0	1
Second partial borrow	0	1	0
Output of OR circuit	0	1	1 = Correct final borrow

4.29. What happens if the subtraction circuit of Fig. 4-12 is offered the problem $0101 - 1011$?

A quick answer is available by thinking in decimal language, in which the problem is equivalent to $5 - 11 = -6$. The appearance of the negative number -6 is a reminder that these numbers play an important role in arithmetic and that we should keep them in mind as we design arithmetical circuitry. This will be our next task, but for the moment it would be useful to follow our subtractor circuit as it processes these two sequences, the A digits now being 0101 and the B digits being 1011. The D digits prove to be 1010, but what we shall focus upon is the fact that there is *an overflow* from the leftmost column. There are various ways in which this output information may be used. One way will be explored in the next few problems, the overflow playing an important role.

4.30. Develop a symbolism for both positive and negative numbers, using only zeros and ones.

One possible system involves attaching an extra value to the binary symbols already in use, perhaps a leading 0 for a positive number and a leading 1 for a negative number. For instance,

$$00101 = +5 \qquad 01011 = +11$$
$$10101 = -5 \qquad 11011 = -11$$

the symbols on the right being decimal. It is important to repeat that the interpretation of these symbols is up to us, 11011 being also usable for the binary equivalent of decimal 27, but that whatever our choice we must carefully "explain" our intentions to our computers by appropriate design. If the leading value of a sequence is to indicate the sign of a number, positive or negative, then this value must clearly be treated differently from the others.

4.31. What are the four cases which may occur in the addition of positive and negative numbers?

They are illustrated by these four examples.

00110	10110	00110	10110
+ 00101	+ 10101	+ 10101	+ 00101
01011	11011	00001	10001

Converted into decimal form these read, from left to right, $(+6) + (+5) = (+11)$, $(-6) + (-5) = (-11)$, $(+6) + (-5) = (+1)$, $(-6) + (+5) = (-1)$. Thus when both numbers have the same sign, their magnitudes (found by deleting signs) are added and the same sign is attached to the sum. But when the two given numbers have opposite signs, one positive and one negative, the smaller magnitude is subtracted from the larger and the result takes the sign of the larger magnitude. This summarizes the addition operation of number arithmetic.

4.32. A circuit which is to add positive and negative numbers must be able to distinguish between the four cases illustrated in the preceding problem and then to take appropriate action. This is a much more sophisticated type of thinking than we have asked of circuitry up to this point, since in a very real sense the machine will have to "decide" which of the four cases confronts it. A key element in making such decisions will be the "gate". Indicate how simple gates might be designed using the same principals involved in the old-fashioned OR, AND, NOT circuits of Chapter 1. More modern gates, and as has already been mentioned, more modern OR, AND, NOT circuits too, use transistors or similar devices.

Fig. 4-13 shows the simplest possible gate. Information passes through from top to bottom, provided that the control input at the left is cold. If this control becomes hot it opens the switch, perhaps by energizing a small magnet, and the flow of information is stopped. It is just as easy to reverse the pattern, or to arrange for several switches to operate together, as Fig. 4-14 shows. Here information passes between the A contacts but not between the B contacts, whenever the control input is cold. If this control becomes hot the reverse is true. Clearly any combination of open and closed switches is easily arranged. The OR, AND, NOT circuits themselves have this character and are often called gates.

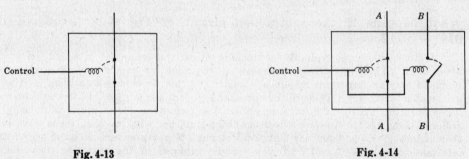

Fig. 4-13   Fig. 4-14

4.33. Design an addition circuit which can handle any combination of positive and negative numbers as in Problem 4.31.

The problem may be symbolized in the form

$$A_5 A_4 A_3 A_2 A_1$$
$$+ \, \underline{B_5 B_4 B_3 B_2 B_1}$$
$$S_5 S_4 S_3 S_2 S_1$$

the leading digit in each case representing the sign of the number, zero for a positive number and one for a negative number, as in Problem 4.30. The circuit of Fig. 4-15 below will appear quite complicated at first glance but, as once or twice before, a careful scrutiny will soon show that it is reasonably simple, and that it does accept the A and B input digits and output the S digits of the required sum. As we study this circuit to see how it goes about carrying out this assignment, it will be particularly interesting to notice the decision process, that is, the determination of which of the four possible cases has arisen and the consequent course of action.

We begin our analysis exactly where we would begin a manual computation, by noting the signs of the two input numbers. Values A_5 and B_5 enter a comparator and, as we know from Chapter 1, the output of this comparator will be hot if the two inputs are different, that is, if the input numbers have different signs. Otherwise, if the signs are the same, the comparator output is cold. This output is applied as the control input to both Gate 1 and Gate 2, which have been arranged so that a cold control sends information through Gate 1 but blocks Gate 2. In different words, when the control is cold (signs the same) the digits A_4 to A_1 and B_4 to B_1 flow through

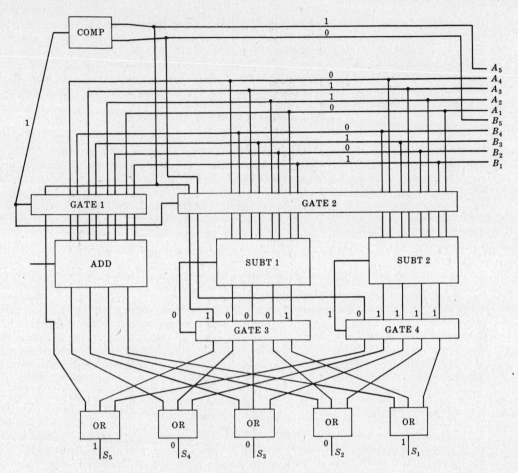

Fig. 4-15

Gate 1 to the ADD unit and not through Gate 2 to the SUBT units. This is just what is wanted since like signs lead to addition, as the first two cases in Problem 4.31 suggest. The sign value A_5 also passes through Gate 1 and eventually provides the sign of the output sum. (B_5 would have served equally well since it is the same as A_5.) Turning to the other possibility, signs different and control input hot, we now find Gate 1 blocked and Gate 2 passing information. In different words, the digits A_5 to A_1 and B_5 to B_1 now enter the SUBT units and not ADD. This also is what is wanted since unlike signs lead to subtraction, as the last two cases in Problem 4.31 suggest. The first decision has already been made, the decision whether to add or subtract, the thinking mechanism consisting simply of a comparator circuit and two gates. The two gates are of course somewhat larger than the miniature models of Figs. 4-13 and 4-14, Gate 1 controlling nine information channels and Gate 2 eighteen.

As already noted, if the sign values A_5 and B_5 are the same, then the ADD unit receives the remaining eight digits of the input numbers. This unit may be taken to be the same as that of Fig. 4-8, outputting the correct sum if there is no overflow. The sign A_5 is also passed by Gate 1 and so the required sum, sign and all, is available just below ADD. Since Gate 2 blocks all information flow, only cold wires emerge from Gates 3 and 4 and the OR circuits at the bottom of the diagram simply transmit the five digit sum.

Suppose, however, that the sign values A_5 and B_5 are different. Then the comparator produces a hot output value, blocking Gate 1 and allowing all ten input digits to pass through Gate 2. The two SUBT units may be assumed to be the same as that of Fig. 4-12. Noticing the arrangement of inputs to these subtractors, one sees that SUBT 1 computes $A_4A_3A_2A_1 - B_4B_3B_2B_1$ while SUBT 2 manages the reverse. In one subtractor, therefore, the larger number (in magnitude) is being taken from the smaller. As observed in Problem 4.29 the subtractor doing this will produce an overflow value of 1. As shown in Fig. 4-15 the overflow from each SUBT unit is used as control input to a gate. Both Gate 3 and Gate 4 have been arranged so that a cold control allows information to pass through, while a hot control value blocks the flow. This now means that the output from one subtractor, the one producing the hot overflow, will not penetrate through to the final OR gates. The other subtractor, the one taking the smaller magnitude from the larger, does not produce a hot overflow and so does not block the flow of its own output information. It will also be seen that the appropriate sign value has been made available at each gate, A_5 at Gate 3 in case the A number proves to be the larger and B_5 at Gate 4 should it prove to be the B number instead. The appropriate sign, that of the larger magnitude, thus accompanies the computed difference through the final gate. Checking back one now sees that in any case only one of the three information channels

Gate 1	SUBT 1	SUBT 2
ADD	Gate 3	Gate 4

transmits an answer, the other two managing only cold values. The terminal OR circuits pass this answer as $S_5S_4S_3S_2S_1$. Note particularly that overflow values have played a part in the decision process, determining whether the B number should be subtracted from the A number or vice versa in a case of unlike signs. It would be easy to turn up one's nose at the primitive kind of thinking being done by the present circuit, but anyone so tempted should remind himself that the human thought process is itself little understood, and that circuits such as this one have been designed by human beings taking as their model certain aspects of human intelligence.

4.34. Show how the addition circuit of Fig. 4-15 solves the last example in Problem 4.31.

Here the A number is 10110, or -6, while the B number is 00101, or $+5$. Various wires in Fig. 4-15, particularly those most important in this case, have been labeled according to the value, hot or cold, which they carry. Since the comparator output is hot, Gate 1 is blocked and the digits all pass through Gate 2. SUBT 1 then computes $6-5$ while SUBT 2 tries $5-6$. Referring back to Fig. 4-12 would show these two subtractors outputting the indicated information. In particular the overflow from SUBT 2 now blocks Gate 4, leaving the 10001 sequence to pass through Gate 3 and the terminal OR circuits to become the correct sum, more simply -1.

4.35. Illustrate the handling of the number zero by the circuit of Fig. 4-15.

Suppose zero represented as 00000, making it a "positive" zero because of the leading 0. If this takes the B position while the A number is, for example, 00001, then because the signs agree the ADD unit will be active. It will execute $0001 + 0000$ and output 0001. The 0 sign value will also pass through Gate 1 and the correct sum 00001 will be given. If on the other hand the A number is negative, say 10001, then because the signs disagree the SUBT units will be active. SUBT 1 will execute $0001 - 0000$ and output 0001. The sign value $A_5 = 1$ will also pass through Gate 3. Since SUBT 2 will overflow and block Gate 4, the sequence 10001 coming through Gate 3 will become the correct final sum. It is curious to note that 10000 can also be used to represent zero, a "negative" zero. A brief analysis will show that this also leads to correct output sums. Either form of zero may also be introduced as the A number, instead of as the B, again with correct results.

4.36. How must the circuit of Fig. 4-15 be changed to handle numbers of larger size?

More full-adders must be attached to the ADD unit, the SUBT units must be similarly enlarged, as must all the gates, more OR circuits included, and so on, but the fundamental ideas are not changed in any way.

4.37. Describe very briefly the role of delay units and amplifiers in a circuit such as that of Fig. 4-15.

As information flows through a circuit, it slowly deteriorates. A current, for example, may become steadily weaker. Amplifiers are used to maintain nearly uniform levels of electrical performance throughout the circuit. Moreover, though information in electrical form travels very fast, it does require a definite amount of time to negotiate each wire and each unit of the circuit. Time delays are inserted in selected places to assure that values which are to reach a certain gate or unit at the same time will actually do so. In the machine of Fig. 4-15 it is also important that the output of the wrong subtractor not pass through the corresponding gate before the hot overflow has had time to block that gate. Delaying the subtractor output for a suitable length of time can prevent this from happening. Practical aspects of machine design such as those just suggested are obviously of great importance, but only this brief mention will be given here as we focus our main effort on other things which are equally important.

4.38. How can the operation of subtraction be handled by an electrical circuit, given any two numbers A and B, positive or negative?

The subtraction circuit of Fig. 4-12, of which the two SUBT units in Fig. 4-15 are copies, makes no allowance for sign values. However, the familiar result of number arithmetic

$$A - B = A + (-B)$$

which is essentially the definition of the subtraction operation, quickly answers the question. It reminds us that by changing the sign of B we may perform an addition instead, and the design of an electrical addition circuit has just been completed. For subtraction of any two numbers, therefore, the sign value of the B number may be passed through a NOT circuit, after which all A and B digits may be processed by the machine of Fig. 4-15, which adds. The output will be the difference

$$A - B = A_5 A_4 A_3 A_2 A_1 - B_5 B_4 B_3 B_2 B_1$$

for numbers having five-value symbols. For instance,

$$6 - 5 = 00110 - 00101$$
$$= 00110 + (10101)$$
$$= 00001$$

the step from the first line to the second being executed by the NOT and the remaining step by the addition circuit of Fig. 4-15. This may seem like a slightly unnatural way to take 5 from 6, but only to a human observer. To a machine the difference between addition and subtraction of any two numbers whatever becomes merely one NOT.

4.39. Find the product of the numbers having binary symbols 1101 and 0110, using only binary language.

For the moment we have omitted sign values to focus upon the magnitudes of the two numbers to be multiplied. The following routine will be reminiscent of a similar decimal procedure.

$$\left.\begin{array}{r}1101 \\ 0110\end{array}\right\} \text{ the given numbers}$$

$$\left.\begin{array}{r}0000 \\ 1101 \\ 1101 \\ 0000\end{array}\right\} \text{ the partial products}$$

$$\overline{1001110} \quad \text{final product}$$

4.40. The multiplication routine just illustrated is more conveniently electrified if a means of *storing* sequences for repeated use as needed is available. Explain what is meant by a flip-flop and a storage register.

Imagine a hinge which can be pushed to either right or left and then rests against a support in either case. (Fig. 4-16.) Whichever of the two possible positions the hinge happens to be in at a given time, it will keep that position until pushed again. In a sense, it remembers that position. Several such hinges arranged in a line, as in Fig. 4-17, could be used to store a Boolean sequence. If we interpret left as zero and right as one, for example, then the sequence shown is 10001 and may be taken to represent the number seventeen or the number minus one among other things.

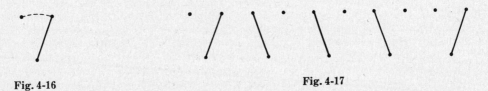

Fig. 4-16   Fig. 4-17

The above hinges flip-flop back and forth between their two possible equilibrium states. In computer science the term flip-flop is applied to an electrical unit which has the same character.

It can take either of two possible states (Fig. 4-18) and will hold that state until changed by the correct sort of input (corresponding to a push in the correct direction for the above hinge). In the figure there are two input terminals, labeled set and reset, and a hot input to either is assumed to make the corresponding output terminal hot and the other output terminal cold. The flip-flop thus remembers which state it is in until another input is applied. Such units can be made from vacuum tubes, transistors or other electrical components, the details being available in engineering literature.

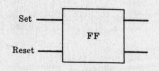

Fig. 4-18.   A flip-flop.

Several flip-flops arranged in a line, as in Fig. 4-19, may be used to store a sequence. If we interpret set as one and reset as zero, for example, then the sequence shown is again 10001, the last hot input to each flip-flop being indicated. An array such as this, capable of storing a sequence, will be called a storage register.

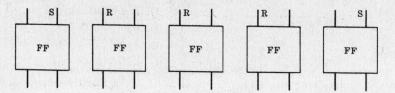

Fig. 4-19.   A storage register.

4.41. Show how flip-flops may be used to make a shifting register.

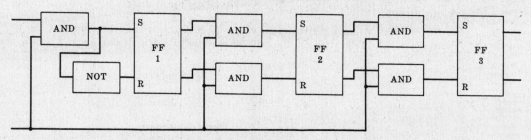

Fig. 4-20

Fig. 4-20 gives the general idea. To load the register a sequence is introduced digit by digit, or to use a popular condensation of binary digit, bit by bit into the AND circuit at the left. Note that this is a different procedure from that used in earlier circuits, where all values of a given sequence were treated more or less at the same time. Simultaneous handling of all bits in a sequence is called parallel information processing. The procedure now being introduced is called serial or sequential information processing. Most general-purpose computers combine the two types of operation, using whichever is more convenient for a particular assignment. A second new operational feature also appears, the control input. For loading purposes this provides a hot value to accompany each arriving bit of information. All AND circuits thus receive a hot input value at their lower terminals. This means that each one will then transmit whatever value arrives at that moment at the upper terminal, the AND thus serving as a gate. Suppose, for instance, that 110 is to be stored. First the zero value arrives at the left, together with the control pulse, giving FF1 the reset (or zero) position. At the next pulse this zero is passed on to FF2 while the incoming one value enters FF1. The third pulse completes the read-in. For longer sequences a longer register would of course be needed, but the idea is the same. Once the register is loaded, the rightmost value of the input sequence is available at the output terminals. The point of the present circuit is that if at any time it is useful to shift the sequence, bringing the next value to the output terminals, and reflection will suggest that this happens often enough in multiplication routines, then another pulse on the control input will shift each value to the right, each flip-flop copying the content of the one to its left. After one such shift the present register would contain 011, assuming no further hot read-in values. Another shift would make the contents 001, and so on. It must also be mentioned that appropriately selected delays must be included, so that the value of a given flip-flop may be copied by the one to its right before being altered by new information coming in from the left.

Many variations are possible. Reversing the pattern of Fig. 4-20 produces a register in which information is shifted to the left instead of to the right. Providing more contacts could allow the register to be loaded by parallel operation, all flip-flops being set or reset at the same time. Still other contacts could allow for the outputs of all the flip-flops to be "read" at the same time. Our basic sequences of zeros and ones may thus be stored in registers or retrieved from them by either serial or parallel means and, as Fig. 4-20 shows, they may also be shifted back and forth as required.

4.42. What is meant by *clearing* a storage register?

Clearing means putting all values to zero, resetting all flip-flops. This could be achieved, for example, by providing for simultaneous access to all reset terminals as suggested in Fig. 4-21. After an input pulse on this access line, the register would be storing 000. This clearing operation is heavily used and will appear in the multiplication circuit about to be designed.

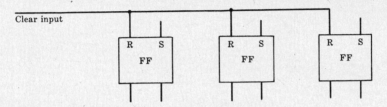

Fig. 4-21

4.43. How may the contents of one storage register be transferred into another?

One procedure clears the recipient register first and then triggers the transfer, as shown in Fig. 4-22. After the upper register has been cleared to 000, any 1 outputs from the lower register, in time with the transfer pulse, will pass through the AND circuits and both registers will have the same content.

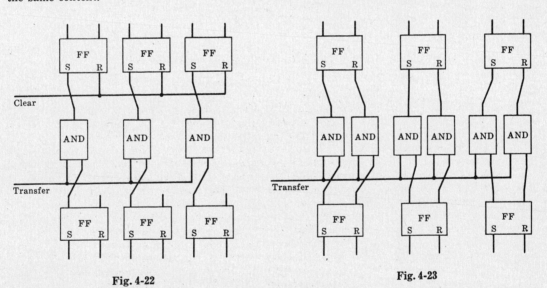

Fig. 4-22   **Fig. 4-23**

Another way is shown in Fig. 4-23. This circuit copies the content of the lower three flip-flops into the upper three, regardless of the previous state of the upper flip-flops and does this upon receipt of only one pulse. When the transfer pulse arrives, all AND circuits receive one hot input. Since each of the lower flip-flops has one hot output terminal and one cold, however, only one of the two AND circuits associated with it will pass a hot value. Thus each upper flip-flop receives either a hot reset input or a hot set input, matching the status of the one directly below it. If an upper flip-flop reads 0 and receives a reset input, it will remain as it was; but if it receives a set input it will then read 1. Either way the two flip-flops will then match. A similar argument holds if the initial reading was 1.

4.44. What is a complementing flip-flop?

This is a modification which has only a single input and always changes state (0 to 1 or vice versa) when a hot input value appears. Several simple designs are available but we omit the engineering details. Fig. 4-24 represents such a flip-flop.

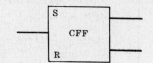

Fig. 4-24. A complementing flip-flop.

4.45. Show how flip-flops, shift registers and an addition unit may be combined to achieve binary multiplication.

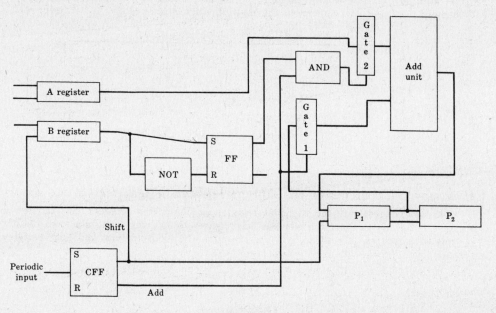

Fig. 4-25

Fig. 4-25 shows one possible multiplier. The two numbers to be multiplied

$$A_4A_3A_2A_1$$
$$B_4B_3B_2B_1$$

are first stored in the A and B shift registers, as described above. With proper timing the complementing flip-flop CFF is then set, and triggers a shift. The bit B_1 is fed to the multiplier bit flip-flop. If the bit is a one it sets the flip-flop; if it is a zero it resets it. Again with proper timing the CFF is now reset and provides a hot input for the control of Gates 1 and 2. This opens Gate 1 and allows the contents of register P_1 to enter the addition unit. If the multiplier bit B_1 is a one, then Gate 2 also opens and the A number enters the addition unit. At the start the content of P_1 must be the sequence 0000, so that after this first step the sum $A_4A_3A_2A_1$ will be in P_1, still assuming that B_1 is a one. If it is a zero then the content of P_1 remains 0000. Now CFF reverts to its set position, the bit B_2 enters the multiplier bit flip-flop, and at the same time the entire content of the double register P_1P_2 is shifted right. (This also occurred on the earlier shift but, all digits in these registers being zeros, nothing of consequence happened here at that time.) Once again CFF changes to reset, and the cycle continues until all four digits of the B number have had their turns as multiplier. At the finish the product is in the double register P_1P_2, the most significant half being in P_1. A summary of the content of the various units at successive stages, using the specific numbers of Problem 4.39, appears as Table 4.1 in Problem 4.46. It will be clear after even a first glance at Fig. 4-25 that no effort has been made in this case to represent every wire and every contact, as has been done up to now. Instead we have only a general plan of the flow of information, with emphasis upon the way in which that flow is controlled. Full details would reveal that the multiplier unit is a reasonably complex information processor.

4.46. Follow the circuit of Fig. 4-25 as it carries out the same computation made by hand in Problem 4.39.

As mentioned above, Table 4.1 summarizes the content of the key registers at successive stages. The A register keeps the same 1101 sequence throughout. B-MB denotes the B register with the attached multiplication bit flip-flop, while P_1-P_2 is the double register in which the product is accumulated. On each shift the contents of B-MB and P_1-P_2 move one place to the right. On each add the content of P_1 is added to 0000 if MB is zero, or to 1101 if MB is one. Notice in particular that the third add step produces an overflow $(0110 + 1101 = 10011)$. This overflow is saved, perhaps in another flip-flop, and then appears at the left end of P_1 on the next shift. The product of two four-digit numbers thus emerges as an eight-digit number, in this case the equivalent of $13 \times 6 = 78$.

A	B-MB	P_1-P_2	
1101	0110 0	0000 0000	Start
1101	0011 0	0000 0000	Shift
1101	0011 0	0000 0000	Add
1101	0001 1	0000 0000	Shift
1101	0001 1	1101 0000	Add
1101	0000 1	0110 1000	Shift
1101	0000 1	0011 1000	Add
1101	0000 0	1001 1100	Shift
1101	0000 0	1001 1100	Add
1101	0000 0	0100 1110	Shift and stop.

Table 4.1

4.47. How may the signs of the two factors be taken into account in a multiplication operation?

Exactly as in the addition circuit of Fig. 4-15, the two sign values (which were omitted in the preceding two problems) may be processed by a comparator circuit. The output may be used as the sign of the product, since it will be hot when the factors have opposite signs and cold when they have the same. Since we have been using a one, or hot, value as a minus sign and a zero, or cold, value as a plus, this is exactly what we want.

4.48. Divide 01001110 by 0110, using binary language only.

Imitating the familiar decimal division routine, we may produce the following layout. Since 0110 exceeds 0100, we place the first 1 of the quotient in position five as shown. (Four zeros may be included in front of it.) The first subtraction then brings 0011 which we enlarge to 0011110 by copying the unused digits from above. This completes the first step and we begin a second of the same sort.

```
            00001101
      0110 ) 01001110
             0110
             0011110
             0110
             000110
             0110
             0000
```

Three steps in all reverse the multiplication operation completed a moment ago, giving us the equivalent of $78/6 = 13$.

4.49. How may the operation of division be carried out by an electrical circuit?

The preceding problem suggests that division is achieved by successive subtractions. Various shifts of sequences are also conspicuous. In general one may already say that a division circuit will consist of a subtractor with associated control assistance. A careful scrutiny of the above example shows that an important part of this control is the decision at each step as to where the next 1 should appear in the quotient, or in other words, whether intermediate zeros must be included. The complexity of this decision process has led to the invention of variations of the familiar subtraction routine, some of which are illustrated in the following problems.

4.50. Illustrate the restoring method of division.

The division of 1101 by 1011 by this method is presented in Table 4.2. Like the more familiar process it is based on successive subtractions. The main difference between the two methods is that here the divisor 1011 is repeatedly subtracted until a negative result is obtained. Since it is so easy to determine visually when enough subtractions have been made it may seem wasteful to go quite so far, but the point is that the negative sign is easy for a machine to recognize and provides a clear signal that it is time to stop. In fact, having made one subtraction too many, it is necessary to restore the proper remainder by adding 1011. A shift then occurs and we are ready for the next step. Notice that we are assuming the subtraction will be made in the correct direction, larger magnitude minus smaller, as in the addition circuit of Fig. 4-15. When the result of the first subtraction is positive, a 1 is recorded for the quotient; when it is negative, a 0 is recorded. The above computation thus produces the sequence 10010 which we interpret as the binary symbol 1.0010. This is equivalent to the fraction 9/8 and is a correct quotient as far as it goes.

1101	
1011	
+0010	Result of first subtraction is positive.
1011	Subtract again.
−1001	Negative remainder, time to stop.
1011	Add.
+0010	Proper remainder restored.
+00100	Shift.
01011	Begin second step.
−00111	Result of first subtraction is negative.
01011	Add.
+00100	Proper remainder restored.
+001000	Shift.
001011	Begin third step.
−000011	Result of first subtraction is negative.
001011	Add.
+001000	Proper remainder restored.
+0010000	Shift.
0001011	Begin fourth step.
+0000101	Result of first subtraction is positive.
0001011	Subtract again.
−0000110	Negative remainder.
0001011	Add.
+0000101	Proper remainder restored.
+00001010	Shift.
00001011	Begin fifth step.
−00000001	Result of first subtraction is negative.
00001011	Add.
+00001010	Proper remainder restored.

Table 4.2

4.51. Illustrate a nonrestoring method of division.

It is fairly clear that the restoring method just used is wasteful. For one thing, if the result of the first subtraction is positive then the next will always be negative, provided we arrange by shifting that both input numbers, dividend and divisor, begin with the digit one. Other simplifications are possible and various routines have been developed. In Table 4.3 one such method is presented. Here the same input numbers 1101 and 1011 of the preceding problem are used. As before we begin with a subtraction, and a positive remainder brings another subtraction. However, after getting a negative remainder there is no restoring. Instead the divisor 1011 is added. Each subtraction or addition is followed by a shift. Each positive remainder brings a 1 to the quotient, and each negative remainder a 0. The same result found in Table 4.2 is reproduced and it is not too hard to analyze the routine and discover why it "works".

1101	
<u>1011</u>	
+0010	First remainder is positive. Record 1.
+00100	Shift.
<u>01011</u>	Subtract again.
−00111	Remainder is negative. Record 0.
−001110	Shift.
<u>001011</u>	Add.
−000011	Sum is negative. Record 0.
−0000110	Shift.
<u>0001011</u>	Add.
+0000101	Sum is positive. Record 1.
+00001010	Shift.
<u>00001011</u>	Subtract.
−00000001	Remainder is negative. Record 0.

Table 4.3

4.52. Diagram the channels of information flow for the nonrestoring routine just illustrated.

Fig. 4-26 gives the general idea. It will be seen at once that no attempt has been made to exhibit every wire. The division circuit is another reasonably complex machine. The diagram follows very closely the path of the computation just completed. The complementing flip-flop alternately opens the gate to allow the next subtraction or addition to be made and triggers the shift left of the dividend (or of the sum or remainder which takes its place). The sign bit of this sum or remainder, reversed in value by a NOT circuit if 1 is to continue to mean negative, is fed to the right end of the quotient register after each computation and then shifts left also, to make room for the next digit. At the finish the entire quotient is available here and the remainder or sum occupies the place of the original dividend.

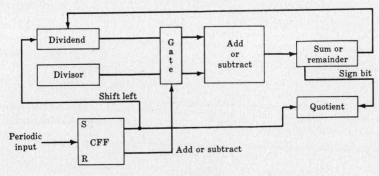

Fig. 4-26

4.53. What is the purpose of *floating-point* symbols for numbers?

The numbers used in most of our earlier problems have been integers, such as decimal 78 and binary 1101. This was done to keep the computations relatively simple. Almost all serious computing, however, involves fractions. The familiar decimal symbols such as 1.44 and .025 represent fractions in what is called a *fixed-point* form. To add in this symbolism we align the decimal points.

```
    1.44          1.44
     .025          .025
    ─────         ─────
    1.465          720
                   288
                   000
                  ─────
                  .03600
```

To multiply we must count the digits to the right of the points and see to it that in the product there are just as many, otherwise treating the numbers as though they were integers. Keeping track of the decimal point in such operations is a form of what is known as scaling. In machine computations scaling also means avoiding overflow, being careful not to shift important digits so that they are lost, and not to allow a sum to exceed the machine's ability to retain. The bookkeeping involved in the scaling of lengthy computations can be substantial. Floating-point symbols have been designed so that scaling can be performed by a systematic routine understandable by an electrical circuit.

4.54. Represent the input and output numbers of the preceding problem in a floating-point decimal language.

There are several alternatives; but one common system, slightly abbreviated, uses the following.

$$1.44 = 0511440 \qquad .025 = 0492500$$
$$1.465 = 0511465 \qquad .036 = 0493600$$

The first digit on the right gives the sign, zero in each case since all four numbers were positive. The last four digits represent the *fraction*, obtained by shifting the decimal point in the standard symbol on the left until it is just before the leftmost non-zero digit. The second and third digits of the floating-point symbol indicate the number of such shifts, above 50 for leftward shifts and below 50 for rightward. Thus 51 means that one leftward shift was made, or what is the same thing, that in the fraction part of the floating-point symbol, so-called because we think of the point as being at the left end, one shift to the right must be made to recover the original 1.44. The use of 50 as reference seems to be more convenient than using positive integers to show shifts in one direction and negative integers for shifts in the other. This part of the symbol is called *the exponent* because of its close relationship to the exponent in another popular symbol for the same number.

$$1.44 = .144 \times 10^1 \qquad .025 = .25 \times 10^{-1}$$
$$1.465 = .1465 \times 10^1 \qquad .036 = .36 \times 10^{-1}$$

4.55. Represent the numbers 144 and 1465 in a floating-point binary language.

For the IBM-7094 computer a sequence of 36 values is used as follows.

> First value: the sign
>
> Next eight: the exponent
>
> All others: the fraction

The idea is much the same as in the preceding problem with 128 serving as reference for the exponents. Similarly in the IBM 360 a sequence of 32 values includes a sign, a seven value exponent and a 24 value fraction, with the option of a 64 value sequence in which the extra 32 values extend the fraction. Choosing 7094 language we find

$$144 = 0\ 10001000\ 10010000\ldots$$
$$1465 = 0\ 10001011\ 10110111001\ldots$$

the spaces being left merely for convenience in reading, and numerous terminal zeros being omitted. Note, for instance, that in the exponent 10001000 the leading one stands for the reference 128 while the other stands for the eight shifts needed to march the binary point to the right end of the sequence 10010000, which then means the same thing as decimal 144.

4.56. Represent the four numbers of Problem 4.54 in the same floating-point binary language.

Here the hardest part is the conversions. By the method of Problem 4.7 or otherwise one may verify that

$$1.44 \ = \ 1.011100001010\ldots$$

$$1.465 \ = \ 1.011101110000\ldots$$

$$.025 \ = \ .000001100110\ldots$$

$$.036 \ = \ .000010010011\ldots$$

more digits being computable if desired. Changing from fixed to floating point symbolism brings

$$1.44 \ = \ 0 \ 10000001 \ 1011100001010\ldots$$

$$1.465 \ = \ 0 \ 10000001 \ 1011101110000\ldots$$

$$.025 \ = \ 0 \ 01111011 \ 1100110\ldots$$

$$.036 \ = \ 0 \ 01111100 \ 10010011\ldots$$

the terminal dots representing digits we have not taken the trouble to compute.

4.57. Add the numbers 1.44 and .025 using the floating-point symbols of the preceding problem.

To find the sum by hand, as in Problem 4.53, one begins by aligning the decimal points. The comparable step in floating-point language is to equalize the exponents. Raising the smaller exponent, and shifting the corresponding fraction rightward by the same amount, these two numbers appear as

$$0 \ 10000001 \ 1011100001010\ldots$$

$$0 \ 10000001 \ 0000001100110\ldots$$

six shifts having been made. Addition now brings

$$0 \ 10000001 \ 1011101110000\ldots$$

the sign and the exponent simply being carried down. Note that it would be impractical to equalize exponents by lowering the larger, since then, to keep the number the same, it would be necessary to shift the fraction leftward, and this would overflow the digits of highest value. Should an overflow occur anyway, even when we proceed as above, then both exponents must be raised by one and the fractions shifted right one value, after which the addition process is repeated.

4.58. How can the addition in Problem 4.57 be carried out by a circuit?

This brings us back to the main point of this chapter, that once a language understandable by both man and machine is in hand the design of circuitry may proceed. We are viewing the above symbols as floating-decimals, but to the machine they are still just sequences of zeros and ones waiting to be processed by AND, OR, NOT circuits and our other basic electrical devices. Careful listing of the steps in the computation of the preceding problem would lead to a circuit capable of duplicating them. The details will be omitted here but notice in particular the use of an overflow as a control signal. When an overflow occurs it triggers the raising of exponents, shifting of fractions, and repetition just mentioned. Floating-point circuits tend to be more complicated than the corresponding fixed point circuitry, but the reward lies in the broad range of numbers which can be represented by using the exponent idea and in the fact that the overflow problem is essentially solved.

4.59. How may the numbers 1.44 and .025 be multiplied using their floating-point symbols?

The fractional parts may be treated as earlier. The product will come double length as it did in the circuit of Fig. 4-25 and the most significant half, the left half, retained. Suppose for simplicity that we truncate the fractional parts to .101110 and .110011. Their product is then .100100101010, the most significant half being .100100 or .100101 if we round up. The exponents are the core of floating-point symbolism. Remembering that 128, the leading 1, is the equivalent of no shifts either way, and noting that 10000001 is one above this reference while 01111011 is five below, we easily compute a net exponent of minus four, which in the present language is 01111100. Our final result is thus

$$0 \ 01111100 \ 100100\ldots$$

agreeing as far as it goes with that of Problem 4.56. The product is of course positive since both factors were positive, and the question of signs in floating-point operations may be answered just as it was earlier for fixed-point. As for the operation of addition, the routine just illustrated may be duplicated by an electrical circuit. The same is true of subtraction and division but details can be omitted in view of the limited objectives of this chapter.

4.60. What is meant by a computer *word*?

This is another name for the sequence of zeros and ones with which the computer operates. Each 36 value floating-point symbol of the sort just discussed might be a computer word. In the memory unit information is usually stored in words, each word occupying one memory location and being addressable by the name of that location.

4.61. What is meant by sequential storing of words?

A frequently used sequential method involves placing the words on the surface of a rotating magnetic drum. Fig. 4-27 shows a miniature model of such a memory device, each word having only five values. To record such words five magnetic tracks must be provided, going completely around the drum. A read-write mechanism records magnetic hots and colds for the ones and zeros and retrieves them as needed. A particular location can be written into or read from only when it is under the read-write mechanism. In general, to retrieve a particular word, it is necessary to sequence through all the intervening words waiting for the right moment, and it is from this that the method gets its name.

Fig. 4-27

4.62. How may sequential storage locations be identified?

From the fact that it is sequential it follows that the integers 0, 1, 2, 3, ... may serve as identification. Converting to binary, and supposing that our miniature drum has 64 locations, we find that the symbols 000000, 000001, ..., 111111 are sufficient. A rotating drum is provided with an extra track which identifies each location. When a particular location is wanted, for reading or writing, control circuitry decides when the identification of that location agrees with that of the location under the read-write mechanism. Fig. 4-27 suggests parallel operation of a drum, an entire word being written or read at one time. Serial operation is also possible with changes in the design.

4.63. What is random access storage?

Here the words are stored in such a way that all of them are equally accessible at any time. In a very common type of random access memory, the basic component is a small ring-shaped piece of magnetic material called a core. These are arranged in planes much as in Fig. 4-28, in which each plane contains eight rows of eight cores each. The planes may then be stacked to a height determined by the word length. The resulting box-shaped unit is a core memory. In this diagram each computer word, or sequence, has been stacked vertically, and one may be reached as easily as another and at any time, assuming that appropriate wiring is provided to sense the value of each core in the stack.

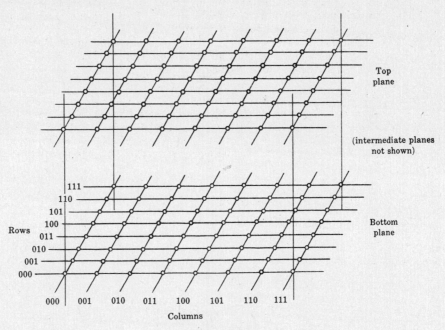

Fig. 4-28

4.64. How may the locations in memory of the type illustrated in Problem 4.63 be identified?

A coordinate system seems most convenient. If for instance there are eight rows and eight columns to each plane, then they may be numbered from 0 to 7, or in binary from 000 to 111. A symbol such as 010101 then serves to identify an entire word, the word stacked vertically above the value in row 010, column 101 of the bottom plane. A decoder such as that of Fig. 4-4 can then be used to accept the first coordinate, say 010, and select the desired row, while another takes the second coordinate, say 101, and selects the proper column. With suitable wiring the word stacked above this position may then be read out or a new word written in its place. Core memory proves to be very fast, in part because of the random access feature, and is extensively used.

4.65. What is the symbol for each number and letter in the alphanumeric code used in Fig. 4-5, page 53?

Fig. 4-29 simulates a piece of punched tape and shows each of the required characters. A few other symbols, for punctuation and clerical matters, are included also to partly round out the picture. The tiny holes are used in drawing the tape through the reading device.

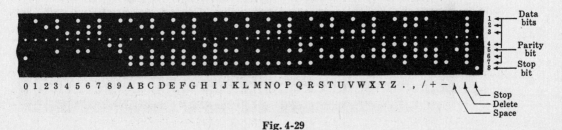

Fig. 4-29

Notice first that the digits 0 to 9 are essentially represented by their binary symbols. The extra punch that occasionally appears in channel five provides what is called an *error detection* feature. All characters in this code use an odd number of punches. This is achieved for the decimal digits by adding the *parity bit* in channel five when needed. Thus 3 becomes the sequence 00010011, 5 becomes 00010101 and so on. The computer itself is taught to check each sequence and indicate if it is faulty. Of course, not all errors can be detected in this way. A punch might be in the wrong channel leaving the total number of punches odd, such as 00100011 appearing where 3 was intended. The sequence is perfectly legal and would be accepted by the machine, even though it means T rather than 3. Certain errors will, however, be detected, and in the transmission of large amounts of data an error detection code may prove useful. Channel eight is used here to signal the end of a particular block of information and stop the reading process.

4.66. Translate the result ARMY 14, NAVY 14 into the code of the preceding problem.

Fig. 4-30 gives the translation, including the spaces, comma and a stop. The symbol 1 stands for a punch.

```
1 1 0 0 0 1 0 1 0 1 1 1 0 0 1 0 0
0 0 0 0 0 0 0 1 0 0 0 0 0 0 0 0 0
0 0 1 0 0 0 1 0 0 1 0 1 0 0 0 1 0
0 1 0 1 0 0 0 1 0 0 0 0 1 0 0 0 0
0 0 1 1 1 0 0 1 1 0 0 0 1 1 0 0 0
1 0 0 1 0 0 0 1 0 0 1 1 1 0 0 0 0
1 1 1 0 0 0 0 0 0 1 1 0 0 0 0 0 0
0 0 0 0 0 0 0 0 0 0 0 0 0 0 0 0 1
```

A R M Y   1 4 ,   N A V Y   1 4

Fig. 4-30

4.67. What is the Hollerith code?

This is an alphanumeric code used with punched cards. Fig. 4-31 shows how the digits 0 to 9 of decimal symbols and the letters of the alphabet are represented. There are several types of cards in use and a variety of codes, the present example being typical. Each column may be used to represent one digit, one letter or special character. Since about eighty columns are usually provided, this is the number of symbols which may be packed onto one card. As will appear later it is often more convenient to be slightly extravagant in the use of cards, since then alterations in data are more easily made. Notice that each digit is very simply coded by a single punch in the row so printed. Each letter requires two punched positions and certain special characters take more. Cards are punched on a specially constructed device having a typewriter-like keyboard. Depressing the proper key produces the punches required for the desired character. Quite often the device also prints the character above the column containing its code, so that a card may be checked without examining the actual punches.

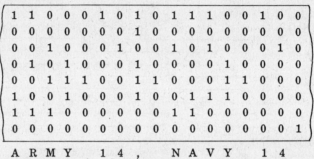

Fig. 4-31

Supplementary Problems

4.68. Convert the following from binary to decimal.

(a) 10111   (d) 110011   (g) 11110000

(b) 11110   (e) 111000   (h) 11001100

(c) 11011   (f) 100011   (i) 10101010

4.69. Convert the following from binary to decimal.

(a) 111   (b) 1111   (c) 11111   (d) 111111   (e) 1111111

Note in each case the next greater number.

4.70. Convert the following from decimal to binary.

(a) 15   (b) 20   (c) 25   (d) 50   (e) 100   (f) 169   (g) 255

4.71. What is the largest number that can be represented by (a) ten binary digits, (b) twenty binary digits, (c) N binary digits?

4.72. Convert these binary fractions to the form A/B, where A and B are integers. (Thus .101 would become 5/8.)

(a) .011   (b) .111   (c) .1101   (d) .1001   (e) .10001   (f) .11001

4.73. Replace the symbols A/B of the preceding problem by decimals, rounding off wherever necessary to three places.

4.74. Represent the following in binary form, rounding off to five places wherever necessary.

(a) 2/3   (b) 1/5   (c) 15/16

4.75. Convert the binary symbols of Problem 4.68 to octal form.

4.76. Hexadecimal symbols use position value 16, the numerals 0 to 9 playing their familiar roles while A, B, C, D, E, F represent 10 through 15. The following equivalent symbols may be verified. Fill the missing places. Note especially that each hexadecimal digit corresponds to exactly four binary digits. Thus the binary

$$10,1101,1110,0101$$

becomes the hexadecimal 2DE5, the commas separating the four hexadecimal digits.

Decimal	Binary	Hexadecimal
12	1100	C
15	1111	...
...	10111011	BB
...	...	ABC
...	1101110	...
43	...	...

4.77. Represent the following by sequences of exactly eight values, the first value being the sign and the rest the binary symbol for the magnitude. (Thus +2 becomes 00000010.)

(a) +1   (b) −1   (c) +15   (d) −15   (e) +0   (f) −127

4.78. Reverse the procedure of the preceding problem, converting the following into decimal form plus sign.

(a) 11000000   (c) 11110000   (e) 00110011

(b) 10101010   (d) 11001100   (f) 01010101

4.79. Use the remainder method of conversion to find the binary equivalents of (a) 175 and (b) 255.

4.80. Perform the following additions using only binary language.

    (a)   1010   (b)   0111   (c)   1011

        + 0011   + 0110   + 0010

4.81. Perform these additions using only binary language.

    (a)   110010   (b)   011100   (c)   011110

        + 000110   + 011100   + 011010

4.82. Show that the circuit of Fig. 4-32 is a suitable half-adder.

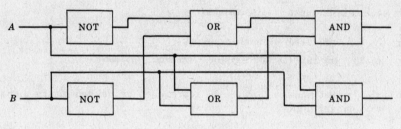

Fig. 4-32

4.83. Follow the machine of Fig. 4-8 as it carries out the addition $1010 + 0011$, labeling each wire according to the value that it carries.

4.84. Follow the machine of Fig. 4-8 as it tries to carry out the addition $0111 + 1011$, noting the overflow. What sum is actually generated?

4.85. What is the largest sum the circuit of Fig. 4-8 can compute without overflow?

4.86. Without referring to Fig. 4-8, simply by thinking through the binary addition process, diagram a five-digit addition circuit. Label all wires according to the value they carry in the computation of $00110 + 01011$. Is there an overflow? What sum is given?

4.87. What is the largest sum that the circuit of the preceding problem can compute without overflow?

4.88. Show that the circuit of Fig. 4-33 is a suitable full-adder.

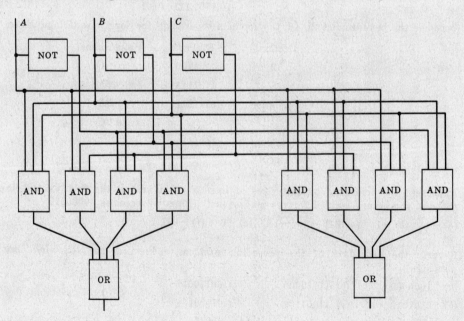

Fig. 4-33

4.89.   Show that the circuit of Fig. 4-34 is also a suitable full-adder, computing $(AB + \bar{A}\bar{B})C + (A\bar{B} + \bar{A}B)\bar{C}$ for record.   What does it compute for carry?

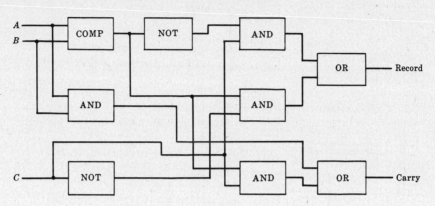

Fig. 4-34

4.90.   The record part of the circuit in the preceding problem also appears in a more light-weight setting in Chapter 3.   In which application did this happen?

4.91.   Find the difference in each of the following cases, using binary language only.

    (a)   1100   (b)   1010   (c)   1010   (d)   1100

          − 0110   − 0111   − 0011   − 0101

4.92.   Perform the following subtractions, using binary language only.

    (a)   111000   (b)   111000   (c)   111000

          − 000111   − 110011   − 100001

4.93.   Show that the circuit of Fig. 4-35 is a half-subtractor.

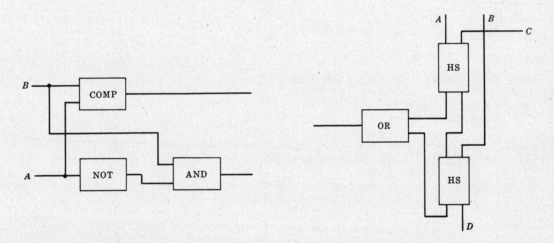

                 Fig. 4-35   Fig. 4-36

4.94.   A full-subtractor is a circuit capable of dealing with one typical column of a subtraction operation.   The machine of Fig. 4-12 includes three such units, one of which is repeated as Fig. 4-36.   By labeling all wires show that the final record for the column involved will be

$$D = (A\bar{C} + \bar{A}C)\bar{B} + (AC + \bar{A}\bar{C})B$$

where C is the borrow made by the next column to the right.   What will be the final borrow made from the next column to the left?

4.95. A full-subtractor must be able to accept three inputs, the given A and B digits of the column in question and the borrow C made by the next column to the right. The usual eight possible combinations arise.

$$A \quad 0\ 0\ 0\ 0\ 1\ 1\ 1\ 1$$
$$B \quad 0\ 0\ 1\ 1\ 0\ 0\ 1\ 1$$
$$C \quad 0\ 1\ 0\ 1\ 0\ 1\ 0\ 1$$

For each such combination, what is the correct record? What is the correct borrow from the next column to the left?

4.96. Verify directly, using the familiar eight column computation, that the full-subtractor of Fig. 4-36 produces the outputs specified in the preceding problem.

4.97. Show that the circuit of Fig. 4-37 is a full-subtractor.

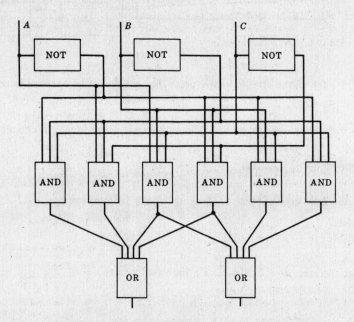

Fig. 4-37

4.98. Show that $\bar{A}B + \bar{A}C + BC$ is also a correct borrow output for a full-subtractor.

4.99. Follow the machine of Fig. 4-12 as it computes $1100 - 0110$, labeling each wire according to the value that it carries.

4.100. What happens if the machine of Fig. 4-12 is offered the problem $0110 - 1100$? Label each wire according to the value that it carries. Note in particular the hot overflow.

4.101. Diagram a five-digit subtractor similar to that of Fig. 4-12 and then label each wire according to the value that it carries in the computation of $10101 - 01110$.

4.102. Compute the following sums, the first value in each sequence being the sign value, 0 for a positive number and 1 for a negative number. Follow the procedure used by the machine of Fig. 4-15.

(*a*)   01100   (*b*)   01100   (*c*)   11100   (*d*)   11100
      + 00011   + 10101   + 00101   + 10011

4.103. Show that in each of the following computations involving "minus zero" the circuit of Fig. 4-15 produces the correct sum. Through which gate does each sum emerge? Assume the top number in each case to be the A number.

(*a*)   00001   (*b*)   10001   (*c*)   10000   (*d*)   10000
      + 10000   + 10000   + 00001   + 10001

4.104. How does the circuit of Fig. 4-15 handle the addition of $A = 00000$ to $B = 10000$ (plus zero and minus zero)?

4.105. Carry out the following *subtraction* by inserting an extra NOT circuit to invert the B_5 value in the *addition* machine of Fig. 4-15, and then labeling all wires according to the value they carry. Which gate leads to the answer?
$$A - B \;=\; 00110 - 10011$$

4.106. Proceed as in the preceding problem with
$$A - B \;=\; 10110 - 10011$$
again noting which gate leads to the answer.

4.107. Consider *the complement method* of adding a positive and a negative number, or what amounts to the same thing, of subtracting two positive numbers. In decimal language the 9s complement of a positive number is found by replacing each digit by nine minus that digit. Thus the complement of 147 is 852 and the complement of 605 is 394. To add 605 and −147 we proceed as follows.

$$
\begin{array}{rll}
+605 & & 605 \\
-147 & \text{complement} & 852 \\
\hline
& (1)457 & \text{temporary sum} \\
& 1 & \text{end-around carry} \\
\hline
& +458 & \text{final sum}
\end{array}
$$

Instead of subtracting, as one would do in a hand computation and as SUBT 1 would do in the machine of Fig. 4-15, we exchange 147 for its complement 852 and actually add. The overflow is then carried into the one's column and added in, the final sum being the correct result. As a second example we reverse the signs.

$$
\begin{array}{rll}
-605 & \text{complement} & 394 \\
+147 & & 147 \\
\hline
& 541 & \text{temporary sum} \\
& -458 & \text{complement}
\end{array}
$$

Here too we complement and then add. This time there is no overflow and a different finish is used. The temporary sum is itself complemented and the result given a minus sign.

Apply this complement method to these examples and perhaps discover why it leads to correct sums.

$$
\begin{array}{ll}
(a) \;\; +372 & (b) \;\; -372 \\
 -198 & +198
\end{array}
$$

4.108. The complement method is also effective in the binary language, complements being found by exchanging zeros and ones. As a first example we add +1011 and −0101.

$$
\begin{array}{rll}
+1011 & & 1011 \\
-0101 & \text{complement} & 1010 \\
\hline
& (1)0101 & \text{temporary sum} \\
& 1 & \text{end-around carry} \\
\hline
& +0110 & \text{final sum}
\end{array}
$$

The routine is the same as in decimal language. Reversing the signs again provides a second example.

$$
\begin{array}{rll}
-1011 & \text{complement} & 0100 \\
+0101 & & 0101 \\
\hline
& 1001 & \text{temporary sum} \\
& -0110 & \text{complement with minus}
\end{array}
$$

Again the routine is the same as in decimal language. Apply this method to the following sums.

$$
\begin{array}{llll}
(a) \;\; +1001 & (b) \;\; -1001 & (c) \;\; +111000 & (d) \;\; -111000 \\
 -0111 & +0111 & -101010 & +101010
\end{array}
$$

4.109. Compute the following products using only binary language. Verify the products by converting to decimal.

(*a*) 1001   (*b*) 1011   (*c*) 101110
     0110   1110   100101

4.110. Verify the following octal language computation of the last product in the preceding problem.

$$
\begin{array}{r}
56 \\
45 \\
\hline
346 \\
270 \\
\hline
3246
\end{array}
$$

4.111. Compute these products in octal language.   Verify the results by converting to decimal.

(*a*) 12×10 (*b*) 44×33 (*c*) 123×45

4.112. Follow the computation of 1001×0110 through the circuit of Fig. 4-25, listing the content of the key registers at each step as in Table 4.1. What product finally appears in register P1?

4.113. Proceed as in the preceding problem with 1011 and 1110. What product finally appears in register P1?

4.114. Divide 01100100 by 1010 using binary language only, as in Problem 4.48.

4.115. Divide 1010 by 1001 using the restoring method of Table 4.2, page 74.   Carry the quotient to five digits.

4.116. Repeat the preceding problem using the nonrestoring method of Table 4.3, page 75.

4.117. To divide 1010 by 0011 using the nonrestoring method, suppose the dividend shifted left two positions to read 1100. Carry the computation to seven or eight digits, noting the repeating nature of the result from there on. Finally shift the binary point two positions toward the right.

4.118. Represent the following decimals in the floating-point language of Problem 4.54.

(*a*) 100   (*b*) 10   (*c*) .1   (*d*) .001

4.119. Carry out the addition

$$
\begin{array}{r}
0531000 \\
+\ 0501000
\end{array}
$$

in the same language, raising the exponent of the lower number and shifting accordingly.   In what form does the sum appear?

4.120. Represent the product of the two numbers in the preceding problem in this floating-point language, remembering that the first digit after the exponent should not be a zero.

4.121. Represent the following in the floating-point language of Problem 4.55.

(*a*) 4   (*b*) 2   (*c*) 1   (*d*) 1/2   (*e*) 1/4

4.122. Proceed as in the preceding problem with the decimal fractions

(*a*) .05   (*b*) .93   (*c*) .88

dropping digits in the fraction after the seventh.

4.123. Carry out the addition .05 + .88 using the floating-point symbols found in the preceding problem. In what form does the sum appear? The fact that this disagrees in the last place with the symbol for .93 as found above is due to the truncation of the fractions. Errors of this sort are very common in computation and are to a large extent unavoidable.

4.124. Follow the same addition method for the sum .93 + .88. Because the two exponents agree there will be no initial shifting, but an overflow will occur. This requires that both exponents be raised and the fractions shifted right. In what form does the sum finally appear?

4.125. Multiply .05 by .88 using their floating-point symbols truncated to seven digits in the fraction. Give the product as a similar floating-point symbol.

4.126. If a magnetic drum has a circumference of 50 inches, a packing density of 90 bits to the inch, and 40 tracks, how many bits of information can be stored on its surface?

4.127. If a magnetic core memory is to store 4096 words of length 36 bits per word, how many cores will be used?

4.128. If the memory of the preceding problem is arranged as in Fig. 4-28, how many rows and columns will there be? Row and column addresses will no longer run from 000 to 111. What will be the new range? How many binary digits are thus needed to identify one storage location?

4.129. If a magnetic tape has 14 tracks, on each of which information can be packed 250 bits to the inch, and if the tape is moved at a speed of 75 inches per second, how many bits can be read per second?

4.130. The following information in the code of Fig. 4-29 contains an error. Which character is incorrect? The machine would not be able to correct the error, even though it could discover it. From the redundancy of ordinary language, however, you will be able to guess what was intended. By transmitting a small amount of redundant information in certain *error-correcting* codes it is possible to have a computer actually correct some errors. (See next problem.)

```
1 0 0 1 1 1 1
0 0 1 1 0 1 0
0 1 0 0 0 0 1
0 0 0 0 1 0 0
1 1 1 0 1 1 1
0 1 1 1 1 1 0
1 0 0 0 1 1 1
0 0 0 0 0 0 0
```

4.131. Occasionally in the transmission of data by magnetic tape several errors may occur in the same track, perhaps due to a speck of foreign matter in the reading device. One scheme which will detect and correct such errors, at least in certain cases, places a parity bit in each character as above and also adds an extra character periodically consisting entirely of parity bits and making the number of ones in each track odd. The information is thus sent in blocks having an odd number of ones in each row and in each column. For example, suppose that a block was intended to read as at the left below but was actually transmitted as seen at the right. Verify that the count of ones is even in one of the eight tracks, and further, that it is even in three of the characters. Then note that changing the three values in these characters and in the track in question will produce the correct block. A machine could easily be taught to make these corrections. Errors in more than one track would be a more severe challenge.

```
1 0 0 1 1 1 1 0        1 0 0 1 1 1 1 0
0 0 1 1 0 1 0 0        0 0 1 1 0 1 0 0
0 1 0 0 0 0 1 1        0 1 0 0 0 0 1 1
0 0 0 0 1 0 0 0        0 0 0 0 1 0 0 0
1 1 1 0 1 1 1 1        1 1 1 0 1 1 1 1
0 1 1 1 1 1 1 1        0 1 1 1 1 1 1 1
1 0 0 0 1 1 1 1        1 0 0 1 0 1 0 1
0 0 0 0 0 0 0 1        0 0 0 0 0 0 0 1
      Correct                 Errors
```

4.132. Verify that the circuit of Fig. 4-38 performs the same function as that of Fig. 4-4, that is, it accepts a three value input such as 000, 001, etc., and decides which of eight possible output channels to activate. This is the work of a decoder. Two of the output channels have been labeled with the input combination which activates them. Provide labels for the others.

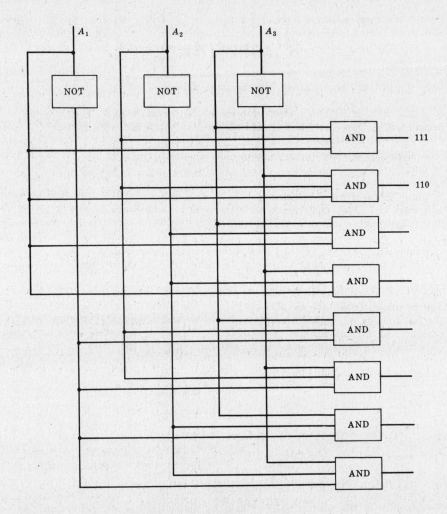

Fig. 4-38

4.133. Extend the design of Fig. 4-4 to accept a four value input and activate one of sixteen possible output channels.

4.134. Extend the design of Fig. 4-38 to make it into a four value decoder, as in the preceding problem. Which design seems simpler?

Chapter 5

Machine Language

Instructions must be provided to a general-purpose computer if it is to carry out an assignment of our choice. Certain other information, perhaps numbers or names, is presumably also needed. In this chapter all this information will be viewed from the machine's standpoint, that is, in terms of electrical hots and colds. For the moment then we ignore the fact that modern circuits will accept inputs in a variety of codes and, following instructions which have been placed permanently in their memories, translate such inputs into their own internal working languages. Instead we shall do the translations ourselves; so to speak, we shall talk *the machine language*. For this purpose imagine a miniature computer in which words are nine values long. This is much shorter than for real machines but it becomes much easier to follow developments. The memory unit is to be capable of storing 64 words of this sort, say in sequential manner since it is troublesome to simulate random access on the printed page. A slightly enlarged version of the drum in Fig. 4-27, page 78, would serve. As pointed out in that chapter certain other memory registers are useful, particularly in the arithmetic unit. One especially important register of this sort is called the accumulator, and several types of instruction will refer to it. Whenever a sequence, or machine word, is to be an instruction the first three values will indicate the type of instruction that it is, while the last six values give the number, or address, of a memory location which will be needed to execute the instruction.

$$\underbrace{\text{x x x}}_{\text{Type}}\underbrace{\text{x x x x x x}}_{\text{Address}}$$

With three values available to designate the type we see that eight types of instruction are possible, one for each of the usual eight combinations. It is now necessary to learn what each combination means in machine language, for the fictitious miniature machine in question. The following list gives the machine language at the left and a brief explanation at the right, the symbol x representing an unspecified 0 or 1. The language will become much clearer as we use it in examples to follow.

000xxxxxx   Stop. In this instruction the last six values are unimportant.

001xxxxxx   Copy the sequence now in memory location xxxxxx into the accumulator, first erasing the previous content of the accumulator. The sequence originally in xxxxxx should be in both locations after this instruction is executed.

010xxxxxx   Add the number in memory location xxxxxx to the number in the accumulator, leaving the content of xxxxxx unchanged. The sum is to be left in the accumulator. (This is to be number addition, not Boolean addition.)

011xxxxxx   Copy the sequence now in the accumulator into memory location xxxxxx, first erasing any previous content of xxxxxx. The sequence originally in the accumulator should be in both locations after this instruction is executed.

100xxxxxx	Punch the sequence now in memory location xxxxxx onto an output card. The sequence also remains in xxxxxx for further use.
101xxxxxx	Take the next instruction from memory location xxxxxx. This breaks the normal routine in which instructions are taken from consecutive locations and is called a jump or branch instruction.
110xxxxxx	Take the next instruction from memory location xxxxxx *if* the number now in the accumulator is negative. Otherwise follow the normal routine.
111xxxxxx	Subtract the sequence in memory location xxxxxx from the sequence in the accumulator, leaving the content of xxxxxx unchanged. The difference is to be left in the accumulator.

Example 5.1.

What is the result of executing the following three instructions in the order given?

$$0\ 0\ 1\ 0\ 1\ 0\ 0\ 0\ 0$$
$$0\ 1\ 0\ 0\ 1\ 0\ 0\ 1\ 1$$
$$0\ 1\ 1\ 0\ 1\ 0\ 0\ 0\ 0$$

To find out we must do just what the machine itself would have to do, analyze each instruction. Since the first three values indicate the type of instruction, we begin by referring back to our list above and decoding 001xxxxxx into "Copy the sequence now in memory location xxxxxx into the accumulator". In this case xxxxxx is 010000, which we may prefer to think of in decimal language as 16. This first instruction then requires the content of memory location 16 to be copied into the accumulator. This brings it to the center of arithmetical action so that presumably it is now to be involved in a computation. Decoding the second instruction brings "Add the number in memory location 010011 (or decimal 19) to the number in the accumulator, leaving the sum in the accumulator". Similarly the last instruction translates into "Copy the sequence now in the accumulator into memory location 010000 (or decimal 16)". Looking back we can now see that the number originally in location 16 has been altered, by adding to it the number in location 19. To achieve this the numbers were brought to the arithmetic unit, where the sum was computed, this sum then being stored in memory. This is a standard pattern of information flow within the machine. The registers in the arithmetic unit are versatile, fast and expensive. They are excellent information processors and data is brought to them for treatment. But these same registers are also very busy and results which are to be saved must be sent to quieter locations for storage.

Control circuitry must be provided so that the computer will be able to analyze instructions and execute them more or less as was suggested in the example just given. Assuming all instructions necessary for a particular assignment to be in the memory unit, control must

(1) select them in proper sequence and copy them into special registers for analysis,

(2) perform the analysis and activate the necessary channels for execution of the instruction.

A general plan for such a control circuit, omitting details, is presented in Fig. 5-1 below. The flip-flop divides the action into the two alternating parts mentioned above, sequencing and execution. At the start the *fetch* output is hot and allows the address of the first instruction, probably 000001, to enter the address decoder, which arranges for the sequence (instruction) in that memory address to be found and sent to the instruction register for analysis. When this step is finished a pulse is communicated to reset the flip-flop, activating the *execute* output. This opens other gates, allowing the type portion of the instruction to enter a decoder much like that in Fig. 4-4, page 52, while the address portion goes to the address decoder so that the needed location in memory may be found. Between these two decoders enough output channels must be triggered to execute the instruction, perhaps sending a word to the arithmetic unit and starting an addition, if the type was 010.

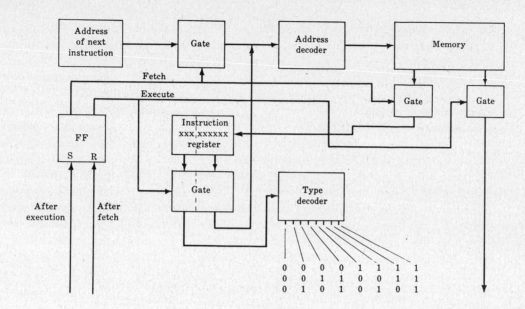

Fig. 5-1

Sometime during this execution step the "address of next instruction" must be increased by one, so that when the next fetch is activated the next instruction in sequence will be located, except when the present instruction happens to be of the jump type, in which case the instruction itself must place the proper address for the one to follow. This also will become clearer as examples are considered. After execution is completed the flip-flop is once again set and another cycle follows.

Example 5.2.

Suppose the three instructions of Example 5.1 are placed in memory locations 1, 2 and 3, or in binary notation, 000001, 000010, 000011. Let us follow developments in the control circuitry of Fig. 5-1 as these instructions are processed.

1. At the start 000001 must be in the address of next instruction register, and the flip-flop in set position.

2. The address 000001 passes through the gate and into the decoder, which finds that location in memory and arranges for the content, our first instruction 001010000, to enter the instruction register.

3. The flip-flop is reset. The first three values in the current instruction, which are 001, pass to the type decoder which activates its 001 output in preparation for a copy from memory. At the same time the last six values of the instruction pass to the address decoder. These values being 010000, the content of memory location 16 is found. Execution from this point on is controlled by circuitry which the 001 output triggers, and which in fact must effect the copy of whatever sequence is in location 16 into the accumulator. When this is done it must also produce an execution completed signal, and increase the address of next instruction by one.

4. The flip-flop is again set. The address 000010 passes into the address decoder which then arranges for the content of that memory location, our second instruction 010010011, to enter the instruction register.

5. The flip-flop is reset. The combination 010 is decoded, activating the 010 output in preparation for an addition. Etc.

A *program* includes all the instructions and data which must be provided to a general-purpose computer if it is to carry out a given assignment. The process of preparing such a program is called programming. When it is ready, a program is read into the memory unit of the machine. In this way it may be executed at the machine's own working speed, and not delayed by frequent human intervention.

This idea of *the stored program* is no doubt one of the real breakthroughs in the early stages of modern computer science. Some of its implications will emerge as we proceed. Table 5.1 is an example of a program. As will be true throughout this chapter, it is in the miniature machine language already used in Examples 5.1 and 5.2. All sequences are in the form of machine words, nine values long, and we must imagine them in machine memory as sequences of magnetic hots and colds, perhaps distributed around the surface of a magnetic drum. Some of these sequences are instructions and some are numbers. Neither man nor machine, except for the programmer himself, could distinguish one from the other at first glance, both having exactly the same form. Sometimes the computer will actually treat an instruction as a number, and just how important this proves to be will be demonstrated among the solved problems. It should be pointed out that only the sequences themselves are in the memory unit, the other information in Table 5.1 such as addresses (both binary and decimal) and certain other symbols being included merely to help us to analyze the program, to discover its purpose. There are 64 locations in this memory unit, with addresses running from 000000 to 111111, but only 50 of these are used in the given program.

	Address	Sequence	
1	0 0 0 0 0 1	0 0 1 0 1 0 0 0 0	
2	0 0 0 0 1 0	0 1 0 0 1 0 0 1 1	
3	0 0 0 0 1 1	0 1 1 0 1 0 0 0 0	
4	0 0 0 1 0 0	0 0 1 0 1 0 0 0 1	
5	0 0 0 1 0 1	0 1 0 0 1 0 0 1 0	
6	0 0 0 1 1 0	0 1 1 0 1 0 0 0 1	
7	0 0 0 1 1 1	1 1 1 0 0 1 1 1 1	
8	0 0 1 0 0 0	1 1 0 0 0 1 0 1 1	
9	0 0 1 0 0 1	1 0 0 0 1 0 0 0 0	
10	0 0 1 0 1 0	0 0 0 0 0 0 0 0 0	
11	0 0 1 0 1 1	0 0 1 0 0 0 0 1 0	
12	0 0 1 1 0 0	0 1 0 0 1 0 0 1 0	
13	0 0 1 1 0 1	0 1 1 0 0 0 0 1 0	
14	0 0 1 1 1 0	1 0 1 0 0 0 0 0 1	
15	0 0 1 1 1 1	0 0 0 1 0 0 0 0 0	
16	0 1 0 0 0 0	0 0 0 0 0 0 0 0 0	
17	0 1 0 0 0 1	0 0 0 0 0 0 0 0 0	
18	0 1 0 0 1 0	0 0 0 0 0 0 0 0 1	
19	0 1 0 0 1 1	0 1 1 0 0 1 1 1 1	X_1
20	0 1 0 1 0 0	1 1 1 1 0 1 0 0 1	X_2
21	0 1 0 1 0 1	0 1 1 0 0 0 0 1 1	X_3
22	0 1 0 1 1 0	1 0 1 0 0 1 1 1 0	X_4

(Locations 23 to 50 contain other sequences that will be called simply X_5, X_6, up to X_{32}.)

Table 5.1

Example 5.3.

The sequence 010010011 in location 2 (Table 5.1) will prove to be an important instruction, the first three values 010 indicating that it activates an addition. It will also be useful to think of this sequence as a number, the first value being a sign value and the rest binary digits. As a number, therefore, the sequence is equivalent to the decimal $+(128+16+2+1)$ or $+147$. At one point in the program the computer will add one to this number, using circuitry of the sort shown in Fig. 4-15, page 67, stretched to accommodate nine values instead of five. The computation runs as follows.

$$
\begin{array}{c}
0\ 1\ 0\ 0\ 1\ 0\ 0\ 1\ 1 \\
0\ 0\ 0\ 0\ 0\ 0\ 0\ 0\ 1 \\
\hline
0\ 1\ 0\ 0\ 1\ 0\ 1\ 0\ 0
\end{array}
$$

In decimal symbols the sum is clearly 148. This new sequence will then replace the old content of location 2. Note that it is of the same type, beginning 010, as the instruction it replaces. The address part has, however, changed from 010011 to 010100, or in decimal language from 19 to 20. The significance of this change will soon become clear.

Example 5.4.

The sequence 101001110 in location 22 (Table 5.1) is intended to be a number. With a leading value of one representing a minus sign, this number would be equivalent to the decimal $-(64 + 8 + 4 + 2)$ or -78. The same sequence does, however, also have meaning as an instruction. The first three values being 101 we find, by referring back to the list of instruction types, that the computer would be asked to break its normal routine for sequencing instructions. Instead of taking its next instruction from the next location, which would have address 23, it must "jump" to the specified location 001110, the equivalent of decimal 14. How far from the intentions of the present program this proves to be, and yet how easily such unwanted developments can be provoked, will be illustrated among the solved problems.

Solved Problems

5.1. Suppose, as suggested in Example 5.2, that the first instruction to be executed is in location 1 (Table 5.1). (We do of course have a memory location with address zero, but since not all the locations will be needed it seems convenient to begin at the traditional number one.) What is achieved by the first three instructions together?

This is basically the issue explored in Example 5.1 but more detail can now be added. These three instructions may be translated, strictly for our own convenience, from machine language to English.

1. Copy the sequence in memory location 16 into the accumulator.
2. Add the number in memory location 19 to the number in the accumulator.
3. Copy the sequence in the accumulator into memory location 16.

As these are executed the following events occur.

1. The sequence 000000000 enters the accumulator, having been copied from location 16.
2. The sum 011001111 appears in the accumulator, being the sum of 000000000 and 011001111.
3. The sequence 011001111 appears in memory location 16, having been copied from the accumulator.

The overall result is that the numbers in locations 16 and 19 have been added together and the sum stored in location 19.

5.2. What is achieved by instructions 4 to 6?

The pattern is the same as for the first three instructions, the addresses being different. These events occur.

4. The sequence 000000000 enters the accumulator, having been copied from location 17.

5. The content of location 18 is added to this, so that the sum 000000001 appears in the accumulator.

6. The sequence 000000001 appears in memory location 17, having been copied from the accumulator.

This may be summarized by saying that the computer has just counted from zero to one and stored the count in location 17.

5.3.   Analyze instructions 7 and 8.

First we must remember that the sequence 000000001 is in the accumulator register, the copy operation just completed not being destructive. Instruction 7 is of type 111 and translates to "Subtract the number in memory location 15 from the one now in the accumulator". It may be easier for us to do this in decimal. The number in the accumulator is +1 while that in location 15 is easily seen to be +32. The difference is thus −31, or in machine language 100011111. This sequence enters the accumulator.

Instruction 8 is of type 110 and translates to, "Take the next instruction from memory location 001011, or decimal 11, *if* the number now in the accumulator is negative. Otherwise proceed as usual". We find −31 in the accumulator and so, following the computer, skip over instructions 9 and 10 to pick up number 11.

5.4.   What is achieved by instructions 11 to 13?

The pattern of instructions 1 to 3 is again repeated, the addresses once again changing. The following events occur.

11. The sequence 010010011 enters the accumulator, having been copied from location 2.

12. The content of location 18 is added to this, so that the sum 010010100 appears in the accumulator. Note that this is precisely the computation made in Example 5.3, and that the content of location 2 is now being treated as a number even though just a few moments earlier it was treated as an instruction. To the computer it is all a question of electrical energy following prescribed paths.

13. The sequence 010010100 appears in memory location 2, having been copied from the accumulator.

The overall result is that instruction 2 has been modified. Though it formerly read "Add the number in memory location 19...", it now reads "Add the number in memory location 20...". And this modification has been made by the computer without outside aid, just following the stored program. The new instruction will be used in a moment.

5.5.   Analyze instruction 14.

This is of type 101 and translates to "Take the next instruction from memory location number 1". This is an unconditional jump, breaking the normal sequencing routine. On instruction 8 the computer also broke routine, but was required first to test the number in the accumulator, at least to see whether the sign value of that number was positive or negative. In a sense the machine was asked to decide whether to break routine or not. Here no decision is involved. The jump is mandatory.

5.6.   What is achieved as instructions 1 to 3 are executed for the second time?

The now familiar pattern is repeated with these consequences.

1. The sequence 011001111 appears in the accumulator, having been copied from location 16 where it was placed during the last execution of instruction 3. This number has also been called X_1.

2. The content of location 20 is added to this, so that the sum $X_1 + X_2$ is computed. This proves to be 100011010 and this sequence enters the accumulator. (It may be more convenient for a human observer to verify this sum in decimal. Since $X_1 = 207$ while $X_2 = -233$, the sum is −26 which translates into machine language as just shown.)

3. The sequence 100011010 appears in memory location 16, having been copied from the accumulator. Notice in particular that the content of this memory location, originally zero and changed to X_1 on the first execution of instruction 3, has now been changed to $X_1 + X_2$. This is the first strong hint at the overall purpose of the program.

5.7.   What is achieved as instructions 4 to 6 are executed for the second time?

Again we have the familiar pattern, and these results.

4. The sequence 000000001 enters the accumulator, having been copied from location 17 where it was placed during the last execution of instruction 6.

5. The content of location 18 is added to this and, $1+1$ being 2, the sequence 000000010 appears in the accumulator.

6. The sequence 000000010 enters memory location 17, having been copied from the accumulator. Notice that the content of this location, originally zero and raised to one on the first execution of instruction 6, has now been raised to two. In this location the computer is counting the X numbers which have been added together.

5.8.   Analyze instructions 7 and 8 for the second time.

As on the first time around, instruction 7 calls for a subtraction. From what is now in the accumulator we must subtract the content of location 15. In decimal language this would be $2-32$ or -30. The computer finds this same difference in its own language and enters 100011110 in the accumulator. Since this is negative, it then decides, following instruction 8, to jump to location 11 for the next instruction.

5.9.   What is achieved as instructions 11 to 13 are executed for the second time?

The content of memory location 2 is again changed, in these three steps.

11. The sequence 010010100 is copied from location 2 into the accumulator.

12. The content of location 18, which is the number 1, is added in and leaves 010010101 in the accumulator.

13. This sum is copied into location 2 where it becomes our new instruction number 2. It translates into "Add the number in memory location 21...".

5.10.   Describe more briefly what occurs on the third cycle through this set of instructions.

The third cycle is triggered as instruction 14 again forces an unconditional jump back to instruction 1. At this point the machine language may begin to look almost readable. The copy-add-copy pattern now changes the sum in location 16 to $X_1+X_2+X_3$ after which it changes the count in location 17 to 3, or to its equivalent in machine language. The subtraction $3-32$ then leaves a negative number in the accumulator, so the computer again decides to skip instructions 9 and 10. The copy-add-copy pattern then modifies instruction 2 once more, leaving it in the form 010010110 which translates into "Add the number in memory location 22...". Instruction 14 then returns the action to the top of the program for still another cycle.

5.11.   What is a *loop*?

A loop is a set of instructions through which a computation cycles repeatedly. In the present program the only loop consists of instructions 1 to 8 and 11 to 14, the last of which closes the loop by returning the action to instruction 1. Most serious programs contain many loops, frequently loops within loops, and this is to be expected because each loop performs a relatively simple routine which is not hard to explain to an electrical machine. The machine can then execute this routine over and over again at electrical speed. This is one of a computer's main skills, the ability to loop through such routines rapidly, accurately and almost endlessly, apparently without boredom.

5.12.   How many times will the loop in the present program be executed and how will the computation finally break out of it?

On the 32nd cycle through the loop the sum in location 16 will become

$$\text{Sum} = X_1 + X_2 + X_3 + \cdots + X_{32}$$

and the count in location 17 will then be raised to 32. The subtraction required by instruction 7 will then yield $32 - 32$ which is clearly zero. At this point in the program the question is whether this difference is negative or not. Unfortunately, as we have seen, a machine language zero may be either positive or negative. To keep things simple it will be assumed here that $32 - 32$ will be $+0$ in our machine, so that the content of the accumulator after this last subtraction is the sequence 000000000. For the first time the computer then executes instruction 8 with a positive number in the accumulator. This causes it to refuse the jump and instead to continue normal sequencing. Instruction 8 is thus followed by the first execution of instruction 9 and the loop is broken after 32 cycles.

5.13. **What will be the output information of the program of Table 5.1?**

Once the loop is broken instruction 9 calls for the punching of the sequence in location 16 onto an output card. This sequence represents the sum of the thirty-two numbers X_1 to X_{32}. Instruction 10, being of type 000, then stops the computation. The purpose of this program was therefore the addition of these thirty-two numbers. It is perfectly true that this purpose could easily be achieved by hand, without appealing to electrical circuits, but the point is that with only minor changes the same program would arrange for the summation of a million numbers. A larger machine with more memory locations and longer sequences would be convenient but the basic ideas of the program would be unchanged. Once the machine language becomes slightly familiar the precise logic of such a program takes on an almost aesthetic appeal.

5.14. **Summarize the information processing called for by the program of Table 5.1 in the form of a** *flow-chart.*

Fig. 5-2 is an example of a flow-chart. It displays in separate boxes the essential steps of the program and shows by means of arrows the directions of information flow. The loop is clearly visible at the center of the flow-chart. Entering at the upper left the computation makes thirty-two cycles around this loop. Every time except the last the question "Is the count less than 32?" is answered "yes" and the looping continues. Finally the answer becomes "no" and the loop is broken. The intended sum is output and the computer stops.

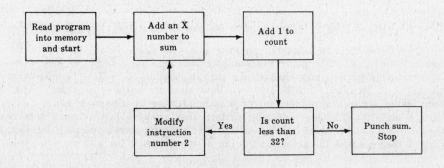

Fig. 5-2

5.15. **What is meant by** *debugging*?

The program presented in Table 5.1 is free from errors. It achieves what it was intended to achieve. It is not hard to see, however, that the tiniest program error, a single 0 where there ought to be a 1 or vice versa, can produce results which are remarkably far from what was intended. As an easy example consider what would happen if the sequence for location 1 were mispunched and entered the computer as 000010000, the only error being in the third digit. One sees almost at once that this makes the very first instruction to be executed a stop instruction. The computation will not even begin. When the start button is pushed it may appear that the computer has not been "plugged in". But experience has shown that when a program fails to run properly it is usually the program and not the machine which is to blame. In the example just given we considered the effect of a known error in a known location. More realistically, and discouragingly often, a programmer has to search for errors in unknown locations, their existence being suggested by the simple fact that when offered to the computer his program did not run as planned. The process of correcting faulty programs is called debugging.

5.16. Suppose it is known that the intended program of Table 5.1 should take only a minute or less of machine time. After punching the program onto cards, reading it into machine memory and starting the computation, however, it is found that computation continues after three minutes. The operator stops the action manually. A program error is suspected. (Most frequently errors are made by the programmer himself in the preparation of his instructions or data, but since in the present example we have already discovered that the program as given in Table 5.1 does achieve its intended goal let us say that an error has been made during punching or during the read-in.) Illustrate debugging procedures for locating this error.

Errors in programs are very common, in part because even the smallest detail must be explained to the machine and certain details are easy to overlook, and in part because of the gulf between human and machine languages which makes error-producing steps such as card punching necessary. As a result most machines have been designed to provide a measure of cooperation in the search for errors. As a simple illustration, the content of some or all memory locations is usually readily accessible to the programmer upon request. It may be displayed in lights on the control panel of the computer or typed out or provided in a variety of other ways, but this information can be very helpful. The present program is so brief that in the event of trouble we could ask for the entire memory to be punched out for our inspection. In a more serious problem such a "memory dump" might be too voluminous to be comfortable and more selective detective work is called for. For example, it is usually helpful to know what the machine was doing when it was stopped, so we can ask for the content of the "address of next instruction" register. Suppose the answer is

$$0\ 1\ 0\ 1\ 1\ 0$$

or in decimal language, location 22. This is surely a discouraging reply. The sequence in location 22 was supposed to be the *number* X_4. To the machine, however, it also makes a perfectly reasonable instruction, assuming it entered as intended. To check this we ask for the content of location 22 to be output, and receive

$$1\ 0\ 1\ 0\ 0\ 1\ 1\ 1\ 0$$

as expected. As an instruction this translates to "Take the next instruction from location 14" just as surely as numerically it means -78. Following the indicated path we next ask for the content of location 14 and are told

$$1\ 0\ 1\ 0\ 0\ 0\ 0\ 0\ 1$$

which is what it should be. Since this sends the action to location 1, let us again follow. The content of location 1 proves to be

$$0\ 0\ 1\ 0\ 1\ 0\ 0\ 0\ 0$$

again as expected. Inquiring about the next instruction, however, we discover the content of location 2 to be

$$1\ 0\ 1\ 0\ 1\ 0\ 1\ 1\ 0$$

which is at least slightly surprising. Only four of the nine values here are what they should be. Instead of the expected addition the machine is being asked to "Take the next instruction from location 22". Now it becomes clear why the computation failed to stop when intended. The computer has been patiently following instructions, jumping from location 22 to 14 to 1 to 2 to 22 over and over again. It is in an unwanted loop from which there is no exit except by outside intervention. Such futile loops have been compared with human insanity. The machine is unable to help itself and requires shock treatment, which was provided when the operator stepped in.

At this point we know what happened to our program but we still do not know how it came about. Either the second instruction was wrong when it entered the computer, or else it was spoiled afterwards. Considering the extent of the damage, suppose we try the second possibility first. It is the instructions in locations 11, 12 and 13 which do the alterations, so we ask to see the content of these registers. The output is

$$0\ 0\ 1\ 0\ 0\ 0\ 0\ 1\ 0$$

$$0\ 1\ 0\ 0\ 1\ 0\ 1\ 0\ 0$$

$$0\ 1\ 1\ 0\ 0\ 0\ 0\ 1\ 0$$

and an error has been found. The middle sequence has a displaced 1. It should read 010010010 instead. This displacement leads to a catastrophe. Instead of altering instruction 2 by adding to it the sequence in location 18, the alteration is made using the sequence in location 20. The computation runs as follows

$$
\begin{array}{ll}
0\ 1\ 0\ 0\ 1\ 0\ 0\ 1\ 1 & +147 \\
\underline{1\ 1\ 1\ 1\ 0\ 1\ 0\ 0\ 1} & -233 \\
1\ 0\ 1\ 0\ 1\ 0\ 1\ 1\ 0 & -86
\end{array}
$$

the decimal equivalent at the right being provided for those who prefer it. The sequence 101010110 thus enters location 2 to become the jump instruction discovered a few moments ago. The misplaced 1 in location 12 fully explains what happened to the program, as may be verified by following the computation from the start to where it enters the unwanted loop. The consequences of this minor error may seem bizarre, but equally strange things happen abundantly and daily in the thought processes of electrical circuits.

5.17. Still assuming that the program of Table 5.1 should take about a minute to run, suppose that after two or three seconds a single sequence is punched out and the machine stops. Conduct debugging procedures to see if there is an error.

Because of the brevity of the computation it seems reasonable to check the final count, the content of location 17. Let us say that this proves to be

$$0\ 1\ 1\ 0\ 0\ 1\ 1\ 1$$

which is surely incorrect, being the equivalent of decimal 207. This suggests checking the counting instructions 4 to 6. The content of these locations is requested and the machine outputs

$$0\ 0\ 1\ 0\ 1\ 0\ 0\ 0\ 1$$

$$0\ 1\ 0\ 0\ 1\ 0\ 0\ 0\ 0$$

$$0\ 1\ 1\ 0\ 1\ 0\ 0\ 0\ 1$$

so that an error does exist in location 5. This sequence should be 010010010. Instead of increasing the count by one (the content of location 18) the machine has been told to increase it by X_1 (the content of location 16 after the first addition). Since this instantly raises the count to $+207$, subtracting 32 leaves a positive number in the accumulator. The very first jump is then refused, the loop broken before it is really formed, the answer X_1 punched out and the machine stops.

5.18. Modify the program of Table 5.1 so that it punches out the final count as well as the final sum. Take this count from location 17, where it is actually computed, not from location 15 which contains the intended final count. In this way a simple check is made available, and a useful one because very often when a program has not run correctly a count of this sort will not attain its intended value.

Patching programs proves to be more delicate work than might at first be supposed. The new instruction to be inserted is easily seen to be

$$1\ 0\ 0\ 0\ 1\ 0\ 0\ 0\ 1$$

the machine language being at this point almost readable. Moreover, the natural place to put this new instruction is beside the present output instruction, number 9. This does require, however, that certain existing sequences be moved to other locations, and since addresses are important we must do this with care. Suppose it is decided to move the top eight instructions upward, using the previously idle location 0 for the first instruction. The new instruction may then be slipped into memory location 8. Table 5.2 shows the new arrangement. No further changes are needed in this part of the program because the addresses referred to in these instructions (11, 15, 16, 17, 18, 19) contain sequences which are not being moved. Even when the second instruction (now in location 1) is altered, it will address **X** numbers which have not been moved. However, the instructions in locations 11 and 13 must now be changed slightly, if they are to continue to perform the intended **alterations**. Their address parts must now read as follows

| 11 | 0 0 1 0 1 1 | 0 0 1 0 0 0 0 0 1 |
| 13 | 0 0 1 1 0 1 | 0 1 1 0 0 0 0 0 1 |

	Address	Sequence
0	0 0 0 0 0 0	0 0 1 0 1 0 0 0 0
1	0 0 0 0 0 1	0 1 0 0 1 0 0 1 1
2	0 0 0 0 1 0	0 1 1 0 1 0 0 0 0
3	0 0 0 0 1 1	0 0 1 0 1 0 0 0 1
4	0 0 0 1 0 0	0 1 0 0 1 0 0 1 0
5	0 0 0 1 0 1	0 1 1 0 1 0 0 0 1
6	0 0 0 1 1 0	1 1 1 0 0 1 1 1 1
7	0 0 0 1 1 1	1 1 0 0 0 1 0 1 1
8	0 0 1 0 0 0	1 0 0 0 1 0 0 0 1

Table 5.2

since their target is now in location 1. A similar change is needed in instruction 14 so that the next cycle through the loop may begin with the first instruction, now in location 0.

14	0 0 1 1 1 0	1 0 1 0 0 0 0 0 0

If the computation is started in location 0 it may now be verified that the intended result is achieved, the final count being punched out followed by the final sum.

5.19. Show how the patch applied to our basic program in the preceding problem can be done without moving instructions, using formerly idle parts of the memory unit.

Ignoring the preceding problem we return to the program as originally given in Table 5.1. Let it remain as it is to the very end, but replace the stop instruction, number 10, by

10	0 0 1 0 1 0	1 0 1 1 1 0 0 1 1

which translates to "Take the next instruction from location 51". This location is beyond all the X numbers, out in unused memory. Two further instructions now complete the patch.

51	1 1 0 0 1 1	1 0 0 0 1 0 0 0 1
52	1 1 0 1 0 0	0 0 0 0 0 0 0 0 0

The first manages the punching out of the count and the second stops the computation.

5.20. Modify the program of Table 5.1 so that both the sum and the count will be punched out at each step.

This time the patch must be applied within the loop. One possible solution is as follows. First we replace instructions 7 to 10 by these substitutes.

7	0 0 0 1 1 1	1 0 0 0 1 0 0 0 0
8	0 0 1 0 0 0	1 0 0 0 1 0 0 0 1
9	0 0 1 0 0 1	1 1 1 0 0 1 1 1 1
10	0 0 1 0 1 0	1 0 1 1 1 0 0 1 1

The first two of these arrange for the punching of the current sum and count immediately after their computation. The third is our subtraction instruction once again. Unfortunately, though only two more instructions are needed we have only location 10 left, unless still more sequences are to be moved. Rather than disturb location 11 and those following it, we place the instruction shown in location 10, and the action jumps to location 51 instead. The program then finishes with

51	1 1 0 0 1 1	1 1 0 0 0 1 0 1 1
52	1 1 0 1 0 0	0 0 0 0 0 0 0 0 0

If the job is not finished this returns the action to instruction 11; if it is finished the computation stops.

5.21. Make a flow-chart for the computation of the preceding problem.

Fig. 5-3 shows the required chart. Comparing with Fig. 5-2, one sees that the only change puts the instructions for punching out information within the loop, so that this will be done on each cycle with the current sum and count.

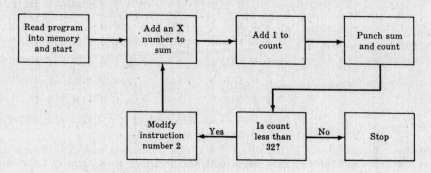

Fig. 5-3

Supplementary Problems

5.22. As the program of Table 5.1 is executed the content of the accumulator as well as of registers 2, 16 and 17 will change. List the content of the accumulator after each instruction is executed and the content of the others whenever there is a change, continuing this for at least two complete cycles through the loop. The list will begin as follows, X_1 being used instead of the actual number since it is perhaps more informative so far as understanding the program is concerned.

Instruction	Accumulator	2	16	17
Start	000000000	010010011	000000000	000000000
1	000000000			
2	X_1			
3	X_1		X_1	
4	000000000			
5	000000001			
6	000000001			000000001
7	100011111			
8	100011111			

5.23. Suppose the first three values in instruction 7 entered the memory unit as 110 instead of 111, the program being otherwise correctly transferred. The first six instructions would still be executed as intended, but what would then happen?

5.24. Suppose the first three values in instruction 7 entered the memory unit as 101 instead of 111, the program being otherwise correctly transferred. What would happen?

5.25. Suppose the first three values in instruction 7 entered as 011 instead of 111, calling for a copy instead of a subtraction. What would be copied and into which location? What would then occur?

5.26. What would be the effect of errors of any sort among the last six values in instruction 10?

5.27. Suppose the sequence for location 15 entered the memory unit as 000010000, making it the equivalent of decimal 16 rather than 32. What would occur? If the time taken by the computer to complete the computation seemed to be short, how might the debugging of the program be started?

5.28. Suppose the sequence for location 15 entered the memory unit as 000100001, making it the equivalent of decimal 33 rather than 32. The unwanted content of location 51 would then be added into the sum. If this happened to be zero a correct output would still be given, otherwise an incorrect one. That is, sometimes this program would "work" and sometimes it would not. Suggest a safeguard, in the way of additional output, which would reveal the error in both this problem and the preceding.

5.29. If the first three values in instruction 10 entered the memory unit as 100 instead of 000, what would occur?

5.30. What would be the consequences if the first three values in instruction 3 entered the memory unit as 111 rather than 011? What sequence would be output?

5.31. If the first three values in instruction 3 were incorrectly entered as 010 instead of 011, changing this from a copy to an addition, what output would be given?

5.32. Suppose the program of Table 5.1 continues computations for two minutes, the expected running time being only one minute. The machine is stopped by the operator and an output of the count is requested. This turns out to be 001000011, or decimal 67, which is consistent with the elapsed time because a count of 32 was anticipated after the first minute. To discover why the machine will not stop by itself the sequence in location 8, the decision instruction, is called for and proves to be 101001011. The second and third digits have been transposed from what was intended. Show that this would explain what happened. If not stopped manually, what further indication would the computer eventually give to show that the computation is in difficulty? Would it ever stop?

5.33. What would happen if the sequence for location 6 entered the computer as 011010000? Plan a debugging procedure for locating this error. (Such a procedure is also known as *a post-mortem*.)

5.34. Modify the program of Table 5.1 to sum 45 numbers, X_1 to X_{45}, which have been stored in memory locations 19 to 63. Except for properly storing those 45 numbers, only one sequence in the entire program would have to be changed. Which one, and what is the alteration?

5.35. Again supposing the program in its basic form of Table 5.1, let instruction 10 be replaced by 101110011 so that after completing its previous assignment the machine turns to location 51 for further instruction. Insert in this and successive locations a program for punching out all the numbers X_1 to X_{32}, beginning with

$$51 \qquad 1\ 1\ 0\ 0\ 1\ 1 \qquad\qquad 1\ 0\ 0\ 0\ 1\ 0\ 0\ 1\ 1$$

which provides for the output of X_1. Use a loop.

5.36. Prepare a flow-chart of the computation in the preceding problem.

5.37. Modify the basic program of Table 5.1 so that at each step the current X number and the current sum are both punched out. This can be done in several ways, one of which involves filling in appropriate sequences below.

7	0 0 0 1 1 1	1 0 0 0 1 0 0 1 1	Punch current X.
8	0 0 1 0 0 0		Punch current sum.
9	0 0 1 0 0 1		Subtract 32.
10	0 0 1 0 1 0		Jump to location 51.
51	1 1 0 0 1 1		Jump (if not done) to location 53.
52	1 1 0 1 0 0		Stop.
53	1 1 0 1 0 1		
54	1 1 0 1 1 0		Modify instruction 7.
55	1 1 0 1 1 1		
56	1 1 1 0 0 0		Jump to location 11.

5.38. Prepare a flow-chart of the computation in the preceding problem.

5.39. The program of Table 5.1 is to be modified so that the current sum and count are output after each group of eight. Verify that the flow-chart of Fig. 5-4 correctly represents these intentions. Note first that the start is unchanged up through the count in box 3. A substantial patch is then needed to count up to eight, determine if it is time for an output, produce that output and reset for the next group. This patch consists of boxes 4, 5, 7 and 8. Notice too that there is a loop within a loop. Seven times the *yes* exit will be taken at box 5, leading to a cycle of the small loop. The eighth time an output is in order so the *no* exit is used, leading to a cycle of the larger loop. This pattern is followed four times in all, after which the large loop is also broken and the computation stops.

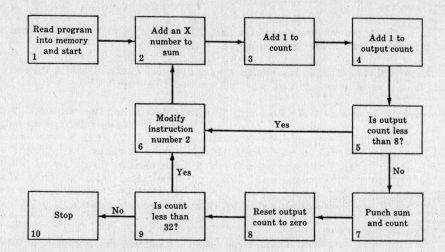

Fig. 5-4

5.40. The instructions needed to carry out the plan of Fig. 5-4 can be placed in the memory unit in various ways. The layout which follows leaves the program of Table 5.1 unchanged except for locations 7 to 10, where the patch begins with the equivalent of box 4 of Fig. 5-4. A jump instruction then sends the action to location 51 and the patch is completed in the formerly idle locations. Supply the details which have been omitted, completing all instructions.

7	0 0 0 1 1 1	0 0 1 1 1 1 1 0 0	⎫
8	0 0 1 0 0 0		⎬ Increase output count.
9	0 0 1 0 0 1		⎭
10	0 0 1 0 1 0		Jump to location 51.
51	1 1 0 0 1 1	1 1 1 1 1 1 1 0 1	Subtract 8.
52	1 1 0 1 0 0		Jump (if) to location 11.
53	1 1 0 1 0 1		Punch current sum.
54	1 1 0 1 1 0		Punch current count.
55	1 1 0 1 1 1	0 1 1	Reset output count to 0.
56	1 1 1 0 0 0	0 0 1	Pick up count.
57	1 1 1 0 0 1		Subtract 32.
58	1 1 1 0 1 0		Jump (if) to location 11.
59	1 1 1 0 1 1		Stop.
60	1 1 1 1 0 0	0 0 0 0 0 0 0 0 0	Output count.
61	1 1 1 1 0 1	0 0 0 0 0 1 0 0 0	8.

5.41.   The flow-chart of Fig. 5-5 represents what is called *a table look-up*. Numbers A_1 to A_{20} have
mates B_1 to B_{20}. One of the A numbers is specified, call it X for the moment. The problem is to
locate this number among the A's, read its mate among the B's and punch out the pair. Convince
yourself that the chart does correspond to the various steps involved. Details will be added in
the next problem, where the actual instructions will be requested. The numbers to be output have
been called X and Y.

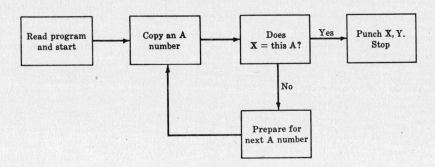

Fig. 5-5

5.42.   Supply the missing details in the following program for a table look-up. **Assume the A numbers**
stored in memory locations 21 to 40 and the B mates in locations 41 to 60. The given number X
has been placed in location 0. A few comments may be helpful. The program begins by copying
the current A number into another location than its assigned storage space. This may seem
unnecessary but it does simplify the program slightly by reducing the number of instructions
which must be modified. Instructions 3 to 8 are all concerned with determining whether or not
the given X equals the current A. If more types of instruction were available, and they would
be in a real computer, this might be done in one step. Here we compute both $X - A$ and $A - X$;
if neither of these is negative the two numbers must be the same.

Location	Sequence	Comment
0	X	The given number.
1	0 0 1 0 1 0 1 0 1	Copy an A number.
2		Store it in location 63.
3		Copy X into accumulator.
4		Subtract current A.
5		If negative jump to location 12.
6		Copy same A into accumulator.
7		Subtract X.
8		If negative jump to location 12.
9		Punch current A = X.
10		Punch B mate = Y.
11		Stop.
12		Copy instruction 1.
13		Add 1.
14		Store new instruction in 1.
15		Copy instruction 10.
16		Add 1.
17		Store new instruction in 10.
18		Jump to location 1.
19		One.

5.43.   The flow-chart of Fig. 5-6 represents *vector addition*, a routine which appears in a variety of applications. Numbers X_1 to X_{10} have mates Y_1 to Y_{10}. Each X number is to be added to its own Y mate and the results stored for future use. There is no immediate output, the present computation being just a part of a larger job. Convince yourself that the chart does suggest the essential steps. Details are to be added in the next problem.

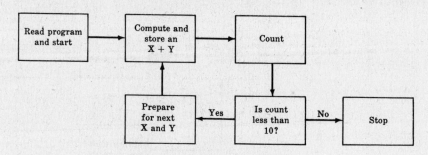

Fig. 5-6

5.44.   Supply the missing details in the following program for vector addition. Assume the X numbers stored in memory locations 31 to 40 and their Y mates in locations 41 to 50. The components of the sum are to be stored in locations 51 to 60.

Location	Sequence	Comment
1	0 0 1 0 1 1 1 1 1	Copy an X number.
2		Add its Y mate.
3		Store X + Y.
4	0 0 1 0 1 0 1 0 0	Copy present count.
5		Add 1.
6		Store new count.
7		Subtract ten.
8		Jump (if) to location 10.
9		Stop.
10		Copy instruction 1.
11		Add 1.
12		Store new instruction in 1.
13		
14		Modify instruction 2.
15		
16		
17		Modify instruction 3.
18		
19		Jump to location 1.
20	0 0 0 0 0 0 0 0 0	Count.
21	0 0 0 0 0 0 0 0 1	One.
22	0 0 0 0 0 1 0 1 0	Ten.

5.45.   The flow-chart of Fig. 5-7 represents the process of finding the largest number in a set consisting of X_1 to X_{32}, this number then being the single output. At the start it is assumed, at least temporarily, that X_1 is the largest. Calling it MAX, we compare it with X_2. If X_2 proves to be greater, it then replaces X_1 in the role of MAX; if not, X_1 continues. MAX is then compared with X_3 and the process continues. Convince yourself that the chart does describe a means of discovering the largest X number, leaving it in the role of MAX at the finish.

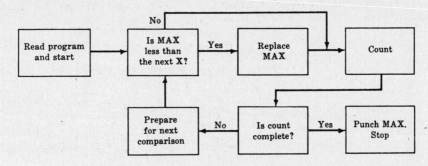

Fig. 5-7

5.46. Supply the missing details in the following program for finding the largest number, implementing the flow-chart of the preceding problem. Notice that since X_1 is started in the role of MAX, only 31 comparisons are needed. The final value of count thus appears as 31 rather than 32. Assume that the numbers X_1 to X_{32} have been stored in memory locations 32 to 63.

Location	Sequence	Comment
1	0 0 1 0 1 0 1 1 0	Copy MAX into accumulator.
2	1 1 1 1 0 0 0 0 0	Subtract next X number.
3		Jump (if) to location 11.
4		
5		Count.
6		
7		Subtract 31.
8		Jump (if) to location 14.
9		Punch out MAX.
10		Stop.
11	0 0 1 1 0 0 0 0 0	Copy current X into accumulator.
12		Store current X as MAX.
13		Jump to location 4.
14		
15		Modify instruction 2.
16		
17		
18		Modify instruction 11.
19		
20		Begin next cycle of loop.
21	0 0 0 0 0 0 0 0 0	Count.
22	X_1	MAX.
23	0 0 0 0 0 0 0 0 1	One.
24	0 0 0 0 1 1 1 1 1	31.

Chapter 6

Programming Languages

The disadvantages of machine languages soon become apparent as one attempts to prepare programs of even moderate complexity. The examples of the preceding chapter are relatively simple but even so they manage to illustrate the principal sources of inconvenience.

1. The biggest disadvantage is the extreme detail which must be included in a machine language program. Arithmetic processes which we are used to thinking of as simple, easily-understood routines must be broken down into a frustrating sequence of primitive steps such as copy, shift, store, etc. Returning to the main example of Chapter 5 for a moment, it was not enough to give the fairly clear single instruction "Add up the following 32 numbers". Instead fourteen instructions were required, some of which must have seemed minuscule at first sight. Even the bookkeeping operation of counting the additions already performed and checking to see if the job was done had to be spelled out in detail, requiring five instructions.

2. The need for keeping track of the specific memory location of every number and instruction in the program creates further difficulties. Every instruction written must include the address of the memory location involved. This means that from the very start the programmer must have addresses in mind. Either he must make tentative assignments (such as X_1 to X_{32} in locations 19 to 50) to be changed if they prove inconvenient, or else he may devise a set of labels for the quantities to be used and write his program in terms of these labels, afterwards translating each label into a specific address. In this spirit, for instance, SUM and COUNT could have been used to represent the *locations* in which certain results of our addition program were stored, these labels eventually giving way to 16 and 17. Both procedures just suggested require close attention to the fine details so that errors may be avoided. Once a machine language program is completed, all information having been assigned its specific memory location, the process of correcting it or modifying it can amount to a substantial undertaking. Thus if an instruction has been omitted, to insert it in its natural place would require the displacement of all subsequent information, initiating a chain of address changes throughout the entire program. The alternative of inserting a jump instruction, transferring the action to a previously unused part of the memory unit where a corrective patch can be applied, seems preferable and was used a number of times in the preceding chapter. Too many such patches, however, can also bring confusion, as more than one hopeful programmer has discovered to his chagrin.

3. A somewhat smaller inconvenience of machine languages is the need to refer to each type of operation or instruction numerically. Thus in the miniature code of Chapter 5, 001 meant "copy from memory" while 010 meant "add" and 111 was "subtract". In a larger repertoire of instructions it would be less easy to commit to memory the full set of numerical equivalents, so that either one continually refers to a table which provides the reminders or else runs the risk of placing something like 111001 where the code 101101 was wanted. In one important code this would put a stop instruction where a jump was wanted.

The development of languages which make man-machine communication increasingly easier for the human partner in the conversation has been one of the major achievements of computer science during the past twenty years. The general trend is toward languages which resemble more and more our familiar human languages and less and less the languages of machines. The key step then involves teaching the machine to make the translations, since otherwise nothing would have been gained. The two essentials in any such system are therefore:

1. *A programming language,* **often** called a symbolic language or a source language, in which the information needed by the machine for the computation in question is presented to its input unit.

2. A machine language program, available within the memory unit of the machine, which allows the computer to translate input information from the programming language into its own machine language. This vital program is known as *the processor.*

To solve a problem in a computing system of the sort just described a prescribed set of steps must thus be followed. First the human programmer prepares his instructions and data in the programming language. The processor, which it must be remembered is itself a machine language program, must be read into the memory unit if it is not already there. Suitably coded on punched cards or some other input device the prepared program, or source program, is also input to the machine. The processor then translates this source program into its own machine language. The translated version is called *the object program* and a copy of this, perhaps on punched cards, may be output from the computer if desired. If the same program is to be used a number of times this would be wise, since the time and expense of a second translation are avoided. Often such a copy is output automatically. The final step is of course the execution of the object program. This may take place at once or may be delayed, the essential machine language program now being in hand.

Assembler systems were the first result of the efforts just mentioned to overcome the disadvantages of machine languages. Appearing first in the late 1950s they succeeded in disposing of the second and third inconveniences listed above, the matter of memory locations and operation codes. Basically they allowed the programmer to refer to sequences in memory by symbolic names rather than by address and to operations by names rather than by number. A suitably prepared processor, called the assembler program, then performed the translations to machine language. Each source instruction thus became a machine language instruction. This means that the source and object programs were of the same length though in different languages and that no reduction in the amount of fine detail had been achieved. The first and major disadvantage listed above thus remained. Though we shall devote only a few moments to assemblers, saving our main effort for a later breakthrough in programming languages, a few minor examples based once again on the addition program of Chapter 5 may be useful.

Example 6.1.
For the miniature and fictitious computer of the preceding chapter the three machine language instructions

$$0\ 0\ 1\ 0\ 1\ 0\ 0\ 0\ 0$$
$$0\ 1\ 0\ 0\ 1\ 0\ 0\ 1\ 1$$
$$0\ 1\ 1\ 0\ 1\ 0\ 0\ 0\ 0$$

began our addition program. In a symbolic language they might perhaps have been written as follows:

COP SUM
ADD X
STO SUM

In such a case the processor, or assembler program, would have to translate these alphabetic characters to the numerical language of the machine. First of all the processor would require a table such as

0 0 0	STP		1 0 0	PUN
0 0 1	COP		1 0 1	JUM
0 1 0	ADD		1 1 0	JIF
0 1 1	STO		1 1 1	SUB

from which it could discover that COP is equivalent to 001 and so on. The alphabetic operation codes are thus easily replaced by their numerical counterparts. The convenience of these alphabetic symbols is not hard to see. Recalling the meaning of each numerical code, one notes that STP now means stop, COP means copy from memory, ADD means add, and so on. The letter combinations are a handy reminder to the human programmer of the function involved in each case, making it less likely that he will select a wrong symbol. Translating the address portions of the source instructions is a greater challenge. In fact, no processor would translate only a fragment of a program such as we have here. It would need to know the length of the entire program in order to assign memory addresses conveniently. This aspect of the assembler system will be presented as a separate example.

Example 6.2.

Suppose the fourteen instructions of the program of Chapter 5 were written in the following programming language (Table 6.1).

(C) COP SUM	STO COUNT	(A) COP (B)
(B) ADD Xn	SUB NUMB	ADD ONE
STO SUM	JIF (A)	STO (B)
COP COUNT	PUN SUM	JUM (C)
ADD ONE	STP	

Table 6.1

Suppose also that the machine is instructed to fill the memory locations named NUMB, SUM, COUNT and ONE with the initial sequences 32, 0, 0 and 1 respectively. Here we have given the machine decimal symbols since this is more convenient for us, and we leave to the processor the task of converting to binary. Finally suppose that with the symbol Xn we instruct the machine to associate thirty-two numbers which we also provide in decimal symbolism. As we then ask the processor to translate this information into its own machine language, just what capabilities are we demanding of it? In other words, recalling that the processor is itself a machine language program, what capabilities must be kept in mind by the human programmer who creates the processor?

In answering this question, even though our present model is miniature and fictitious, we obtain a somewhat clearer view of the origins of modern programming systems. Assume that the fourteen basic instructions are first allocated by the processor to memory locations 1 to 14, and that after this locations are assigned in the order listed for initial values. That is, following the basic instructions come NUMB, SUM, COUNT and ONE plus the thirty-two Xn. (Checking back one would find this to be the order of memory allocations used in Chapter 5.) It is then no severe challenge for either man or machine to identify NUMB with 15, SUM with 16, COUNT with 17, and so on. In particular Xn is identified with locations 19 to 50 inclusive, initially with 19. Both we and the machine must realize that this symbol is to stand for different locations at different times. Let us say that the processor has been taught to expect this of the lower case letter n, noting that lower case letters have not been used in any other way in the source program. Assume also that the symbols (C), (B) and (A) appearing in the program will be identified with the locations in which the corresponding instructions ultimately appear. Here this quickly makes them 1, 2 and 11 in that order. At this point both we and the processor are ready for the final translated version of the program, the object program. Replacing COP by 001 and SUM by 010000, the latter converted from decimal 16, the first instruction becomes our old

$$0 \ 0 \ 1 \ 0 \ 1 \ 0 \ 0 \ 0 \ 0$$

and similarly replacing ADD by 010 and Xn by 010011, the second instruction becomes the familiar sequence

$$0 \ 1 \ 0 \ 0 \ 1 \ 0 \ 0 \ 1 \ 1$$

Continuing the translation process reproduces the original machine language program, now called the object program. Looking backward over this example, one sees that the processor of an assembler system must be able to look up operation codes in a given table and must also be able to identify symbols occurring in the source program with specific memory locations. To be sure the human programmer could do these same things himself, but they are an example of the kind of routine to which circuits are well adapted.

Compiler systems were the next step forward in the development of the art of programming, and a giant step from the point of view of both convenience and complexity. Their main objective is the reduction of the amount of detail which the human programmer must consider. Once again this is achieved by transferring a still larger part of the communication effort to the machine. The source languages of compiler systems resemble rather closely the alphabetical and arithmetical languages used by human beings in their efforts to solve the world's problems. Often they are called problem-oriented languages because of this resemblance. In contrast, assembler languages reflect the structure of the particular machines for which they were created. They are machine-oriented, being essentially modified machine languages. After all, the difference between

COP SUM

and the machine language　　　　　0 0 1 0 1 0 0 0 0

is mostly a matter of bookkeeping, of knowing that COP means 001 and SUM means 010000. Even the COP SUM version reflects the fact that the computer in question contains hardware which diverts the COP to one decoder and the SUM to another. In theory at least, compiler languages are machine-independent; they do not reflect the structure of a particular computer. In this connection, however, it must be recalled that the problem of translating a source program into a machine language object program is still present. To achieve this a processor is required. For a compiler system the processor is called a compiler, and proves to be a very complex and lengthy machine language program.

One problem-oriented language will be our main concern from here on; it is known as Fortran, and is probably the most extensively used programming language. As will be seen one Fortran instruction usually represents a significant step in problem solution, so that recalling our recent experiences with machine language instructions, it will be easy to believe that one such Fortran instruction often translates into a whole set of machine language instructions. It is the task of the processor, or compiler, to split the operation in question into the elemental copy, shift, store and other steps which the computer is to execute. This is one example of fine detail being transferred from human hands to the machine. Together with numerous similar efforts to reduce our own labors at the machine's expense this explains the great complexity of modern compilers. Often these programs occupy a disheartening fraction of the computer's total memory unit, leaving a programmer who has a problem with voluminous data feeling somewhat cramped. The question has actually arisen whether bigger and more expensive memory units are in order or whether our demands for compiler sophistication should be limited. Considering human nature and the history of computer science it is almost certain the first path will be taken. Compiler systems, and this will in part summarize the message of recent paragraphs, thus have a number of advantages over direct machine language programming.

1. Source programs are written in a language which resembles the familiar arithmetical and alphabetical languages of the programmer.

2. The programmer needs to know almost nothing about the internal structure of the machine that he is to use.

3. The number of instructions which must be provided to the machine is greatly reduced, most of the fine detail being supplied during the translation or compiling process. (Here we do not count the enormous number of instructions in the compiler itself, but these are provided by professional programmers and not by the average user.)

4. Allocation of specific memory addresses to the various instructions and data is left to the machine.

5. Extensive aid for the debugging, or detection of errors in programs is usually provided.

6. A variety of input-output devices may be called upon, and the format or arrangement of data may be specified rather freely.

Clearly this is asking much more of the machine than was the case in the miniature programs offered earlier. These points will be brought out in more detail as we use the Fortran language.

Monitors represent an effort to make as efficient use as is possible of a particular computer considering the varying needs of its users and the variety of languages in which their programs may be written. A monitor is a program which controls or supervises the machine's activity. A typical sequence of jobs that might be processed under the supervision of a monitor program is as follows:

1. A program written in Fortran which is to be compiled, the object program being output. Execution is to be postponed.

2. A Fortran program which is to be compiled and, if no errors are at once apparent, executed.

3. A machine language program which is to be executed.

4. A program written in a symbolic language which is to be assembled and executed.

5. For a specified time period programs are to be accepted only from certain remote consoles. The users of these consoles remain in constant communication with the computer, their instructions being accepted according to priorities determined by the monitor program. This process is called time-sharing. The computer's high operating speed allows almost any number of users to introduce, run and modify their own programs as though each were the only user. Dispensing machine time as called for by the different consoles, or explaining delays, is the monitor's function.

6. A set of object programs, previously compiled, is to be executed one after another. This is called batch processing.

To carry out such an important assignment a monitor must be a program of some complexity. As with assemblers and compilers, however, we make no effort here to go into the details, leaving these to the professionals and continuing to adopt the consumer's rather than the producer's point of view. In preparing programs our principal contact with monitors will be the need to include information indicating the programming language used and how much processing we require.

Solved Problems

6.1. In Problem 5.18 we modified the basic program of Chapter 5 to punch out the final count as well as the final sum. This required moving certain instructions to new memory locations with corresponding changes of address. Show that this modification can be made more conveniently if the symbolic programming language of Examples 6.1 and 6.2 is used.

The program in Example 6.2 may still be used with

PUN COUNT

added just after PUN SUM. In Problem 5.18 it was necessary to make specific allocations in memory for all instructions and data. The insertion of a new instruction of this sort required in particular that the address portions of instructions 11, 13 and 14 be changed after the insertion. Here these addresses are called simply (B) and (C) which may be left as they are. The assembler will eventually replace them by specific addresses.

6.2. In Problem 5.20 we modified the basic program of that chapter to punch out the sum and count at each step. Show that this same modification can be made more conveniently if the programming language of Example 6.2 is used.

From the flow-chart provided in Fig. 5-3 the following program may be prepared (Table 6.2). Note that, as earlier, each box in the flow-chart corresponds to a set of instructions. With symbolic programming, however, there is no need to concern ourselves with addresses. It is the assembler's job to provide them afterward. This same program could be achieved by making a few alterations in the symbolic program of Example 6.2. In addition, all the initial values of that example must be repeated.

(C) COP SUM	STO COUNT	STP
(B) ADD Xn	PUN SUM	(A) COP (B)
STO SUM	PUN COUNT	ADD ONE
COP COUNT	SUB NUMB	STO (B)
ADD ONE	JIF (A)	JUM (C)

Table 6.2

6.3. In Problem 5.37 the basic program of that chapter was modified to punch out the current X number and the current sum at each step. How can this be done in the symbolic programming language of Example 6.2?

The program of Table 6.3 suggests the essential steps. It must be kept in mind that any such program assumes an assembler with appropriate capabilities.

(C) COP SUM	PUN SUM	ADD ONE
(B) ADD Xn	(D) PUN Xn	STO (B)
STO SUM	SUB NUMB	COP (D)
COP COUNT	JIF (A)	ADD ONE
ADD ONE	STP	STO (D)
STO COUNT	(A) COP (B)	JUM (C)

Table 6.3

6.4. In Problem 5.40 the basic program of that chapter was modified to punch out the correct sum and count after each group of eight. Following the same flow-chart prepared in Problem 5.39, write a corresponding program using the symbolic language of Example 6.2.

Such a program is given in Table 6.4. It is equivalent to the one in Problem 5.40 but no specific memory addresses are involved. The symbol OUTCT stands for output count. When this reaches eight an output occurs after which this count is reset to zero. The same initial values as in Example 6.2 are to be used, with the additions OUTCT equals 0 and EIGHT equals 8.

(C) COP SUM	STO OUTCT	JIF (A)
(B) ADD Xn	SUB EIGHT	STP
STO SUM	JIF (A)	(A) COP (B)
COP COUNT	PUN SUM	ADD ONE
ADD ONE	PUN COUNT	STO (B)
STO COUNT	STO OUTCT	JUM (C)
COP OUTCT	COP COUNT	
ADD ONE	SUB NUMB	

Table 6.4

6.5. Suppose that 45 numbers rather than 32 are to be summed. How does this affect the symbolic program prepared in Example 6.2?

The main instructions themselves are unaffected. The assembler must be told, however, that the value of NUMB is now 45 and it must be offered 45 numbers to be associated with the symbol Xn. In the Fortran language that we turn to next the compiler will want to know as soon as possible the size of any such collection of numbers, so that a comparable segment of the memory unit may be set aside for it.

Supplementary Problems

6.6. In Problems 5.41 and 5.42 a machine language program for a table look-up was prepared. Write a corresponding program in the language of Example 6.2. What numbers must be made available to the computer?

6.7. In Problems 5.43 and 5.44 a machine language program for vector addition was prepared. Write a corresponding program in the symbolic language of Example 6.2.

6.8. In Problems 5.45 and 5.46 a machine language program for finding the largest number in a given set was prepared. Write a corresponding program in the language of Example 6.2.

6.9. Review the disadvantages of machine languages and note how to some extent these are overcome by the symbolic language of Example 6.2. Notice also that the programs just prepared in Problems 6.6 to 6.8 have the same length as their counterparts in Chapter 5, so that there has been no reduction in the detail that the program must include.

6.10. What is the main difference between an assembler system and a compiler system? Historically which came first?

6.11. What is the role of a monitor program?

Chapter 7

Introduction to Fortran

The Fortran language, the name being an abbreviation of the two words formula translation, is a problem-oriented programming language. In contrast to the fictitious languages used in our earlier examples, Fortran is extensively used throughout the world. Because it resembles familiar arithmetical language, it greatly simplifies the preparation of problems for machine computation. Data and instructions may be organized in the form of a sequence of Fortran statements. This is the source program. The Fortran compiler, also called the translator or processor, then analyzes these statements and translates them into an object program in machine language. A program written in Fortran language can be processed on any machine which has a Fortran compiler. In this sense the language is machine independent. However, the compiler must in each case be prepared with the particular machine in mind. Because machines do differ in their internal organization, a number of "dialects" of Fortran have developed, each dialect being suited to a class of machines. The differences between dialects are not severe and one easily adjusts from one to another. The dialect to be presented here is known as Fortran IV.

The alphabet of Fortran includes the following characters, all of which are familiar symbols of handwriting and of typewriter keyboards as well as of the special keypunch devices made for use in Fortran systems.

Letters

A B C D E F G H I J K L M N O P Q R S T U V W X Y Z

Digits   0 1 2 3 4 5 6 7 8 9

Other characters   + − * / = . , ( ) $

From this alphabet all our symbols, expressions and statements in the Fortran language are to be constructed.

NUMBERS

Numbers may be represented in a variety of ways, all of which resemble the symbols of ordinary arithmetic. There are, however, certain conventions due to the fact that Fortran provides for both fixed-point and floating-point computations. As was pointed out in Chapter 4 these two types of computation involve different types of hardware, different arithmetical circuitry. It is important that no confusion arise in the selection of circuitry for processing individual numbers, and symbols for numbers are chosen with this in mind. Fixed-point symbols are to be distinguishable from floating-point symbols. The first will be used only with integers and such computations will be called integer arithmetic, or integer mode. Otherwise the arithmetic of real numbers will be done in floating-point form and will be referred to as real arithmetic, or real mode. Since it is also convenient to distinguish constants (numbers which do not change throughout the execution of the program) from variables (numbers which may change) four kinds of symbols for numbers arise.

1. *Integer constants.* These are represented by one to eleven digits *without* a decimal point. The maximum number of allowed digits varies slightly with the dialect of Fortran being used. A minus sign must precede the digits if the integer is negative. If it is positive, a preceding plus sign is optional. The absence of the decimal point causes the compiler to treat such numbers in fixed-point form.

Example 7.1.
   Proper symbols for integer constants include

$$1492 \quad +1492 \quad -1492 \quad 0 \quad +1$$
$$3000000000 \quad 007 \quad +007 \quad -10 \quad -1$$

Improper symbols for integer constants include

   1492.   (decimal point not allowed)

   123456789000   (more than eleven digits)

2. *Real constants.* These are represented by one to nine significant digits *with* a decimal point. The maximum number of allowed digits varies slightly with the dialect. The decimal point may be placed at the beginning, at the end, or between any two digits. Its presence leads to floating-point treatment of the number involved. A minus sign must precede the digits if the number is negative; if it is positive, a preceding plus sign is optional.

Example 7.2.
   Proper symbols for real constants include

$$123.456 \quad -123.456 \quad +123.456 \quad 1.492$$
$$.0000001492000 \quad .007 \quad -.007 \quad -.0001$$

Notice that leading zeros are not considered to be significant digits.

   The following are also allowable:

$$0. \quad 1. \quad 1492. \quad -1492. \quad 2.00$$

Improper symbols for real constants, not slated to be treated as integers, include the following:

   1492   (decimal point missing)

   123456789.99   (more than nine significant digits)

There is a second way in which real constants may be represented. It is called the exponential form. To a symbol of the sort just described, and illustrated in Example 7.2, one may append the letter E and a one or two digit integer constant, positive or negative. This integer constant, or exponent, indicates that the decimal point is to be shifted a corresponding number of places, leftward if the exponent is negative and rightward if positive. For a negative exponent the minus sign must be used; for a positive exponent + is optional. In Fortran IV the presence of an exponent even makes the use of the decimal point optional, the exponent serving to tell the compiler that the constant involved is not to be given integer treatment.

Example 7.3.
   Proper symbols for real constants in exponential form include the following, the nonexponential form also being listed for comparison.

Exponential	Nonexponential
1.23456E + 02	123.456
1.23456E2	123.456
123.456E00	123.456
+1.492E − 02	+.01492
−1.492E + 03	−1492.
−1000E − 3	−1.000

Improper symbols include

$$+1.492E3. \quad \text{(no decimal point allowed in exponent)}$$
$$1.492E123 \quad \text{(three digits in exponent)}$$

3. *Integer variables.*   These are represented by combinations of one to six letters and digits, the other characters not being allowed.   The first character must be one of the letters I, J, K, L, M or N.   This first character distinguishes an integer variable from other real variables, symbols for which will not be allowed to start in this way.   During execution of the program integer variables must be restricted to integer values.

Example 7.4.
   Proper symbols for integer variables include

INTVAR	ICOUNT	I1	I2	I	KOUNT
JOHN	NUMBER	LL	M10	N	N1492

   Some improper symbols are

COUNT	(first character must be I, J, K, L, M or N)
INTEGER	(too many characters)
J.000	(illegal character).

4. *Real variables.*   These are represented by combinations of one to six letters and digits, other characters not being allowed.   The first character must be a letter other than I, J, K, L, M or N.   During execution of the program such variables must be restricted to real, nonintegral values.   (Thus 1. would be a suitable value but 1 would not.)

Example 7.5.
   Proper symbols for real variables include the following.

A	FORCE	X1	COST15	ALPHA	SUM
Z	SPEED	Y2	PRICE4	BETA	TAX

Some improper symbols are

MASS	(first character cannot be M)
1A	(first character must be a letter)
VOLTAGE	(too many characters)
X$	(illegal character).

Since numbers are the ingredients from which computations are made, it is clearly important to have a well specified symbolism for them, and this has now been provided. It is also convenient, when possible, to choose variable names which suggest the quantities involved, such as the KOUNT, PRICE, TAX and other illustrations above. In this connection, however, the agreement on leading letters must be respected. Thus KOUNT may stand for an integer while COUNT may not, and XMASS may represent a real mass while MASS may not. Using such names simplifies programming and also simplifies the search for errors.

ARITHMETIC OPERATIONS

   Arithmetic operations and the symbols which the Fortran language assigns to them are the following.

Addition	+
Subtraction	−
Multiplication	*
Division	/
Exponentiation	**

The sum and difference of two numbers A and B are thus represented by A + B and A − B exactly as in ordinary arithmetical language. Their product must, however, be written A*B instead of in the more familiar AB or A × B forms. This amounts to a minor concession made to simplify the work of the compiler. Similarly the quotient must be written A/B instead of as A ÷ B or $\frac{A}{B}$. Exponentiation is also called raising to a power. Thus $A^2 = AA = A \times A$ can be written in Fortran as A*A or as A**2 while $A^3 = AAA$ becomes A**3 in Fortran exponential form.

ARITHMETIC EXPRESSIONS

It is now possible to translate arithmetical combinations of numbers, or arithmetical expressions, into Fortran symbolism. Various rules which must be observed while doing this will be listed below.

Example 7.6.

A few expressions are listed below in both Fortran and ordinary arithmetical language.

Fortran	Ordinary
A + B − 3.*C	A + B − 3C
A**2 + B**2	$A^2 + B^2$
B**2 − 4.*A*C	$B^2 − 4AC$
(A + B)/2.	$\frac{1}{2}(A + B)$
I + J − 3*K	I + J − 3K

Rules governing the formation of arithmetic expressions will now be listed, their purpose being either the accurate transmission of the programmer's intentions to the compiler or the simplification of such expressions consistent with such accuracy.

Rule 1.

All the constants and variables in an expression must be in the same mode, that is, all must be integers or else all must be real. (One exception to this rule will be mentioned in Rule 2.) Example 7.6 has already provided illustrations. In the first line the numbers A, B, C are in the real mode, which requires the constant to conform as 3., the decimal point being necessary. In the last line, however, the variables I, J, K are in integer mode, and here the constant appears as 3, the decimal point being necessarily absent. (Note: In some systems a certain amount of mode-mixing is allowable. For details see your local computing center staff. Here we shall obey the rule religiously.)

Rule 2.

A**B, A**I, I**J are all acceptable exponentiations. In particular, the middle form mixes modes by raising a real number to an integer power. This exception to Rule 1 has been provided for in the Fortran compiler because integer powers involve only successive multiplications (thus A**4 = A*A*A*A) while noninteger powers call for much more sophisticated computations. In Example 7.6 the terms A**2 and B**2 illustrate this exception. Note that I**A, an integer to a noninteger power, is not allowed.

Rule 3.

Operations are executed with these priorities.

1. Exponentiation
2. Multiplication and division
3. Addition and subtraction

This means that if no further information is provided the exponentiations in an expression will be computed first of all, then the multiplications and divisions, finally the additions and subtractions. Among operations of equal priority the order of execution is from left to right. The form A**B**C is not, however, allowed. Here parentheses are required to indicate the priority. The use of parentheses is described in the next rule.

Example 7.7.

Suppose that A = 5., B = 8. and C = 2., all three being in the real mode as the letters themselves suggest. The computation of the expression A + B − 3.*C then proceeds in these steps:

$$3.*2. = 6. \qquad 5. + 8. = 13. \qquad 13. - 6. = 7.$$

Similarly for A**2 + B**2 the computer will perform

$$5.**2 = 25. \qquad 8.**2 = 64. \qquad 25. + 64. = 89.$$

while for B**2 − 4.*A*C the steps are the following:

$$8.**2 = 64. \qquad 4.*5. = 20. \qquad 20.*2. = 40. \qquad 64. - 40. = 24.$$

Rule 4.

Parentheses may be used in Fortran to designate operations which are to be executed first, much as in ordinary arithmetic. The natural order of priorities given in Rule 3 may thus be altered to suit the programmer's intentions. When one set of parentheses occurs within another the inner set has priority, the operations within it being executed first.

Example 7.8.

Suppose that A = 5., B = 8., C = 2. and D = 1.6. Then the computation of (A + B)/C would take these two steps

$$5. + 8. = 13. \qquad 13./2. = 6.5$$

the natural order of priority being reversed by the parentheses. In contrast the expression A + B/C would bring

$$8./2. = 4. \qquad 5. + 4. = 9.$$

In the same way (A + C)**2 would lead to

$$5. + 2. = 7. \qquad 7.**2 = 49.$$

while A + C**2 brings instead

$$2.**2 = 4. \qquad 5. + 4. = 9.$$

Still another elementary example makes

$$(A*B)/(C*D) = 40./3.2 = 12.5$$

while in the absence of parentheses operations would be performed from left to right leading to

$$A*B/C*D = 40./C*D = 20.*D = 32.$$

Finally to illustrate parentheses within other parentheses, take

$$(A*(B + C))**2 = (A*10.)**2 = 50.**2 = 2500.$$

the inner parentheses giving B + C the highest priority. Omitting the inner parentheses changes the meaning of the expression to

$$(A*B + C)**2 = (40. + C)**2 = 42.**2 = 1764.$$

the remaining parentheses still having priority over the exponentiation. Omitting the outer parentheses instead leads to

$$A*(B + C)**2 = A*10.**2 = A*100. = 500.$$

Omitting all parentheses would produce the result 44. Clearly the programmer must know exactly which meaning he wants and must use parentheses carefully to obtain his goal.

Rule 5.

An operation symbol must not precede a positive or negative sign. This is another minor concession to simplify the problem of compiling the program. Parentheses may be used to enclose the sign and its associated constant or variable.

Example 7.9.

The unacceptable symbols

$$A* - B \qquad I + -J \qquad M - +N \qquad A/-B$$

should be replaced by $\qquad$ A*(−B) $\qquad$ I + (−J) $\qquad$ M − (+N) $\qquad$ A/(−B)

STATEMENTS

Statements are the basic units from which Fortran programs are constructed. They may be classified into groups according to their function, perhaps as follows.

1. Arithmetic
2. Control
3. Input-output
4. Specifications

A few examples from each group will be enough to allow the preparation of a variety of nontrivial programs.

1. *Arithmetic statements* are formed from the expressions just presented and their function is of course to specify the particular computations which must be made. The form to be used is

$$\text{Variable} = \text{Expression}$$

and resembles fairly closely an arithmetical equality. The meaning of the = sign is, however, somewhat different in Fortran. It requires that the value of the expression on the right be computed, and that this value then be assigned to the variable named on the left. In other words, the value is stored in the memory location which has been allocated to that variable. An arithmetic statement thus calls for both a computation and a storage operation.

Example 7.10.

Recalling the computations already made in Example 7.8, the arithmetic statements

$$X = (A + B)/C$$
$$POWER = (A + C)**2$$
$$FRACT = (A*B)/(C*D)$$

would cause the numbers 6.5, 49., 12.5 in that order to be stored in memory locations set aside for the variables X, POWER and FRACT, assuming the same values for A, B, C and D. Slightly more surprising at first sight is a statement such as

$$A = A + 1.5$$

which would be impossible in ordinary arithmetical language. In Fortran the expression on the right is computed, taking the value 6.5 if we continue to assume A given as 5., and this new value is then assigned to the variable A, being stored in A's memory location. After execution of this statement, therefore, A no longer has the value 5. but the new value 6.5 instead. Similar, and reminiscent of an earlier chapter, would be the statements

$$SUM = SUM + X$$
$$ICOUNT = ICOUNT + 1$$

the letter I being added to the second of these because it is an integer operation.

Under arithmetic statements we may also include certain special computations which the compiler will recognize by name. The statement

$$Y = SQRT(9.)$$

will, for instance, provoke the computation of the positive square root of 9., which is 3. The compiler identifies the code SQRT with the square root idea and calls upon a previously prepared program for making the calculation. Similarly the arithmetical expression

$$Z = \sqrt{X^2 + Y^2}$$

can be obtained in Fortran by the statement

$$Z = SQRT(X**2 + Y**2).$$

For those with recollections of trigonometry a second example of this sort is provided by the statement

$$\text{ALPHA} = \text{SIN(BETA)}$$

in which the code SIN calls for the computation of the sine of BETA, the resulting value then being stored under the name ALPHA. The compiler responds to the code SIN by calling upon a previously prepared program which produces the required sine. A generous variety of such routines is available to Fortran programmers. Known as *functions,* or subroutines or subprograms, they may be requested by statements of the form

$$\text{A} = \text{CODE(B)}$$

where CODE is the code identifying the desired function. A partial list of available functions will be accumulated as we proceed. It is not necessary to know the details of the method by which each of these is computed, but one should at least learn in each case if the subprogram places any restrictions on the value B. Thus for

$$\text{A} = \text{SQRT(B)}$$

the value B must not be negative. Often there is an upper limit to the size of B. Failure to observe such restrictions can lead to serious error. For most functions the value B must also be in real rather than integer mode.

2. *Control statements* play a number of critical roles. For instance, Fortran statements are usually executed in the same order in which they appear in the source program. As seen in Chapter 5, however, it is often important to be able to alter this normal routine, to jump elsewhere for the next instruction or to jump if a certain condition is satisfied. For this purpose the Fortran language provides for the numbering of key statements. In fact all statements could be numbered if desired though this might mean wasted effort. *A statement number* must be a one to five digit integer constant without plus or minus sign. The number is placed to the left of the statement in the program. The examples

$$2 \ \ \text{ICOUNT} = \text{ICOUNT} + 1$$

$$99 \ \ \text{A} = \text{SQRT(B)}$$

are probably sufficient for the moment. One control statement which requires statement numbers is the following.

The GO TO statement. This takes the form

$$\text{GO TO N}$$

where N is a statement number. A GO TO statement produces an unconditional jump. Thus GO TO 2 sends the action to statement number 2, which might be the above counting instruction. GO TO 99 brings a jump to statement number 99, say the above square root statement.

Example 7.11.

Consider this miniature program.

$$\text{I} = 1$$

$$\text{INTSUM} = 0$$

$$1 \ \ \text{INTSUM} = \text{INTSUM} + \text{I}$$

$$\text{I} = \text{I} + 1$$

$$\text{GO TO 1}$$

The first two statements assign initial values to the variables I and INTSUM. The next two increase INTSUM by the amount I and I by the amount 1, at which point the GO TO returns the action to statement number 1. It quickly becomes clear that the last three statements will be executed repeatedly, with I running through the sequence of values $1, 2, 3, \ldots$ and INTSUM through the sequence $0, 1, 3, 6, 10, 15, 21, \ldots$. This second sequence displays the sums of positive integers, and these are presumably the objective of the program. It is also clear that the loop which is present in this program has no built-in exit. This flaw can be removed by using a different control statement.

The IF statement. This takes the form

$$\text{IF (A) } L, M, N$$

where A is any arithmetic expression and L, M, N are statement numbers. During execution the expression A is first computed. Then

(1) if A is negative, statement number L is executed next,

(2) if A is zero, statement M is executed next,

(3) if A is positive, statement number N is executed next.

An IF statement amounts to a conditional jump, everything depending upon the current value of A. The form just given may be altered by replacing A by I, meaning that an expression taking integer values rather than real values may be used in this place. Parentheses and commas must appear where shown. Before turning to another example, one further type of control statement will be presented.

The STOP statement. This appears simply as

$$\text{STOP}$$

and terminates execution of the program. If the computer is under the control of a monitor program, then control returns to that monitor. Otherwise the computer just stops.

Example 7.12.

Suppose Example 7.11 modified as follows.

```
      I = 1
      INTSUM = 0
   1  INTSUM = INTSUM + I
      I = I + 1
      IF (I − 100) 1, 1, 2
   2  STOP
```

The first four statements are unchanged, but an IF now replaces the GO TO. As a result, if I is less than 100 the first statement number will be active and a jump back to statement number 1 occurs. If I equals 100, the second statement number is active and the same exact jump is made. If, however, I is greater than 100, then the third statement number brings a jump to statement number 2 and the computation stops. This happens just after I has been increased to 101, so it is the integers from one to a hundred that will be summed.

Perhaps the most popular way for constructing program loops and providing for exit at the proper time is by use of the following statement.

The DO statement. This takes the forms

$$\text{DO K I} = L, M, N$$

$$\text{DO K I} = L, M$$

the second and simpler form applying if $N = 1$, as it usually does. In the DO statement K stands for a statement number, I an integer variable, and L, M, N are integer variables or constants without sign. The DO causes repeated execution of all statements following, up to statement number K inclusive. The first time these statements are executed the variable I equals L; on each succeeding pass I will have been increased by the amount N, until on the final pass it equals M. At this point the DO loop is terminated and control passes to the statement just after statement number K. Thus L is the initial value of the variable I and M is its terminal value. This variable I is called the *index* of the DO statement and its current value may be used in computations during execution of the loop. The statements which form the loop, those following the DO up to and including statement number K, are called the *range* of the DO.

Future examples will make the use of DO statements more clear but a few restrictions should be mentioned at once. The index I is sequenced automatically during execution of the loop, when it may be treated as any other integer variable except that no effort must be made to redefine it. In other words, I should not appear as the left side of an arithmetic statement or in an input list of the sort to be described in a moment. Its value must be left as defined automatically by the DO loop. After completion of the loop, however, the index I is undefined and the symbol becomes available for general use. Essentially the same remarks apply to the integers L, M, N. As a second restriction, the final statement in the range of a DO, the statement with number K, should not be a specification statement or a transfer of control. This excludes such things as GO TO, IF and DO as well as FORMAT, END and other types to be introduced shortly. Third, at no place in the overall program should a transfer be made into the range of a DO statement. Entry to the DO loop should always be through the DO statement itself since otherwise the value of the index may be undefined. It is perfectly all right to transfer out of a DO loop, however, before its cycle is finished and an example in which this is useful will be given. Finally, it is quite common for one DO loop to be entirely within another or for both to share the same final statement. In such cases the loops are called "nested". During execution the inner loop will be treated as part of the range of the outer. But one DO loop may not be partially inside and partially outside another; loops must be completely nested or not at all.

Example 7.13.

The program of Example 7.12 can be replaced by the following.

```
            INTSUM = 0
            DO 1 I = 1,100
          1 INTSUM = INTSUM + I
            STOP
```

The range of this DO is the single statement with number 1, which is executed first with I = 1 and last with I = 100, the increase each time being 1. The sum of the integers from 1 to 100 is thus obtained.

3. *Input-output statements* are obviously designed for getting information into and out of the computer. There is an abundance of procedures for doing this but only one type of statement for transmitting information in each direction will be presented at this time.

The READ statement.   This has the form

$$READ\ (I, N)\ LIST$$

I and N being integers and LIST representing a list of variable names for which values are to be read. The integer I designates the type of input device to be used. The code may vary from one computer installation to another, but for present purposes let us say that I = 5 designates a card reader. The integer N is the statement number of an associated FORMAT statement to be described under specifications.

Example 7.14.

The statement

$$\text{READ (5, 8) A, B, C, D, E}$$

will cause the reading of five numbers from cards. These five numbers will be stored in the memory locations which have been assigned to variables A, B, C, D, E in that order. The commas separating these variable names are necessary. The numbers must be made available at the card reader in a format consistent with that described in statement 8. (See the section on specification statements below.) Similarly

$$\text{READ (5, 3) AMOUNT, PRICE, TAX}$$

will cause the read-in of three numbers to be stored under the names shown. The numbers must be made available in a format consistent with that of statement 3.

The WRITE statement. This has the form

$$\text{WRITE (I, N) LIST}$$

I and N being integers and LIST representing a list of variable names for which values are to be written. The integer I designates the type of output device to be used. The code may vary from one computer installation to another but for present purposes let us say that $I = 6$ designates a printer. The integer N is the statement number of an associated FORMAT statement.

Example 7.15.

The statement

$$\text{WRITE (6, 8) A, B, C, D, E}$$

will cause the printing of the current values of variables A, B, C, D, E in the format specified by statement number 8. The commas separating these variable names are necessary. The values will be output in the order prescribed in the list, after having been brought from the memory unit and transformed into the specified form. Similarly

$$\text{WRITE (6, 9) INTSUM}$$

will cause the printing out of the current value of the integer variable INTSUM. The format specified in statement number 9 must in this case be an integer format. (See below.)

4. *Specification statements* do not themselves initiate computations or bring control jumps or stimulate information flow, but instead provide the compiler with essential details for proper translation of the Fortran program into the object program or for proper conversion of data at input or output. Several types of specification are included in the Fortran language, of which two will be presented at this point. First consider the problem of getting numerical data into the computer. Including a statement such as

$$A = 14.92$$

in the Fortran program will surely result in the value 14.92 being assigned to the variable A, after conversion from decimal language to the machine's own language. Values for other variables could also be assigned by similar program statements. All such values would in this case pass through the compilation process and be imbedded in the object program. To run the same program again, using different values for A and certain other variables, would then require a new compilation. Reruns of this sort are very common in a broad variety of applications, and the repeated compilations are both expensive and time-consuming. To avoid them the READ statement may be used. To be specific consider the statement

$$\text{READ (5, 7) A}$$

which causes the computer to "call" for a value of the variable A. The integer 5 means that A is available on *a data card* in the card reader. But the conventional card has 80 columns, each of which may contain a letter or digit or other character, as already suggested in Fig. 4-31. In which columns is the value of A to be found, and in what form? The answer to this question is vital for correct read-in and conversion to machine language. It is made available to the computer in a FORMAT statement.

The FORMAT statement. This has the form

$$N \; \text{FORMAT} \; (\; , \; , \; , \;)$$

in which N is the statement number of the FORMAT statement and corresponds to the N in the forms given above for READ and WRITE statements. The spaces between the commas are available for specifications to be described, the number of such spaces being one or more depending upon the programmer's needs.

The I specification: Iw

Here I denotes an integer value and w is an integer which indicates the number of columns, or *field width*, which that integer occupies on the input card. If a sign is included, + being optional, that column must be counted in determining w. The following examples are no doubt sufficient.

Data value	1492	+1491	−1492	0	+1
Specification	I4	I5	I5	I1	I2

The F specification: Fw.d

Here F denotes a real value, in familiar decimal form, and as above w indicates the field width, the number of columns which that value occupies on the input card. The sign, if any, and the decimal point must be counted in determining w. The integer d denotes the number of digits which appear to the right of the decimal point.

Data value	123.456	−.007	1492.	+.1492
Specification	F7.3	F5.3	F5.0	F6.4

The E specification: Ew.d

Here E denotes a real value in exponential form and w again indicates the field width, which this time must include the sign, if any, decimal point and exponent. The integer d denotes as before the number of digits which appear to the right of the decimal point, not counting the exponent.

Data value	.123456E02	−.7E−02	.1492E+04
Specification	E10.6	E7.1	E9.4

Example 7.16.

The two statements

$$\text{READ} \; (5, 7) \; A$$

$$7 \; \text{FORMAT} \; (F7.2)$$

will cause the computer to call for a single number from the card reader, that number being located in the first seven columns of the card in reading position. It is to be in ordinary decimal form with two digits to the right of the decimal point. Such a card is shown in Fig. 7-1 below. From this card the value 14.92 would be read into the memory location assigned to variable A. Note that this value has been punched in the five rightmost columns of the seven allocated by the FORMAT statement.

In this position it is said to be right-justified, which means simply that it has been placed as far to the right as is possible within its designated field. A number in the F specification does not have to be right-justified; it can be placed anywhere within its designated field. Here, for instance, the 1 could take any one of the first three columns. Even more room would have been available if the specification F10.2 or F20.2 had been used, the variable A being given the same 14.92 value in each case. Though right-justification of values is not necessary in F specification, it is not a bad habit to develop.

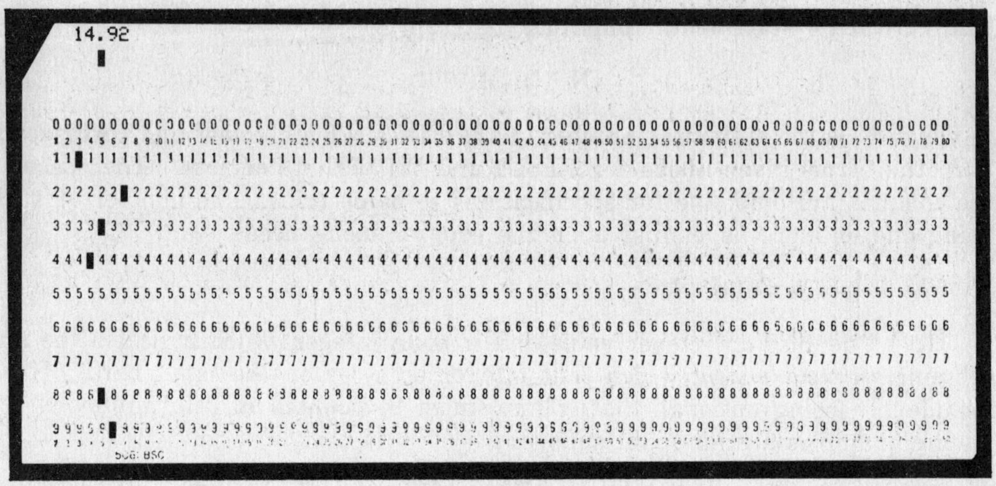

Fig. 7-1

Example 7.17.

The two statements   READ (5, 3) AMOUNT, PRICE, TAX

3 FORMAT (F10.0, F6.2, F5.1)

will cause the computer to call for three numbers from the card reader, to be stored under the variable names indicated. Though three separate cards might be used it seems reasonable to punch the three numbers on one card, AMOUNT in the first ten columns, PRICE in the next six columns, and TAX in the next five. Thus if 24,000 items were sold at a price of 14.98 each, with an added tax of 12.5 per cent, the ingredients for computing the total charge could be packaged in the combined format shown in Fig. 7-2. Here all three values have been right-justified, even though this was not necessary. Note that the choice of field widths leaves at least one space between values, making it easier for the programmer to read the printed version of his data at the top of the card.

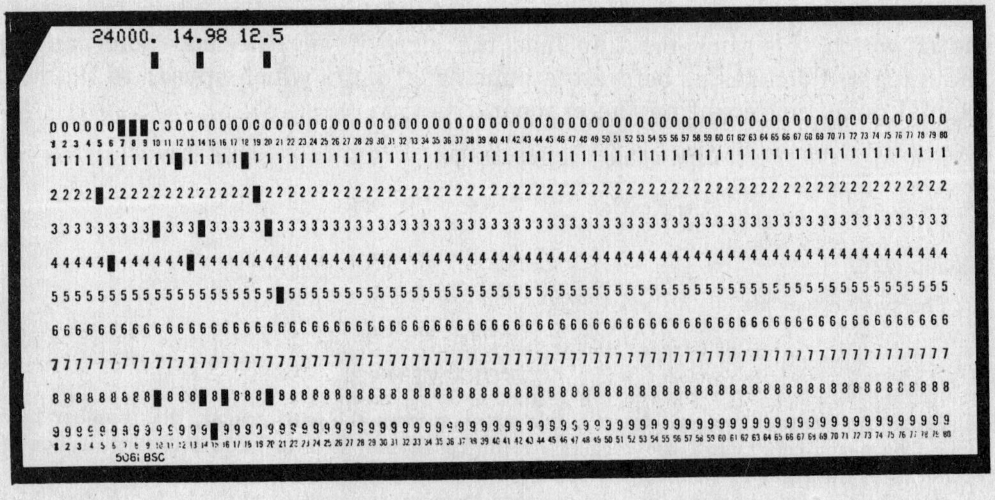

Fig. 7-2

Example 7.18.

The two statements

$$\text{READ (5, 4) I, J, K, L, M, N}$$

$$\text{4 FORMAT (6I5)}$$

introduce a minor modification which is available for FORMAT statements. Here six integers are to be read, all six having the same I5 specification. Instead of FORMAT (I5, I5, I5, I5, I5, I5) the almost natural abbreviation shown above is allowed. A suitable input card might have the following information punched in the first 30 columns.

$$\text{sss95sss92sss86sss83sss78sss70}$$

The letter s is being used here to denote a space. On the card itself the corresponding columns would be left clear. Note that in each of the six fields in action the value has been right-justified. In the I specification this *must* be done. Since each integer uses only two digits, a narrower field could have been used, but again the spaces facilitate reading of the card by the programmer.

For getting information out of the machine the FORMAT statement and I, F, E specifications are essentially the same as for input. In choosing the field width w it is wise, if not always totally necessary, to make allowance for the following.

1. A sign, even though a + is usually not printed.

2. A decimal point for F and E specifications.

3. At least one digit to the left of the decimal point, since many systems will print a 0 there if no other digit occurs.

4. Four places for the exponent of the E specification.

5. Enough places for all desired significant digits, since digits for which no room is allowed will be truncated or rounded off.

6. The first place to be left blank (for the time being). This position controls print spacing and a blank means normal single spacing. Other options will be mentioned later.

Example 7.19.

The two statements

$$\text{WRITE (6, 7) A}$$

$$\text{7 FORMAT (F7.2)}$$

will cause the computer to output the current value of the variable A as a line of print. Suppose we assume that values in memory are converted to eight digit decimals, and that in the present case the result of conversion is A = 14.926789. Format number 7 would then reduce this to

$$\text{ss14.92}$$

which would appear as far to the left as possible on the print line. As earlier, the letter s denotes a space. In some systems the extra decimal digits would not be truncated, but rounded off, the output then being ss14.93. The specification F10.6 would output the entire eight decimal digits, plus the decimal point and an implied though not printed + sign.

Example 7.20.

The two statements

$$\text{WRITE (6, 5) KOUNT, SUM, X}$$

$$\text{5 FORMAT (I4, 2F9.2)}$$

will lead to the output of current values of KOUNT, SUM and X on a single line of print. Note that KOUNT is an integer variable and that the corresponding place in the FORMAT statement contains an integer specification. Suppose that the values in memory are KOUNT = 27, SUM = +123.45600 and X = −115.15100 or their equivalent in machine language. The line

$$\text{ss27sss123.46ss−115.15}$$

will be printed, and placed as far to the left as possible on the print line.

The second and last specification statement to be included in this introductory chapter on the Fortran language is the following.

The END statement. This reads simply

$$END$$

and tells the Fortran compiler that the end of the source program has been reached. The END statement must be the very last statement of every Fortran program.

Notice that END is entirely different from STOP. The latter terminates the execution of the object program; the former is not present in the object program, no machine language instructions being generated from it. END is just a signal to the compiler that no more Fortran statements are involved in the program in question.

Operating procedure provides the link between a computation as programmed by the human user and that same computation in actual execution by the machine. It is a vital link in the chain of communication since it makes the various statements and data available in electrical form as input information to the computer, and at the other end of the job, arranges for the output information to be collected. There are variations in procedure from one computing facility to another but the general plan remains basically the same. Here we discuss first the procedure in which punched cards play the central input role. The principal alternative is the time-sharing console, and remarks concerning its use will follow.

In card operations the first step toward electrification of the program may be its transfer to a coding form. If the programmer plans to punch his own cards this step is probably not necessary. Otherwise the similarity between card and form layout allows the programmer to make his intentions perfectly clear to the punch operator. Although a card has 80 columns the coding form has only 72, since procedure places limits on where Fortran statements may be punched. As mentioned earlier numerical data may be punched anywhere in the 80 columns, the format being explained to the computer in an accompanying FORMAT statement. Fortran statements, however, do not extend beyond column 72 and usually begin in column 7.

Example 7.21.
The six statements of Example 7.12 would appear on a coding form as shown in Fig. 7-3.

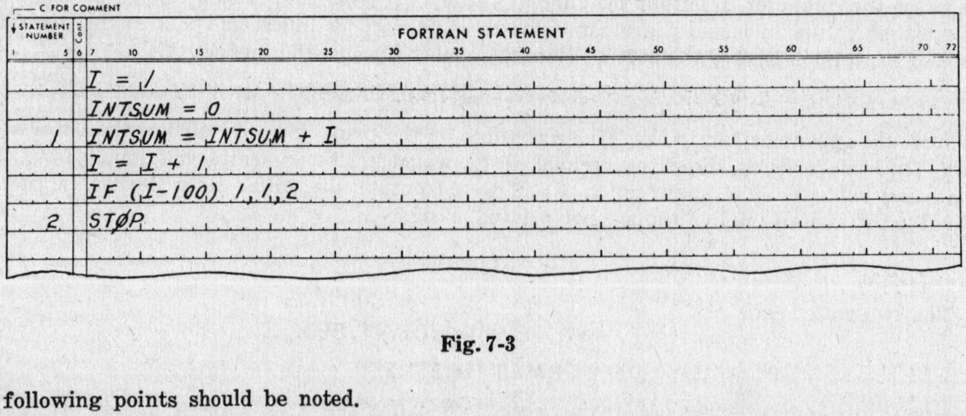

Fig. 7-3

The following points should be noted.

1. Each character is placed in the column it is to occupy on the card, including the equality sign, plus sign, parentheses, comma, etc. Note that the letters O and I are represented as $\emptyset$ and I respectively since they can be easily confused with digits 0 and 1.

2. Each statement appears on its own line, even though there may have been an abundance of space left on the preceding line. Since each line of the coding form corresponds to a card, this also implies that each statement will appear on a separate card.

3. Statements are written between columns 7 and 72, the area designated for them on the form. Though it is not strictly essential to begin them all in column 7, this is usually done.

4. Spaces have been left blank here and there. This may be done at the programmer's pleasure to facilitate reading by either him or the person who will punch the corresponding cards. Only in certain special circumstances are spaces significant in the Fortran language and these circumstances will be carefully described later. This means that spaces could also have been left if wanted in the statements as presented in Examples 7.11, 7.12 and so on, or in handwritten preliminary versions.

5. The statement numbers 1 and 2 have been placed in the five columns designated for them on the form. Any columns in this area would have been suitable but a consistent and neat policy has often been found to minimize errors and is recommended on that basis.

As already mentioned the second step in operating procedure is the transferral of information as recorded on the coding form to a set of punched cards. Because of the similarity in layouts this can be done by someone unacquainted with the program. Using a device called a card-punch, somewhat similar to an ordinary typewriter, each line of the coding form is copied character by character. Depressing the key corresponding to any particular character causes a combination of holes to be punched in the card column currently in position, the combination being determined according to the code illustrated in Fig. 4-31.

Example 7.22.
    The six statements on the coding form of Fig. 7-3 would be punched on six cards. Two of these cards are shown in Fig. 7-4. Notice the correspondence between columns from the form to the cards.

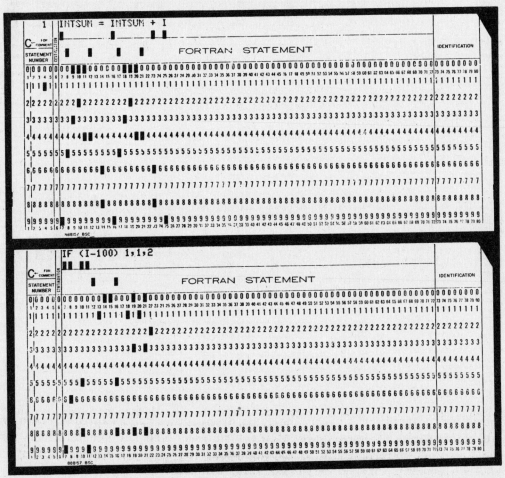

Fig. 7-4

Control cards are another necessary element of operating procedure. To avoid confusion it should be mentioned at once that the word control, as used here, has a meaning somewhat different from what it signifies in the expression "control statement". The latter is a statement in the Fortran language, perhaps a GO TO or an IF. A control card serves a purpose outside the Fortran language. Most modern computer centers offer a variety of opportunities and services to their customers. The programmer who enters with his Fortran cards in hand must tell the machine that it is the Fortran language which he has used, rather than some other language in which the machine is also fluent. He must also indicate precisely what he wants done. Is the program to be compiled and an object program in machine language punched out? Or is the program, assuming it proves to be free of errors, to be executed as soon as possible? If errors are found during compilation, which of the many aids to "debugging" is the machine requested to output? These are just a few examples of questions the programmer must answer. The answers to such questions are communicated to the machine by means of control cards. Because the precise nature of such cards varies so much from one computing center to another, no effort will be made to offer details here. They must be obtained by consulting the operating staff of the particular center to be used. Generally speaking, control cards may be needed at any of three places in the supply of input information: at the beginning, just after the Fortran cards but before the data cards and at the end. Fig. 7-5 suggests this same pattern.

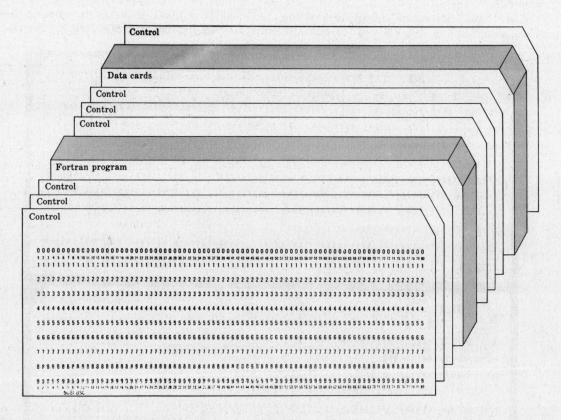

Fig. 7-5

Time-sharing operation involves the same procedural steps as in card operations, the cards being replaced by lines typed at the terminal. The statements which form the program and other necessary data are typed directly and enter the machine through special input-output circuitry. Instead of control cards one uses certain control commands which also are typed directly at the terminal. These serve to identify the user, to indicate when a program is to be typed, when compilation is expected and by which processor, when data are to be entered, when execution should begin, and so on. Perhaps the most significant difference between card and terminal operations is that with the latter the computer often types responses to the commands given, signaling that information has been received, that it is being processed, or perhaps explaining delays. The result is an almost conversational relationship between programmer and computer.

Solved Problems

7.1. Which of the following are not proper symbols for integer constants in the Fortran language?

$$1620 \quad +1620 \quad -1620 \quad 1O \quad 1A \quad 2*3 \quad 0. \quad 001$$

The fourth, fifth and sixth symbols cannot be used for integer constants because they involve characters which are not digits, specifically the O, A and *. The seventh symbol must also be disallowed because of the decimal point, which indicates the real rather than the integer mode.

7.2. Which of the following are not proper symbols for real constants in the Fortran language? Assume that the integer mode is not wanted.

$$1620. \quad +1620. \quad -1620. \quad 16.20 \quad -0.1620 \quad 0.$$

$$1620 \quad REAL \quad 1620.16201620 \quad \tfrac{1}{2} \quad 1/2 \quad .5$$

The first five symbols of the second row are all improper. The first lacks the decimal point which is the identifying feature of real constants. The second is suitable for a real variable but only digits, and of course sign and decimal point, may be used for a real constant. The third contains more than the allowed nine significant digits, while $\tfrac{1}{2}$ and / are again forbidden characters. The symbol $\tfrac{1}{2}$ does not exist in the Fortran language. The slash / does exist and is used for other purposes.

7.3. Express the following in ordinary decimal form.

$$.16200000E+04 \quad -.16200000E+02 \quad -.16200000E-04$$

$$.10000000E+01 \quad -.10000000E-02 \quad .10000000E-05$$

Dropping unnecessary zeros for simplicity, we have

$$1620. \qquad -16.2 \qquad -.0000162$$

$$1. \qquad -.001 \qquad .000001$$

the exponent indicating as usual the number of places which the decimal point is to be shifted right or left.

7.4. Which of the following are not proper symbols for real constants in exponential form?

$$1620.E-02 \quad 16.20E+02 \quad .1620E4 \quad 1620E4.$$

Only the last one is incorrect, and not because a decimal point is lacking in the 1620 since this is accepted by the compiler, but instead because a decimal point is present in the exponent.

7.5. Which of the following may not be used as names for integer-variables?

$$\text{ONE} \quad \text{NINE} \quad \text{NONE} \quad \text{MONEY} \quad \text{METOO} \quad \text{ME2} \quad \text{I+J}$$

The first because it starts with a disapproved letter and the last because it contains a character other than letters and digits.

7.6. Which of the following may not be used as names for real variables not in integer mode?

$$\text{REAL} \quad \text{VARIABLE} \quad \text{ONE} \quad \text{1UP} \quad \text{INCOME} \quad \text{A+B} \quad \text{K9}$$

The second symbol is too long. The fourth, fifth and last start with disapproved characters. The sixth contains the + character. Only the first and third symbols are acceptable.

7.7. Convert the following into Fortran expressions.

(a) $2I + 3J$ (c) $A^2 - 4B$ (e) $(A + B + C)^2$ (g) $\left(\dfrac{A}{B}\right)^2$ (i) $\dfrac{A + B}{C + D}$ (k) $\dfrac{A}{B} + \dfrac{C}{D}$

(b) $2A + 3B$ (d) $2(A + B)$ (f) $\frac{1}{2}(I + J)$ (h) $I^2 - 4J$ (j) $2IJK$ (l) $-AB$

Assuming that I, J denote integers while A, B denote real mode, we have

$$(a) \quad 2*I + 3*J \qquad \text{and} \qquad (b) \quad 2.*A + 3.*B$$

the presence or absence of decimal points being important. The following columns translate into Fortran language as

(c) $A**2 - 4.*B$ (e) $(A + B + C)**2$ (g) $(A/B)**2$ (i) $(A + B)/(C + D)$ (k) $(A/B) + (C/D)$

(d) $2.*(A + B)$ (f) $(I + J)/2$ (h) $I**2 - 4*J$ (j) $2*I*J*K$ (l) $(-1.)*A*B$

Entry (f) requires a further comment. Presumably the sum $I + J$ is to be an even integer, in which case division by 2 will produce another integer. If, however, $I + J$ happens to be odd, then the integer mode of operation will retain only the integer part of the quotient, the extra $\frac{1}{2}$ being truncated. Thus $(1 + 2)/2$ will prove to be 1.

Note that in every case some acceptable alternatives exist.

7.8. What is wrong with each of the following Fortran expressions?

(a) $A**I + 2$ (c) $A*B + A* - C$ (e) $4*A*C$

(b) $(A + B**2$ (d) $AB + C/D$ (f) $A**(I + 2.)$

As it stands (a) mixes the real mode $A**I$ with the integer mode 2 and so is not allowed. The intended result might be either $A**I + 2.$ or $A**(I + 2)$, the meanings of the two being of course quite different. (b) has an incomplete set of parentheses. If no parentheses were intended then the form $A + B**2$ would be allowed, while $(A + B)**2$ is also intelligible Fortran. It would be hard to guess from the given form which of these two was intended, and one should not expect the Fortran compiler to make such guesses. For (c) the expression $A*B + A*(-C)$ seems clearly indicated. Rule 5, page 117, requires that the parentheses be used here. The alternative $A*(B - C)$ is still simpler. In (d) we find a missing multiplication sign, the correct and intended result apparently being $A*B + C/D$. Then another example of mixed modes occurs in (e), and the correct expression is $4.*A*C$, showing the missing decimal point. The final expression in (f) also mixes the modes and this time we remove a decimal point to obtain $A**(I + 2)$, which brings us back to where the problem began.

7.9. With A = 6., B = 5., C = 3. and D = 2. evaluate the Fortran expressions of Problem 7.7 which contain these variables. Keep in mind the priority of arithmetic operations given in Rule 3, page 116, and Rule 4, page 117.

We find

(b) 2.*A + 3.*B = 12. + 15. = 27.

(c) A**2 − 4.*B = 36. − 4.*B = 36. − 20. = 16.

(d) 2.*(A + B) = 2.*11. = 22.

(e) (A + B + C)**2 = 14.**2 = 196.

(g) (A/B)**2 = 1.2**2 = 1.44

(i) (A + B)/(C + D) = 11./5. = 2.2

(k) (A/B) + (C/D) = 1.2 + 1.5 = 2.7

(l) (−1.)*A*B = −30.

7.10. With I = 7, J = 3 and K = 2 evaluate the Fortran expressions of Problem 7.7 which contain these integer variables.

We find

(a) 2*I + 3*J = 14 + 9 = 23

(f) (I + J)/2 = 10/2 = 5

(h) I**2 − 4*J = 49 − 4*J = 49 − 12 = 37

(j) 2*I*J*K = 14*J*K = 42*K = 84

the multiplications in the last expression being taken from left to right.

7.11. Using the results of the preceding two problems describe the action taken by the computer in executing the following arithmetic statements.

$$SUM = 2.*A + 3.*B$$
$$FORCE = A**2 − 4.*B$$
$$Z = 2.*(A + B)$$
$$KOUNT = 2*I + 3*J$$

The execution of an arithmetic Fortran statement involves computation of the expression on the right side followed by storage of the value obtained in the memory location assigned to the variable whose name appears on the left side. Thus the real values 27., 16. and 22. would be stored under the names SUM, FORCE and Z in that order, and the integer value 23 would be stored as KOUNT.

7.12. Again using the values A = 6. and B = 5., what would be the effect of the Fortran statements

$$A = A + B$$
$$B = (A + B)**2$$

executed one after the other as part of a larger program?

At the start the real values 6. and 5. are in memory under the names A and B. The first instruction replaces A by the new

$$A = 6. + 5. = 11.$$

The second instruction then replaces B by the new

$$B = (11. + 5.)**2 = 16.**2 = 256.$$

The point is that the current value of any variable is the one which participates in the computation. In fact it is the only value the variable then has, any previous values having been erased from memory. In the same spirit, if the third instruction

$$SUM = A + B$$

were to follow next it would place in the memory location assigned to the variable SUM the value

$$SUM = 11. + 256. = 267.$$

7.13. Suppose the following are consecutive statements of a Fortran program, the initial values of A, B, C also being provided. Supply the missing values of each variable after execution of each statement.

	A	B	C
Initial values	5.0	1.0	2.0

$$B = A/C$$
$$A = B + C$$
$$C = B**2 - A**2$$
$$A = A - B$$
$$B = B**A$$
$$C = 2.*B + A**2 + C$$
$$A = A*B$$

This sequence of statements has no particular significance, serving merely as an exercise in the continual use of current values of variables. At each step only the variable named on the left side of the statement being executed will change. First we compute

$$B = A/C = 5.0/2.0 = 2.5$$

and store this in place of the old value of B. Next comes the new

$$A = B + C = 2.5 + 2.0 = 4.5$$

followed by

$$C = 2.5**2 - 4.5**2 = -14.0, \quad A = 4.5 - 2.5 = 2.0$$

$$B = 2.5**2.0 = 6.25, \quad C = 2.*6.25 + 2.**2 + (-14.) = 2.5$$

and finally

$$A = 2.*6.25 = 12.5$$

so that the terminal values are $A = 12.5$, $B = 6.25$ and $C = 2.5$.

7.14. What is achieved by execution of the following program?

```
        I = 1
        INTSUM = 0
      1 INTSUM = INTSUM + I
        IF (I - 100) 2, 3, 3
      2 I = I + 1
        GO TO 1
      3 STOP
        END
```

The integers from 1 to 100 will again be summed, as in Examples 7.12 and 7.13. To see this note first that I and INTSUM are initialized in the first two statements. INTSUM is then increased by 1 and the IF sends the computation to statement 2. Here I is raised to 2, after which the GO TO returns the action to statement 1. INTSUM is now increased by 2 and the second pass through the loop has begun. Ultimately statement 2 raises I to 100 and the action returns to statement 1 for the last time. INTSUM is increased by 100 and the IF then diverts control to statement 3. The difference between this program and that of Example 7.12 is minor. The IF and I = I + 1 statements appear in reversed order. The middle exit of the IF must therefore stop the computation now being analyzed, because I = 100 will already have been added to INTSUM. Note also that the END statement has been included as the very last statement, to signal to the compiler that no further statements need be sought.

7.15. What is achieved by execution of the following program?

$$I = 1$$
$$ISODSQ = 0$$
$$1 \quad ISODSQ = ISODSQ + I*I$$
$$I = I + 2$$
$$IF (I - 100) \, 1, 2, 2$$
$$2 \quad STOP$$
$$END$$

The first two statements provide initial values for the variables I and ISODSQ. The second of these is then increased by the amount 1*1, after which I is raised to 3. The IF then returns the computation to statement 1 which increases ISODSQ by 3*3. The loop is fairly conspicuous and will continue until ISODSQ has been increased by 99*99, at which point I will be raised to 101 and the IF will divert control to the STOP. The sum of the squares of odd integers from 1 to 99 is thus computed. In this program the middle exit of the IF never operates, but some statement number occurring in the program must be placed there even so to satisfy the Fortran compiler. The same remark applies to the third exit of the IF in the preceding problem.

7.16. What is achieved by execution of the following program?

$$J = 1$$
$$ISPROD = 0$$
$$1 \quad I = 1$$
$$2 \quad ISPROD = ISPROD + I*J$$
$$I = I + 1$$
$$IF (I - 10) \, 2, 2, 3$$
$$3 \quad J = J + 1$$
$$IF (J - 10) \, 1, 1, 4$$
$$4 \quad STOP$$
$$END$$

The first three statements provide initial values for the variables J, ISPROD and I. The second of these is then increased by the amount 1*1, after which I is raised to 2 and the IF returns the computation to statement 2. ISPROD is now increased by 2*1 and the loop consisting of the fourth, fifth and sixth statements is cycled until 3*1, 4*1, ..., 10*1 have all been added to ISPROD. At this point the IF sends the action to statement 3 which raises J to 2. The second IF then diverts control back to statement 1 which restores I to its initial value of 1. Now ISPROD is increased by 1*2 and the loop referred to above is again cycled until 2*2, 3*2, ..., 10*2 have also been added to this variable. It is then once again time for statement 3, which raises J to 3. The pattern continues with this new value of J, the variable ISPROD being increased by 1*3, 2*3, ..., 10*3. Finally J will reach 11, and the second IF will call upon statement 4 which is the STOP. When this happens ISPROD will be the sum of all products of the form I*J, where I and J are the integers from 1 to 10. This program illustrates what is called a loop within a loop, as the flow-chart of the next problem will make still clearer. Loops within loops are handled even more conveniently by use of the DO statement. Examples of this will be provided shortly.

7.17. Prepare a flow-chart for the computation of the preceding problem.

The chart of Fig. 7-6 below displays the essential features of the computation. After providing initial values the computation enters the inner loop at the upper right corner, cycles this loop until I reaches 11, then starts leftward across the bottom row. After J is increased to 2 the upward turn is taken, I is reset to 1, and the inner loop is again cycled until I regains the value 11. At this point J is increased to 3 and the pattern of ten cycles of the inner loop for every one of the outer loop continues until J reaches 11, when the STOP statement is encountered. The chart makes the loop within the loop fairly clear.

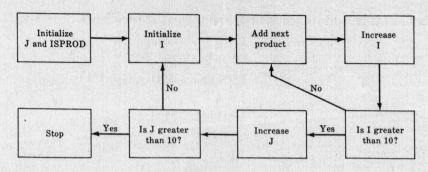

Fig. 7-6

7.18. What will be the ultimate value of SUM in this program?

$$X = 1.$$
$$SUM = 0.$$
$$1 \quad IF (10. - X) \, 3, 3, 2$$
$$2 \quad SUM = SUM + 1./X$$
$$X = X + 1.$$
$$GO \; TO \; 1$$
$$3 \quad STOP$$
$$END$$

Notice first that X and SUM are in real rather than integer mode, and that their initial values and certain other constants are also given in real mode. The first two statements again provide initial values. The IF sends the action to statement 2 and the reciprocal of 1. is added to SUM. Then X is raised to 2. and the GO TO returns the action to statement 1. The loop consisting of the third through sixth statements is now traveled until X attains the value 10. at which point the IF diverts control to the STOP. At this point SUM will be the sum of the reciprocals of all integers from one to nine inclusive. The real mode is needed here since such reciprocals are surely not integers.

7.19. Prepare a flow-chart for the computation of the preceding problem.

Fig. 7-7 shows the course of action. This chart is simpler than that of Problem 7.17 in that there is only a single loop. In fact, what we have here may be considered the classic pattern for a machine computation. After certain preparations, assignment of initial values or whatever, the computation enters a loop, which it cycles some specified number of times and then leaves. This classic pattern may be found twice in the chart of Problem 7.17, once for each loop, and larger programs will be seen to be more intricate combinations of the same pattern.

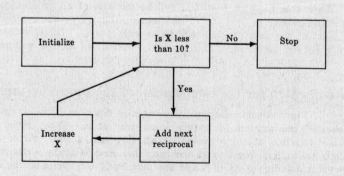

Fig. 7-7

7.20. Where does the END statement figure in the flow-charts just presented?

It does not. These charts represent the course of the computation made in executing the object program, the computation which has been the programmer's objective all along. The END statement is involved in the translation process which converts the programmer's Fortran statements into machine language, and its job is finished before the computation represented by the chart can begin.

7.21. Replace the program of Problem 7.15 by one which achieves the same result using a DO statement, and then prints this result.

Various possibilities exist, including the following.

```
        ISODSQ = 0
        DO 1 I = 1, 99, 2
1       ISODSQ = ISODSQ + I*I
        WRITE (6, 9) ISODSQ
9       FORMAT (I10)
        STOP
        END
```

After ISODSQ has been initialized at 0, the DO statement arranges for all the odd squares from 1*1 to 99*99 to be added to it. The terminal 2 in this DO provides for the index I to be increased by 2 at each step, rather than by 1 which is more often the case, thus assuring that only odd integer values will arise. The WRITE then activates output unit number 6, say a printer, and the terminal value of ISODSQ is printed in format 9. It will be seen that the companion FORMAT statement does specify a single integer output and allows ten positions for it. A simple estimate will show that this is more than enough space.

7.22. Replace the program of Problem 7.16 by one which achieves the same result using two DO statements, and then prints this result.

Here is one possibility.

```
        ISPROD = 0
        DO 1 J = 1, 10
        DO 1 I = 1, 10
1       ISPROD = ISPROD + I*J
        WRITE (6, 9) ISPROD
9       FORMAT (I10)
        STOP
        END
```

Here we have an example of "nested" DO statements, meaning that the entire range of one DO statement is located within the range of another DO. In such a case execution proceeds in this order. First J takes the value 1 and the inner DO runs its course, that is, the index I of the inner DO runs through the values 1 to 10. Control then returns to the outer DO and J becomes 2, the inner DO then running its course once again. This continues until J becomes 10 and the inner DO runs for the last time. At this point both DO statements have run their course. It will be seen that in a sense it is the outer DO which takes control, the inner being treated as just another statement in its range. The range of the first DO thus consists of the two statements which follow it, including the second DO. The range of the second DO is simply statement number 1. The WRITE statement then arranges for ISPROD to be printed, the format specification again being more than ample.

7.23. Replace the program of Problem 7.18 by one which achieves the same result using a DO statement, and then prints this result.

Such a program introduces a feature of the Fortran arithmetic statement not mentioned up to this point.

$$
\begin{aligned}
&\text{SUM} = 0. \\
&\text{DO 1 I} = 1, 9 \\
&\text{X} = \text{I} \\
1\ \ &\text{SUM} = \text{SUM} + 1./\text{X} \\
&\text{WRITE (6, 2) SUM} \\
2\ \ &\text{FORMAT (F10.6)} \\
&\text{STOP} \\
&\text{END}
\end{aligned}
$$

The statement referred to above is, of course, $X = I$. Since the computation must be made this time in the real mode, and since the index I is in integer mode, the statement

$$\text{SUM} = \text{SUM} + 1./\text{I}$$

would clearly violate the rule about mixing modes in an arithmetic expression. The Fortran compiler will, however, accept and translate $X = I$ so that the integer I will be represented in real form as the new variable X. More generally, a statement such as

$$X = \text{integer mode expression}$$

will lead to the computation indicated on the right followed by the storing of the integer which results, with a decimal point added, as the value of X. Similarly a statement such as

$$I = \text{real mode expression}$$

will bring computation of the expression and storage of its integer part, discarding any fraction, as the value of I. The remainder of the above program presents no new features. The final value of SUM will be printed to six decimal places. Since it is slightly less than 3 the allotted ten spaces will be sufficient.

7.24. An airplane flying at altitude A passes directly **over a point P.** If its speed is S compute its distance from point P at times $T = 1, 2, 3, \ldots, 60$ after the pass.

Fig. 7-8 may be helpful. The distance traveled by the airplane after passing over point P is ST, and the required distance has been called D. An ancient geometric result then guarantees that these three distances are related to each other. Specifically

$$D = \sqrt{A^2 + (ST)^2}$$

or in the Fortran language

$$D = \text{SQRT}(A**2 + (S*T)**2).$$

A program to achieve the given objective may now be written.

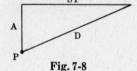

Fig. 7-8

$$
\begin{aligned}
&\text{READ (5, 1) S, A} \\
1\ \ &\text{FORMAT (2F7.2)} \\
&\text{WRITE (6, 1) S, A} \\
&\text{DO 2 I} = 1, 60 \\
&\text{T} = \text{I} \\
&\text{D} = \text{SQRT}(\text{A**2} + (\text{S*T})**2) \\
2\ \ &\text{WRITE (6, 5) T, D} \\
5\ \ &\text{FORMAT (F5.0, F10.3)} \\
&\text{STOP} \\
&\text{END} \\
&\text{Data card for S and A}
\end{aligned}
$$

Notice first that the values of S and A are not written into the program itself, but are to be supplied on a data card which the READ statement will call for when the program is executed. This is one way of allowing for the possibility that various combinations of S and A values may be needed. A new combination can be accommodated simply by changing the data card. Since this data card follows the END statement, it is not involved in the compiling process, which means that one compilation is sufficient, the object program being reusable as desired. It is convenient to print out the values of S and A so that they will appear with the computed distances. The DO statement then takes care of the computation in question and also the printing out of the T, D pairs. It is not necessary for us to know how the square root is to be found, this being accomplished by a standard subroutine already in machine memory, but some details of this process will be brought out in a later chapter. The statement $T = I$ plays the same sort of role as the $X = I$ of the preceding problem. Returning briefly to the matter of the data card, suppose that $S = .10$ and $A = 3.00$ are the desired values. Then according to FORMAT statement 1 each of these should occupy seven columns of the card, which takes the form shown in Fig. 7-9 if each value is right-justified in its own field.

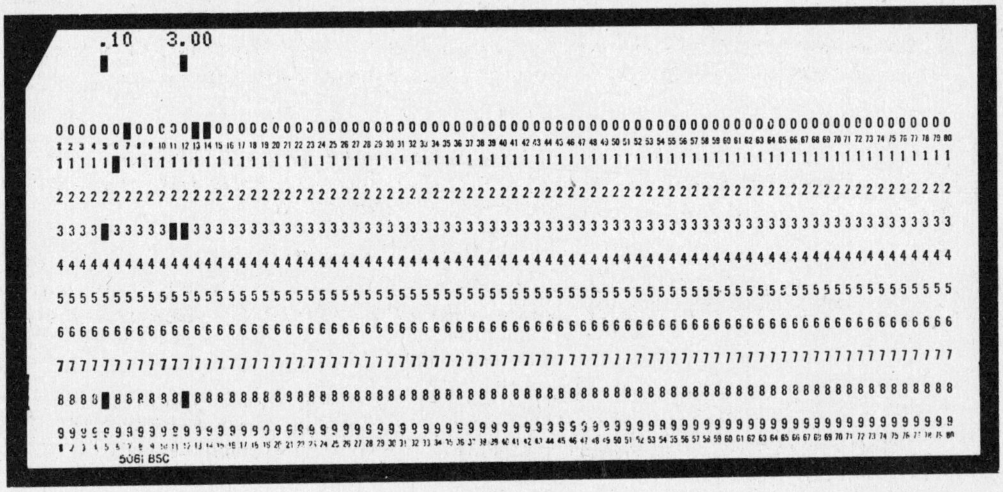

Fig. 7-9

In view of FORMAT statement 5 the final output pattern will be as appears in Table 7.1, the top line giving S and A while the other sixty lines display the T, D pairs. Providing five spaces for T and ten for D leaves room between them and facilitates reading the printed page. Here as before the letter s, which is *not* printed during actual output, serves to indicate a blank space, while the letter x denotes digits to be supplied by the computer. All lines of print will be placed as far to the left as the printer can manage.

sss0.10sss3.00

sss1.sssss3.xxx

sss2.sssss3.xxx

. . . .

ss60.sssss6.xxx

Table 7.1

7.25. The preceding problem is to be changed so that the three values $S = .10, .15$ and $.20$ are treated, in each case A taking the values $3.00, 3.05, 3.10, \ldots, 5.00$. Though the program just considered could be used, a quick count shows that 123 pairs of S, A values are involved. Rather than punch 123 data cards, prepare a new program.

As usual there are many possibilities. Each of the three variables S, A, T must now run through a sequence of values and the following program achieves this in a different way for each one.

```
1  READ (5, 2) S
2  FORMAT (2F7.2)
   A = 3.00
3  WRITE (6, 2) S, A
   DO 4 I = 1, 60
   T = I
   D = SQRT(A**2 + (S*T)**2)
4  WRITE (6, 5) T, D
5  FORMAT (F5.0, F10.3)
   IF (A − 5.00) 6, 1, 1
6  A = A + .05
   GO TO 3
   END
   Data card (S = .10)
   Data card (S = .15)
   Data card (S = .20)
```

A number of comments are in order. Starting at the top, though only one number is to be read the accompanying FORMAT statement provides for two. This sort of generosity in specifying format will not lead to error. The various specifications included in the FORMAT statement will be used from left to right in so far as they are needed; if more are present than are needed the excess will be ignored. In the present case both specifications are the same and S will be read according to F7.2. Notice that the WRITE which follows a moment later uses the FORMAT statement full strength. The DO loop then arranges for T to run through its sequence of values exactly as in the preceding problem, and for the output of the T, D pairs in the same format used there. It is then the turn for the IF to play its role. For A less than five control passes to statement number 6, which increases A to the next required value, after which the GO TO returns the action to statement 3 for a repetition with the same S but a new A. Many such repetitions follow, with A finally taking the value 5.00, when the IF produces a jump to the original READ. The entire pattern is then repeated with each remaining S value. In retrospect one sees that the computation contains three loops, one within the other. The innermost loop sequences the T values, and is controlled by the DO statement. Enclosing this loop is another which sequences the A values, and is governed by the IF. Enclosing both is the outermost loop, which sequences the S values through use of the READ. Clearly there exists a variety of techniques for creating loops and the programmer must choose what he feels the most suitable for the occasion. As a final comment, the present program contains no STOP statement. Computation will end when the READ statement finds no data cards left in the card reader.

The output from this program will be fairly substantial. First the content of Table 7.1 will appear, since the present computation begins just like that of the preceding problem. This is already 61 lines of print. But then a similar table will appear for every other S, A combination, beginning with S = .10, A = 3.05 and finishing with S = .20, A = 5.00, and as pointed out a moment ago this amounts to 123 combinations altogether. With 61×123 lines of print anticipated it might be well to check the paper supply before pushing the start button.

7.26. Prepare a flow-chart of the computation of the preceding problem.

Many programmers make preparation of the flow-chart the first step in programming. For the moment they are being used here mostly to obtain a second view of a program already studied. With more complex programs to appear later, we shall reverse this order of operation. The present chart appears in Fig. 7-10 below. Note especially the three loops, each within the next. The innermost loop is simply the DO loop.

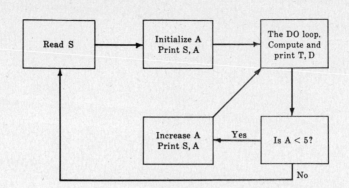

Fig. 7-10

7.27. A new road is to be built linking highways 1492 and 1620 and passing through the town of Plymouth which is located as suggested in Fig. 7-11. Exactly where should this road be placed if it is to be as short as possible?

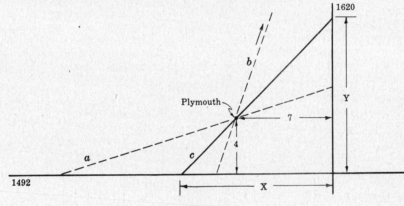

Fig. 7-11

A brief experiment with paper and ruler shows that extreme positions such as a and b make the new road very long and that an intermediate position such as c seems to minimize its length. To determine the minimum position more precisely let X and Y be distances as labeled. The same theorem of geometry used in the airplane problem now assigns the length

$$L = \sqrt{16 + (X - 7)^2} + \sqrt{49 + (Y - 4)^2}$$

to the new road. Since the road is to be straight it is also true that

$$(Y - 4)/7 = 4/(X - 7)$$

making $(Y - 4) = 28/(X - 7)$ and consequently

$$L = \sqrt{16 + (X - 7)^2} + \sqrt{49 + (28/(X - 7))^2}.$$

A few simple trial computations are now in order. For instance, if $X = 9$ we easily find

$$L = \sqrt{20} + \sqrt{245} = 20 \text{ (approximately)}$$

while for $X = 11$ and $X = 14$,

$$L = \sqrt{32} + \sqrt{98} = 15 \text{ (approximately)}$$
$$L = \sqrt{65} + \sqrt{65} = 16 \text{ (approximately)}$$

in that order. It would seem that the minimum length for the road is near 15 and that the distance X which achieves this minimum is about 11. This is useful information for programming a more detailed search. It suggests computing the values of L for a selection of X values running from roughly 9 upwards, and observing the decrease from a length of near 20 to one nearer 15 followed by a steady increase. The program below has this objective. Notice at once that the letter L, which seemed so natural for the length of the road, has been abandoned in favor of ROAD. This is due of course to the fact that in Fortran L would denote an integer mode variable.

```
      X = 9.
    1 Z = X - 7.
      ROAD = SQRT(16. + Z**2) + SQRT(49. + (28./Z)**2)
      WRITE (6, 2) X, ROAD
    2 FORMAT (2F7.2)
      IF (X - 14.) 3, 4, 4
    3 X = X + .01
      GO TO 1
    4 STOP
      END
```

The values of X run from 9 to 14, which by our trial computations should be more than sufficient. They are spaced .01 units apart. If the unit is a mile this is an interval of about fifty feet, which should be fine enough for the purpose. The variable Z is not really needed, and has been introduced only to make the expression for ROAD a little easier to read. The subroutine for evaluating square roots will be called upon twice for each computation of this expression, but again the inner workings of this routine need not concern us at the moment. Once more, however, we are open to the criticism that our demands for output are fairly greedy. A quick count shows that 501 pairs of numbers X, ROAD are to be printed, each on its own line. Since output is one of the slower operations, each programmer must struggle with his conscience and make a compromise between greed, necessity and economy. The 501 lines requested here will have the form indicated in Table 7.2, where as before the letter s denotes a blank space and the letter x a digit to be supplied by the computer.

```
sss9.00ss20.xx
sss9.01ss20.xx
.............
ss11.00ss15.xx
.............
ss13.99ss16.xx
ss14.00ss16.xx
```

Table 7.2

7.28. How may the program of Problem 7.24 be recorded on the Fortran coding form?

Although this is largely a matter of copying a handwritten or typed version, one or two further examples using the coding form may be useful, if only to show once again the columns which are reserved for the various ingredients. Fig. 7-12 shows the result for the program in question. Notice that information for the data card has also been included so that this necessary item will also be punched. The prescribed format for data must be observed, in this case F7.2.

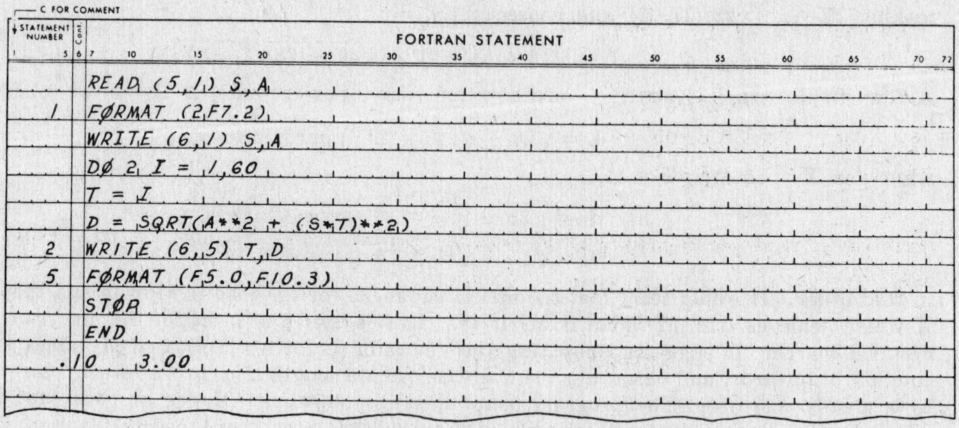
C FOR COMMENT
STATEMENT NUMBER
Cont.
FORTRAN STATEMENT
READ (5, 1) S, A
1 FØRMAT (2F7.2)
WRITE (6, 1) S, A
DØ 2 I = 1, 60
T = I
D = SQRT(A**2 + (S*T)**2)
2 WRITE (6, 5) T, D
5 FØRMAT (F5.0, F10.3)
STØP
END
.10 3.00

Fig. 7-12

7.29. Record the program of Problem 7.25 on a coding form.

The result appears in Fig. 7-13, the remarks made in the preceding problem being once again appropriate.

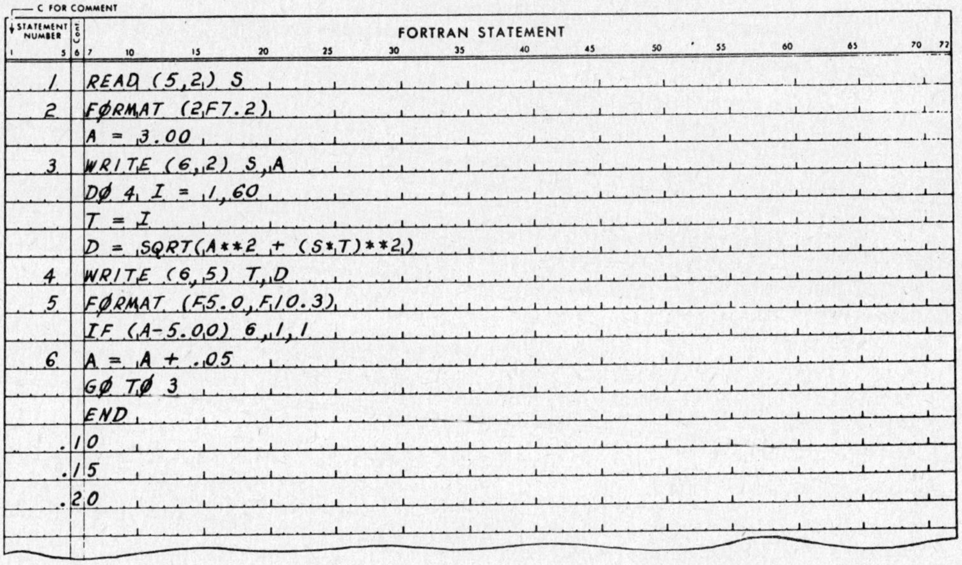

```
C FOR COMMENT
STATEMENT NUMBER          FORTRAN STATEMENT
   1     READ (5,2) S
   2     FORMAT (2F7.2)
         A = 3.00
   3     WRITE (6,2) S,A
         DO 4 I = 1,60
         T = I
         D = SQRT(A**2 + (S*T)**2)
   4     WRITE (6,5) T,D
   5     FORMAT (F5.0,F10.3)
         IF (A-5.00) 6,1,1
   6     A = A + .05
         GO TO 3
         END
  .10
  .15
  .20
```

Fig. 7-13

Supplementary Problems

7.30. Identify each of the following as an integer constant, a real constant, or an improper symbol.

$$0.1 \quad .200 \quad 200 \quad -0.0 \quad +0 \quad 1492.1620E-04$$
$$\#9 \quad \$1.98 \quad 1.1E1.1 \quad 1492- \quad 1+1 \quad 1.23E123$$

7.31. Which of these pairs represent the same number?

(a) 3.14   +03.14

(b) 3.14   +.314E+01

(c) .00314   314.E−05

(d) 3140   3.14E+03

7.32. Identify each of the following as an integer variable, a real variable, or an improper symbol for any variable.

ABCDEF	ITEM	VARIABLE	1A
THING	NO	AND/OR	A**2
DOLLAR	N0	A.B	A + B

7.33. Translate these Fortran expressions into ordinary arithmetic language.

$$A + B**2 \quad 2.*A*B \quad A**(I+2) \quad A + B/C \quad 2. + 3.*X$$

7.34. Convert the following into Fortran expressions.

$$3I + 4J \qquad N(N+1)/2 \qquad \tfrac{1}{2}LW \qquad 1/X^2 \qquad 1/(A+B)$$
$$3A + 4B \qquad 1 + 3.14R^2 \qquad AB + CD \qquad \frac{1}{A} + \frac{1}{B} \qquad X^2 + (2Y)^2$$

7.35. What is wrong with each of these Fortran expressions?

$$X{**}2 + 2 \qquad 2{*}X{*}Y{*}Z \qquad (A + B/C)) \qquad (1/2)(A + B)$$

7.36. With A = 6., B = 5., C = 3. and D = 2. evaluate the Fortran expressions below, keeping in mind the priorities of arithmetic operations.

$$A + 2.{*}B \qquad A/3. + B \qquad (A + B){**}2 \qquad A{**}2/(B + C + 2.{*}D)$$
$$C + D{**}2 \qquad A{**}2/C \qquad A + B{**}2 \qquad (A + B)/2. + C - D$$

7.37. Using the results of the preceding problem, describe the action taken by the computer in executing these arithmetic statements.

$$AL = A + 2.{*}B \quad BOB = (A + B){**}2 \quad CARL = A{**}2/C \quad DAN = A + B{**}2$$

7.38. Again using A = 6. and B = 5., what would be the result of

$$A = A + 2.{*}B \quad B = A/(B - 3.) \quad AB = A - 2.{*}B$$

being executed one after another?

7.39. Suppose the following are consecutive statements of a Fortran program, the initial values of A, B, C also being provided. Supply the missing values of each variable after execution of each statement.

	A	B	C
Initial values	6.0	5.0	3.0

```
C = A/B
A = B**2 - 3.*A
B = B + A
C = 10.*C - B
A = B
B = A*B*C
```

7.40. What is achieved by execution of the following program?

```
      I = 1
      INTSUM = 0
    1 INTSUM = INTSUM + I
      I = I + 1
      IF (I - 101) 1, 2, 2
    2 STOP
      END
```

7.41. What will be the ultimate value of INTSUM in this program?

```
      I = 1
      INTSUM = 0
    1 INTSUM = INTSUM + I
      I = I + 2
      IF (I - 100) 1, 2, 2
    2 STOP
      END
```

7.42. How could the program of the preceding problem be altered to sum the even integers from 2 to 100?

7.43. Modify the program of Problem 7.41 so that the final value of INTSUM is output.

7.44. What will be printed by this program?

```
          I = 1
          J = 1
      1   J = I*J
          I = I + 1
          IF (I − 10) 1, 1, 2
      2   WRITE (6, 3) J
      3   FORMAT (I10)
          STOP
          END
```

7.45. Replace the program of the preceding problem by one which uses a DO statement.

7.46. Using a DO statement, prepare a program for summing the reciprocal squares of the integers from 1 to 100, to six places.
$$\frac{1}{1^2} + \frac{1}{2^2} + \frac{1}{3^2} + \cdots + \frac{1}{100^2}$$

7.47. Replace the program of Problem 7.41 by one which uses a DO statement.

7.48. In Problem 7.24 how would the three separate cases A = 3.00, S = .10, .15 and .20 be handled?

7.49. Suppose a data card punched as follows,

ssss123ss4567

the first 13 columns being used. Which of these format specifications would lead to correct reading of the integers 123 and 4567?

FORMAT (2I7)   FORMAT (I7, I6)

FORMAT (I9, I4)   FORMAT (2I6)

What would be read by the other formats?

7.50. Suppose a data card punched as follows,

ss12.3ssss4.5

the first 13 columns being used. Which of these format specifications would lead to correct reading of 12.3 and 4.5?

FORMAT (F6.1, F7.1)   FORMAT (2F7.1)

FORMAT (F10.1, F3.1)   FORMAT (2F6.1)

7.51. Suppose a data card punched as follows,

sss.1234E+02sss.5670E−01

the first 24 columns being used. Which of these format specifications would lead to correct reading of 12.34 and .05670?

FORMAT (2E12.4)   FORMAT (2E13.4)

FORMAT (F12.4, F12.4)   FORMAT (E12.4, E12.4)

7.52. The integer 123 and the real number 1.234567 are to be printed out, the integer going as far to the left as possible on the line and two spaces being left between the two numbers. What format specifications will achieve this?

7.53. The integers 123 and 45, together with the numbers 14.92000 and 16.20000 are to be printed out. If two spaces are to be left between numbers, complete the following specification.

FORMAT (2I___, 2F_____)

7.54. Suppose that a computer stores each number in a form that is equivalent to eight decimal digits plus sign plus exponent. The example

$$-.12345678E-01$$

might be typical. (In actual memory this could very well be in binary rather than decimal form, but since in the Fortran language we use decimals and leave to the machine the task of translating to its own language this need not concern us here.) Often enough the programmer will not even know the approximate size of the results which his program is to output. This makes it hard to choose the integers w and d of the Fw.d specification, and explains the popularity of the E specification. For the above computer, what integers w and d should be chosen for the specification Ew.d?

7.55. Record the program of Problem 7.18 on a Fortran coding form.

7.56. Record the program of Problem 7.27 on a coding form.

7.57. A coin is tossed until heads finally appears, the tosser then being paid as many dollars as he has made tosses. If this is done over and over, what should be the average winning? Probability theory shows that this average is the limit of the sequence of numbers

$$S(N) = (\tfrac{1}{2})(1) + (\tfrac{1}{2})^2(2) + (\tfrac{1}{2})^3(3) + \cdots + (\tfrac{1}{2})^N(N).$$

Prepare a program for computing these S(N) one after another up to S(30) and outputting every fifth one. The theoretical limit is exactly 2. What does S(30) prove to be?

7.58. The numbers

$$P(N) = 4\left(1 - \frac{1}{3} + \frac{1}{5} - \frac{1}{7} + \cdots \pm \frac{1}{2N-1}\right)$$

are known to converge to π. The convergence proves to be terribly slow, however. Write a program to compute the P(N) up to P(1000), outputting every hundredth one. The thousandth should turn out to be 3.1405776, which is off in the third decimal place.

Chapter 8

Arrays

An array can be loosely described as a group of numbers. The simplest kind of array to be considered here is the one-dimensional array, or more briefly a *list*. The test scores

$$94, 63, 84, 72, 61, 96, 74, 76, 79, 69$$

present a familiar example. The numbers which form an array are called the *elements* and in applications they are usually related to each other in some way, perhaps being measurements of like kind as is the case with the above scores. Almost always the elements of an array are to be processed according to some computational pattern which is an outgrowth of the relationship between them; as a trivial example the test scores might all be added together as a first step toward finding their average value. For this reason it is convenient to be able to refer to an array, the entire group of numbers, by a single name. The above list could, for instance, be represented by the name LIST, or more simply by the single letter L. The name SCORE also suggests itself but with Fortran in mind it is important to recall the I, J, K, L, M, N convention for integer variables.

If we choose LIST to represent the entire array, then the individual elements may be denoted LIST(1), LIST(2), LIST(3) and so on, the number in parentheses indicating the position of the element in the array. Again taking the above example, LIST(1) would be the score 94, while LIST(2) would be 63, and so on. The integer within the parentheses is called a *subscript*, the word being carried over from the traditional form in which elements of a list are represented in ordinary arithmetic or algebra as $L_1, L_2, L_3, \ldots$ where the subscript actually appears on a lower level.

Somewhat more interesting is the two-dimensional array, or *matrix*. The numbers

27.25	30.50	31.25
48.50	48.75	46.25
74.00	78.50	82.25
2.50	7.00	25.00

present a typical example. Each row might represent the prices of a particular stock on January 1, April 1 and July 1 of a given year. Each column would then pertain to a single date. If we use the symbol PRICE to stand for the entire array, or matrix, then each individual element can be represented in the form PRICE(I, J) with I indicating the row of that element and J the column. For the matrix given, this would make

$$\text{PRICE}(1, 1) = 27.25 \qquad \text{PRICE}(1, 2) = 30.50$$
$$\text{PRICE}(2, 2) = 48.75 \qquad \text{PRICE}(4, 3) = 25.00$$

among others. The integers within the parentheses are again called subscripts, the common arithmetical symbol being of the form

$$P_{I,J}$$

with the subscripts at a lower level.

145

Both systems provide a convenient name for the array itself and for each individual element. The general idea of either system is easily extended to accommodate arrays of three or more "dimensions".

Arrays are represented in the Fortran language by variable names, observing the rules prescribed earlier. The individual elements of an array are indicated by attaching to the array name from one to three subscripts, enclosed in parentheses as in the examples of the preceding paragraph, and separated by commas if there is more than one. The variable itself is then called a *subscripted variable*. A number of rules must be observed in using subscripted variables.

Rule 1.

A subscript must be an integer. It may itself be a variable or one of these arithmetic combinations

$$a*v + b \qquad a*v - b$$

in which v is an integer variable and a, b are unsigned integer constants.

Example 8.1.

Acceptable subscripts include

$$1 \quad 1492 \quad I \quad INT \quad 2*I \quad 10*KOUNT$$
$$2*I + 3 \quad 2*I - 3 \quad 10*KOUNT + 2 \quad 1492*I - 3$$

whereas the following may not be used.

$$1 + I \quad -I \quad 2 - 10*KOUNT \quad -1492 - INTSUM$$

The sum $1 + I$ must be reversed so that the variable term leads, becoming $I + 1$. The remaining three combinations use negative multipliers, or place the constant term first, or involve subtraction of the variable term, all of which are forbidden by the Fortran compiler.

Rule 2.

A subscript must take only positive values. In a sense this could be considered as implied in Rule 1 but it is important enough to warrant special mention.

Rule 3.

A subscript must not itself be subscripted. Thus A(I(3)) is not allowed.

Rule 4.

A symbol that represents an array, a subscripted variable, should not also be used without subscripts to represent a different variable in the same program. Thus A(I) and A should not refer to different variables. In fact, only in certain special circumstances should an array itself be referred to by its own name without subscripts.

Example 8.2.

Symbols for real subscripted variables might include

$$A(INT) \quad A(I, J) \quad SUM(K + 2) \quad SUM(K + 3) \quad A(I, 2*J + 1) \quad X(I) \quad PRICE(I, J, K)$$

while for integer variables the following are suitable:

$$I(J) \quad INT(M, N) \quad KOUNT(2*I - 1)$$

The DIMENSION statement. This statement provides a way of telling the Fortran compiler how much memory space to set aside for subscripted variables. It takes the form

$$DIMENSION \ u, v, w, \ldots$$

where u, v, w... are variable names, each being followed by the maximum number of elements in the corresponding array. With this information the compiler can make adequate memory space available for the variables involved. The following rules must be observed.

Rule 1.

Every subscripted variable must be mentioned in a DIMENSION statement before its first use in the program.

Rule 2.

The symbols represented above by u, v, w, ... must have the form

variable name (maximum number of elements)

the variable name conforming to rules given earlier and the number in parentheses being an integer constant.

Rule 3.

The particular array to be used may have fewer elements than specified in the covering DIMENSION statement, but not more.

Rule 4.

The variable as it appears in the DIMENSION statement should have exactly the same number of subscripts as it has elsewhere in the program.

Example 8.3.

The variable LIST(I) where I is to take on 100 different values can be dimensioned by

DIMENSION LIST(100)

which will cause the compiler to reserve 100 memory locations under the name LIST. If I were to take on fewer than 100 values the same DIMENSION statement would suffice, though a certain amount of memory space would be left idle. Several variables can be dimensioned by the same DIMENSION statement. If, for instance, X(I), Y(I), Z(I) are all to be used with I running through 100 values, then

DIMENSION X(100), Y(100), Z(100)

would accommodate all three. Of course three separate DIMENSION statements could also be used. If X(I) and Y(J) were to have 100 and 50 values respectively, then

DIMENSION X(100), Y(50)

could be used. The point is to reserve enough memory space for all values involved without being too wasteful, that is, without keeping idle a large number of memory locations.

Example 8.4.

The matrix which was named PRICE(I, J) just a few moments ago could be dimensioned by

DIMENSION PRICE(4, 3)

since there were four rows and three columns of numbers in the array. If also A(M, N) were a 10×10 square array, meaning that it had ten rows and ten columns, then both could be covered by

DIMENSION PRICE(4, 3), A(10, 10)

all commas being necessary. Similarly the statement

DIMENSION LIST(100), PRICE(4, 3), A(10, 10)

would cover three subscripted variables, reserving a total of 212 memory locations under the three separate names. Notice that the variable A should not be dimensioned as A(100) even though the correct number of places would be reserved; the form A(10, 10) should be used since it follows the A(M, N) pattern of this two-dimensional array.

Input and output of arrays can be simplified by the use of extensions of the READ and WRITE statements presented earlier. For one-dimensional arrays the form

$$\text{READ } (5, 1) \text{ (LIST(I), I} = 1, 100)$$

would cause the reading of 100 numbers to be assigned to the memory locations reserved earlier for the variable LIST. All parentheses and commas shown in this form are necessary. This extension of the READ statement thus contains a sort of built-in DO loop which cycles the integer I through its 100 values and reads LIST(1), LIST(2), LIST(3), ... consecutively in the order of appearance in the card reader. The format must of course be given in statement number 1. In the same way the statement

$$\text{WRITE } (6, 1) \text{ (LIST(I), I} = 1, 100)$$

would bring the 100 values of the array LIST in the form of printed output. Again there is a built-in, or implied, DO loop in this extension of the WRITE statement presented earlier. Clearly the use of these two forms shortens the programmer's work in handling the input or output of large lists. An even simpler form is available for the (most common of all) case in which the size of the list to be read is precisely the size dimensioned for that variable, the maximum size. These two statements

$$\text{DIMENSION LIST(100)}$$

$$\text{READ } (5, 1) \text{ LIST}$$

could be used to read 100 values of the subscripted variable LIST. Notice that here the name of this variable appears without its subscript, simply as LIST and NOT as LIST(I). This is one of the rare situations in which the compiler will stand for omission of the subscript; in fact, here it *must* be omitted. In the same way the two statements

$$\text{DIMENSION LIST(100)}$$

$$\text{WRITE } (6, 1) \text{ LIST}$$

could be used to output this same list of 100 values. In all cases an appropriate FORMAT statement must accompany the READ or WRITE.

For two-dimensional arrays the form

$$\text{READ } (5, 1) \text{ ((PRICE(I, J), I} = 1, 4), J = 1, 3)$$

would cause the reading of 12 values to be assigned to the memory locations reserved for PRICE. The various parentheses and commas are again necessary, serving as indicators to the compiler that a DO loop within a second DO loop is actually involved. As usual it is the inner loop which runs the fastest, the I values cycling once for each fixed value of J. Another way of saying this is that the twelve values of PRICE will be called for column-wise, the entire J = 1 column being read, then the entire J = 2 column, and so on. The data must therefore be made available at the reader in this same order. In the same way the statement

$$\text{WRITE } (6, 1) \text{ ((PRICE(I, J), I} = 1, 4), J = 1, 3)$$

could be used for output of the PRICE matrix. Moreover, if the array to be read in or printed out is precisely of the size dimensioned in the covering DIMENSION statement, then simplification is again possible as above. The two statements

$$\text{DIMENSION PRICE(4, 3)}$$

$$\text{READ } (5, 1) \text{ PRICE}$$

would lead to the reading of the entire array of twelve elements. The order of input would be column-wise as before.

Similarly
$$\text{DIMENSION PRICE}(4,3)$$
$$\text{WRITE }(6,1)\text{ PRICE}$$
could be used to print out the entire array. As always, a suitable FORMAT statement
must accompany any READ or WRITE.

Often at the time a program is written the exact size of arrays in question will not be
known, or perhaps the program is to be capable of handling arrays up to a certain maximum size. Another extension of the input-output vocabulary is useful in such situations.
The pair of statements
$$\text{READ }(5,1)\text{ N},\ (X(I),\ I=1,N)$$
$$1\ \ \text{FORMAT }(I5/(10F6.3))$$
will, for instance, result in the following steps. First an integer will be read and stored
under the name N. As indicated in the companion FORMAT statement this integer will
occupy the first five columns of the input card, and must as always be right-justified in
this field. The second phase of the READ can then begin, the input of N values to be
stored under the name X. The symbol / which appears in the FORMAT statement means
that these values are not to be taken from the same card which provided the integer N,
but from the cards which follow. Suppose that N were 50. Then with the format shown,
which provides for ten values in specification F6.3 to each card, five more data cards must
be available. A covering DIMENSION statement is also needed, though not shown here,
to provide the maximum anticipated size of the array X. If this were 100 as suggested
earlier, then any N up to 100 would now be suitable. Moving up one dimension, the three
statements
$$\text{DIMENSION A}(10,10)$$
$$\text{READ }(5,1)\text{ K, L},\ ((A(M,N),\ M=1,K),\ N=1,L)$$
$$1\ \ \text{FORMAT }(2I5/(10F6.3))$$
will produce first the reading of two integers to be stored as K and L. These integers must
be available in the 2I5 specification on the first available card. Because of the / in the
FORMAT statement this card will then be abandoned, and the second phase of the READ
will input K*L numbers to be stored under the name A. These numbers are to be made
available ten to a card in specification 10F6.3, the last card perhaps not containing a full
ten. Thus if K = L = 8 in a particular case, eight data cards are needed for the complete
reading. The first must contain K and L; the next six have full quotas of ten values each;
the last card brings the final four values of A. Since the row index M is involved in the
inner loop, the read-in will proceed column-wise and values of A must be arranged in this
order on the cards.

Solved Problems

8.1. Why must each of the following be avoided in naming subscripts?

(a) $2 + I$ (b) COUNT (c) -1492 (d) $I(3)$ (e) $-2*I + 1$

(a) The $2 + I$ must be written with the variable first as $I + 2$. (b) The symbol COUNT does not represent an integer. (c) Subscripts must be positive, ruling out -1492. (d) They cannot themselves be subscripted, ruling out $I(3)$. (e) The negative multiplier -2 disallows the remaining entry.

8.2. Suppose that any three consecutive elements of a one-dimensional array are related by the equation

$$N(I + 2) = N(I + 1) + N(I)$$

If $N(1) = 1$ and also $N(2) = 1$, compute the next eight elements.

This problem provides an opportunity to become better acquainted with the symbolism for subscripted variables. Notice first that the three subscripts given are all of the form allowed by rules 1 to 4, and then that they are consecutive integers. This is what is meant by consecutive elements of the array; their subscripts are consecutive integers. To compute $N(3)$ from the given equation we now put I equal to 1 and find

$$N(3) = N(2) + N(1) = 1 + 1 = 2$$

which sets the pattern for the rest of the computation. Setting I equal to $2, 3, 4$ in succession brings

$$N(4) = N(3) + N(2) = 2 + 1 = 3$$
$$N(5) = N(4) + N(3) = 3 + 2 = 5$$
$$N(6) = N(5) + N(4) = 5 + 3 = 8$$

one after another. It soon becomes clear that in this array each element is the sum of the two just before it, so that $N(7) = 13$, $N(8) = 21$, $N(9) = 34$ and $N(10) = 55$ complete the required computation, though plainly the array could be extended to any desired length. The numbers of this array are called Fibonacci numbers and have appeared in a variety of applications.

8.3. If the array of the preceding problem is to be computed by machine for $I = 1, 30$, how may the variable $N(I)$ be dimensioned?

The statement
$$\text{DIMENSION N(30)}$$
would be sufficient.

8.4. Verify that the array

$$0 \quad 5 \quad 10 \quad 15 \quad 20 \quad 25$$

which will be represented by $M(J)$ for $J = 1, 6$ has the property

$$M(J) = \tfrac{1}{2}(M(J - 1) + M(J + 1))$$

or in words, that each element is the average of its two neighbors. In this equation J is restricted to the values $2, 3, 4, 5$.

Notice first that the subscripts $J - 1$ and $J + 1$ on the right make these two elements the neighbors of the element $M(J)$ on the left, which has subscript J. For $J = 2$ this average becomes

$$\tfrac{1}{2}(M(1) + M(3)) = \tfrac{1}{2}(0 + 10) = 5$$

and does equal $M(2)$. Similarly for $J = 3$ the average is

$$\tfrac{1}{2}(M(2) + M(4)) = \tfrac{1}{2}(5 + 15) = 10$$

which agrees with $M(3)$. For $J = 4, 5$ the verification is achieved in the same way.

8.5. Suppose that $A(I, J)$ are the elements of a two-dimensional array. The first row consists of the five numbers $1, 1, 1, 1, 1$. In the symbolism of subscripted variables

$$A(1, J) = 1 \qquad J = 1, 5$$

where I has been replaced by 1 to denote the first row and J takes the integer values 1 to 5. Suppose also that the rest of the first and fifth columns consist of zeros. In symbols

$$A(I, 1) = A(I, 5) = 0 \qquad I \neq 1$$

where J has been replaced by 1 and 5 to denote the two columns in question and $I \neq 1$ excludes the first row. Finally suppose that the relationship

$$A(I, J) = \tfrac{1}{2}(A(I-1, J-1) + A(I-1, J+1))$$

holds for $I \neq 1$ and $J = 2, 3, 4$. Use this relationship to compute values of $A(I, J)$ in the second to fourth columns.

As in the preceding two problems the purpose here is to develop familiarity with the subscript language. To begin, set I equal to 2 and rewrite the equation as

$$A(2, J) = \tfrac{1}{2}(A(1, J-1) + A(1, J+1))$$

Recalling that the first row consists entirely of 1s, this can at once be reduced to $A(2, J) = 1$. The J here must be restricted to the values $2, 3, 4$ so the first two rows of the array, or matrix, take the following form,

$$1 \quad 1 \quad 1 \quad 1 \quad 1$$
$$0 \quad 1 \quad 1 \quad 1 \quad 0$$

the two zeros having been specified earlier. Now set I equal to 3. The equation becomes

$$A(3, J) = \tfrac{1}{2}(A(2, J-1) + A(2, J+1))$$

With $J = 2, 3, 4$ successively this produces

$$A(3, 2) = \tfrac{1}{2}(A(2, 1) + A(2, 3)) = \tfrac{1}{2}(0 + 1) = \tfrac{1}{2}$$
$$A(3, 3) = \tfrac{1}{2}(A(2, 2) + A(2, 4)) = \tfrac{1}{2}(1 + 1) = 1$$
$$A(3, 4) = \tfrac{1}{2}(A(2, 3) + A(2, 5)) = \tfrac{1}{2}(1 + 0) = \tfrac{1}{2}$$

making the third row of the array $0, \tfrac{1}{2}, 1, \tfrac{1}{2}, 0$. Eventually it becomes clear that our basic equation here makes each interior value in the array the average of its two neighbors in the next row above and in adjacent columns. Each row thus determines all values in the row below it and the computation may be continued as long as desired. The next two rows, for instance, will prove to be $0, \tfrac{1}{2}, \tfrac{1}{2}, \tfrac{1}{2}, 0$ and $0, \tfrac{1}{4}, \tfrac{1}{2}, \tfrac{1}{4}, 0$. Computations of this sort, though on a much larger scale, occur often in applications involving the diffusion of one substance through another or the diffusion of energy.

8.6. If the matrix of the preceding problem is to be computed for 20 rows, how should the variable $A(I, J)$ be dimensioned?

Since 100 values of A will result, the statement

DIMENSION A(20, 5)

which reserves 100 memory locations will be adequate.

8.7. Compare the following two program fragments. What difference will there be in execution?

DIMENSION A(100)	DIMENSION A(100)
READ (5, 1) (A(I), I = 1, 100)	READ (5, 1) (A(I), I = 1, 100)
1 FORMAT (10F6.3)	1 FORMAT (5F6.3)

Only the FORMAT statements differ, so both will read in 100 values of the subscripted variable A. In the format at the left ten values appear on each card, so ten cards will be read. In the format at the right only five values appear on each card and so twenty cards are needed.

8.8.   Compare the two program fragments:

          DIMENSION A(100)   DIMENSION A(100)
          READ (5, 1) N   READ (5, 3) N, (A(I), I = 1, N)
        1 FORMAT (I5)   3 FORMAT (I5/(10F6.3))
          READ (5, 2) (A(I), I = 1, N)
        2 FORMAT (10F6.3)

They have the same effect. Even the arrangement of data cards should be the same, one card
for the integer N followed by others bringing ten values of A per card until N values have been
provided. If N is not a multiple of ten, the last card will not contain a full set. Of course N must
not exceed 100.

8.9.   What is achieved by these statements?

                    DIMENSION A(100)
                    READ (5, 1) N
                  1 FORMAT (I5)
                    DO 4 I = 1, N
                  4 READ (5, 2) A(I)
                  2 FORMAT (10F6.3)

The effect is the same as in the preceding problem. The DO loop which is implied in the symbolism of the READ statements of Problem 8.8 is brought out into the open in this problem.

8.10.   Compare these two program fragments:

          DIMENSION A(10, 10)   DIMENSION A(10, 10)
          DO 1 J = 1, 10   READ (5, 2) ((A(I, J), I = 1, 10), J = 1, 10)
          DO 1 I = 1, 10   2 FORMAT (10F6.3)
        1 READ (5, 5) A(I, J)
        5 FORMAT (F6.3)

The same values will be read in. The nested DO loops which are implied in the symbolism of
the READ statement on the right are displayed openly at the left. The only difference is in format,
there being one value to a card in the left program and ten to a card in the other.

8.11.   What is achieved by the following statements?

                    DIMENSION A(10, 10)
                    DO 1 J = 1, 10
                  1 READ (5, 2) (A(I, J), I = 1, 10)
                  2 FORMAT (10F6.3)

They have the same effect as the programs of the preceding problem. Here one DO loop is
implied and one is open. In all three cases values are taken column-wise, the index I cycling
faster than J, so they must be made available in this same order.

8.12.   Compare the program fragment below with those of the last two problems.

                    DIMENSION A(10, 10)
                    READ (5, 2) A
                  2 FORMAT (10F6.3)

This is equivalent to the earlier programs, the matrix A being read at its full as-dimensioned
size.

8.13. What form will the output take if produced by these statements?

$$\text{WRITE } (6, 2) \ (X(I), I = 1, 50)$$

$$2 \ \text{FORMAT } (5F20.3)$$

The fifty values of X will appear five to a line, each printed in a field of width twenty spaces. There will be three digits to the right of the decimal point. The number 20 in the FORMAT statement provides ample room between the columns of print.

8.14. Describe the output produced by the statements

$$\text{WRITE } (6, 7) \ (I, X(I), I = 1, 50)$$

$$7 \ \text{FORMAT } (I5, F20.3)$$

The integer variable I is now paired with X(I) inside the parentheses of the WRITE statement. Each line of print will thus contain such a pair, the value of I appearing in the first five columns and that of X(I) in the next twenty. All values will be right-justified as usual. Fifty lines will be required.

8.15. Describe the output produced by the following.

$$\text{WRITE } (6, 8) \ (X(I), Y(I), Z(I), I = 1, 50)$$

$$8 \ \text{FORMAT } (3F20.3)$$

Now X(I), Y(I), Z(I) all appear inside the parentheses, so they will all be output for each value of the index I. The accompanying FORMAT statement arranges each of these triples on one line, twenty spaces to a number. There will be fifty lines of this sort.

8.16. What is the effect of the symbol / in an output operation such as the following?

$$\text{WRITE } (6, 10) \ I, X(I), Y(I), Z(I)$$

$$10 \ \text{FORMAT } (I5/3F20.3)$$

In a read operation the / has been used to skip from one card to the next. In a print operation it will mean skipping from one line to the next. In the present example the value of I will be placed on one line, in the first five columns. The / then causes X(I), Y(I), Z(I) to be placed on the next line, each in its own field of width twenty spaces. The double slash // would have left an unused line between the integer I and the X, Y, Z triple.

8.17. A switching path between parallel railroad tracks A and B, as shown in Fig. 8-1, is to provide a reasonably smooth crossing. It must leave Track A tangentially, to avoid a sharp corner there, and join Track B at a point 4 units of distance to the east and 2 units to the north, again tangentially.

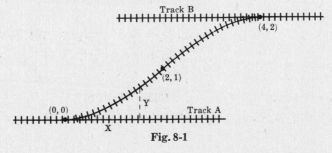

Fig. 8-1

One relatively simple curve which meets the above requirements and also has the desirable feature of being symmetric about the central point labeled (2, 1) is the "cubic polynomial" on which

$$Y = (6. - X)X^2/16.$$

As shown in the figure X and Y here represent distance eastward and northward from (0, 0). For laying the track the values of Y at positions $X = .01, .02, \ldots, 2.00$ are wanted, the other half then being determined by the symmetry. Write a program to output these values.

One such program could have been written in the preceding chapter, since it makes no use of subscripted variables.

```
      X = .01
  1   Y = (6. - X)*X**2/16.
      WRITE (6, 2) X, Y
  2   FORMAT (F6.2, F10.5)
      IF (X - 2.) 3, 4, 4
  3   X = X + .01
      GO TO 1
  4   STOP
      END
```

Here each X, Y pair is output the moment it is available and the same exact names may then be used for the succeeding pair. Computation and output thus follow each other repeatedly. It is often desirable to avoid this alternation, to complete as much computation as one can before turning to output. This can be done here by converting X and Y to subscripted variables, perhaps using a program such as this one.

```
      DIMENSION X(200), Y(200)
      DO 1 I = 1, 200
      A = I
      X(I) = A/100.
  1   Y(I) = (6. - X(I))*X(I)**2/16.
      WRITE (6, 2) (X(I), Y(I), I = 1, 200)
  2   FORMAT (F6.2, F10.5)
      STOP
      END
```

This time all values X(I), Y(I) are computed non-stop, so to speak, and stored in memory locations set aside by the DIMENSION statement. The first DO achieves this. When it is finished, the second DO, implied in the WRITE statement, outputs both the X and the Y array, again non-stop. With the format specified that output will begin with these two rows, the letter s again denoting a blank space.

```
      sss.01ssss.00004
      sss.02ssss.00015
```

The values of X(I) appear in the first six spaces and those of Y(I) in the next ten. There will be 200 such lines.

8.18. The switching path of the preceding problem involves what are called discontinuities in "curvature" at both ends. Though tracks A and B are both perfectly straight, the cubic polynomial bends in a way which would be very noticeable to passengers, particularly at these two points. Theory suggests that the transitions can be made smoother by use of the "fifth degree polynomial"

$$Y = (80X^3 - 30X^4 + 3X^5)/256$$

which can be shown to have zero curvature at $X = 0$ and $X = 4$. Write a program to compute and output the values of X and Y in the pattern of the preceding problem.

Only the fifth statement in the program just presented needs to be changed, its replacement being

1 $Y(I) = (80.*X(I)**3 - 30.*X(I)**4 + 3.*X(I)**5)/256.$

8.19. Polynomials appear in a startling variety of mathematical settings, their applications ranging from medicine to physics to economics. As a result their values must be computed often. Prepare a program for doing this efficiently for an arbitrary polynomial of degree 20 or less.

The degree of a polynomial is the highest power appearing in it, the general polynomial

$$P(X) = A_1 X^N + A_2 X^{N-1} + A_3 X^{N-2} + \cdots + A_{N+1}$$

thus having degree N. In computing a value of P(X) for a given X, it is not terribly efficient to proceed as was done in the last two problems. There each power was handled separately, X^5 being calculated without reference to X^4, for instance. But it takes only a moment to see that the product XXXXX requires four multiplications, while if $X^4 =$ XXXX is already in hand the same result is available by the single multiplication $X^4 X$. Clearly there are opportunities to economize in polynomial computation, and generating each power from the next smaller power by a single multiplication is one such possibility. A second possibility has, however, proved to be more popular. It involves rearranging the original form of the polynomial into the pattern

$$P(X) = ((\ldots(A_1 X + A_2)X + A_3)X + A_4)X \ldots + A_{N+1}$$

which at first glance is almost certain to seem less, rather than more, attractive. The idea is that, beginning with the innermost parentheses as standard procedure dictates, one first computes the expression $A_1 X + A_2$; in the second step this is multiplied by X and the result added to A_3; another multiplication by X is then followed by the addition of A_4 and the routine continues until a final multiplication by X is followed by the addition of A_{N+1}. Each step thus involves one multiplication and one addition, making a final count of N operations of each type. This is a substantial improvement over the count one would reach by considering the original form. The above rearrangement, in which $((\ldots($ denotes $N - 1$ consecutive open parentheses, is thus substantially more efficient.

The succession of multiplications and additions also proves to be a pleasure to program. Taking $N = 4$ for a first illustration, the necessary steps may be displayed as follows.

$$P = A_1 {*} X \qquad P = P{*}X$$
$$P = P + A_2 \qquad P = P + A_4$$
$$P = P{*}X \qquad P = P{*}X$$
$$P = P + A_3 \qquad P = P + A_5$$

Here the first column comes before the second, and the final value of P is the value of the polynomial. The Fortran statements needed to achieve this same result are easy enough to find.

$$P = 0.$$
$$DO\ 1\ I = 1, 5$$
$$1\ \ P = P{*}X + A(I)$$

Variations certainly exist but a simple DO loop is definitely sufficient. This fragment now forms the core of the required program.

```
        DIMENSION A(21)
        READ (5, 11) N, X
 11     FORMAT (I5, E20.7)
        NPLUS1 = N + 1
        READ (5, 12) (A(J), J = 1, NPLUS1)
 12     FORMAT (4E20.7)
        P = 0.
        DO 1 I = 1, NPLUS1
```

$$1 \quad P = P*X + A(I)$$

WRITE (6, 12) X, P

STOP

END

Notice first that the subscripted variable A is dimensioned for 21 memory locations, since a polynomial of degree 20 would have that many coefficients. The values of N, X and the numbers A(J) are then read from cards. This allows the same program to be used for any assortment of these values. The slightly mysterious fourth statement is explained by the fact that the integer variable name NPLUS1 is allowable in the READ statement which follows, while an arithmetic expression such as $N + 1$ cannot be used in this place. With the required information inside the machine, the fragment already displayed computes the value of the polynomial. The pair of values X, P is printed and the job is done. The E format selected allows a wide range for the numbers X, P and A(J). The next problem provides a few further details in this regard.

8.20. How would the data of Problem 8.17 be presented for input to the program of Problem 8.19, choosing $X = .01$?

The values to be read are $N = 3$, $X = .01$, $A(1) = -1/16$, $A(2) = 3/8$ and $A(3) = A(4) = 0$. The first card to be read could therefore take the form

sssss3ssssssss.1000000E−01

the value of N occupying the field consisting of the first five columns while X appears in the next twenty. The four coefficients A(I) are all presented on one card, their fields exhausting the entire eighty columns; here it is more convenient to display them in column form.

ssssssss−.6250000E−01

ssssssss .3750000E 00

ssssssss .0000000E 00

ssssssss .0000000E 00

Again the letter s denotes a space, or blank column. Although the data of this problem are very simple, an effort has been made to use a standard form of presentation, the first significant digit appearing just to the right of the decimal point and the exponent taking its full four places. Some such standardization is useful to reduce errors.

8.21. What form would the output of the program of Problem 8.19 take?

One line of the form

sssssss0.1000000E−01sssssss0.3xxxxxxE−04

would be printed, the letter x denoting digits to be supplied by the computer. A zero before the decimal point has been included since many printers furnish this automatically.

8.22. Suppose the values of a polynomial are required not at one single X but at a range of equally spaced X values, as in the problems of the railroad switching paths (Problem 8.17). Modify the general program of Problem 8.19 to produce them.

Here is one possibility.

```
          DIMENSION A(21)
          READ (5, 11) N
       11 FORMAT (I5)
          NPLUS1 = N + 1
          READ (5, 12) (A(J), J = 1, NPLUS1)
       12 FORMAT (4E20.7)
          READ (5, 12) XINIT, XDIFF, XTERM
          X = XINIT
```

```
         2  P = 0.
            DO 1 I = 1, NPLUS1
         1  P = P*X + A(I)
            WRITE (6, 12) X, P
            X = X + XDIFF
            IF (X − XTERM) 2, 2, 3
         3  STOP
            END
```

The modifications are not violent. The range of numbers X is accommodated in the third READ statement where initial and terminal values are given as well as the difference between consecutive values. After initializing X the computation of P then proceeds as before and the X, P pair is printed out. The familiar routine of increasing X by the specified amount and then using an IF statement to properly route the remaining action completes the program.

8.23. How would the data of Problem 8.18 be presented for input to the program just written?

The numbers to be read are N = 5, A(1) = 3/256, A(2) = −30/256, A(3) = 80/256, A(4) = A(5) = A(6) = 0, XINIT = .01, XDIFF = .01 and XTERM = 2. The first card is to contain only the number N

```
                        ssss5
```

which appears in the first five column field as just shown. The coefficients A(J) are then packaged four to a card, each in its own twenty column field. We have only six such coefficients this time and in E20.7 specification they appear as

```
            ssssssss .1171875E−01
            sssssss−.1171875E  00
            ssssssss .3125000E  00
            ssssssss .0000000E  00
            ssssssss .0000000E  00
            ssssssss .0000000E  00
```

so the first four of these will be punched on one card and the remaining two on the left half of another. The fourth and last data card then contains the information needed to describe the range of X, in the form

```
            ssssssss.1000000E−01
            ssssssss.1000000E−01
            ssssssss.2000000E  01
```

and located in the first sixty columns. The four cards must be in the order just listed.

8.24. What form would the output of the program of Problem 8.22 take?

There would be 200 lines of print of the sort already illustrated in Problem 8.21, which would again be the first line. Notice that although only two values are being printed to a line FORMAT statement 12, which covers four values, is being used. As remarked earlier, there is no harm in this; a FORMAT statement may be more ample than is needed in a particular output operation. In the present case only the left half of the 4E20.7 specification is used, the rest being ignored.

8.25. How might the first two READ statements of Problem 8.22 be combined?

The two statements

```
        READ (5, 13) NPLUS1, (A(J), J = 1, NPLUS1)
     13 FORMAT (I5/(4E20.7))
```

would be sufficient. As pointed out in the introduction, they will cause NPLUS1 to be read from a first card and then, as the second stage of the reading process, the coefficients A(J) from subsequent cards under the control of an implied DO.

8.26. Recalling Problems 8.2 and 8.3, prepare a program for computing and printing these values of N(I).

> The core of such a program must be the repeated use of the basic equation relating successive values. This could be arranged by use of a single DO loop.

$$
\begin{aligned}
&\text{DIMENSION N(30)}\\
&\text{N(1) = 1}\\
&\text{N(2) = 1}\\
&\text{DO 1 I = 1, 28}\\
&1\ \ \text{N(I + 2) = N(I + 1) + N(I)}\\
&\text{WRITE (6, 2) N}\\
&2\ \ \text{FORMAT (I10)}\\
&\text{STOP}\\
&\text{END}
\end{aligned}
$$

After initial values have been established the DO loop disposes of the main computation; output follows and the machine stops. Notice that in the WRITE statement the array is being referred to simply as N, without the subscript. This is possible since it is to be printed as dimensioned, the full 30 values.

8.27. Recalling Problems 8.5 and 8.6, prepare a program for computing and printing the values of A(I, J). The initial values A(1, J) are to be left unspecified, to be read in **from cards.**

> Here too the core of the program must be the basic equation which relates neighboring values of the matrix A. This time two nested DO loops are sufficient.

$$
\begin{aligned}
&\text{DIMENSION A(20, 5)}\\
&\text{READ (5, 14) (A(1, J), J = 1, 5)}\\
&14\ \ \text{FORMAT (5F10.4)}\\
&\text{DO 1 I = 2, 20}\\
&\text{A(I, 1) = 0.}\\
&1\ \ \text{A(I, 5) = 0.}\\
&\text{DO 3 I = 2, 20}\\
&\text{DO 3 J = 2, 4}\\
&3\ \ \text{A(I, J) = .5*(A(I − 1, J − 1) + A(I − 1, J + 1))}\\
&\text{WRITE (6, 14) ((A(I, J), J = 1, 5), I = 1, 20)}\\
&\text{STOP}\\
&\text{END}
\end{aligned}
$$

As required the READ statement inputs the initial values of A, belonging to the row I = 1. These appear on a single card. The DO loop which follows then sets the rest of columns J = 1 and J = 5 to zero. These are what are known as the "boundary values". The two DO's remaining are nested and manage the brunt of the computation, filling in all the "interior" values of the array. The WRITE statement then prints the entire matrix in the same format used for reading in the initial row. Here one further comment may be useful. In this program it is more convenient to output the array row by row, since then each row will truly look like a row on the printed page. This is achieved by putting the column subscript J in the innermost parentheses, as shown. This WRITE statement of course contains two implied DO loops, one nested within the other. The overall program thus involves *six* such loops, including one passed over without mention in the READ.

8.28. If the five initial values for the preceding problem are to be 1, as in Problem 8.5, how should these be presented to the computer?

> In view of the 5F10.4 specification the appropriate card should be punched as follows.

ssss1.0000ssss1.0000ssss1.0000ssss1.0000ssss1.0000

8.29. Using the initial values of Problem 8.28, and recalling the computations made in Problem 8.5, what form will the output of the preceding program take?

Since the output specifications are the same as used for input there will be twenty lines of print, the first duplicating on the printed page the line just displayed in the preceding problem as input. The next few lines would be the following.

ssss0.0000ssss1.0000ssss1.0000ssss1.0000ssss0.0000

ssss0.0000ssss0.5000ssss1.0000ssss0.5000ssss0.0000

ssss0.0000ssss0.5000ssss0.5000ssss0.5000ssss0.0000

8.30. Two square arrays, or matrices, are to be read from cards and a third matrix of the same size, each element of which is the sum of the corresponding elements of the input matrices, is to be computed and printed. This third matrix is known as the sum of the other two. Write a program to produce this sum.

Suppose that the maximum size anticipated for these matrices is 20×20. Here is one possible program.

```
      DIMENSION A(20, 20), B(20, 20), C(20, 20)
      READ (5, 11) N
   11 FORMAT (I2)
      READ (5, 12) ((A(I, J), J = 1, N), I = 1, N)
   12 FORMAT (4E20.7)
      READ (5, 12) ((B(I, J), J = 1, N), I = 1, N)
      DO 1 I = 1, N
      DO 1 J = 1, N
    1 C(I, J) = A(I, J) + B(I, J)
      WRITE (6, 12) ((C(I, J), J = 1, N), I = 1, N)
      STOP
      END
```

The matrices involved are of size $N \times N$ where N may be any integer from 1 to 20. The input matrices are read row by row, because the column subscript J appears in the innermost position of the READ statements. The elements of matrix A should be presented four to a card, one row following the next, the last card of all perhaps being incomplete. Since matrix B is then handled by a separate READ statement, the element B(1, 1) starts a new card and B is presented in exactly the same way as A. The two indicated DO's then compute the sum matrix C, also row by row, which is then output in the same way that A and B were read. In the language of matrices the computation involved here is written simply as $C = A + B$. The difference of A and B, written as $D = A - B$, could be produced by exchanging the + of the above program for a −, no other alterations being needed; for our own peace of mind it might also be worth a moment's effort to replace C by D. Computations with matrices appear in a wide variety of applications, and other aspects of "matrix arithmetic" will be included as we proceed.

Supplementary Problems

8.31. Suppose the values of a subscripted variable are related according to the equation
$$N(I + 1) = I*N(I) + I**2$$
and that $N(1) = 1$. Compute the next three values.

8.32. Write a program to compute and print $N(I)$ of the preceding problem for $I = 1, \ldots, 10$. Estimate the size of $N(10)$ in advance to obtain an idea of what format should be adequate for the output.

8.33. Suppose the values of a subscripted variable are related according to the equation
$$Y(I + 1) = Y(I) + X**I$$
where X is a number to be specified, perhaps .2 as a first example. Using the initial value $Y(1) = 1$, compute the next five values of $Y(I)$.

8.34. Write a program to compute and print the $I, Y(I)$ pairs of the preceding problem for $I = 1, \ldots, 15$. Use specification F10.6 for the values of Y, thus saving six decimal digits. What will be true of the last several values?

8.35. Modify the program of the preceding problem so that the number X is not specified in the program itself but instead is read from a data card, using specification F5.2.

8.36. Modify the program of the preceding problem so that the number X takes successively the values .05, .10, .15, \ldots, .50, using an IF statement to control the cycling of these values.

8.37. Problem 8.5 involved a matrix A having the property
$$A(I, J) = \tfrac{1}{2}(A(I - 1, J - 1) + A(I - 1, J + 1))$$
together with certain initial and boundary conditions. Now consider a larger matrix of nine columns having this same property. The initial row is to have
$$A(1, J) = 1$$
for $J = 1$ to 9 and the boundary columns are to have
$$A(I, 1) = A(I, 9) = 0$$
for $I \neq 1$. Compute the next four rows. In certain classical applications of the central equation being used here the present computation would be considered a more accurate approximation to the solution of a fundamental problem than the one obtained in Problem 8.5. In particular the fifth row here represents an improvement over the second row of the earlier matrix. Compare the two. (For further details see, for example, page 389 of reference 1.)

8.38. Supply the missing details of the following program for duplicating the manual computation of the preceding problem and continuing it to 77 rows. This somewhat mysterious number of rows is chosen since in the applications mentioned above an advance of four rows here corresponds to an advance of one row in Problem 8.5. As a result rows $1, 5, 9, \ldots, 77$ may be considered for such applications to be improvements over rows $1, 2, 3, \ldots, 20$ of the earlier matrix.

```
          DIMENSION A(77, 9)
          DO 1 J = 1, 9
        1 A(1, J) =
          DO 2 I = 2, 77
          A( , ) = 0.
        2 A( , ) = 0.
          DO 3 I = 2, 77
          DO 3 J = 2, 8
        3 A(I, J) =
          WRITE (6, 4)
        4 FORMAT (9F10.7)
          STOP
          END
```

ARRAYS

8.39. For certain applications the following equation may also be thought of as an improvement over that of the preceding two problems:

$$A(I, J) = (A(I-1, J-1) + 4A(I-1, J) + A(I-1, J+1))/6$$

Given the initial values $A(1, J) = 1$ for $J = 1$ to 9 and the boundary values $A(I, 1) = A(I, 9) = 0$ for $I \neq 1$, compute the next three rows of the matrix A.

8.40. Supply the missing details of the following program for duplicating the manual computation of the preceding problem and continuing it for a total of 49 rows. This number is chosen since in the applications in question an advance of twelve rows here corresponds to an advance of one row in Problem 8.5. As a result rows $1, 13, 25, 37, 49$ may be considered for such applications to be improvements over rows $1, 2, 3, 4, 5$ of that problem and also over rows $1, 5, 9, 13, 17$ of Problem 8.38.

```
      DIMENSION A(49,9)
      DO
   1  A(1, J)
      DO
      A(I, 1) = 0.
   2  A(I, 9) = 0.
      DO
      DO
   3  A(I, J) =
      WRITE (6, 4) ((A(I, J), J = 1, 9), I = 1, 49)
   4  FORMAT (9F10.7)
      STOP
      END
```

8.41. An array of numbers which appear in an astonishing variety of applications is known as Pascal's triangle.

```
1   1
1   2   1
1   3   3   1
1   4   6   4   1
. . . . . . . . . . . . . . .
```

The elements are also called the binomial coefficients, and the feature of interest at the moment is that each of them is the sum of two elements of the preceding row, except for the boundary elements which are all 1. To be more precise the equation

$$K(I, J) = K(I-1, J-1) + K(I-1, J)$$

holds whenever the subscripts have meaning. Use this equation to continue the array to another four rows.

8.42. (a) Supply the missing details in this program for computing the binomial coefficients. Also find one error.

```
      DIMENSION K(20, 21)
  11  FORMAT (12I8)
      DO
      K(I, 1) = 1
   1  K(I, I + 1) = 1
      DO
      DO
   2  K(I, J) = K(I-1, J-1) + K(I-1, J)
      DO
   3  WRITE (6, 11) (K(I, J), J = 1, I + 1)
```

(b) How many rows of Pascal's triangle are to be computed. (c) How many elements will be printed on a given line? (d) How will the twelfth and succeeding lines be printed? (e) How was the I8 specification chosen?

8.43. Refer to Problem 8.7. If the first ten values of A(I) were

.123   .456   .789   .012   .345   .678   .901   .234   .567   .890

how should these be presented to the card reader

(a) for the program at the left in that problem,

(b) for the program at the right?

The other 90 values, not given here, receive similar treatment.

8.44. Refer to Problem 8.8. If $N = 75$ and the A(I) are as in the preceding problem how should the data cards be presented?

8.45. Refer to Problem 8.10. How many data cards are needed for the program at the left? How many for the program at the right? If $A(I, J) = 1/(2I + J)$, how should the first three cards be prepared for each of these programs?

8.46. For the switching path of Problems 8.17 and 8.18, suppose the fourth degree polynomial

$$Y = (4 - X)X^3/16$$

is selected for the part from $(0, 0)$ to $(2, 1)$ and a symmetric section forms the other half. Supply the missing details in the following program for computing and printing the X, Y pairs.

```
        X = .01
    1   Y =
        WRITE
    2   FORMAT (F6.2, F10.5)
        X = X
        IF (X − 2.)
    3   STOP
        END
```

8.47. Modify the second program of Problem 8.17 to accommodate the fourth degree polynomial of Problem 8.46.

8.48. To compute the polynomial

$$Y = 1 + X + \tfrac{1}{2}X^2 + \tfrac{1}{6}X^3 + \tfrac{1}{24}X^4$$

for $X = 1$, using the program of Problem 8.19, what data cards would be needed?

8.49. For certain polynomials of special character which appear in many applications it is useful to prepare special programs, rather than to appeal to a standard routine such as that of Problem 8.19. The polynomial of the preceding problem is in this select group. Consider this program for evaluating it and certain relatives:

```
        P = 1.
        TERM = 1.
    1   READ (5, 11) X
    11  FORMAT (E20.7)
        WRITE (6, 11) X
        DO 2 I = 1, 20
        A = I
        TERM = TERM*X/A
        P = P + TERM
    2   WRITE (6, 12) I, TERM, P
    12  FORMAT (13,2E20.7)
        GO TO 1
        END
```

(*a*) What is the degree of the polynomial being used?　(*b*) What is the role of the statement A = I?
(*c*) What stops execution of the program?　(*d*) How is each new term actually produced?　(*e*) If
X = 1, what will be the first five lines of output?

8.50. Supply the missing details in this program for adding N numbers.

```
        DIMENSION X(1000)
        READ (5, 11) N, (X(I),
   11   FORMAT (I4/(4E20.7))
        SUM =
        DO
    1   SUM = SUM
        WRITE (6, 12) SUM
   12   FORMAT (E20.7)
        STOP
        END
```

8.51. What change may be made in the program of the preceding problem if SUM is to be printed
after each step rather than only at the very end?

8.52. What change should be made in the same program if I, X(I) and SUM are all to be printed at
each step?

8.53. What is achieved by the following program?

```
        SUM = 0.
    1   READ (5, 11) X
   11   FORMAT (E20.7)
        SUM = SUM + X
        WRITE (6, 11) SUM
        GO TO 1
        END
```

Chapter 9

Sorting

Applications to various fields such as engineering, business and military strategy were among the original sources of inspiration from which computers, programming and related matters have emerged. Like so many other creations of the human mind the world of computers is a response to a well-documented need, in this case the need for fast and accurate processing of large volumes of information. While it is true that many fascinating questions have appeared, and much effort has been expended trying to answer them, which are more or less internal affairs of this world of computers, such as the development of efficient machine languages or the ability of machines to learn or to intercommunicate, it remains true also that applications continue to point the way toward progress. In earlier chapters a few miniature applications have been introduced. In the chapters now to follow a selection of slightly more sophisticated applications will be presented. Since our objective continues to be, however, the gradual development of familiarity with the different aspects of computer science, the treatment of large-scale modern applications is beyond our reach. Each such application requires reasonable familiarity with the field involved, and after that a noteworthy programming effort. Certain problems of interest are still accessible, and in this chapter we consider such things as finding the largest number in a given assortment and of putting an entire array into increasing order. Such jobs often prove to be a part of a larger assignment. In the process of solving these problems we shall take the occasion to introduce a few further items from the Fortran language.

Comment lines offer the programmer a means for indicating what a given program is supposed to accomplish, or what different parts of that program are supposed to accomplish. They are an enormous convenience to someone other than the programmer who may have occasion to use the program in question; they will also be welcomed whole-heartedly by the programmer himself who returns to reread his masterpiece after a short absence. A comment line in a program is identified by placing the letter C in column 1 of the coding sheet. Though this column is in the field usually reserved for statement numbers, or data, the compiler will recognize this identification. It will then completely ignore the information punched on the card in question. This information, or comment, simply appears on the coding sheet for the convenience of the reader. If the corresponding cards are used to produce a printed version of the program, on an auxiliary device, the same comments will appear in the printed version and for the same purpose, the convenience of the reader. It may be worth repeating that comment lines are not processed by the compiler, and consequently are not involved in the execution of the program. They should not be confused with WRITE statements, which remain the way to obtain output information from the computer.

Example 9.1.

The switching path program of Problem 8.17 is hardly big enough to require comment lines, but for purposes of illustration Fig. 9-1 below reproduces it with three such lines added. The first gives the program a title and the other two identify two main parts. Once again, these lines have no influence upon the output of the program, which is produced by the WRITE statement. They are an attempt to summarize the purpose of the program itself.

```
C     SWITCHING PATH PRØGRAM
C     CØMPUTE AN X,Y PAIR
      X = .01
    1 Y = (6.-X)*X**2/16.
      WRITE (6,2) X,Y
    2 FØRMAT (F6.2,F10.5)
C     SET UP FØR NEXT PAIR
      IF (X-2.) 3,4,4
    3 X = X+.01
      GØ TØ 1
    4 STØP
      END
```

Fig. 9-1

Format statements have been included in our sample programs almost from the very beginning, which is only natural since they are necessary for getting answers out of the computer. The I, F and E specifications have been used. Two further types of specification will now be added, the first of which makes it possible to include explanatory comments in the output much as the comment lines do for the input program. It may also be used for reading such comments.

The H specification: wH____

Here w denotes the number of characters and spaces which follow the H, in this case represented only by the empty line. Notice that the spaces are to be counted in determining w. This is one case in which they are not ignored by the Fortran compiler.

Example 9.2.

The pair of statements

```
  WRITE (6,1)
1 FORMAT (15H SWITCHING PATH)
```

would cause the heading SWITCHING PATH to be printed in positions 2 to 15 of the print line. Notice that the WRITE statement has no list attached to it. It does not appear in a form such as

```
WRITE (6,1) X, Y
```

which has been our general model heretofore. Notice also that the spaces in the above heading have specifically been included in the count of fifteen characters. If the length of the message following the H does not conform with the count w, the Fortran compiler will reject the program and signal an error.

Example 9.3.

The H specification may be used together with the earlier I, F, E specifications to identify numerical output data. The two statements

```
  WRITE (6,1) INTSUM
1 FORMAT (8H INTSUM=I10)
```

would cause, assuming the actual value of INTSUM to be 5050, the output sINTSUM=ssssss5050 to be printed. The letter s is again being used here to denote a blank space, six of them completing the ten position field allocated for the integer INTSUM. The printer would leave these positions truly blank. Notice that the WRITE statement has regained its list, even though only one item long, and that the I specification for this one item immediately follows the eight character message of the H specification. Changing the format to

```
1 FORMAT (9H INTSUM =I5)
```

would have brought the output line sINTSUMs = s5050 in which two spaces are accounted for in the H specification and the other in the I.

Example 9.4.

Only slightly more complicated is the pair of statements

WRITE (6, 1) X, Y

1 FORMAT (4H X =F5.2, 6H, Y =F10.5)

two spaces being left before the Y. If the actual values of X and Y were .01 and .00004 respectively, then the output would be

sXs=ss.01,ssYs=ssss.00004

and would occupy the first 25 positions on the print line. Another glance at the FORMAT statement shows that $4 + 6 = 10$ of these positions are accounted for by the two H specifications and $5 + 10 = 15$ by the two F specifications. A word about the various commas is in order and once again illustrates the care with which programs must be prepared. The first comma in the FORMAT statement is necessary to separate the parts of that statement, just as commas have been used in the same place earlier. The second comma, however, is one of the six characters governed by the second H specification and so appears in the output line as the leading character of the ,ssYs= pattern. Further commas could have been inserted if wanted to separate the H parts of the FORMAT statement from the F parts. Such commas are optional. Thus we could have used

1 FORMAT (4H X =,F5.2, 6H, Y =,F10.5)

instead of the above. Only the third comma will appear in the output information. One could be pardoned for wondering how the computer keeps everything straight, particularly as increasingly complicated formats are designed. Why, for instance, might it not output a line beginning (the above example still serving)

sXs=,

or even worse the following mysterious message?

sXs=,F5.2, 6H

The answer is that obeying specific rules it dissects the format indicated and takes each part in its turn. First the 4H dictates the output of sXs= and no more, only these four characters. Then the F5.2 plays its now familiar role and ss.01 appears. The 6H and F10.5 in their turns then finish up. By playing according to exactly the same rules as the computer, or more accurately, by speaking the language that it understands, the programmer can obtain from the machine the output format he requires.

Example 9.5.

The effect of an H specification on a read operation may be illustrated by these two statements:

READ (5, 1)

1 FORMAT (11H   )

If the message TRIAL NO. 4 is then made available at the card reader, these eleven characters will be substituted for the blank spaces in the format. Actually any eleven characters could have been placed after the H, since they are to be replaced by characters read in.

The X specification: wX

Here again w is an unsigned integer constant. This time it denotes a number of positions to be left blank, that is, a number of spaces. The X specification thus provides a simpler way of indicating how much spacing is wanted between other format elements.

Example 9.6.

The statements

WRITE (6, 1)

1 FORMAT (40X, 14HSWITCHING PATH)

would cause the heading SWITCHING PATH to be printed in positions 41 to 54 of the print line, thus approximately centering it on the page. The same result is accessible by using 54H and leaving 40 spaces after the H, but the use of the X specification seems more convenient. The comma following the X is optional.

Example 9.7.

The statements

$$\text{WRITE } (6, 1) \text{ X, Y}$$

$$1 \text{ FORMAT } (4H \text{ X} = F5.2, 10X, 3HY = F10.5)$$

assuming X = .01 and Y = .00004 as before, would output the line

$$sXs = ss.01sssssssssssYs = ssss.00004$$

beginning in position 1.

Example 9.8.

The statements

$$\text{READ } (5, 1) \text{ A, C, E}$$

$$1 \text{ FORMAT } (F10.5, 10X, F10.5, 10X, F10.5)$$

would cause values of A, C, E to be read from columns 1 to 10, 21 to 30, and 41 to 50 respectively. The computer is asked to ignore the intervening columns, which perhaps contain the values of B and D.

Continuation lines provide a means for handling statements which are too long to fit on a single card. If one finds column 72 of the coding form approaching, it is permissible to continue the statement on a second line, breaking off at a convenient place. Only in the case of a FORMAT statement using H specification is it essential to completely use one line before continuing onto the next. To show that the new line is a continuation of the old, one places the digit 1 in column 6 of the continuation line. Should another continuation be required the digit 2 is placed in column 6 of the second continuation, and so on up to the limit imposed by a particular computing facility, perhaps between six and nineteen lines. The digits in column 6 will cause the computer to continue reading and interpreting all the lines as a single statement. Letters of the alphabet may be used once the supply of digits has been exhausted.

The CONTINUE statement. This always reads simply

$$\text{CONTINUE}$$

and is sometimes referred to as a dummy statement since it plays no active role, serving merely as a point of reference. It provides the programmer with a way of inserting a statement number into his program without generating any further instructions. The most common use of the CONTINUE statement is as the last statement in the range of a DO when otherwise the last statement would be a transfer of control. It was mentioned earlier that certain types of statement must not terminate the range of a DO. The use of CONTINUE in this connection will be amply illustrated in the solved problems. It is sometimes recommended that a CONTINUE be associated with each DO, just for safety, using this pattern:

$$\text{DO 1 I} = \text{etc.}$$

(statements forming the loop)

$$1 \text{ CONTINUE}$$

Solved Problems

9.1. Given a set of numbers A(I), devise a procedure for finding the largest.

For a relatively short list of numbers, orderly displayed, the eye can tell rather quickly which is the largest. The idea here is to work out a step by step routine which can accept a set of almost any size and which can be programmed for machine execution. Such a routine will prove to be useful in slightly more complex problems to follow. One historical solution begins by temporarily assuming the first number of the list to be the largest. This may seem unnecessarily optimistic but the point is that if incorrect, as it probably is, this assumption may quickly be discarded in favor of a better. We begin then by trying out A(1) in the role of BGST, the biggest number of the list. The difference

$$BGST - A(2)$$

is then computed. If it is positive then BGST exceeds A(2) and we pass to the computation of BGST $-$ A(3) to compare BGST with the next member of the list. If, however, BGST $-$ A(2) is negative then A(2) exceeds A(1) and takes over the role of BGST, A(1) having proved unsuitable. As in the previous case the next step will still be the computation of BGST $-$ A(3), but with a new element playing the role of BGST. Similar comparisons follow until the entire list has been processed, and the element which finally plays the role of BGST is actually the largest. A flow-chart of this procedure appears as Fig. 9-2.

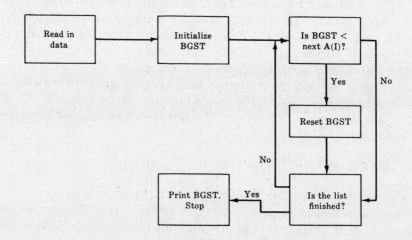

Fig. 9-2

9.2. Prepare a program based on the analysis and flow-chart of the preceding problem.

One possibility is as follows.

```
C       THIS PROGRAM FINDS THE LARGEST NUMBER IN A GIVEN SET
        DIMENSION A(1000)
        READ (5, 1) N, (A(I), I = 1, N)
    1   FORMAT (I5/(4E20.7))
        BGST = A(1)
        DO 2 I = 2, N
        IF (BGST − A(I)) 3, 2, 2
    3   BGST = A(I)
    2   CONTINUE
        WRITE (6, 4) BGST
    4   FORMAT (22H THE LARGEST NUMBER IS, E20.7)
        STOP
        END
```

The comment which heads the program merely identifies it and does not influence the output. The C must be placed in column 1 of the coding form, the rest of the comment appearing as desired. The integer 1000 in the DIMENSION is entirely arbitrary and could be replaced by whatever seemed suitable. The reading process allows for a list of size N, the value of this variable to be presented on the first data card. The list of A(I) then follows packaged four to a card in E specification. The sequence of comparisons described in the preceding problem is then introduced, with the DO providing the central control. Notice here the role of the CONTINUE. Without it there would be some question of which statement should be referred to in the DO itself, and in the final two exits from the IF. As it stands the program uses the statement number of the CONTINUE in all three places. Finally, the output format involves the H specification. Should the largest number actually prove to be 1492, just to be definite, then the line

$$\text{sTHE LARGEST NUMBER ISsssssss0.1492000Es04}$$

would appear, the s again being used to denote a space. On the printed line this s would not appear.

9.3. Referring to Problem 9.2, prepare an alternate program based upon the same flow-chart and identifying both the largest number and its position in the given list.

Only minor modifications are needed.

```
C       THIS PROGRAM FINDS THE LARGEST NUMBER IN A GIVEN SET
C               AND THE POSITION OF THAT NUMBER IN THE SET
        DIMENSION A(1000)
        READ (5, 1) N, (A(I), I = 1, N)
      1 FORMAT (I5/(4E20.7))
        M = 1
        DO 2 I = 2, N
        IF (A(M) − A(I)) 3, 2, 2
      3 M = I
      2 CONTINUE
        WRITE (6, 4) A(M)
      4 FORMAT (22H THE LARGEST NUMBER IS, E20.7)
        WRITE (6, 5) M
      5 FORMAT (16H ITS POSITION IS, I5)
        STOP
        END
```

The principal difference between these two programs is that in the first we keep in our hands the current candidate for the role of largest number, which now has the two names BGST and A(M), while in the second it is the position M of that candidate which is our main object of attention. Apart from this the steps taken by the two programs are essentially the same. In the problems which are now to follow, however, the idea of this second program will be found to hold some substantial advantages.

9.4. Suppose that each item in an industrial warehouse is given a number NUM(I) and that the current supply, or inventory, of that item is represented by INV(I). The content of the warehouse can then be summarized as a double list, consisting of the pairs NUM(I) and INV(I). In other words, the warehouse records form what is familiarly known as a table. Suppose further that the current inventory of one particular item is wanted, the number of that item being ITEM. Devise a routine for extracting the desired information from the table.

In principle this is an easy and familiar assignment. A comparison of the number ITEM with the members NUM(I) of one of our lists is in order to locate the particular item in question in the table. The companion number INV(I) in the other list is then to be printed out. For a warehouse with many items we shall imagine the table as a set of punched cards, each card containing one NUM(I), INV(I) pair, so that the required routine must be suitable for programming. This is not, however, hard to arrange since the key comparison can be made in considering the difference ITEM − NUM(I) for the various items. Fig. 9-3 shows a flow-chart of the action. Notice that provision has been made for the possibility that no number NUM(I) agrees with ITEM. The computation may therefore stop in either of two ways, one a success and the other a failure.

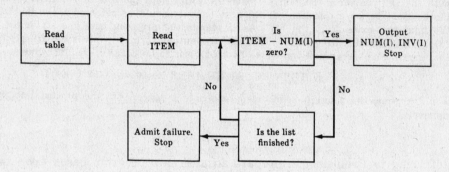

Fig. 9-3

9.5. Prepare a program for looking up inventory values in a table, based upon the analysis and flow-chart of the preceding problem.

Here is one possibility.

```
C       SEARCH FOR INVENTORY
        DIMENSION NUM(1000), INV(1000)
        READ (5, 1) N, (NUM(I), INV(I), I = 1, N)
1 FORMAT (I5/(2I10))
        READ (5, 2) ITEM
2 FORMAT (I10)
        DO 3 I = 1, N
        IF (ITEM − NUM(I)) 3, 4, 3
3 CONTINUE
        WRITE (6, 5)
5 FORMAT (23H THERE IS NO SUCH ITEM.)
        STOP
4 WRITE (6, 6) NUM(I), INV(I)
6 FORMAT (9H FOR ITEM, I10, 17H THE INVENTORY IS, I10)
        STOP
        END
```

Again a comment line provides a title for the program. Though this title was begun in column 7, where statements must begin, this was not necessary. The comment could appear anywhere on the line. Reading of the table requires an initial card giving the length of the table, not to exceed 1000, and then N cards bearing the NUM(I), INV(I) pairs. After ITEM is read in the DO loop checks each item number NUM(I) searching for the right one, the one that equals ITEM. When found the center exit from the IF leads the action to statement number 4 and a successful finish. In this case the DO loop will not have run its full N cycles. (Even if the item in question were the last one of the list, corresponding to I = N, the last cycle of the loop would not reach the final statement in the range of the DO, the CONTINUE.) This is important because it means that at the moment when the action passes to the WRITE, statement number 4, the index I of the DO loop will still be meaningful. This index is visible in the WRITE. When a DO loop has run its full quota of cycles its index I becomes meaningless. In such a case it would be unwise, there is no doubt a stronger word, to depend upon it for output. As things stand here, however, the index remains available and is put to use. Should no NUM(I) be found to agree with ITEM, the DO will do its full duty and the action will flow through the CONTINUE to output the sentence

THERE IS NO SUCH ITEM.

The failure is thus brought out into view. Returning to the success option for another moment, suppose that the item of interest bore the number ITEM = NUM(I) = 31416 and that the corresponding supply, or inventory, was 1492 copies of this item. The output line generated by statements 4 and 6 would then be

FOR ITEMsssss31416 THE INVENTORY ISssssss1492

with blank spaces where the letter s has been inserted.

9.6. A list of numbers A(I) is to be sorted, the largest number being placed in first position, then the next largest and so on. Devise a procedure for doing this by computer.

This application, in principle not much more complicated than those just considered, is the main objective of this chapter. Sorting a list into descending order can be accomplished by repeated use of the procedure for finding the largest number. The central idea can be summarized in these three steps.

1. Find the largest number in a given list.
2. Record it somewhere else and then delete it from the given list.
3. Repeat steps 1 and 2 with the smaller list.

Continuing this procedure down to a list of length one will result in all members being recorded in descending order. These three steps themselves amount to a sort of rough flow-chart of the computation to be made.

9.7. Write a program which implements the procedure outlined in the preceding problem.

Such a program need not be much longer than those just presented. Though probably not needed, a few comments will be included to separate the parts.

```
C     SORTING WITH PLENTY OF STORAGE ROOM
C     READING IN THE GIVEN LIST
      DIMENSION A(1000), B(1000)
      READ (5,1) N, (A(I), I = 1, N)
    1 FORMAT (I5/(4E20.7))
C     BEGIN THE SEARCH, ASSUMING A(1) IS LARGEST
      DO 2 I = 1, N
      B(I) = A(1)
      M = 1
C     MAKE THE NECESSARY COMPARISONS
C     KEEP TRACK OF LARGEST NUMBER AND ITS ORIGINAL POSITION
      DO 3 J = 2, N
      IF (B(I) − A(J)) 4, 3, 3
    4 B(I) = A(J)
      M = J
    3 CONTINUE
C     DELETE LARGEST NUMBER AND REPEAT WITH NEW LIST
    2 A(M) = −1.E 38
C     OUTPUT AND STOP
      WRITE (6,5) (I, B(I), I = 1, N)
    5 FORMAT (I5, E20.7)
      STOP
      END
```

A certain amount of explanation may be welcome. In the first place the heading itself points out that the program requires a little more storage space than may really be necessary. The given list A is completely rewritten as a second list B, taking 2N storage locations for the two lists together.

An alternate program, more frugal in this respect, will be described in the following problem. The core of the present program, consisting of the two DO loops, deserves a moment's thought. First setting $I = 1$, it searches for the largest element of all, which is to be known as $B(1)$. This search is basically the same as in Problems 9.2 and 9.3, the features of both those problems being included. Thus at the start we assume the largest element to be the first one in the list, $A(1)$, and note its position as $M = 1$. Comparisons with the other $A(J)$ then follow, and if a better candidate is found, we replace the current $B(1)$ by that $A(J)$ and the current M by that J. The inner DO takes care of these comparisons and replacements, and when it has run its course $B(1)$ will actually be the largest number of the A list and M will give its position in that list. It is then the turn of statement number 2. To delete the largest number $A(M)$, we must replace it by something. An attractive possibility exists; perhaps another element can be put in its place and the list made one element shorter. The next step, involving the search for the second largest element $B(2)$, would then be a little shorter. Further economies would also be available by continuing the same policy every time. Something of this sort will be realized in the variations to come, but the present program is not so ambitious. It merely replaces $A(M)$ by the number $-1.E\,38$, which is -1 followed by 38 zero digits. This is an extremely small number, because of the minus. Words can hardly describe how deeply it plunges into the supply of negative numbers. One might go deeper still, but some machines limit exponents to size 38 and this should be sufficient to prevent the new $A(M)$ from winning any of the remaining competitions for largest number. (In fact, it would be enough to replace $A(M)$ by any number smaller than all members of the list. If all the $A(I)$ were known to be positive, for instance, then zero could be used in place of the more exotic $-1.E\,38$.) Whatever replacement is made, the range of the first DO will have been executed once and the second cycle can begin. In all there will be N such cycles, all more or less identical, the largest number in each case being replaced by $-1.E\,38$. At the finish the $B(I)$ are the original numbers sorted into descending order and form the output information. Notice that step 3 as listed in the preceding problem has been executed in spirit if not to the letter. The A list does not grow physically smaller, but the part of it which is significant does shrink by one element each time.

9.8. **Prepare an alternate program for the sorting problem in such a way that the list remaining to be sorted does actually become shorter with each cycle.**

Once again comments will be inserted to separate and identify the various parts.

```
      C     SORTING WITH LIMITED STORAGE ROOM
      C     READING IN THE GIVEN LIST
            DIMENSION A(1000)
            READ (5, 1) N, (A(I), I = 1, N)
          1 FORMAT (I5/(4E20.7))
      C     BEGIN ITH SEARCH, ASSUMING A(I) IS ITH LARGEST
            NM1 = N - 1
            DO 2 I = 1, NM1
            IP1 = I + 1
            M = I
      C     MAKE THE NECESSARY COMPARISONS
      C     KEEP TRACK OF POSITION OF ITH LARGEST NUMBER
            DO 3 J = IP1, N
            IF (A(M) - A(J)) 4, 3, 3
          4 M = J
          3 CONTINUE
      C     SHIFT ITH LARGEST NUMBER TO ITH PLACE
            TEMP = A(I)
            A(I) = A(M)
          2 A(M) = TEMP
      C     ITH SEARCH IS NOW FINISHED
      C     OUTPUT AND STOP
            WRITE (6, 5) (I, A(I), I = 1, N)
```

```
5 FORMAT (I5, E20.7)
  STOP
  END
```

And once again a certain amount of explanation may be welcome. As the heading points out this program is more economical of memory space, the entire B array of the preceding program having been eliminated. The reading process which then begins the action is just the same as before. Ignoring the new variable NM1 for a moment consider the first cycle of the outer DO, when I = 1. Setting M = 1, the number A(1) is momentarily offered the role of largest number A(M). The usual comparisons with A(J) for J = 2, N then follow. If any A(J) proves to exceed the current candidate A(M) then it replaces that candidate, the statement M = J effecting the replacement. The comparisons then continue. When the inner DO has run its full quota of cycles the last A(M) will be the largest number. Up to this point the routine is the same as in the preceding program. Now, however, comes the essential difference. The largest number A(M) is *interchanged* with A(1). This requires three statements since the "obvious" interchange

$$A(I) = A(M)$$
$$A(M) = A(I)$$

would result in A(I) being obliterated as the first step. (Both locations would contain A(M) after this pair of statements was executed.) The statement TEMP = A(I) saves A(I) in a temporary location as A(M) is shifted into the Ith place. The interchange is then completed by A(M) = TEMP. The first cycle of the outer DO has then been completed and the second begins with I = 2. Here it is important to observe two things. First, the statement M = 2 makes A(2) the initial candidate for the role of second largest number. Second, this A(2) is compared with A(J) for J = 3, N. This shortening of the working list is possible because the very largest number has been shifted into first place, out of range of the present action. When the inner DO has again run its course, A(M) will be the second largest number. It is then interchanged with A(2) and still another cycle of the outer DO begins, with I = 3 and a still shorter list. The process is repeated NM1 = N − 1 times, bringing the N − 1 largest numbers in descending order into the N − 1 top positions of the list. A moment's thought is then enough to bring conviction that the smallest number will have automatically sunk to the lowest place, making an Nth cycle unnecessary. The sorted A list can then be output.

It is not too hard to discover that the present method of sorting involves just half as many comparisons as the earlier method, and that it is consequently twice as fast, or at least approximately so. With the added advantage of economizing memory requirements, it appears to be clearly superior. The sorting problem has a long history and many other variations exist, some of them still more efficient than this one.

9.9. **The monthly performance of a sales force** is recorded on punched cards, two numbers to a card, the first being the identification number of a particular salesman and the second the number of sales he made. Let these two numbers be represented as MAN(I) and NUM(I) respectively. Prepare a program for sorting the list NUM into descending order and outputting an ordered sales record for the entire force.

The general plan already used needs only minor modifications.

```
C     AN ORDERED SALES RECORD
C     READING IN THE DATA
      DIMENSION MAN(1000), NUM(1000)
      READ (5, 1) N, (MAN(I), NUM(I), I = 1, N)
    1 FORMAT (I5/(2I10))
C     BEGIN ITH STEP OF SORTING PROCESS
      NM1 = N − 1
      DO 2 I = 1, NM1
      IP1 = I + 1
      M = I
C     MAKE THE COMPARISONS
C     KEEP TRACK OF POSITION OF LARGEST NUMBER OF SALES
      DO 3 J = IP1, N
      IF (NUM(M) − NUM(J)) 4, 3, 3
    4 M = J
    3 CONTINUE
```

```
C      SHIFT BOTH MAN(M) AND NUM(M) TO ITH PLACE
       ITEMP = MAN(I)
       MAN(I) = MAN(M)
       MAN(M) = ITEMP
       ITEMP = NUM(I)
       NUM(I) = NUM(M)
    2  NUM(M) = ITEMP
C      ITH STEP IS NOW FINISHED
C      OUTPUT AND STOP
       WRITE (6, 5) (NUM(I), MAN(I), I = 1, N)
    5  FORMAT (2I10)
       STOP
       END
```

The modifications appear in the input and output statements and in the fact that parallel interchanges are made in both the MAN and NUM lists. In this sense the MAN list has also been sorted, not into descending order but into an order dictated by what happens to the companion NUM list.

Supplementary Problems

9.10. Complete the following program for identifying the salesman who has achieved the largest number of sales. The output is to be the identification number MAN(I) of this man plus the number of sales NUM(I) that he made.

```
C      THE BEST SALESMAN
       DIMENSION MAN(1000), NUM(1000)
       READ (5, 1) N,
    1  FORMAT (I5/(2I10))
       MAXNUM = NUM(1)
       MAXMAN = MAN(1)
       DO 2 I = 2, N
       IF
    3  MAXNUM =
       MAXMAN =
    2  CONTINUE
       WRITE (6, 4)
    4  FORMAT (   H THE BEST SALESMAN IS,     )
       WRITE (6, 5) MAXNUM
    5  FORMAT (   H HIS RECORD IS,     )
```

9.11. Complete the following alternative to the program of the preceding problem. This one is more economical, because when a comparison shows that the maximum NUM(I) has not yet been found only one replacement rather than two needs to be made. This program imitates the one in Problem 9.3 while the program of the preceding problem imitates the one in Problem 9.2.

```
C      THE BEST SALESMAN, IMPROVED VERSION
       DIMENSION MAN(1000), NUM(1000)
       READ
       FORMAT
       M = 1
       DO 2
       IF
```

```
                            3 M = I
                            2
                                WRITE (6, 4)
                            4 FORMAT
                                WRITE (6, 5)
                            5 FORMAT
```

9.12. Complete the program below for sorting a list of numbers A(I). It is more efficient than that of Problem 9.7 but not as efficient as the one in Problem 9.8.

```
            C     SORTING WITH LIMITED ROOM, VARIATION
                  DIMENSION A(1000)
                  READ (5, 1)
                1 FORMAT (I5/(4E20.7))
                  NM1 =
                  DO 2 I =
                  IP1 = I + 1
                  DO 2 J =
                  IF (A(I) − A(J))
                3 TEMP =
                  A(I) =
                  A(J) =
                2 CONTINUE
                  WRITE (6, 5) (I, A(I), I = 1, N)
                5 FORMAT (I5, E20.7)
```

9.13. Complete the following program for producing an ordered sales record. It is not quite as efficient as the one in Problem 9.9.

```
            C     AN ORDERED SALES RECORD, VARIATION
                  DIMENSION
                  READ
                1 FORMAT (I5/(2I10))
                  NM1 = N − 1
                  DO 2 I =
                  IP1 =
                  DO 2 J =
                  IF (NUM(I) − NUM(J))
                3 ITEMP =
                  NUM(I) = NUM(J)
                  NUM(J) =
                  ITEMP = MAN(I)
                  MAN(I) =
                  MAN(J) =
                2 CONTINUE
```

9.14. Complete the following statements for outputting the heading ORDERED SALES RECORD FOR THE MONTH.

```
                  WRITE (6, 11)
                11 FORMAT (
```

9.15. Complete the statements below for printing HIS RECORD IS _____ SALES, with the correct value of NUM(I) to be placed in the position designated by the blanks. (See Problem 9.11.)

```
                  WRITE (6, 11)
                11 FORMAT (
```

9.16.   Complete the statements below for printing THE TOP MAN IS   WITH   SALES, the
        correct value of MAN(I) to be placed where the first blank appears and the correct value of
        NUM(I) in place of the second.

                                    WRITE (6, 11)

                               11   FORMAT (

9.17.   What would be printed by the following statements?   Assume that the winner has number 1492
        and made 162,000 sales.

                               WRITE (6, 11) MAN(M), NUM(M)

                   11   FORMAT (10H WINNER IS, I10, 10X, 8H HE MADE, I10, 6H SALES)

9.18.   Which columns of a card would be read by the following statements?

                               READ (5, 11) I, MAN(I), NUM(I)

                          11   FORMAT (5X, I5, 5X, I10, 5X, I10)

9.19.   The numbers A(I) of a list have been punched in columns 16 to 35, one number to a card.   The
        specification used was E20.7.   Use the X specification to produce a correct reading format.

9.20.   The following heading is to be printed.   THE COLUMN AT THE LEFT BELOW LISTS ALL
        SALES FIGURES FOR THE MONTH OF FEBRUARY IN DESCENDING ORDER.   THE
        COLUMN AT THE RIGHT LISTS IDENTIFICATION NUMBERS OF THE CORRESPOND-
        ING SALESMEN.   How should the appropriate instructions appear on the coding form?

Chapter 10

Classifying

Problems of classifying data which is input in large quantity, putting each data element into an appropriate subset, offer a surprising variety of program complications in view of the relative simplicity of the arithmetic involved. The underlying simplicity is explained by the fact that most often the major item of interest is to count the elements which fall into the different subsets, or perhaps to subject such counts to minor arithmetical maneuvers. Complications enter, however, as the number of subsets is increased, making it more and more delicate to separate them. The examples to be presented in this chapter require no new types of Fortran statement. They have been chosen because they illustrate at a reasonably low level of complication the nature of the classification problem, still retaining a modest measure of interest. Included are:

1. Counting the test scores which fall between given limits.
2. Completely classifying a set of test scores into adjoining intervals.
3. Counting the vote for each candidate in an election.
4. Analyzing responses to a poll involving several questions.
5. Ranking student records for a term.

In problems of this sort control statements such as DO, IF and GO TO become particularly prominent, the program logic being more intricate than the arithmetic. Some care must also be given to the input and output aspect, good format being conducive both to correct programming and to clear understanding of the output information.

Solved Problems

10.1. A set of N test scores is available on punched cards. The first eight columns of each card are used to record the number of the student in question and the next four columns contain his score. Prepare a program to discover how many scores fall between 70 and 80 inclusive.

Since the number of scores is given as N, it is possible to use an IF with a counter to control the number of steps.

```
      KOUNT = 0
      READ (5, 1) N
    1 FORMAT (I5)
      K = 0
    6 READ (5, 2) MARK
    2 FORMAT (8X, I4)
      IF (MARK − 70) 5, 4, 3
```

      3 IF (MARK − 80) 4, 4, 5
      4 K = K + 1
      5 KOUNT = KOUNT + 1
         IF (KOUNT − N) 6, 7, 7
      7 WRITE (6, 8) KOUNT
      8 FORMAT (17H NUMBER OF SCORES, 2X, I5)
         WRITE (6, 9) K
      9 FORMAT (25H NUMBER BETWEEN 70 AND 80, 2X, I5)
         STOP
         END

The variable KOUNT represents the number of scores processed and should ultimately reach N. The variable K counts the scores in the target interval. Note that the first data card will be expected to contain the integer N. The main action begins with the fifth statement, the reading of a score. Since scores are assumed here to be integers, we switch to the name MARK which starts with a suitable letter for an integer name. The specification 8X in the FORMAT arranges for the first eight columns of each such card, bearing the student's number, to be overlooked. The two IF statements which then follow perform the central function of classifying the MARK just read, determining whether or not it falls inside the specified interval. The statement number 5 appears wherever the MARK fails to qualify, being either less than 70 or greater than 80. The action then passes to KOUNT = KOUNT + 1 and the question of whether or not the job is done. Otherwise the exit from this pair of IFs is to statement number 4, where K is increased to record that the MARK in process does qualify, and then on to statement 5 as above. The last IF returns the computation to the MARK reading statement until all scores have been processed, after that to the output operations. A typical output from this program might be as follows:

NUMBER OF SCORESsss1000

NUMBER BETWEEN 70 AND 80ssss400

10.2. Suppose the number of test scores of the preceding problem to be unknown. As the last card of the data deck we insert one new card bearing a 1 punch in column 13, a column which remains blank on all the others. Modify the program just analyzed using this new card to determine when the job is finished.

There is no harm in retaining the KOUNT variable since it will probably be useful to know at the finish just how many test scores have been handled, but under the circumstances we cannot depend upon this variable to stop the classification process and start the output. Instead suppose we begin as follows:

         KOUNT = 0
         K = 0
      6 READ (5, 1) MARK, LAST
      1 FORMAT (8X, I4, I1)
         IF (LAST − 1) 10, 7, 10

Both KOUNT and K are initialized to zero as before. Because of the I1 specification which appears in the FORMAT, a value for the variable LAST is then read from the current data card along with the MARK appearing there. If the thirteenth column is blank, as it usually is, then LAST will have the value 0 and the IF will pass the action to statement number 10. We assign this number to the first of our pair of IFs so that the program continues with

      10 IF (MARK − 70) 5, 4, 3
       3 IF (MARK − 80) 4, 4, 5
       4 K = K + 1
       5 KOUNT = KOUNT + 1

as before. The current MARK will thus be classified and the necessary counting done. It is then time to start the next cycle and

GO TO 6

achieves this. Should this new cycle happen to be the one on which the last card of the data deck is read, then LAST will finally be given the value 1. The first IF above will then exit to statement number 7 and output will begin. This part of the program, from statement number 7 down, will be just the same as before. Notice that the statements involving N no longer appear. These include the opening READ of Problem 10.1 with its accompanying FORMAT, and the final IF which was used to trigger the output. The only other change made was the expansion of the remaining READ to accommodate the new variable LAST, together with its own accompanying FORMAT.

10.3. Extend the program of the preceding problem to completely classify the test scores, determining how many fall in each of the intervals 0 to 10, 11 to 20, 21 to 30, and so on up to the interval 91 to 100.

The essential steps are:

1. Set all counters initially to zero.
2. Read a card.
3. If it is not the last card, classify the MARK, counting it in the proper interval. Then raise KOUNT and return to step 2.
4. If it is the last card, begin output.
5. Output and stop.

These steps amount to a flow-chart of the computation. The only one which presents new features is the third, and here it seems clear that some sort of extension of the classification mechanism used in the preceding two problems is called for. Such an extension might be explored in a direct, if not stylish, manner such as this.

```
        IF (MARK − 10) 10, 10, 11
   10   K(1) = K(1) + 1
        GO TO 4
   11   IF (MARK − 20) 20, 20, 21
   20   K(2) = K(2) + 1
        GO TO 4
   21   IF (MARK − 30) 30, 30, 31
   30   K(3) = K(3) + 1
        GO TO 4
        . . . . . . . . . . . . . . . . . . . . . .
   81   IF (MARK − 90) 90, 90, 91
   90   K(9) = K(9) + 1
        GO TO 4
   91   K(10) = K(10) + 1
        GO TO 4
```

The dots indicate the numerous similar statements not shown explicitly and dealing with the intervals from 31 to 80. The symbols $K(1)$ to $K(10)$ represent the counts for the various intervals. If any MARK is too large for a given interval it is passed along to the next larger until it finds its place, at which time the corresponding $K(I)$ is increased and an exit is made to statement number 4. A glance at the steps listed a moment ago shows that this exit must lead to the increase in KOUNT and a return for new data.

Even the most casual study of the extension just exhibited will be enough to suggest that simplification is possible. So many of the statements are duplicates or near duplicates. In the program which follows, a single DO loop is used to replace our effective but unstylish first effort.

```
   C    THIS IS A PROGRAM FOR CLASSIFYING TEST SCORES
   C    FIRST WE SET ALL COUNTERS TO ZERO
        DIMENSION K(10)
        DO 1 I = 1, 10
   1    K(I) = 0
        KOUNT = 0
```

```
C     NOW WE READ A CARD AND TEST FOR FINISH
   2  READ (5, 3) MARK, LAST
   3  FORMAT (8X, I4, I1)
      IF (LAST − 1) 12, 5, 12
C     THIS IS THE CLASSIFICATION LOOP
  12  DO 11 I = 1, 10
      LIM = 10*I
      IF (MARK − LIM) 10, 10, 11
  10  K(I) = K(I) + 1
      GO TO 4
  11  CONTINUE
C     AFTER CLASSIFICATION KOUNT AND RETURN
   4  KOUNT = KOUNT + 1
      GO TO 2
C     OUTPUT OF RESULTS
   5  WRITE (6, 6) KOUNT
   6  FORMAT (17H NUMBER OF SCORES, 2X, I5)
      WRITE (6, 7)
   7  FORMAT (24H NUMBER IN EACH INTERVAL)
      WRITE (6, 8) (K(I), I = 1, 10)
   8  FORMAT (10I6)
      STOP
      END
```

With the comments that have been included, very little further explanation may be needed. On the first cycle of the DO loop the index I takes the value 1; this makes LIM = 10 and the IF tests to see if MARK is inside the first interval. If so K(1) is increased; if not the CONTINUE triggers the second cycle. Now I is 2 and LIM becomes 20. Since MARK was not in the first interval the IF now tests to see if it is in the second. If so K(2) is increased, and so on it goes. The ultimate exit from this DO loop is to statement number 4 followed by a return to the READ. When the value LAST = 1 is encountered the first IF transfers control to statement number 5 and output begins. That output might appear in this form.

NUMBER OF SCORESsss1000
NUMBER IN EACH INTERVAL
ssss10ssss50ssss90sss150sss200sss210sss170ssss80ssss30ssss10

10.4. In all of the preceding problems the test scores were assumed to appear one to a card. Suppose now that they have been packaged 20 to a card, each in its field of four columns. (The numbers of the students involved may be available elsewhere.) There are 50 such cards. Modify the program of Problem 10.1 for this new form of input information.

The principal difference will be that we now treat the scores on each card as an array of twenty elements. We shall also use a DO instead of an IF to control the number of cards read, although either way is suitable.

```
      DIMENSION MARK (20)
      K = 0
C     THIS DO CONTROLS THE NUMBER OF CARDS READ
      DO 5 I = 1, 50
      READ (5, 1) (MARK(J), J = 1, 20)
   1  FORMAT (20I4)
C     THIS DO CLASSIFIES THE MARKS
      DO 5 J = 1, 20
      IF (MARK(J) − 70) 5, 4, 3
```

```
          3 IF (MARK(J) − 80) 4, 4, 5
          4 K = K + 1
          5 CONTINUE
    C    TIME FOR OUTPUT
            WRITE (6, 8)
          8 FORMAT (22H NUMBER OF SCORES 1000)
            WRITE (6, 9) K
          9 FORMAT (25H NUMBER BETWEEN 70 AND 80, 2X, I5)
            STOP
            END
```

Notice that an entire card is read and its 20 scores retained in memory. The outer DO arranges that this be done 50 times, the index I of this outer DO serving no other purpose than to count these 50 cycles. The inner DO takes each of the 20 values of MARK(J) in its turn from memory and determines whether it is to be counted; after all 20 have been processed the inner DO yields to the outer and another card is read to refill the same memory locations with new values of MARK(J). The output information is similar to that of the earlier problem.

10.5. There were six candidates in a presidential election. Each voter used a punched card with his identification number in the first eight columns and punched 1, 2, 3, 4, 5 or 6 in column 10 according to his choice of candidate. Write a program for counting these ballots, outputting the final count for each candidate and announcing the winner.

This may be done using the number of each candidate as a subscript.

```
    C    BALLOT COUNTING
    C    SET ALL COUNTS TO ZERO
            DIMENSION K(6)
            DO 1 I = 1, 6
          1 K(I) = 0
            KOUNT = 0
    C    READ A CARD AND TEST FOR FINISH
          2 READ (5, 3) KAND, LAST
          3 FORMAT (9X, I1, 2X, I1)
            IF (LAST − 1) 4, 5, 4
    C    RECORD THE VOTE
          4 K(KAND) = K(KAND) + 1
            KOUNT = KOUNT + 1
            GO TO 2
    C    FIND THE WINNING TOTAL
          5 MAX = K(1)
            DO 7 I = 2, 6
            IF (MAX − K(I)) 6, 7, 7
          6 MAX = K(I)
          7 CONTINUE
    C    OUTPUT THE WINNER
            DO 10 I = 1, 6
            IF (MAX − K(I)) 10, 8, 10
          8 WRITE (6, 9) I
          9 FORMAT (24H THE WINNER IS CANDIDATE, I2)
         10 CONTINUE
    C    OUTPUT THE VOTING PATTERN
            WRITE (6, 11) KOUNT
```

```
11 FORMAT (19H THE TOTAL VOTE WAS, I8)
   WRITE (6, 12)
12 FORMAT (28H THE VOTE FOR EACH CANDIDATE)
   WRITE (6, 13) (K(I), I = 1, 6)
13 FORMAT (6I8)
   STOP
   END
```

The various comments almost serve as a flow-chart of the computation. The number of voters not being known in advance, it has been decided to again use the device of a final coded card to signal the end of the data supply. The READ and its accompanying FORMAT extract the actual vote, here called KAND, from column 10 and a value for LAST from column 13. As before, this thirteenth column is to be left blank on the actual data cards, making LAST zero and causing the first IF to exit to statement number 4 for recording the vote just read. On the extra card inserted at the very end, however, this column is to be punched with a 1; the vote then having been fully counted, the IF exits to statement number 5 instead and the search for the winner is begun. This search is much the same as the maximum-hunting routines of the preceding chapter, and when it is completed the output procedure begins. A typical output might run as follows.

THE WINNER IS CANDIDATE 4

THE TOTAL VOTE WASssss5000

THE VOTE FOR EACH CANDIDATE

sssss400ssss1900sssss500ssss2000ssssss50sssss150

Note that in case of a tie each of the leading candidates would be announced as the winner, the opening statement of the output being repeated for each one.

10.6. A poll is taken to determine the opinion of the general public on ten questions of current interest. The response to each question is to be one of the following.

1. In favor

2. Opposed

3. No opinion

For each person polled the responses are punched (1, 2 or 3) in the first ten columns of a card. Prepare a program to tabulate and print the results of the poll.

The device of an extra coded card at the end of the data supply may serve to detect the proper moment for terminating analysis and starting output.

```
C    THE PUBLIC OPINION POLL
C    SET ALL COUNTS TO ZERO
     DIMENSION N(10, 3), M(10)
     DO 1 I = 1, 10
     DO 1 J = 1, 3
   1 N (I, J) = 0
C    READ A CARD AND TEST FOR FINISH
   2 READ (5, 3) (M(K), K = 1, 10), LAST
   3 FORMAT (11I1)
     IF (LAST − 1) 4, 5, 4
C    RECORD THE TEN RESPONSES
   4 DO 6 I = 1, 10
     J = M(I)
     N(I, J) = N(I, J) + 1
   6 CONTINUE
C    RETURN FOR ANOTHER CARD
     GO TO 2
```

C   OUTPUT THE RESULTS
```
      5  WRITE (6, 7)
      7  FORMAT (29H TABULATION OF POLL RESPONSES)
         WRITE (6, 8)
      8  FORMAT (12X, 9H IN FAVOR, 1X, 8H OPPOSED, 1X, 11H NO OPINION)
         DO 9 I = 1, 10
      9  WRITE (6, 10) I, (N(I, J), J = 1, 3)
     10  FORMAT (9H QUESTION, I3, 2X, I5, 5X, I5, 5X, I5)
         STOP
         END
```

Once again the comments serve as a basic flow-chart. The matrix $N(I, J)$ is first set up to record the response pattern, each row to correspond to one of the questions and each column to one of the three kinds of response. The array $M(K)$ consists of the ten responses on a given card and is changed each time a new card is read. The first FORMAT statement indicates that LAST will be read from column 11, so the final card must be punched with a 1 in this column. As the IF shows, this 1 will trigger the output of results which begins with statement number 5. All the actual data cards will be processed by the central DO loop. To see this in action suppose the first card reads 1212123333, indicating that this person was alternately in favor and opposed on the first six questions and had no opinion on the last four. These ten values are then the $M(K)$. As the DO loop is cycled for the first time I has the value 1, so the first row of matrix N is involved. But setting $J = M(1) = 1$ also activates the first column. The counting step

$$N(1, 1) = N(1, 1) + 1$$

then adds 1 to the first row, first column element of this matrix. On the second cycle I will be 2 and the second row has its turn. Setting $J = M(2) = 2$ also activates the second column. Thus

$$N(2, 2) = N(2, 2) + 1$$

records this "opposed" response to question 2. This routine is continued until finally with $I = 10$ and $J = M(10) = 3$ the statement

$$N(10, 3) = N(10, 3) + 1$$

records a "no opinion" response to question 10. The CONTINUE, not really necessary here, and the GO TO then lead to the reading of a new card and a repetition of the routine.

The output of results follows the pattern we have been using, the various X specifications serving to align the columns of the matrix under the corresponding headings. Because the index I belongs to the outer DO loop of the printing procedure, and the index J to the inner loop implied in the final WRITE, the matrix will be written row by row. The Ith row will begin with the label QUESTION I. One possible output pattern is presented as Table 10.1.

TABULATION OF POLL RESPONSES

		IN FAVOR	OPPOSED	NO OPINION
QUESTION	1	12000	8000	1000
QUESTION	2	17000	3000	1000
QUESTION	3	5000	14000	2000
QUESTION	4	10000	10500	500
. . . .				
QUESTION	10	18000	2900	100

Table 10.1

10.7. The scores made by students in a large class are to be recorded on punched cards. At the end of the term these scores, four for each student, are to be added together to measure his overall achievement, the fourth score counting double since it corresponds to the final term examination which was twice as long as the others. Prepare a program for displaying the class record, showing the rank of each student.

Suppose that each data card contains the number of the student involved, in the first ten columns, and the four scores he made in columns 11 to 15, 16 to 20, 21 to 25, and 26 to 30.

The steps to be taken include the following.

1. Reading the data.
2. Computing the sums of scores.
3. Sorting the sums.
4. Computing and printing the ranks.

Using these steps as a rudimentary flow-chart, the required program might take the form

```
C     A PROGRAM FOR RANKING TEST SCORES
C     READING THE DATA AND COMPUTING THE SUMS
      DIMENSION IDEN(1000), ISUM(1000), MARK(4)
      READ (5, 1) N
    1 FORMAT (I4)
      DO 5 I = 1, N
      READ (5, 6) IDEN(I), (MARK(J), J = 1, 4)
    6 FORMAT (I10, 4(I5))
      ISUM(I) = MARK(1) + MARK(2) + MARK(3) + 2*MARK(4)
    5 CONTINUE
C     SORTING THE SUMS FROM HIGHEST TO LOWEST
C     PARALLEL TREATMENT FOR IDEN AND ISUM
      NM1 = N - 1
      DO 2 I = 1, NM1
      IP1 = I + 1
      M = I
      DO 3 J = IP1, N
      IF (ISUM(M) - ISUM(J)) 4, 3, 3
    4 M = J
    3 CONTINUE
      ITEMP = IDEN(I)
      IDEN(I) = IDEN(M)
      IDEN(M) = ITEMP
      ITEMP = ISUM(I)
      ISUM(I) = ISUM(M)
    2 ISUM(M) = ITEMP
C     COMPUTING AND PRINTING THE RANKS
      WRITE (6, 7)
    7 FORMAT (3X, 8H STUDENT, 3X, 5H RANK)
      DO 8 I = 1, N
      A = I
      B = N
      RANK = 100.*(A - B)/(1. - B)
      WRITE (6, 9) IDEN(I), RANK
    9 FORMAT (1X, I10, 2X, F6.2)
    8 CONTINUE
      STOP
      END
```

The variable IDEN(I) represents the **identification number of** the Ith student and ISUM(I) the **sum of his test scores**. Both arrays have been dimensioned for 1000, but this figure is entirely arbitrary. The actual size of the class is N and is read from the first data card. The first DO loop then controls the reading of the N student cards. As each is read the corresponding ISUM(I) is computed, so that when the reading is finished both **arrays IDEN** and ISUM are available in machine memory.

The central part of the program then follows, the sorting of the elements of ISUM. But this is precisely the job which was undertaken in Problem 9.9 to analyze the monthly performance of a sales force. This part of our present program has been lifted from the one presented there, the variable names IDEN and ISUM replacing MAN and NUM. Not only will the numbers ISUM(I) be sorted from highest to lowest but, just as in Problem 9.9, the companion numbers IDEN(I) will be rearranged into matching positions. Thus ISUM(I) and IDEN(I) will still refer to the same student. After sorting is completed the output process begins with the printing of headings. The final DO loop accommodates one student at a time, computing his RANK and printing it alongside his identification number. The two statements $A = I$ and $B = N$ manage conversions to real, rather than integer, arithmetic. The formula for RANK then assigns the top student, for whom A and I are both one, a rank of 100. It also assigns the bottom student, for whom A and I are both N, a rank of 0. The others are ranked in appropriate order between these two extremes. The various X specifications constitute an effort to align the printed results under the already available headings. The general nature of the output is suggested by Table 10.2, for which N was taken to be 800.

STUDENT	RANK
001492	100.00
001620	99.87
001066	99.75
001969	99.62
. . . .	
014920	0.25
000044	0.13
031416	0.00

Table 10.2

Certain other factors might have been considered in the construction of this program. For one thing, no allowance has been made for the possibility that two students will have identical values of ISUM(I). As things stand they will receive different ranks, and this will not be a popular output. It might also be useful to give letter grades of HONORS, PASS, FAIL or A, B, C, D, F in reasonable proportions. The necessary program changes to meet such goals involve nothing which is basically different from the patterns of program logic already presented.

Supplementary Problems

10.8. Modify the program of Problem 10.1 using a DO to control the processing instead of the final IF.

10.9. Modify the program of Problem 10.1 to count the scores which are greater than 70.

10.10. Modify the program of Problem 10.1 to count the scores which are less than 50.

10.11. Modify the program of Problem 10.3 to determine how many of the scores fall in each of the intervals 0 to 5, 5 to 10, 10 to 15, and so on up to 95 to 100.

10.12. Modify the ballot counting program of Problem 10.5 if there are only three candidates rather than six.

10.13. Modify the program for tabulating the public opinion poll presented in Problem 10.6 to permit five possible responses.

1. Excellent   2. Good   3. Fair   4. Bad   5. Impossible

10.14. Suppose that an array NUM(I) is already in machine memory, and that it has already been sorted into descending order. The following partial program is designed to detect any elements of this array which are equal.

```
C     TO FIND BLOCKS OF EQUAL ELEMENTS
C     LOOKING FOR THE TOP OF A BLOCK
      I = 1
    3 IF (NUM(I) − NUM(I + 1)) 1, 2, 1
    1 I = I + 1
      IF (I − N) 3, 4, 4
    2 ITOP = I
C     LOOKING FOR THE BOTTOM OF A BLOCK
    6 I = I + 1
      IF (I − N) 8, 5, 5
    8 IF (NUM(I) − NUM(I + 1)) 5, 6, 5
    5 IBOT = I
C     OUTPUT OF THE BLOCK
      WRITE (6, 7) ITOP, IBOT
    7 FORMAT (7H ITOP = , I5, 5X, 7H IBOT = , I5)
C     CONTINUE OR STOP
      GO TO 1
    4 STOP
```

If for instance NUM(1) = NUM(2), then the first IF already exits to statement number 2 which sets ITOP equal to 1 to mark the top of a block of equal elements. Then I is raised to 2 and the search for the bottom of the block begins. If NUM(2) = NUM(3), then statement number 6 is repeated and I becomes 3. Suppose now that NUM(3) ≠ NUM(4). Then IBOT is given the current value of I, which is 3, to mark the bottom of this block. The output line

$$\text{sITOPs=ssss1ssssssIBOTs=ssss3}$$

will then appear and the computation returns to statement number 1 where I is raised to 4. Since this is probably smaller than the size N of the array NUM, the action begins again at statement number 3 and the search for another block is on. Supposing that the second such block of equal elements consists of NUM(6) through NUM(9), follow the computer as it finds its way through the relevant statements of the program. In what order will the numbered statements be encountered? What would be the total output if NUM were the following list?

$$95, \ 95, \ 95, \ 92, \ 90, \ 88, \ 88, \ 88, \ 88, \ 85, \ 80, \ 80, \ 75, \ 73, \ 71, \ 65, \ 65, \ 65, \ 65, \ 60$$

10.15. The program of Problem 10.7 for ranking test scores may be modified to allow for the possibility that some students may have the same values of ISUM(I). No changes are needed except in the part for computing and printing the ranks. We may thus make use of the partial program of the preceding problem which assumes that the array involved, this time ISUM, is in the computer memory and has been sorted. Some alterations are necessary in this partial program due to the nature of present output requirements, but the essential features of this block hunting routine remain the same.

```
C     COMPUTING AND PRINTING THE RANKS
C     WRITE THE HEADINGS AND INITIALIZE I
      WRITE (6, 7)
    7 FORMAT (3X, 8H STUDENT, 3X, 5H RANK)
      I = 1
C     IS THIS THE TOP OF A BLOCK OF EQUAL ELEMENTS
   13 IF (ISUM(I) − ISUM(I + 1)) 19, 12, 19
C     IF NOT, PRINT RANK OF ONE STUDENT
   19 A = I
      B = N
```

```
                    RANK = 100.*(A − B)/(1. − B)
                    WRITE (6, 9) IDEN(I), RANK
                  9 FORMAT (1X, I10, 2X, F6.2)
      C     INCREASE I AND TEST FOR FINISH
                 11 I = I + 1
                    IF (I − N) 13, 19, 20
                 20 STOP
      C     IF TOP OF BLOCK, LOOK FOR BOTTOM
                 12 ITOP = I
                 16 I = I + 1
                    IF (I − N) 18, 15, 15
                 18 IF (ISUM(I) − ISUM(I + 1)) 15, 16, 15
      C     PRINT SAME RANK FOR ENTIRE BLOCK OF STUDENTS
                 15 A = ITOP
                    B = N
                    RANK = 100.*(A − B)/(1. − B)
                    WRITE (6, 9) (IDEN(J), RANK, J = ITOP, I)
      C     INCREASE I AND TEST FOR FINISH
                    GO TO 11
                    END
```

(a) In what order will the numbered statements be encountered if the top five students have the following ISUM(I) values?

$$490, \quad 485, \quad 485, \quad 485, \quad 480$$

(b) What form will the corresponding part of the output take?

10.16. The classification Problem 10.3 could also be solved by first sorting all the numbers MARK(I) into descending order. Prepare a program to do this. Which method appears to be better?

Chapter 11

Scheduling

Preparation of class schedules for the students in a large university is a particularly complicated problem of the general type introduced in the preceding chapter. A substantial list of courses is available and each student is expected to make his selections consistent with university regulations. Many courses are offered at more than one time, in essentially duplicate sections, because of high demand. Once a student has made his selections there remains the task of finding sections which do not conflict with one another. This is complicated further by the fact that each section can accommodate only a certain number of students, and some may already have been filled by earlier registrants. Basically this is a problem of classifying students into sections, but with interesting complications. To what extent can a computer help? The answer to this question is not yet fully known. Perhaps it could be asked to keep track of each student's record, noting his unfilled obligations, suggesting courses at a level of difficulty consistent with his past performance or in a field that he seems to handle well. Or from the administration's point of view perhaps it could keep track of available classrooms and instructors as well as of registration numbers. Our objective here will be much more modest. Assuming the student has made his selections, we will ask the computer to check for conflicts and filled sections. Even this will be a much more complex task than any we have so far attempted. Once again it is not arithmetic which produces the complication but program logic, effective use of control statements to reach the intended goal.

The computed GO TO statement. This adds another element of flexibility to the Fortran language and will be useful in solving the scheduling problem. It takes the form

$$\text{GO TO } (I, J, K, \ldots), INT$$

where $I, J, K, \ldots$ represents a list of statement numbers of any reasonable length and INT is a nonsubscripted integer variable. All the commas are necessary. The computed GO TO allows control to move in any one of several directions, depending upon the value of INT. If $INT = 1$ at the time of execution, then the next statement executed will be the one with number I; if $INT = 2$ the next statement executed will be the one with number J, and so on down the list. Where an IF statement such as

$$\text{IF (INT) } I, J, K$$

may send control to any one of the three statements numbered I, J, K a computed GO TO allows a wider range of options $I, J, K, \ldots$. It is true that coupled IFs could achieve the same sort of result. For instance, the pair

$$\text{IF (INT} - 2) \text{ I}, J, 1$$

$$1 \text{ IF (INT} - 4) \text{ K}, L, M$$

will lead to statements I, J, K, L, M according as the value of INT is $1, 2, 3, 4, 5$. The computed GO TO is clearly more convenient. The example

$$\text{GO TO } (200, 105, 106, 107), NPROC$$

will occur in a moment, and sends control to statements numbered $200, 105, 106, 107$ according as the integer variable NPROC has the value $1, 2, 3$ or 4.

Solved Problems

11.1. Suppose that a university offers N courses, of which some are duplicates meeting at different times, such duplicates to be called sections. To be specific let us say that N does not exceed 5000 and that no more than 20 sections exist having duplicate content. Devise a code for representing each such course, showing in each case the number of duplicating sections and the meeting times of each.

Usually courses bear names something like HI107 for an elementary history or MA444 for something slightly advanced in mathematics. If there happens to be more than one section then symbols such as HI107A and HI107B are popular choices. The times of meeting are often represented by adding MWF10 or TTH8 to achieve

HI107A MWF10

or something similar. Such a code could be made understandable to a computer, but for the examples of this chapter it will be more convenient to have a completely numerical code instead. Accordingly we shall imagine the list of N courses to take the form suggested in Table 11.1. The first three digits of each row indicate the subject matter and the next two the section. If there is only one section in the subject it is numbered 01, a second becomes 02, and so on. The first five digits together therefore represent the combined course-section number and will be denoted by the Fortran symbol NUMCOR(K). From the course list it can be seen that

$$NUMCOR(1) = 14901$$

while
$$NUMCOR(2) = 39701$$
$$NUMCOR(3) = 39702$$

both being sections in the same subject. It will also be convenient to require that in the course list the separate sections in any subject follow one another, in the natural order 01, 02, 03 and so on. This requirement has been observed in the fragment of the list exhibited as Table 11.1. Thus NUMCOR(1) is the only section in that particular subject, and the next two courses are the only two sections of that kind.

14901 01 12
39701 02 05
39702 02 10
54901 04 13
54902 04 12
54903 04 02
54904 04 07
22201 01 12
10701 01 07
. . . .

Table 11.1

The next two digits in the code for each course are slightly redundant but will simplify the programming effort which lies ahead. They give the number of duplicating sections in the subject involved, and will be called NUMSEC(K). Thus NUMSEC(1) is 01 and reaffirms that there is only one section. But NUMSEC(2) and NUMSEC(3) are both 02 since here two parallel sections exist. In the same spirit NUMSEC(4) through NUMSEC(7) are all 04, showing that there are four sections in this popular area. It may be recalled that we are anticipating up to 20 sections in some cases, making this the maximum value possible for NUMSEC(K), though this figure was chosen merely to have something definite for dimensioning purposes and could easily be changed.

The last two digits of the code concern the times of meeting. In preparing his own tentative program each student may prefer to imagine a two-dimensional layout in which each column represents an hour of the day and each row a day of the week, or vice versa. It will be simpler here to choose a one-dimensional array instead. To simplify still further it will be supposed that time is to be used only in specific blocks, each block represented by a two digit symbol as displayed in Table 11.2 below. Each course, or section, the two words being used interchangeably here, must fit into one of these blocks. This is slightly unrealistic since certain subjects may traditionally receive more time than others but for our own programming comfort we shall insist.

01 MWF 8-9	06 MWF 1-2	11 TTh 930-11
02 MWF 9-10	07 MWF 2-3	12 TTh 11-1230
03 MWF 10-11	08 MWF 3-4	13 TTh 1230-2
04 MWF 11-12	09 MWF 4-5	14 TTh 2-330
05 MWF 12-1	10 TTh 8-930	15 TTh 330-5

Table 11.2

Referring back to Table 11.1 we now see that the course 14901 meets in time block 12, or TTh 11-1230. These two digits will be called INTIME(1) since they pertain to the course having $K = 1$. Thus INTIME(1) = 12. Courses 54902 and 22201 also meet in this same time block, making INTIME(5) = 12 and INTIME(8) = 12. In the same spirit the duplicate sections 39701 and 39702 are scheduled in time blocks INTIME(2) = 05 and INTIME(3) = 10 respectively.

11.2. Prepare a partial program to read the course list of the preceding problem into the computer.

This is now a routine assignment.

```
        DIMENSION NUMCOR(5000), NUMSEC(5000), INTIME(5000)
        READ (5, 1) N
      1 FORMAT (I4)
        READ (5, 2) (NUMCOR(K), NUMSEC(K), INTIME(K), K = 1, N)
      2 FORMAT (I5, 1X, I2, 1X, I2)
```

Note that the first card is to contain only the total number of courses, or sections, N. Each of the remaining N cards is to introduce the relevant information for one of those courses. The two X specifications arrange for the layout on each card to conform with that of Table 11.1. Thus from the first such card the computer learns that

NUMCOR(1) = 14901   NUMSEC(1) = 01   INTIME(1) = 12

and so on. When this reading is completed the computer knows the full schedule of available courses together with their times of meeting.

11.3. Suppose that no section is to have more than 30 students. Greater flexibility is possible here by having a separate maximum for each, perhaps represented by MAX(K) and read in along with the other data of the preceding problem, but once again we shall elect to simplify. Set up counters to keep track of the registrations for each section.

This is also a routine assignment.

```
        DIMENSION KOUNT(5000)
        DO 3 K = 1, N
      3 KOUNT(K) = 0
```

The count for each section has been initialized at zero.

11.4. Referring to the preceding problems, devise a procedure for reading the course selections of a particular student into the computer.

As usual there are many options but let us suppose that the essential information is arranged on one card in the format of Fig. 11-1 below. The identification number of the student appears in columns 1 to 10, right-justified as always. Assume that a student is limited to four courses. The numbers of these courses are then punched in the next four fields, each five columns wide. The actual selection of courses is of course dependent upon the interests of the individual involved. It would also be convenient to allow each student to indicate his choice of section, in cases where duplicate sections exist, but to reduce our programming burdens it will be asked that this choice be left to the computer. The last two columns in each of the four fields are to contain the digits

01, implying that section 01 will be assigned if possible. If this proves to be impossible because it is already full, or because there is a conflict with another choice, then section 02 will be tried, then 03, and so on. But the computer will do this itself. It may even be desirable to have the four 01 pairs punched in advance, perhaps the identification number too, presenting the registrant with a pattern such as

$$ssss001492sss01sss01sss01sss01$$

into which he must merely insert appropriate choices in place of the four sss groups. The card of this sort for student 001492 is shown in Fig. 11-1. In making these insertions it might be recommended that courses which are particularly important to the student be put first in field 1, then field 2, etc., since if conflicts are found it is these which are less likely to be rejected. At least, the chances of getting registered in such courses will have been slightly improved.

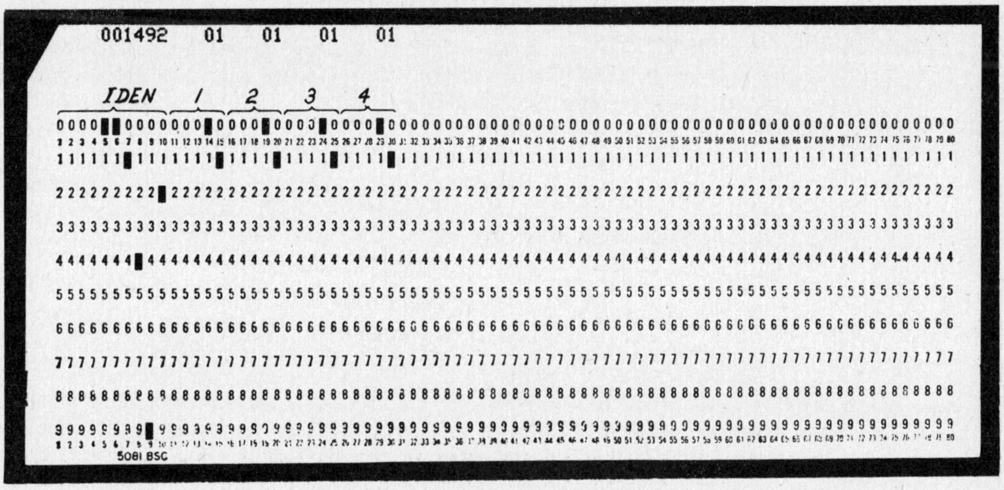

Fig. 11-1

Now we turn to the reading of the selections made. The name IDEN will be used for the identification number and MY(I) for the four selections, the index I thus running from 1 to 4. The following three statements are then sufficient.

DIMENSION MY(4)

10 READ (5, 4) IDEN, (MY(I), I = 1, 4)

4 FORMAT (I10, 4I5)

The format conforms to that of Fig. 11-1. Note that MY(I) is read according to specification I5, which means that the entire field is picked up and not only the three digits supplied by the student. This will be convenient in a moment. The statement number 10 on the READ is also for future use.

11.5. The information read in preceding problems provides the computer with all the information necessary for checking the selected schedule, to determine whether conflicts exist or whether certain sections have reached capacity, all information except of course the instructions which explain how this is to be done. Begin this programming effort by identifying in the master course list the NUMCOR(K) which correspond to the selections made.

Basically this identification amounts to a table look-up operation. The selection MY(1) presumably corresponds to one of the listed courses, but which one? And are there duplicate sections? The same questions arise for the other MY(I). We proceed very much as in Problem 9.4.

DIMENSION KTOP(4), KBOT(4)

DO 5 I = 1, 4

DO 6 K = 1, N

IF (MY(I) − NUMCOR(K)) 6, 8, 6

```
   6 CONTINUE
     WRITE (6, 7) IDEN, MY(I)
   7 FORMAT (1X, I10, 10X, 22H NO COURSE WITH NUMBER, 1X, I5)
     GO TO 10
   8 KTOP(I) = K
     KBOT(I) = K + NUMSEC(K) − 1
   5 CONTINUE
```

The first DO assures that all four selections will be considered. The second DO arranges the search or look-up operation. The list of courses is scanned from top to bottom (K = 1 to K = N) until the NUMCOR(K) which matches MY(I) is found. Exit 8 from the IF then leads to the recording of the successful value of K as KTOP(I) and to the value of K corresponding to the last section which duplicates MY(I) as KBOT(I). This assures that this set of duplicate sections will be readily accessible when needed. Should no course be found to match MY(I), because of misunderstanding or incorrect punching by the student involved, then the inner DO runs its full number of cycles and the action passes through the first CONTINUE to write an error message. The GO TO then refers back to the reading of another student's card. (With a somewhat greater effort we could arrange that only the incorrect selection be skipped, the rest being processed, which would be less severe on student morale.)

11.6. Referring to Problem 11.5 what steps are involved in processing the first selection, which is now both MY(1) and NUMCOR(K) for K = KTOP(1)?

Here there is no question of conflicts since this is the first selection to be considered. Some sections may, however, have reached the maximum of 30 registrations as earlier cards were processed. The necessary action is suggested in the flow-chart of Fig. 11-2. The loop at the upper right represents the search for a section that is still open for more registrations, assuming that the initial section with K1 = KTOP(1) has been filled. When K1 exceeds KBOT(1), all duplicate sections will have been tried and the student's first choice cannot be accommodated. The computation then switches to the next selection.

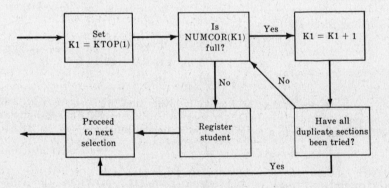

Fig. 11-2

11.7. Write a partial program to achieve the purpose of the preceding problem.

The part of the flow-chart which has been called "register student" deserves some preliminary comment. This could be interpreted to mean preparing a list of registrants for each section, printing a pass to admit the student to the first meeting of the class, and various other things. Here it will be limited, however, to the record keeping which is essential to our immediate purpose, checking for conflicts and full sections. Even the second of these can be postponed momentarily, as we focus first on the final program of the student whose selections are in process. This student must be told which courses have been scheduled for him and in which time blocks. Accordingly we let MYSKED(I) stand for his schedule, the index I running from 1 to 15 since there are fifteen time blocks, and initialize all elements of this array to zero to show that at the start he is registered for nothing.

C   INITIALIZE MYSKED ARRAY

DIMENSION MYSKED(15)

DO 9 I = 1, 15

9 MYSKED(I) = 0

This finally puts us in position to begin the attack upon our ultimate objective, checking and recording the course selections.

Consider this set of statements:

K1 = KTOP(1)

100 IF (KOUNT(K1) − 30) 101, 102, 102

101 IN1 = INTIME(K1)

MYSKED(IN1) = NUMCOR(K1)

GO TO 200

102 K1 = K1 + 1

IF (K1 − KBOT(1)) 100, 100, 103

This parallels the flow-chart above. If course NUMCOR(K1) is not yet full, the first IF exits to statement number 102 and the number of this course is entered in the student's schedule. Using K1 and IN1 avoids double subscripts such as MYSKED(INTIME(K1)) which are not allowed in the Fortran language. After recording this course the computation passes to statement number 200 which will appear in the treatment of the next selection. If on the other hand course NUMCOR(K1) is full, then statement number 103 arranges for the next duplicate section to be tried, not going beyond K1 = KBOT(1). Notice that when the computation leaves this program fragment the value of K1 continues to represent the first successful section encountered. This will be useful in the next step. If no section is successful, then K1 will reach and remain at the value KBOT(1) + 1 and this can be used as an indicator that this course is not worth further consideration. Since this was the student's top choice, the tragic aspect of the situation is slightly heightened. (See also Problem 11.9.)

11.8. The analysis presented in Problem 11.7 for treatment of the first selection is not entirely adequate. To see this fairly clearly explore the steps involved in processing the second selection, which is now both MY(2) and NUMCOR(K) for K = KTOP(2).

There will of course be a strong similarity with the steps just described for the first selection, but we have the added feature that sections may now be rejected momentarily because of conflicts with the NUMCOR(K1) already scheduled. The word momentarily is used here since it is quite possible that no section like MY(2) is both unfilled and conflict-free. In this case we must go back to the first selection in the hope that a different section of this course may lead to success in scheduling both. This would involve testing the sections of selection two all over again. The indicated flow-chart appears in Fig. 11-3 below.

First the search for an unfilled section is undertaken. If none exists then the action plunges down the right-most column of the chart and proceeds to the third selection without disturbing any registration which may have been made for the preceding course selection. In this case the value of K2 will be left as KBOT(2) + 1 and will serve as a reminder that further attention to this course is useless. If, however, an unfilled section is found, then it is tested for conflict with any previously registered course. If no conflict is found the computer registers the student in NUMCOR(K2) for the current K2 and proceeds, this time on a note of success instead of failure, to the third selection. In case of conflict the next duplicate section is tried, and then another if needed until perhaps a success is achieved. If all sections have been tried then this course is incompatible with the NUMCOR(K1) registered, which is then deleted from the student's schedule and the action returns to selection one in the hope that a better value of K1 can be found.

Glancing back at Fig. 11-2 for a moment, one sees that after a new choice of K1 processing returns to the top of Fig. 11-3 for a repetition of the events just described. There are two ways out of this big loop. Hopefully a compatible pair of sections will ultimately be found, in which case we leave Fig. 11-3 at the lower right corner in high spirits. If this hope is not to be realized, however, then K1 will reach the value KBOT(1) + 1. This development is now not due to all sections of the top selection being filled but to conflicts with the second selection.

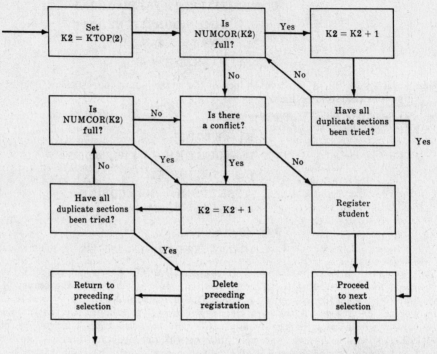

Fig. 11-3

It now becomes possible to see that our analysis of the processing of the top selection was incomplete. In fact, it will not be complete until we have considered all four selections, since conflicts anywhere along the way may force reconsideration of this top selection. The complications promised in the introduction have begun to appear. To return to our present analysis, faced with an unavoidable conflict between the first two choices we must abandon the second, revive the first, and then carry on to the third selection for further processing. The following final version of part one of our program has thus been at least partly explained.

11.9. Write the program fragment for processing the first selection.

The following statements will be adequate.

```
C     INITIALIZE TO TAKE TOP SECTIONS FIRST
      K1 = KTOP(1)
      K2 = KTOP(2)
      K3 = KTOP(3)
      K4 = KTOP(4)
C     PROCESS THE FIRST SELECTION
      NPROC = 1
100   IF (KOUNT(K1) − 30) 101, 102, 102
101   IN1 = INTIME(K1)
      MYSKED(IN1) = NUMCOR(K1)
      GO TO 200
102   K1 = K1 + 1
      IF (K1 − KBOT(1)) 100, 100, 103
103   GO TO (200, 104, 105, 106), NPROC
104   K2 = KBOT(2) + 1
      GO TO 107
```

```
        105  K3 = KBOT(3) + 1
             GO TO 107
        106  K4 = KBOT(4) + 1
        107  K1 = KTOP(1)
             GO TO 100
```

A fair amount of explanation is surely necessary. Of the opening initializations only the first, dealing with K1, may seem necessary at this point. The other three will be clearer when the corresponding selections are processed. The variable NPROC keeps track of how far the computation has penetrated down the list of four selections. It will prove to be useful to have this information available. Here it is set to one since we are taking the first selection for the very first time. The next six statements are the same as in Problem 11.7 and dispose of the actual processing of this selection. Notice that exit 103 leads to a computed GO TO. If NPROC = 1, then the computation has reached this point because all sections of the top choice are filled. There is then nothing to be done but move on to the next selection, leaving K1 = KBOT(1) + 1 as a reminder of failure. Exit 200 takes care of this. But, as pointed out just a moment ago, we can also arrive at this point because of an unresolvable conflict between the top two selections, and then a different type of action is demanded. But such a conflict means that we have at least begun the processing of the second selection and, as will appear in a moment, the value of NPROC will then have been changed to 2. The second exit, number 104, will then be used and will set K2 permanently equal to KBOT(2) + 1 as a reminder that the second selection need not be given further attention. The same exit also resets K1 at its initial value and leads back to the reprocessing of the top selection. In exactly the same way exits 105 and 106 from the computed GO TO remove a later selection which proves to be the cause of unresolvable conflicts. Further details will be given as the later selections are taken up.

11.10. Program the processing of the second selection.

Many of the details are similar to those just given but the level of complexity increases somewhat.

```
        C     PROCESS THE SECOND SELECTION
        C     HAS THIS ALREADY BEEN REJECTED
        200  IF (K2 − KBOT(2)) 201, 201, 300
        C     HAS THIS BEEN ENCOUNTERED BEFORE
        201  IF (NPROC − 2) 202, 203, 203
        202  NPROC = 2
        C     IS THIS SECTION FULL, IF SO TRY ANOTHER
        203  IF (KOUNT(K2) − 30) 204, 205, 205
        205  K2 = K2 + 1
             IF (K2 − KBOT(2)) 203, 203, 300
        C     IF NOT FULL TEST FOR CONFLICT AND PERHAPS REGISTER
        204  IN2 = INTIME(K2)
             IF (MYSKED (IN2)) 206, 207, 206
        207  MYSKED(IN2) = NUMCOR(K2)
             GO TO 300
        C     IF CONFLICT TRY ANOTHER SECTION
        206  K2 = K2 + 1
             IF (K2 − KBOT(2)) 208, 208, 209
        208  IF (KOUNT(K2) − 30) 204, 206, 206
        C     RETURN TO FIRST SELECTION IF STILL ACTIVE
        209  IF (K1 − KBOT(1)) 210, 210, 211
        210  MYSKED(IN1) = 0
             K2 = KTOP(2)
             GO TO 102
        211  ITEMP = NPROC − 1
             GO TO (300, 212, 213), ITEMP
```

212 K3 = KBOT(3) + 1
     K2 = KTOP(2)
     GO TO 200
213 K4 = KBOT(4) + 1
     K2 = KTOP(2)
     GO TO 200

Notice first that the entry to this part of the program, statement 200, is an IF. If at the time of entry K2 happens to be KBOT(2) + 1, the computation simply bounces off the top of this section to statement 300 which begins the next. The second selection has then been permanently rejected, though this bouncing process may be repeated many times. It is then the turn of NPROC. If it was 1 it will be reset to 2, to show that the second selection is now in process; otherwise it will be left as it was. In this way we keep track of how far the computation has penetrated. The next three statements are similar to those for K1. If an unfilled section is found we move on to statement 204 to investigate conflicts: if none exists then K2 reaches KBOT(2) + 1, permanently rejecting this selection, and the action passes to statement 300 without disturbing any registration which may have been made for the top choice. The test for conflict merely asks if MYSKED continues to have the zero value it was given originally in time block INTIME(K2), using the current K2. If so there is no conflict and statement 207 registers the section NUMCOR(K2) which is both unfilled and conflict-free. If, however, MYSKED is not zero for this time block, it is because some section of the top selection has already been scheduled there; statement 206 then continues search for a better section. If no value of K2 brings success, then appeal must be made to the earlier selection and statement 209 asks if this would be of any use. If alternative sections of that course exist, then statement 210 cancels the registration previously made and we go back to try the next value of K1, stopping first to reset K2 at its initial value so that the sections of choice two may be paired with the new registration in choice one. If, on the other hand, it is useless to return to the top selection then the course of action depends upon NPROC. If it is equal to 2 we must abandon the second selection and move on to statement 300, leaving K2 permanently at KBOT(2) + 1. Exits 212 and 213 are present in case the conflicts which trouble us here are the fault of the third or fourth selections. In such case the offending course is rejected permanently and the computation returns to statement 200 to recover earlier options. A similar remark applies to the closing section in Problem 11.9. It may be worth a moment to list the four possible results that may occur as the top two selections are processed.

1. Compatible sections of both courses may be found. They will then be recorded in MYSKED and the corresponding values of K1 and K2 will be preserved.

2. Only the top course can be registered, either because all sections of the other are full or because conflicts have caused this course to be abandoned in favor of the first, which has higher priority. Here K2 is left at the value KBOT(2) + 1.

3. Only the second course can be registered, all sections of the first being filled. Here K1 is left at the value KBOT(1) + 1.

4. Neither course can be registered, all sections of both being full. Here K1 = KBOT(1) + 1 and K2 = KBOT(2) + 1.

11.11. Program the processing of the third selection.

There is not much difference between what is needed here and what was needed in handling the second selection. The flow-chart of Fig. 11-3 may again be used, all 2s being replaced by 3s. A certain amount of care is helpful at the exits but the program statements themselves are perhaps enough to clarify the transitions involved.

```
C     PROCESS THE THIRD SELECTION
C     HAS THIS ALREADY BEEN REJECTED
300  IF (K3 − KBOT(3)) 301, 301, 400
C     HAS THIS BEEN ENCOUNTERED BEFORE
301  IF (NPROC − 3) 302, 303, 303
302  NPROC = 3
C     IS THIS SECTION FULL, IF SO TRY ANOTHER
303  IF (KOUNT(K3) − 30) 304, 305, 305
305  K3 = K3 + 1
     IF (K3 − KBOT(3)) 303, 303, 400
```

```
        C     IF NOT FULL TEST FOR CONFLICT AND PERHAPS REGISTER
        304  IN3 = INTIME(K3)
             IF (MYSKED(IN3)) 306, 307, 306
        307  MYSKED(IN3) = NUMCOR(K3)
             GO TO 400
        C     IF CONFLICT TRY ANOTHER SECTION
        306  K3 = K3 + 1
             IF (K3 − KBOT(3)) 308, 308, 309
        308  IF (KOUNT(K3) − 30) 304, 306, 306
        C      RETURN TO EARLIER SELECTION IF STILL ACTIVE
        309  IF (K2 − KBOT(2)) 310, 310, 311
        310  MYSKED(IN2) = 0
             K3 = KTOP(3)
             GO TO 206
        311  IF (K1 − KBOT(1)) 312, 312, 313
        312  MYSKED(IN1) = 0
             K3 = KTOP(3)
             GO TO 102
        313  ITEMP = NPROC − 2
             GO TO (400, 314), ITEMP
        314  K4 = KBOT(4) + 1
             K3 = KTOP(3)
             GO TO 300
```

The parallel between this part of the program and the preceding part is almost complete. The only noteworthy difference appears in the closing statements, and even there a strong resemblance is apparent. If K3 has not run past its limit of KBOT(3) then a new section of this same course is tried, in the hope that conflicts encountered in reaching this point can be removed. This is similar to the corresponding earlier step. Suppose, however, that all such sections have been exhausted. In this event exit 309 carries us back for a possible change in K2. Statement 310 prepares the way for such a change. If this path is also blocked, then statement 311 asks if there is any use in returning to the topmost selection. If so, statement 312 makes the necessary arrangements; if not, statement 313 leads to an effort to place the blame. The finish is similar to that of the preceding part of the program.

11.12. Program the processing of the last selection.

Again the details are similar.

```
        C     PROCESS THE FOURTH SELECTION
        C      HAS THIS ALREADY BEEN REJECTED
        400  IF (K4 − KBOT(4)) 401, 401, 500
        C      HAS THIS BEEN ENCOUNTERED BEFORE
        401  IF (NPROC − 4) 402, 403, 403
        402  NPROC = 4
        C      IS THIS SECTION FULL, IF SO TRY ANOTHER
        403  IF (KOUNT(K4) − 30) 404, 405, 405
        405  K4 = K4 + 1
             IF (K4 − KBOT(4)) 403, 403, 500
        C     IF NOT FULL TEST FOR CONFLICT AND PERHAPS REGISTER
        404  IN4 = INTIME(K4)
             IF (MYSKED(IN4)) 406, 407, 406
        407  MYSKED(IN4) = NUMCOR(K4)
             GO TO 500
```

```
C     IF CONFLICT TRY ANOTHER SECTION
406   K4 = K4 + 1
      IF (K4 − KBOT(4)) 408, 408, 409
408   IF (KOUNT(K4) − 30) 404, 406, 406
C     RETURN TO EARLIER SELECTION IF STILL ACTIVE
409   IF (K3 − KBOT(3)) 410, 410, 411
410   MYSKED(IN3) = 0
      K4 = KTOP(4)
      GO TO 306
411   IF (K2 − KBOT(2)) 412, 412, 413
412   MYSKED(IN2) = 0
      K4 = KTOP(4)
      GO TO 206
413   IF (K1 − KBOT(1)) 414, 414, 500
414   MYSKED(IN1) = 0
      K4 = KTOP(4)
      GO TO 102
```

Once again the closing statements show the only alterations worth mentioning. If conflicts occur then one probes back as far as is necessary in the effort to remove them, always being careful to cancel the earlier registration and reactivate K4 at its initial value. Ultimately the computation finds its way, by one path or another, to exit 500 where the finishing touches are to be applied.

11.13. Complete the program of this chapter by arranging for the counting of any registrations made and for the output of schedules.

Only a few more statements are needed.

```
C     COUNTING THE REGISTRATIONS
500   IF (K1 − KBOT(1)) 501, 501, 502
501   KOUNT (K1) = KOUNT(K1) + 1
502   IF (K2 − KBOT(2)) 503, 503, 504
503   KOUNT (K2) = KOUNT(K2) + 1
504   IF (K3 − KBOT(3)) 505, 505, 506
505   KOUNT(K3) = KOUNT(K3) + 1
506   IF (K4 − KBOT(4)) 507, 507, 508
507   KOUNT(K4) = KOUNT(K4) + 1
C     OUTPUT OF THE SCHEDULE
508   WRITE (6,509) IDEN
509   FORMAT (1X, I10)
      WRITE (6,510) (MYSKED(I), I = 1, 15)
510   FORMAT (15(1X, I5))
      GO TO 10
      END
```

Each counting statement is preceded by a check to see whether or not that particular selection was actually registered. As for the output, the format indicated puts the student's identification number on one line and the schedule on the next, perhaps as follows.

```
sssss001492
sssss0s54903sssss0sssss0s39701sssss0s10701...
```

Though only seven time blocks have been displayed, all fifteen would be included on the second line. A zero means that no course has been scheduled for that time. After output the computation returns to statement number 10 to read another student's card.

11.14. Summarize the entire program by means of a flow-chart.

Fig. 11-4 amounts to a simplified version of such a chart. Each box stands for one of the program fragments already presented.

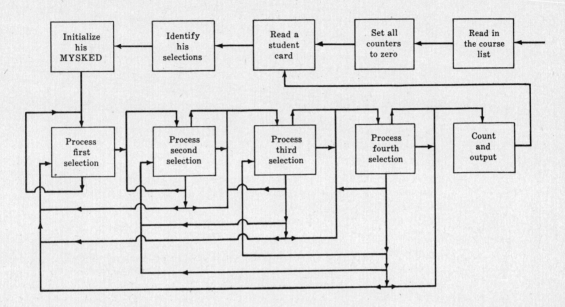

Fig. 11-4

Beginning at the upper right of the chart the computation first makes the initial preparations. Once a student card has been read, the lower half of the chart is soon encountered and a bewildering assortment of loops within loops becomes available. Cards which are processed early should provoke little complication since few if any sections will be full. Occasional conflicts will be resolved quickly and the exits at the right sides of the selection processing boxes will lead the way to output and another student's card. Note that these exits always lead to the top of the next box. The top has been used to suggest that processing always begins with the number one section of that course.

Cards presented later, after many students have been accommodated, will make the computer work harder. For these the bottom exit from a selection processing box will be used rather often. This exit corresponds to the exhaustion of all sections of the course involved. It leads the computation back to the reconsideration of earlier selections, if such selections are still active, in the hope that a successful combination may be discovered. Running the eyeball around the various possible loops appearing under these processing boxes, and simultaneously thinking through what each such loop means, is one way of unraveling the complex possibilities. Another way is to run the program for certain sets of circumstances which are designed to trigger the use of the different loops. This is also a good way to test a program of this sort, to see whether or not it is doing what was intended. Some opportunities of this nature will be suggested among the supplementary problems.

Supplementary Problems

11.15. Identify the following in Table 11.1, page 189.

NUMCOR(5)   NUMSEC(5)   INTIME(5)

NUMCOR(9)   NUMSEC(9)   INTIME(9)

For the next eight problems assume the course list to be as given in Table 11.1, page 189. These problems may be used to test various parts of the program.

11.16. A student selects courses 149, 397, 549 and 107, in that order of priority. That is, $MY(1) = 14901$, $MY(2) = 39701$, and so on. None of the sections have yet been filled. Indicate the course that processing takes by listing the successive changes in K1, K2, K3, K4. What will be the output? It might be advisable to start by identifying the KTOP(I) and KBOT(I).

11.17. The selections are the same as in Problem 11.16, but now the first three sections of course 549 are filled. Indicate the course that processing takes by listing the successive changes in K1, K2, K3, K4.

11.18. Proceed as in Problem 11.17 but with the priorities of the selections reversed. That is, $MY(1) = 10701$, $MY(2) = 54901$, $MY(3) = 39701$ and $MY(4) = 14901$. The first three sections of course 549 are still filled.

11.19. Again proceed as in Problem 11.17 but with these priorities: $MY(1) = 54901$, $MY(2) = 14901$, $MY(3) = 10701$, $MY(4) = 39701$.

11.20. Suppose the selections $MY(1) = 54901$, $MY(2) = 22201$, $MY(3) = 39701$, $MY(4) = 10701$ are made. What are the KTOP(I) and KBOT(I)? In what order will sections be processed if 54901 is already filled?

11.21. Proceed as in the preceding problem but with these priorities: $MY(1) = 39701$, $MY(2) = 54901$, $MY(3) = 22201$, $MY(4) = 10701$.

11.22. Proceed as in the preceding problem but with sections 54901 and 54903 both filled and this order of priorities: $MY(1) = 22201$, $MY(2) = 54901$, $MY(3) = 10701$, $MY(4) = 39701$.

11.23. How many courses will be registered under the conditions of Problem 11.22 if $MY(1) = 10701$, $MY(2) = 54901$, $MY(3) = 14901$, $MY(4) = 22201$? Indicate the course that processing follows.

11.24. Studying examples of the sort just offered in Problems 11.16 to 11.23 not only suggests ways to test a program for correctness, but also may point the way to improvements. For example, is it necessary to let the variable K1 of our program run to $KBOT(1) + 1$ in the case of conflicts? This destroys registrations made for this top choice and requires reprocessing. Similar questions apply to K2 and K3.

11.25. Prepare statements for printing out the registration KOUNT in each course after each thousand student cards are processed.

Chapter 12

Subprograms

Subprograms are in fact programs which have been written and labeled in such a way that they may be called into use as needed by other programs. Sometimes known also as subroutines, their development has been a perfectly natural step forward in programming technique. If a particular set of statements is found to be repeated often, it is only human nature to want to represent the entire set by a single symbol and to teach the computer itself, acting as compiler, to replace the symbol by the statements themselves. As a bonus, once the subprogram has been prepared correctly the user is spared the danger of making errors in an effort to achieve the same result by his own hand. And further, in preparing a subprogram, aware that many users are anticipated, one is likely to make a supreme attempt at near perfection, to analyze the problem involved in depth. The result is that most of the common subprograms are not only correct in their Fortran grammar but represent the best paths known to computer scientists for reaching the given objective.

Library functions include a variety of heavily used subprograms, available upon demand to any Fortran programmer. Most of the functions of interest in the basic applications of mathematics to science and engineering, such as the trigonometric and logarithmic functions, together with such things as absolute values, or the maximum and minimum values in a set, plus a long list of others, will be computed when asked for by name. Most computer centers try to add regularly to their library holdings and the programmer should check locally to learn what is available. A partial list of library functions usually available is given in Appendix 2. In requesting any such subprogram the user must simply:

(1) call for it by its correct name,

(2) have input and output variables in the correct arithmetical mode.

Example 12.1.

One of the most heavily used library functions appeared earlier in Problem 7.27, the square-root function. If the square root of a positive number X is needed, it will be computed automatically if SQRT(X) is imbedded in an arithmetical statement. The letters SQRT form the *name* of this function for the Fortran language. The *argument* for which it is to be evaluated is here X, and appears immediately after the name of the function and in parentheses. This is the procedure for all library functions. In the problem just mentioned the statement

$$\text{ROAD} = \text{SQRT}(16. + \text{Z**2}) + \text{SQRT}(49. + (28./\text{Z})\text{**2})$$

was used. The square-root function is called for twice. Note that in each case the argument inside parentheses is in the real mode, and that the symbol for the output, namely ROAD, is also in the real mode. This is required for the square-root function. For each library function one must know the correct name and modes.

Example 12.2.

The sine and cosine functions have applications in almost all scientific fields. Their traditional symbols sin X and cos X are adopted in the forms

$$\text{SIN}(X) \qquad \text{COS}(X)$$

by the Fortran language. The argument **X** and the values of the two functions are in real mode. Thus the arithmetic statement

$$WAVE = SIN(T) + .5*SIN(2.*T) + .25*COS(3.*T)$$

calls for the computation of two sines and one cosine of given real arguments and for the blending of the three real values obtained into the number WAVE.

Example 12.3.

The statement

$$I = MAX0 \ (J, K, L)$$

calls upon an integer subprogram for finding the largest among the numbers J, K, L and assigning this largest value to the variable I. As with all library routines there is no absolute need for the programmer to know how the maximum will be found. It is enough to call for it by name. In the same way

$$Y = AMAX1 \ (A, B, C, D, E)$$

calls for the largest among the real numbers A, B, C, D, E to be stored under the name Y. Any reasonable number of arguments from two up is permitted in these routines. The digits 0 and 1 indicate integer and real arguments respectively. The leading A before MAX indicates the real mode of the output value.

Home-made subprograms may also be prepared, to deal with situations not covered by library facilities. This may be done in more than one way, depending upon the complexity of the task.

1. *Arithmetic statement functions* are the simplest sort of homemade subprogram. If it is found that a certain series of computations is being repeatedly used, and if this series can be expressed in a single arithmetic statement, then the programmer may choose a name for the output of the series and define his own function.

Example 12.4.

The quadratic formula

$$R = \frac{-B \pm \sqrt{B^2 - 4AC}}{2A}$$

will be more or less familiar to all who have withstood a program in algebra. It occurs very often in applications. To avoid translating it several times into Fortran within the same program, one might want to define the function

$$QUAD(A, B, C) = (-B + SQRT(B**2 - 4.*A*C))/(2.*A)$$

and perhaps also a second function which subtracts the root instead of adding it. This home-made function may then be used just as the library functions, for the program in hand. When needed it is called for by name, the arguments of the moment being provided. Thus

$$R = QUAD(2., 4., 1.5)$$

would cause the value $-.5$ to be stored under the name R. The advantage of the home-made function is the same as that of the library function: the computation involved need only be programmed once. The type of subprogram now being considered consists of only a single arithmetic statement, but that statement might be quite complicated. Programming it only once could represent a considerable economy of effort and perhaps avoid copying errors.

It is important to notice the difference between the two statements above. The first *defines* the function; it tells the compiler to associate the name QUAD with the series of computations on the right, or rather with the output of that series. The second statement *uses* the function as defined; it provides specific arguments A, B, C and assigns a memory location in which the output is to be placed.

2. *Function subprograms* involving more than a single statement may also be home-made. If the required output is accessible only via a combination of logic and computation, then no single statement could possibly be sufficient. The subprogram now resembles very closely an ordinary program, with two important distinguishing features. First, the opening statement must be

The FUNCTION statement. This has the form

$$FUNCTION \ NAME(ARGUMENTS)$$

the NAME being an appropriate Fortran variable name and ARGUMENTS denoting the input information. Since NAME denotes the output of the subprogram, this must appear somewhere within it at the left side of an equality sign. There may be several arguments, separated by commas, and these may include array names (without the subscript) or names of other subprograms.

The second distinguishing feature of function subprograms is that in place of a STOP statement one uses

The RETURN statement. This has the form

$$RETURN$$

and indicates that execution of the subprogram has been completed. Control then passes back to the master program from which the call was made.

Example 12.5.

The factorial of a positive integer is the product of all consecutive integers from itself down to 1. The factorial of N is usually denoted N! Thus $3! = 3 \times 2 \times 1 = 6$ and $4! = 4 \times 3 \times 2 \times 1 = 24$. A subprogram to compute factorials might run as follows.

```
        FUNCTION IFACT(N)
        IFACT = 1
        DO 1 I = 2, N
      1 IFACT = IFACT*I
        RETURN
        END
```

The input is the argument N. This is to be supplied by the master program when it calls for this subprogram. The output is the value of IFACT. Both input and output are in integer mode. Apart from the FUNCTION and RETURN statements this is a normal program, even including the END.

Example 12.6.

To use the routine of the preceding example it is only necessary to imbed the name of the function in an arithmetic statement. Thus

$$NCOMB = IFACT(N)/(IFACT(K)*IFACT(N - K))$$

calls for this subprogram three times in producing the number of combinations of size K in a set of size N.

3. *Subroutines* bring still more flexibility to the art of subprogramming in that they allow more than one value to be returned to the master program. The various subprograms described under the title of function are all single-valued, producing a single output value. The need for multiple output is frequent and subroutines are the answer. To use them two further types of Fortran statement are needed. In preparing a subroutine the first statement must be the following.

The SUBROUTINE statement. This has the form

$$SUBROUTINE NAME(ARGUMENTS)$$

with NAME and ARGUMENTS playing exactly the same roles as for the FUNCTION statement just introduced, except that arguments whose values are desired by the master program should also be included. The preparation then proceeds as for any other program except that a RETURN is used in place of a STOP.

The second new type of statement is used in calling the subroutine into action.

The CALL statement. This has the form

$$CALL NAME(ARGUMENTS)$$

in which NAME denotes the name of the subroutine wanted and ARGUMENTS the specific input and output variables upon which that subroutine depends. These arguments may be in the form of arithmetic expressions.

Example 12.7.

The sorting program of Problem 9.8 can be converted to a subroutine by making only minor changes.

```
          SUBROUTINE SORT(N, A)
          DIMENSION A(1000)
          NM1 = N − 1
          DO 2 I = 1, NM1
          IP1 = I + 1
          M = I
          DO 3 J = IP1, N
          IF (A(M) − A(J)) 4, 3, 3
       4  M = J
       3  CONTINUE
          TEMP = A(I)
          A(I) = A(M)
       2  A(M) = TEMP
          RETURN
          END
```

The SUBROUTINE statement provides the name SORT for this subprogram and also indicates the input and output variables N, A. The integer N gives the size of the array A. When the RETURN is executed this array will be available to the master program sorted into descending order.

Example 12.8.

In Problem 9.9 the monthly performance of a sales force was considered. Among other things the number of salesmen N and the number of sales made by each man NUM(I) were read into the computer from cards. The sorting of these NUM(I) could have been achieved by converting to real mode, say ARRAY(I) = NUM(I), and then

$$\text{CALL SORT(N, ARRAY)}$$

if the SORT subroutine had been available.

Example 12.9.

It will be observed that the array A of the SORT subroutine and the array NUM which is substituted in its place by the CALL statement have the same dimension of 1000. This is required by some Fortran compilers. It is often convenient, however, to use subroutines written by another programmer or upon an earlier occasion. In such cases the dimensions of arrays may be different. To avoid a great deal of rewriting and recompiling, provision has been made for adjustable dimensioning in subroutines. The program of Example 12.7 could have begun

$$\text{SUBROUTINE SORT(N, A, K)}$$

$$\text{DIMENSION A(K)}$$

making the size K of the maximum permissible array one of the arguments to be transmitted by the master program. The CALL statement of Example 12.8 would then be changed to

$$\text{CALL SORT(N, ARRAY, 1000)}$$

the specific size 1000 thus being transmitted. In this way the dimensions of A in master program and subroutine are sure to conform.

Variable names in subprograms may duplicate those of the master program or those of other subprograms. If this were not true every programmer would face the nightmare of continually seeking names not thought of by others in the preparation of subprograms. The compiler keeps a separate tabulation of the set of variable names for each subprogram. It is useful to remember at this point that a Fortran name actually represents the content of a particular memory location, rather than a particular number. This is why a statement such as K1 = K1 + 1 can make sense in Fortran but not in ordinary arithmetic. If the name N is used in both a master program and a subprogram, different memory locations are set aside for the two N's and they remain essentially distinct variables. The preceding remark applies to what are called the "local" variables of the subprogram, those which are defined locally within the subprogram itself, such as the NM1, IP1, M and TEMP of Example 12.7.

The arguments which are listed after the name of a subprogram are treated somewhat differently. Often the names of such arguments are called "dummy" names, the idea being that the actual values to be used will be indicated by the master program when it makes its call. The N and A of Example 12.7 are of course such dummies. As for local variables, these two names may also be duplicated in the program which calls this subprogram, but to economize on storage space it is not customary to set aside extra memory locations under the dummy names. Since many subprograms process arrays, often of substantial size, this can amount to quite a saving. Statement numbers in subprograms may also duplicate those of the master program or of other subprograms. In brief, all such programs may be thought of as being for the most part independent of one another.

Communication between programs is, however, essential if subprograms are to serve their purpose, so the independence just referred to is far from complete. One important means of communication has already been introduced, the list of arguments. The library program that we refer to, for instance, as SQRT(X) is written in terms of the dummy variable X. If called for by

$$Y = SQRT(16. + Z**2)$$

the actual argument 16. + Z**2 is computed and made available to play the role of X. The output of the subprogram is then stored under the name Y and two-way communication with the subprogram has been achieved. Similarly the statements

SUBROUTINE SORT(N, A)

DIMENSION A(1000)

begin the sorting routine in terms of two dummy variables N and A. If called for by

CALL SORT(N, ARRAY)

then values N and ARRAY(I) must be available in the calling program, and will play the roles of N (name the same in this case) and A. The sorted array becomes available to the calling program, still by the name ARRAY, and again two-way communication has been achieved. It is probably clear enough, but takes only a moment to mention, that the actual arguments should appear in the calling statement in the same order as the dummies they are to replace, and with matching arithmetical modes. It must also be pointed out that if one of the dummy variables appears on the left side of an arithmetical statement, in the subprogram, then the value of the corresponding actual variable will be changed. This is due to the fact that when the subprogram is called, only the addresses of these variables are transmitted to it, the variables themselves remaining in their normal memory locations. This consequence of the decision to economize storage space, mentioned a moment ago, can lead to frustration if not kept in mind by the programmer.

A second method of communication is available in

The COMMON statement. This takes the form

COMMON LIST

where LIST denotes a list of variable names. The variables in the list will be assigned memory locations which from then on are identifiable by the name COMMON. Two such statements, one in a master program and one in a subprogram, will cause corresponding elements of the two lists to share the same common memory location. This, for computing purposes, makes such elements the same.

Example 12.10.

The statement

COMMON A, B, C

would cause variables A, B, C to be assigned to the first three locations of common storage. If followed later by

COMMON I, J

then I and J would be assigned to the next two such locations. If now the statement

COMMON X, Y, Z, NUM, KOUNT

appeared in a subprogram called by the above master program, then X, Y, Z, NUM, KOUNT would share the same five locations of common storage. Thus A and X would be treated as the same variable, B and Y, C and Z, and so on. Communication is achieved not by reading an argument from the main program into the proper memory location of the subprogram, but by using the same common location for both variables right from the start.

Example 12.11.

The statement

COMMON NUM, LIST

in a master program matched with

COMMON N, L

in a subprogram would make NUM and N share the first location of common storage while the elements of the arrays LIST and L share the locations that follow. Suitable DIMENSION statements must appear in both programs. Note that this is one of the few places in which an array name can appear without a subscript.

Example 12.12.

It is possible to use a COMMON statement to provide dimension information. Thus

COMMON A(1000), B(50, 50)

will reserve 1000 locations for the array A and 2500 for B, just as a DIMENSION statement would do. These locations will be identified as common storage. When an array is dimensioned in a COMMON statement it must not also be included in a DIMENSION statement.

Example 12.13.

Parts of common storage may be further identified by giving them names. Any block so named may be referred to by its name in a master program and any of its subprograms. Such blocks are called *labeled common* storage, the rest of common storage being *blank common*. Names are placed between slashes in a COMMON statement. Thus

COMMON /ALPHA/A, B, C/BETA/D, E/GAMMA/F, G, H

assigns variables A, B, C to block ALPHA, D, E to block BETA and F, G, H to block GAMMA. Block names may be any suitable Fortran variable names and should not be used for other purposes in the same program. Suppose the above COMMON statement appeared in a master program and the following three

COMMON /ALPHA/S, T, U

COMMON /BETA/V, W

COMMON /GAMMA/X, Y, Z

in three separate subprograms. Then A, B, C would share the same memory locations as S, T, U; similarly D, E would share the same locations as V, W and F, G, H would share the block GAMMA with X, Y, Z. Communication with all three subprograms is thus established without having to duplicate the entire common storage assignment in each. In using labeled common storage, one must be sure to keep corresponding lists compatible. Thus the dimensions of A, B, C above should conform to those of S, T, U since both lists refer to block ALPHA.

Linking a main program with the appropriate subprograms is the task of what is called *the loader*. This is itself a program, much as compilers and monitors are programs. Subprograms are compiled in a special way which makes them relocatable and the loading program provides the specific memory addresses for each use. The homemade subprograms prepared under the FUNCTION and SUBROUTINE labels, and many of the library subprograms as well, are handled as *closed* routines. This means that they are copied into memory just once for a given master program. Communications are then established as just described, the addresses of necessary arguments being made available to the subprogram and its output information being directed to locations specified by the master program.

Certain other library subprograms are handled as *open* routines. This means that such routines are imbedded, each time they are called for, into the master program itself. Since they thus become an integral part of the master program, no further problem of communications exists.

If several applications are to be made and the subprogram is rather long, it is clearly uneconomical of memory space to use the open method of linking a subprogram to its master.

Appendix 2 will indicate which library routines belong to each category, though this is an issue of greater interest to the loader than to the individual programmer. As an item of interest, the loader will first assume that any subprogram name corresponds to a routine provided by the programmer himself, and only if no such routine is defined by him will it search for a library equivalent. This means that the programmer does not have to worry about duplicating a library name. If there is duplication, then his own candidate will get the nod.

The method of successive approximations provides the skeleton around which many of the more sophisticated programs and subprograms of modern computer science have been constructed. This is perfectly natural because, faced with a problem which is too complex to be solved exactly in a few or finite number of steps, one soon decides to seek an approximate solution instead. The question of how good the approximation actually is then leads to a further search for improvements. Computation of the standard elementary functions of mathematics, such as the square root, sine, logarithm functions among others, offers a conspicuous example. Library subprograms for these produce successive approximations until a specified accuracy has been achieved, some examples being given in the solved problems. Finding roots of equations, solving differential equations, evaluating integrals, these are just a few of the basic problems of today's technology for which successive approximations constitute the only realistic hope. Except for a few examples involving straight lines, sorting and other things of the same conceptual simplicity, the problems of this chapter amount to variations on the successive approximations theme and require therefore a broader acquaintance with mathematical ideas than has been the case in earlier chapters.

Solved Problems

12.1. Prepare a subprogram to produce the absolute value of a real number.

$$|X| = \begin{cases} X, & \text{if X is positive or zero} \\ -X, & \text{if X is negative} \end{cases}$$

Crudely speaking, any minus sign is simply discarded to make the absolute value. Since only one output value is needed, a function subprogram will serve.

```
        FUNCTION ABS(X)
        IF (X) 1, 2, 2
    1   ABS = −X
        RETURN
    2   ABS = X
        RETURN
        END
```

Most libraries will include the equivalent of this simple program.

12.2. Prepare a subprogram to **produce** the positive square root of a positive real number, approximately.

This is again of course an assignment which is covered by a standard library routine, but it serves to illustrate how such results are obtainable by successive approximations. Choosing a first approximation A, a sequence B, C, D, ... is then generated in the form

$$B = \frac{1}{2}\left(A + \frac{Q}{A}\right), \quad C = \frac{1}{2}\left(B + \frac{Q}{B}\right), \quad \dots$$

the members of this sequence drawing steadily nearer and nearer to the exact square root of the number Q. (See page 317 of Reference 1, for further details.) Consider the following program.

```
        FUNCTION SQRT(Q)
        A = 1.
    1   B = (A + Q/A)/2.
        IF (ABS(B − A) − .000001) 2, 2, 3
    2   SQRT = B
        RETURN
    3   A = B
        GO TO 1
        END
```

Choosing A = 1 as initial approximation, this computes B as suggested a moment ago. A test to determine whether or not this B is already good enough then follows. The results given in Table 12.1 for the case Q = 2 may aid in understanding this test. For the first two approximations ABS(B − A) = .5, and since this clearly dominates the .000001, exit 3 from the IF will be taken. In words, the difference between these first two approximations is too great; we expect it to grow smaller as the correct square root is approached.

$$A = 1.0000000$$
$$B = 1.5000000$$
$$C = 1.4166667$$
$$D = 1.4142157$$
$$E = 1.4142136$$
$$F = 1.4142136$$

Table 12.1

Statement 3 now shows that instead of pursuing the letters of the alphabet it is simpler to rework A and B. The present B becomes the new A, and returning to statement 1 a new B is computed. This time ABS(B − A) is about .08 and, though much smaller than before, it still dominates .000001. Exit 3 is again taken and the process repeats until for the fifth and sixth approximations, E and F in the earlier symbolism, we find ABS(B − A) zero to seven decimal places. Exit 2 then assigns the current value of B to SQRT and a return to the master program is in order. Notice the appearance of the library subprogram for absolute values in the IF. We have here an example of one subprogram calling another. Asking that this absolute value be less than .000001 as the condition for breaking out of the loop is typical of many programs for successive approximations. For greater accuracy this tolerance could be made still smaller, but it is unwise to press too closely the last decimal place that a machine is capable of carrying, since round-off errors may cause this digit to fluctuate unpredictably.

As a final comment, it is often wise to make provision against an occasional attempt to use a subprogram under circumstances that were never intended. Here, for instance, the number Q must not be negative, such Q not having real square roots. If a negative Q were inadvertently input to this subprogram, an endless loop could be encountered. To avoid this a test for the sign of Q, and possibly an error message, could be built into the early part of the routine.

12.3. Prepare a subprogram for computing sin(X).

The basis of most routines for computing sine values is the polynomial approximation

$$P(X) = X - \frac{1}{6}X^3 + \frac{1}{120}X^5 - \cdots \pm \frac{1}{(2N+1)!}X^{2N+1}$$

which for increasing N draws arbitrarily close to the exact sin(X). (See page 159 of Reference 1 and any calculus text for further details.) A program based on this polynomial might run as follows.

```
       FUNCTION SINE(X)
       SUM = X
       TERM = X
       A = 1.
     1 TERM = TERM*(−X**2)/((2.*A)*(2.*A + 1.))
       IF (ABS(TERM) − .000001) 2, 2, 3
     2 SINE = SUM
       RETURN
     3 SUM = SUM + TERM
       A = A + 1.
       GO TO 1
       END
```

The underlying idea is the same as for the square root routine, the details seeming different because of a change in symbolism. Here a new approximation is found by adding another term to the polynomial. TERM thus measures the difference between the two approximations, as B − A did in Problem 12.2, and it is ABS(TERM) which now replaces ABS(B − A) in determining when the loop is to be broken. When this is less than the given tolerance of .000001 the current value of SUM is assigned to SINE and a return is in order.

One other point must be mentioned. Although the method just presented works in theory for any real number X, it works best for relatively small X. When X is large the number of terms needed to construct a good approximation is also large. It is more efficient to accommodate such values by using the periodicity of the sine function. Most professional subprograms for computing sines thus begin by replacing the input argument X by a substitute which falls inside a basic interval, perhaps the interval between 0 and $\pi/2$. This effects the sign of the result under certain circumstances, but it is no major problem to supply the correct sign at the last moment. For the basic interval suggested seven terms of the available supply will guarantee eight decimal place accuracy, the computation thus being very efficient. The details of reducing the argument to this interval are not difficult.

12.4. Variables X and Y are known to satisfy a straight line relationship. If the pairs X = A, Y = B and X = C, Y = D are known, prepare a subprogram for computing the mate Y of an arbitrary X.

This is a fundamental problem of analytic geometry, the required formula being the familiar

$$Y(X) = B + S(X - A)$$

with S = (D − B)/(C − A). The single statement

$$Y(X, A, B, C, D) = B + (D − B)*(X − A)/(C − A)$$

provides the required Y value. This arithmetic statement function may be defined directly in the master program.

12.5. Variables X and Y are known to satisfy a parabolic relationship. If the three pairs (A, B), (C, D), (E, F) are known, prepare a subprogram for computing the Y mate of an arbitrary X.

This and the preceding problem may be viewed as the simplest special cases of the general problem of finding the polynomial of degree N which includes N + 1 specified points. The classic solution appears in Reference 1, Chapter 6, and reduces in the present case to

$$Y(X) = B + S(X − A) + T(X − A)(X − C)$$

with S = (D − B)/(C − A) as before and T = (F − 2D + B)/2(C − A)². A single statement in Fortran could again represent Y, just as in the preceding problem, but the following alternative is also possible.

```
FUNCTION PARAB(X, A, B, C, D, E, F)
S = (D − B)/(C − A)
T = (F − 2.*D + B)/2.*(C − A)**2
PARAB = B + S*(X − A) + T*(X − A)*(X − C)
RETURN
END
```

Notice that the value E does not appear. This is due to the fact that the formula used here assumes A, C, E to be equally-spaced. If this is not true a more complicated formula must be used.

12.6. How is the subprogram for computing sines used to generate a table of values of the following oscillation which blends three different frequencies?

$$Y = \sin X + \tfrac{1}{2}\sin(2X) - \tfrac{1}{4}\sin(3X)$$

Since sines are available by library routines, they may be used simply by writing the name SIN with appropriate arguments directly in the arithmetic expression involved.

```
C     BLENDING THREE FREQUENCIES
      READ (5, 1) A
1 FORMAT (F4.0)
      H = 2.*3.1416/A
      X = 0.
2 Y = SIN(X) + .5*SIN(2.*X) − .25*SIN(3.*X)
      WRITE (6, 3) X, Y
3 FORMAT (1X, 2F10.6)
      X = X + H
      IF (X − 2.*3.1416) 2, 2, 4
4 STOP
      END
```

Pairs of X, Y values will be printed for one period of the oscillation, spaced at an interval determined by the number A which is read from a card. As suggested, communication with the library subprogram is established by writing SIN followed by the desired argument, such as 3.*X, in parentheses.

12.7. A straight line includes the two points $(0, 5)$ and $(1, 8)$. Use the function of Problem 12.4 to compute its values for $X = 2$ to $X = 10$.

This is not a library function and so its definition must appear in the program.

$$Y(X, A, B, C, D) = B + (D - B)*(X - A)/(C - A)$$
$$DO\ 1\ I = 2, 10$$
$$X = I$$
$$S = Y(X, 0., 5., 1., 8.)$$
$$1\ \ WRITE\ (6, 2)\ X, S$$
$$2\ \ FORMAT\ (1X, 2F10.6)$$
$$STOP$$
$$END$$

Being an arithmetic statement function, however, the definition requires only one line. After its definition such a function may be called just as a library function. To use it in a different program it would have to be redefined in that program.

12.8. A parabolic path includes the three points $(0, 5)$, $(1, 8)$ and $(2, 11)$. Use the function of Problem 12.5 to compute its values for $X = 3$ to $X = 10$.

The master program might be simply this.

$$DO\ 1\ I = 3, 10$$
$$X = I$$
$$P = PARAB(X, 0., 5., 1., 8., 2., 12.)$$
$$1\ \ WRITE\ (6, 2)\ X, P$$
$$2\ \ FORMAT\ (1X, 2F10.6)$$
$$STOP$$
$$END$$

It is clear, however, that the name PARAB must be identified to permit its use. This may be done by appending the subprogram of Problem 12.5 to this master.

12.9. A positive integer is called prime if no smaller positive integer other than 1 divides it evenly. Thus the first few primes are 2, 3, 5, 7, 11, 13, 17, 19, 23 and so on. To determine if a particular integer is a prime, one may divide it by all smaller integers and look for remainders. Prepare a subprogram to do this.

We may use the fact that in Fortran division of integers any remainders are automatically discarded. The computation
$$(N/I)*I$$
will therefore produce exactly N in the case that I divides N evenly, since then no remainder has been discarded. In case I does not divide N evenly the result will be less than N, because of the discard. For instance,
$$(6/3)*3 = 2*3 = 6$$
whereas
$$(7/3)*3 = 2*3 = 6$$
In the first case the 6 is recovered; in the second case the 7 is not. This fact may be exploited as follows.

$$FUNCTION\ IPRIME(N)$$
$$I = 2$$
$$1\ \ IF\ ((N/I)*I - N)\ 2, 3, 2$$
$$2\ \ I = I + 1$$
$$IF\ (I - N)\ 1, 4, 4$$

```
      3 IPRIME = 0
        RETURN
      4 IPRIME = 1
        RETURN
        END
```

If I divides N, then exit 3 from the first IF sets IPRIME to zero as an indication that N is not prime. If no such I divides N, then exit 4 from the second IF eventually sets IPRIME to one to show that N is prime. Only these two values are used for this function.

12.10. In the year 1225 Leonardo of Pisa studied the equation

$$F(X) = X^3 + 2X^2 + 10X - 20 = 0$$

and found the solution X = 1.368808107 to nine decimal places. His method of achieving this result is unknown but it was a remarkable accomplishment for the time. Today there exists a variety of procedures for discovering such "roots" of equations. One of the oldest assumes two arguments A and B to be known such that F(A) and F(B) are of opposite sign. A root X must then lie between these arguments. An approximation to this root is then found by linear interpolation, which means that temporarily the polynomial with values F(X) is replaced by the straight line function which includes the points A, F(A) and B, F(B) as shown in Fig. 12-1. This line reaches the zero level at argument

$$C = A - \frac{(A-B)F(A)}{F(A) - F(B)}$$

This argument now replaces either A or B, the choice being made so as to once again have two arguments at which the polynomial takes values of opposite sign. The process may then be repeated with a new line. (Further details are given on page 318 of Reference 1.) Prepare a subprogram for carrying out this root-finding operation.

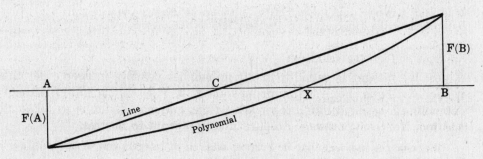

Fig. 12-1

As usual there are variations, depending upon the amount and accuracy of the output information wanted. Consider this possibility:

```
        SUBROUTINE ROOT(N, COEFF, AINIT, BINIT, X, P)
        DIMENSION COEFF(21)
        A = AINIT
        B = BINIT
        F1 = POLY(A, N, COEFF)
        F2 = POLY(B, N, COEFF)
      1 C = A - (A - B)*F1/(F1 - F2)
        F3 = POLY(C, N, COEFF)
        IF (ABS(F3) - .000001) 2, 2, 3
```

```
       2  X = C
          P = F3
          RETURN
       3  IF (ABS(A − B) − .000001) 2, 2, 4
       4  IF (F1*F3) 5, 5, 6
       5  B = C
          F2 = F3
          GO TO 1
       6  A = C
          F1 = F3
          GO TO 1
          END

          FUNCTION POLY(X, N, A)
          DIMENSION A(21)
          NPLUS1 = N + 1
          POLY = 0.
          DO 1 I = 1, NPLUS1
       1  POLY = POLY*X + A(I)
          RETURN
          END
```

First it must be observed that what we have here is a combination of two programs. The last eight statements identify the function POLY and reproduce the routine of Problem 8.19 for computing the value at argument X of the polynomial of degree N having coefficients A(I). This function subprogram is called for three times in the subroutine ROOT. For this subroutine a polynomial of degree N with coefficients represented by the array name COEFF is assumed. The variables A, B, C, F and X play the roles suggested by Fig. 12-1. All three appeals to POLY transmit N and COEFF to take the places of N and A, with A, B, C in turn taking the place of the argument X. Note that the symbol X plays different roles in the two subprograms.

The logic of the subroutine deserves further comment. The first IF terminates this computation if F3, which is the value of the polynomial at C, is near zero. This makes some sense since our objective has been to find an argument for which F is zero. Exit 2 then identifies the root as X = C and preserves the value of F3 as P. These two numbers are then the available output information from the subroutine. The second IF can also terminate the computation, provided that A − B is near zero. This also makes some sense since the root X will then have been located fairly precisely. Exit 2 then applies as before. (In fact the symbols X and C, though representing the exact and approximate roots in Fig. 12-1 and the accompanying analysis, are redundant in the program which deals only with approximations. Either one could be discarded, making the statement X = C also unnecessary. A similar remark applies to P and F3.)

One could be pardoned for wondering why two methods of terminating the subroutine have been included. Actually, in a particular application one or the other may be preferable. It is quite true that A − B and F3 will both move steadily nearer to zero, so that in theory either is adequate for detecting a successful finish. The point is, however, that these two indicators may approach zero at quite different rates. For a very steep curve A − B could be quite small while F3 remained moderately large; for an almost level curve the situation would be reversed. Moreover, if the tolerance is reduced from our .000001 to something near the lowest nonzero number in the machine language, then it is perfectly possible that small fluctuations due to rounding off may prevent one of these IFs from ever activating exit 2. Most experienced programmers have encountered such obstacles often enough so that they are no longer entirely unexpected. The two IFs have been included here mostly to raise the alert. It might be better to have two separate subroutines, one terminating when A − B becomes small and the other when F3 becomes small. The programmer could then choose which type of precision seems more suitable for his problem. To finish, the last IF prepares the way for another step by determining whether F3 has the same sign as F1 or not. If so, exit 6 leads to the rejection of approximation A; if not, exit 5 rejects approximation B instead. The opposition of sign is thus preserved and the action goes back to statement 1 to find a better approximation.

12.11. Use the subroutine of the preceding problem to solve Leonardo's equation.

Here our job involves providing the specific information needed by the subroutine ROOT and printing out the answers which the subroutine produces.

```
C     LEONARDOS EQUATION
      DIMENSION A(21)
      A(1) = 1.
      A(2) = 2.
      A(3) = 10.
      A(4) = -20.
      CALL ROOT (3, A, 1., 2., X, P)
      WRITE (6, 1) X, P
    1 FORMAT (2F10.6)
      STOP
      END
```

12.12. One of the most common problems in the applications of mathematics calls for the solution of a system of simultaneous equations of the form

$$A(1,1)X(1) + A(1,2)X(2) + \cdots + A(1,N)X(N) = B(1)$$
$$A(2,1)X(1) + A(2,2)X(2) + \cdots + A(2,N)X(N) = B(2)$$
$$\cdots\cdots\cdots\cdots\cdots\cdots\cdots\cdots\cdots\cdots\cdots\cdots\cdots\cdots\cdots\cdots\cdots$$
$$A(N,1)X(1) + A(N,2)X(2) + \cdots + A(N,N)X(N) = B(N)$$

known as a linear system. The coefficients $A(I,J)$ being given, along with the numbers $B(I)$, it is required to discover the values of the $X(J)$. A staggering variety of methods for doing this has been accumulated, which testifies to the importance of the problem as well as to the numerous difficulties which have been encountered. One of the oldest methods, and still one of the most heavily used, is known as the Gauss elimination method. It replaces certain equations of the system by combinations of other equations to produce a triangular system such as

$$C(1,1)X(1) + C(1,2)X(2) + \cdots + C(1,N)X(N) = D(1)$$
$$C(2,2)X(2) + \cdots + C(2,N)X(N) = D(2)$$
$$\cdots\cdots\cdots\cdots\cdots\cdots\cdots\cdots$$
$$C(N,N)X(N) = D(N)$$

in which the $X(J)$ are the same as before. This system is easily solved by "backsubstitution", the last equation yielding $X(N)$ at once, the preceding equation then yielding $X(N-1)$, and so on. (For further details, and a selection of alternate methods, see Reference 1, Chapter 26.) Prepare a flow-chart of the Gauss elimination method.

To avoid excessive dedication to any particular dogma of flow-charting, suppose we arrange this one in the form of a simple list of necessary steps. This may serve to reemphasize that there is no unusual merit or magic in a pattern of boxes or arrows; what is important is that the computation be planned with care, and in sufficient detail that it may be described to a machine. The steps to be taken are these.

1. Name the subroutine and set dimensions.

2. Dispose of the simple case $N = 1$ separately.

3. For other N set $I = 1$ initially.

4. Find the largest in absolute value of the coefficients in column I and no higher than row I. Suppose this coefficient is in row L. (If all such coefficients are zero jump to step 9.)

5. Interchange row I and row L. (The point of this and the preceding step is that the absolutely largest coefficient in positions I, I to N, I will have been moved to position I, I. This is known as the *pivot* coefficient and making it large has been shown to be good for the control of round-off errors during the computation.)

6. Reduce all coefficients in column I and below position I, I to zero. This is one step in the triangularization process.

7. Increase I by 1. If the new I does not exceed $N - 1$ return to step 4. If it does, go to step 8.

8. The back-substitution step. Solve the Nth equation for $X(N)$. Using this value solve the $(N - 1)$th equation for $X(N - 1)$. Using both these values solve the $(N - 2)$th equation for $X(N - 2)$. Continue in this way until the first equation has been solved for $X(1)$. The computation is then finished.

9. Indicate that the given system is "singular".

12.13. Program the computation flow-charted in Problem 12.12.

Here is one possibility.

```
C     GAUSSIAN ELIMINATION
      SUBROUTINE GAUSS(N, A, B, X, ILL)
      DIMENSION A(N, N), B(N), X(N)
      ILL = 0
C     THE CASE N EQUALS ONE
      IF (N − 1) 4, 1, 4
    1 IF (A(1, 1)) 2, 3, 2
    2 X(1) = B(1)/A(1, 1)
      RETURN
    3 ILL = 1
      RETURN
C     THE GENERAL CASE, FINDING THE PIVOT
    4 NLESS1 = N − 1
      DO 13 I = 1, NLESS1
      BIG = ABS(A(I, I))
      L = I
      IPLUS1 = I + 1
      DO 6 J = IPLUS1, N
      IF (ABS(A(J, I)) − BIG) 6, 6, 5
    5 BIG = ABS(A(J, I))
      L = J
    6 CONTINUE
C     INTERCHANGE IF NECESSARY
      IF (BIG) 8, 7, 8
    7 ILL = 1
      RETURN
    8 IF (L − I) 9, 11, 9
    9 DO 10 J = 1, N
      TEMP = A(L, J)
      A(L, J) = A(I, J)
   10 A(I, J) = TEMP
      TEMP = B(L)
      B(L) = B(I)
      B(I) = TEMP
C     REDUCE COEFFICIENTS TO ZERO
   11 DO 13 J = IPLUS1, N
      QUOT = A(J, I)/A(I, I)
      DO 12 K = IPLUS1, N
```

```
        12  A(J, K) = A(J, K) − QUOT*A(I, K)
        13  B(J) = B(J) − QUOT*B(I)
   C        THE BACK SUBSTITUTION STEP
            IF (A(N, N)) 15, 14, 15
        14  ILL = 1
            RETURN
        15  X(N) = B(N)/A(N, N)
            I = N − 1
        16  SUM = 0.
            IPLUS1 = I + 1
            DO 17 J = IPLUS1, N
        17  SUM = SUM + A(I, J)*X(J)
            X(I) = (B(I) − SUM)/A(I, I)
            I = I − 1
            IF (I) 18, 18, 16
        18  RETURN
            END
```

The dimension N of the linear system has been left as an input to the subroutine. The variable ILL serves as an indicator of the solvability of the system. It is set initially to zero and keeps this value if a unique set of X(I) is found. If, however, the system is singular, meaning that a unique set of X(I) cannot be found, then ILL will be changed to one. There exist cases in which the given system is "nearly-singular" and which, due to round-off errors made in the process of combining equations, are replaced by singular substitutes. In such cases ILL will also be changed to one, this value thus indicating failure to obtain the desired X(I). The simplest example of this appears when N = 1 and A(1, 1) = 0. Statement 3 then records failure. For any other A(1, 1) statement 2 produces X(1). Either way leads to a RETURN.

For the general case the first DO divides the triangularization process into N − 1 stages, the index I noting which column is currently being treated. Finding the pivot in that column, using the library ABS subprogram, is very similar to the maximum-hunting programs of Chapter 9. The pivot ultimately proves to be of size BIG and is located in row L. The second DO supervises the job of finding it. If BIG turns out to be zero, no unique set of X(I) can be found and ILL = 1 records this failure. Otherwise an exchange is made to bring the discovered pivot to the I, I position unless of course it is already there (L = I), in which case a jump to statement 11 is in order.

The actual triangularization is achieved by the five statements beginning with number 11. Notice especially that putting K = I in statement 12 would make A(J, I) zero, for J = I + 1 to J = N. The new coefficients in column I and below position I, I are thus truly zero. This fact is recognized by skipping K = I entirely and applying statement 12 only from K = I + 1 to K = N. A careful look will reveal that this statement computes the coefficients in a new Jth equation obtained by subtracting from the old Jth equation the Ith equation multiplied by QUOT. Such an operation has no effect upon the numbers X(I) which are our target. Statement 13 similarly computes the new B(J). When triangularization has been completed back-substitution can generate the X(I) one by one beginning with X(N). The possibility A(N, N) = 0 shows that failure must still be provided for even at the brink of success, and exit 14 takes appropriate measures. More optimistically, the shrinking value of I marks the emergence of the X(I) in reverse order until I = 0 signals the finish.

12.14. Boundary value problems of differential equations are one of the richest sources of linear systems, which enter when certain discrete methods of approximate solution are attempted. Probably the most famous example is the Dirichlet problem, which may arise from a background of fluid flow, stretched membranes, electrical energy or heat flow, to mention just a few of the possibilities. In a common approximation to this problem one seeks the values of a function at the interior points of a lattice such as that of Fig. 12-2, the values on the boundary being known. Each

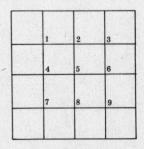

Fig. 12-2

interior value is to be the average of its four neighbors. Suppose all boundary values are zero except along the bottom, where they are one. Then it is easy to verify that the following nine equations must be satisfied, the index J in X(J) corresponding to the number assigned in Fig. 12-2 to each interior point.

$$
\begin{aligned}
4X(1) \quad -X(2) \qquad\qquad -X(4) \qquad\qquad\qquad\qquad\qquad\qquad &= 0 \\
-X(1) + 4X(2) \quad -X(3) \qquad\qquad -X(5) \qquad\qquad\qquad\qquad &= 0 \\
-X(2) + 4X(3) \qquad\qquad\qquad -X(6) \qquad\qquad\qquad &= 0 \\
-X(1) \qquad\qquad +4X(4) \quad -X(5) \qquad -X(7) \qquad\qquad &= 0 \\
-X(2) \qquad -X(4) + 4X(5) \quad -X(6) \qquad -X(8) \qquad &= 0 \\
-X(3) \qquad -X(5) + 4X(6) \qquad\qquad -X(9) &= 0 \\
-X(4) \qquad\qquad +4X(7) \quad -X(8) \qquad &= 1 \\
-X(5) \qquad\qquad -X(7) + 4X(8) \quad -X(9) &= 1 \\
-X(6) \qquad\qquad -X(8) + 4X(9) &= 1
\end{aligned}
$$

Use the subroutine of the preceding problem to solve this system.

Our task consists mostly of making the coefficients $A(I, J)$ and the numbers $B(I)$ available to the subroutine. One familiar way is to punch all this data onto cards in some suitable format and use one or more READ statements. Because of the fact that only the numbers 4, −1 and 0 are involved, an alternate procedure can be illustrated.

```
C       INPUT OF THE SYSTEM
        DIMENSION A(9, 9), B(9), X(9)
        DO 1 I = 1, 5
        IPLUS4 = I + 4
        DO 1 J = IPLUS4, 9
     1  A(I, J) = 0.
        DO 2 I = 1, 6
     2  A(I, I + 3) = −1.
        DO 3 I = 1, 7
     3  A(I, I + 2) = 0.
        DO 4 I = 1, 8
     4  A(I, I + 1) = −1.
        A(3, 4) = 0.
        A(6, 7) = 0.
        DO 5 I = 1, 9
     5  A(I, I) = 4.
        DO 6 I = 2, 9
        ILESS1 = I − 1
        DO 6 J = 1, ILESS1
     6  A(I, J) = A(J, I)
        DO 7 I = 1, 6
     7  B(I) = 0.
        DO 8 I = 7, 9
     8  B(I) = 1.
C       CALL FOR THE SUBROUTINE
        CALL GAUSS(9, A, B, X, ILL)
C       OUTPUT OF RESULTS
        IF (ILL − 1) 11, 9, 11
     9  WRITE (6, 10)
    10  FORMAT (18H NO SOLUTION FOUND)
    11  WRITE (6, 12) (X(I), I = 1, 9)
```

```
                12 FORMAT (1X, 9F7.4)
                   STOP
                   END
```

The diagonal structure of the coefficient matrix is exploited by the various DO statements, the two deviations at positions 3, 4 and 6, 7 being repaired afterward. The triangle below the main diagonal is filled by symmetry. Though this system is known to have a unique solution, the ILL output of the subroutine is checked anyway. If no error has been introduced, exit 9 from the IF will be idle and exit 11 will output the numbers $X(I)$.

12.15. Illustrate the use of the COMMON statement for establishing communications between programs.

A subprogram is written for adding two matrices.

```
             SUBROUTINE MADD(X, Y, Z, M, N)
             DIMENSION X(20, 20), Y(20, 20), Z(20, 20)
             DO 1 I = 1, M
             DO 1 J = 1, N
           1 Z(I, J) = X(I, J) + Y(I, J)
             RETURN
             END
```

This can then be called in the now familiar way of the argument list.

```
             DIMENSION A(20, 20), B(20, 20), C(20, 20)
             ........................................
             CALL MADD(A, B, C, I, J)
             ........................................
             END
```

The subroutine will thus be run with **the actual arguments A, B, C, I, J** in place of the dummies X, Y, Z, M, N. The first row of dots in **the calling program** must include the specific determination of the actual arguments, the necessary statements not being detailed here. The second row of dots presumably consists of statements which use the output of the subroutine.

The point at the moment is that the same result could be achieved in another way, the subroutine appearing as

```
             SUBROUTINE MADD
             COMMON X(20, 20), Y(20, 20), Z(20, 20), M, N
             DO 1 I = 1, M
             DO 1 J = 1, N
           1 Z(I, J) = X(I, J) + Y(I, J)
             RETURN
             END
```

and the calling program as follows.

```
             COMMON A(20, 20), B(20, 20), C(20, 20), I, J
             ........................................
             CALL MADD
             ........................................
             END
```

The COMMON statements would cause the A, B, C, I, J of the calling program to share the same memory locations as the X, Y, Z, M, N of the subroutine. The two sets of names refer to exactly the same things. This is sometimes referred to as implicit transmission of the arguments, in contrast with the explicit transmission provided by the earlier argument lists. Notice that the name of the subroutine now appears without an argument list. The rules of Fortran do not permit a name which occurs in the argument list of a subprogram to occur also in a COMMON statement.

Supplementary Problems

12.16. Write a subprogram to compute the sum of N numbers.

12.17. Write a program which uses the result of the preceding problem to find the average of 50 numbers available on cards, one to a card in specification F10.5.

12.18. Describe the action of the following subroutine.

$$\text{SUBROUTINE QUADS}(A, B, C, I, X1, X2)$$
$$D = B*B - 4.*A*C$$
$$\text{IF } (D) \ 1, 2, 2$$
$$1 \quad I = 1$$
$$\text{RETURN}$$
$$2 \quad I = 0$$
$$X1 = (-B + SQRT(D))/(2.*A)$$
$$X2 = (-B - SQRT(D))/(2.*A)$$
$$\text{RETURN}$$
$$\text{END}$$

12.19. Describe developments in a calling program which contains the following two statements, among others.

$$\text{CALL QUADS}(1., 2., 3., I, ROOT1, ROOT2)$$
$$\text{IF } (I) \ 5, 6, 5$$

12.20. Indicate two purposes which are served by the local variable X in this function subprogram.

$$\text{FUNCTION FACT}(K)$$
$$X = K$$
$$\text{FACT} = 1.$$
$$1 \quad \text{FACT} = \text{FACT}*X$$
$$X = X - 1.$$
$$\text{IF } (X - 1.) \ 2, 2, 1$$
$$2 \quad \text{RETURN}$$
$$\text{END}$$

12.21. Complete the following program for determining the largest element in absolute value in a specified row NR of a two-dimensional array, the number of columns being NC.

$$\text{FUNCTION PIVOT}(X, NR, NC)$$
$$\text{DIMENSION X}(50, 50)$$
$$\text{PIVOT} = \text{ABS}(X(NR, 1))$$
$$\text{DO } 1 \ I = 2, NC$$

12.22. The area shown in Fig. 12-3, under the curve and above the X axis, between arguments A and B, may be approximated by a set of trapezoidal areas. The total area of all the trapezoids is

$$T(N) = \tfrac{1}{2}H(Y(1) + 2Y(2) + 2Y(3) + \cdots + 2Y(N) + Y(N+1))$$

where N is the number of trapezoids, all of which have width H, and the Y(I) are the various heights.

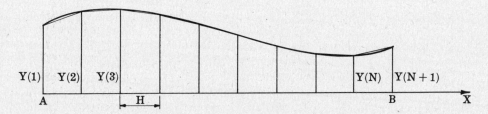

Fig. 12-3

Complete the following subprogram for computing this approximate area.

$$\text{FUNCTION TRAP}(Y, \text{NPLUS1}, A, B)$$
$$\text{DIMENSION } Y(\text{NPLUS1})$$
$$N = \text{NPLUS1} - 1$$
$$H = (B - A)/\text{FLOAT}(N)$$

The name FLOAT refers to a library subprogram for converting from integer to real mode. The fourth statement above is thus the equivalent of the two statements

$$\text{XN} = N$$
$$H = (B - A)/\text{XN}$$

and provides an alternate way to avoid mixing modes.

12.23. Apply the subprogram of the preceding problem to the case in which the $Y(I)$ are values of $SIN(X)$. Let $A = 0$ and $B = \pi/2$. Begin with $N = 1$ and then continually double N until successive approximations differ by less than .001. **At what value of N does this happen?**

12.24. A truck can travel a distance of one "leg" on the maximum load of fuel it is capable of carrying. It is not too hard to deduce (see page 168 of Reference 1) that if an unlimited supply of fuel is available at the edge of a desert, then the truck can manage to cross the desert no matter what its width is, the maximum penetration on N loads being

$$1 + \frac{1}{3} + \frac{1}{5} + \cdots + \frac{1}{2N - 1}$$

Use the subprogram of Problem 12.16 to determine how many loads are needed to cross a desert of width 3 legs.

12.25. The average scores reported by golfers of various handicaps on a difficult par-three hole are as follows.

Handicap	6	8	10	12	14	16	18	20	22	24
Average	3.8	3.7	4.0	3.9	4.3	4.2	4.2	4.4	4.5	4.5

These number pairs may be charted as shown in Fig. 12-4, each pair being represented by one spot.

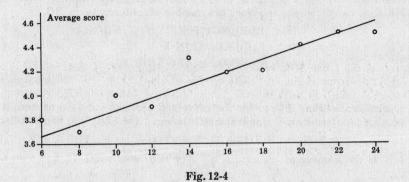

Fig. 12-4

Clearly the spots do not fall along a straight line. Often, however, it proves convenient to assume that spots obtained from observational data of this sort should line up, the discrepancies being due to certain unpredictable factors such as the natural fluctuations in a golfer's game. If one accepts this assumption, the question of "which line" must be answered. An ancient nomination is the "least squares line"

$$Y = AX + B$$

for which

$$A = (S_0 T_1 - S_1 T_0)/(S_0 S_2 - S_1^2)$$
$$B = (S_2 T_0 - S_1 T_1)/(S_0 S_2 - S_1^2)$$

where the data points (X_i, Y_i) determine

$$S_0 = N = \text{number of points}$$
$$S_1 = \text{sum of the } X_i$$
$$S_2 = \text{sum of the } X_i^2$$
$$T_0 = \text{sum of the } Y_i$$
$$T_1 = \text{sum of the products } X_i Y_i.$$

(See page 239 of Reference 1 for details.) Complete the following subprogram for a least squares line.

```
FUNCTION YLSQ(XARG, X, Y, N)
DIMENSION X(100), Y(100)
S0 = N
S1 = 0.
S2 = 0.
T0 = 0.
T1 = 0.
DO 1 I = 1, N
S1 = S1 + X(I)
S2 = S2 + X(I)**2
................................
YLSQ = A*XARG + B
RETURN
END
```

12.26. Apply the subprogram of the preceding problem to the golf data, the $X(I)$ being the handicaps and the $Y(I)$ the **average scores**. Output the values of YLSQ for $XARG = 6, 8, 10, \ldots, 24$. These are called the *smoothed* values, since they fall precisely along the least squares line. (Use output format F6.2.)

12.27. The product of two matrices having elements $A(I, J)$ and $B(I, J)$ is a third matrix with elements

$$C(I, J) = A(I, 1)B(1, J) + \cdots + A(I, N)B(N, J)$$

it being assumed that the number of columns in matrix A and the number of rows in matrix B are both N. Complete the following subroutine for computing a matrix product.

```
SUBROUTINE MAPROD(A, B, C, N)
DIMENSION A(N, N), B(N, N), C(N, N)
DO 1 I = 1, N
DO 1 J = 1, N
C(I, J) = 0.
```

Notice that the name MAPROD begins with a letter usually reserved for integer names, though the intended output of the routine is the set of numbers $C(I, J)$. With subroutine names this convention is dropped, in part because the output may include information in more than one mode. Notice also that A and B have been taken to be square matrices, of size N by N, making the product C of the same size. This is the most important case of matrix multiplication.

12.28. Apply the subroutine of the preceding problem to the case

$$A = \begin{pmatrix} 1 & 1/2 & 1/3 \\ 1/2 & 1/3 & 1/4 \\ 1/3 & 1/4 & 1/5 \end{pmatrix} \qquad B = \begin{pmatrix} 9 & -36 & 30 \\ -36 & 192 & -180 \\ 30 & -180 & 180 \end{pmatrix}$$

12.29. Apply the subroutine of Problem 12.13 to solve the system

$$1.00X(1) + .50X(2) + .33X(3) = 1$$
$$.50X(1) + .33X(2) + .25X(3) = 0$$
$$.33X(1) + .25X(2) + .20X(3) = 0$$

in which a two decimal place approximation to the matrix A of the preceding problem appears.

12.30. In Problem 12.2 a square root subprogram was prepared. A similar routine for cube roots can be based on the formula

$$B = \frac{1}{3}\left(2A + \frac{Q}{A^2}\right)$$

in which B represents a better approximation than A to a cube root of Q. Write the corresponding program and then apply it to the case Q = 2. (See page 317 of Reference 1, for further details.)

12.31. In Problem 12.3 a subprogram for computing values of sin(X) was prepared. A similar routine for "the powers of e" may be based upon the approximation

$$P(X) = 1 + X + \frac{1}{2}X^2 + \frac{1}{6}X^3 + \cdots + \frac{1}{N!}X^N$$

which for increasing N draws arbitrarily close to the exact e^X. (See page 159 and Chapter 11 of Reference 1.) Write the corresponding program and then apply it to the case X = 1.

12.32. Theoretically the value of π is accessible by the series

$$\pi/4 = 1 - \frac{1}{3} + \frac{1}{5} - \frac{1}{7} + \cdots$$

Use the subprogram of Problem 12.16 in an attempt to obtain the well-known approximation 3.1416.

12.33. Values of "the arctangent function" may be approximated by the polynomials

$$P(X) = X - \frac{1}{3}X^3 + \frac{1}{5}X^5 - \cdots \pm \frac{1}{N}X^N$$

N being an odd integer. Prepare a subprogram based on these polynomials and perhaps compare it with the library routine available for the arctangent function. Use your program to approximate the value of π by the following formula.

$$\pi/4 = 2 \arctan(1/5) + \arctan(1/7) + 2 \arctan(1/8)$$

12.34. For large integers N the formula

$$\sqrt{2\pi N}\,(N/e)^N$$

gives approximately the value of N factorial. (See page 169 of Reference 1.) Use library subprograms to evaluate this formula for N = 20.

12.35. Refer to pages 268-272 of Reference 1 for a discussion of the "min-max" line. Then prepare a subprogram based upon the exchange method. Finally apply that subprogram to the data given in Problem 22.8 to reproduce the indicated results.

12.36. Refer to page 340 of Reference 1 for an example of the Gauss-Seidel method of solving systems of equations. Prepare a subroutine to implement this method and apply it to the system of the example in question, duplicating the results obtained there.

12.37. What is the effect of the following two statements?

COMMON A, B, C, I

COMMON SUM, PROD

12.38. What is the effect of the following two statements?

DIMENSION A(10, 10), B(5)

COMMON I, J, A, B, SUM

12.39. Replace the two statements of the preceding problem by a single COMMON statement.

12.40. What is the effect of placing the statement

COMMON A(20)

in a master program and

COMMON B(10), C(10)

in a subprogram?

12.41. What is the effect of placing

COMMON I, J/NAME1/A, B, C/NAME2/K, L

in a master program and

COMMON /NAME1/ALPHA, BETA, GAMMA

COMMON KOUNT1, KOUNT2/NAME2/INTSUM, ISODSQ

in two separate subprograms?

12.42. What is the effect of placing

COMMON /NAME1/A(10, 10)//I, J

in a master program and

COMMON KOUNT1, KOUNT2/NAME1/ARRAY(10, 10)

in a subprogram? (The double slash assigns following elements to unlabeled common storage.)

12.43. Refer to Problem 19.12 of Reference 1 for an account of the Runge-Kutta method of solving differential equations. Program this method in terms of a function subprogram F(X, Y) and certain other function subprograms corresponding to the derivatives of this function. Then apply your program to duplicate the results of Problem 19.14.

12.44. Refer to Problem 26.17 of Reference 1 for an extension of the Gaussian elimination method which produces the inverse of a matrix. Then modify the program of Problem 12.13 to compute such an inverse. Finally apply your program to invert

$$\begin{pmatrix} 1 & .50 & .33 \\ .50 & .33 & .25 \\ .33 & .25 & .20 \end{pmatrix}$$

and compare with the result of Problem 12.29.

12.45. Refer to Chapter 27 of Reference 1 for a presentation of the simplex method of solving linear programs. Try to develop a subprogram for implementing this method. Compare with library routines for doing the same thing.

Chapter 13

Logical Computations

Logical computations may also be programmed by means of the Fortran language, the procedures being very similar to those already presented for number arithmetic. There are just two logical constants

.TRUE.   .FALSE.

the dots being necessary. Any logical variable or expression must take one or the other of these two values, just as the variables and expressions of ordinary arithmetic take numerical values. A natural interpretation of logical elements is as statements, their values being .TRUE. or .FALSE. according as the corresponding statements are true or false, but as was shown in Chapter 3 interpretations in terms of electrical circuits and subsets are equally valid. Logical variables are assigned Fortran names in the same general manner as integer or real variables. There is no restriction on the leading alphabetic character, the logical nature of the variable being made clear to the compiler by means of a *type declaration statement* of the form

LOGICAL A, B, INPUT

which identifies A, B and INPUT as logical variables. Logical expressions in Fortran may blend constants and variables of both logical and numerical type. The familiar operations of ordinary arithmetic may be used along with the following.

The logical operations: .NOT.   .AND.   .OR.

The relation operations: .LT.   .LE.   .EQ.   .NE.   .GE.   .GT.

as will now be illustrated.

Example 13.1.

The expression .NOT.A will have the opposite value as variable A. The expression A.AND.B will have the value .TRUE. only when both A and B have that value. Similarly A.OR.B will have the value .FALSE. only when both A and B have that value. This corresponds to conventions adopted in Chapter 2 for Boolean algebra.

Example 13.2.

The expression

A.AND..NOT.B.OR..NOT.A.AND.B

is called the *exclusive or*, since it takes the value .TRUE. only if one or the other, but not both, of A and B has that value. In contrast, A.OR.B is called the inclusive or since it takes the value .TRUE. also when both A and B have that value.

Example 13.3.

The expression A.LT.B is read "A less than B". The symbols A and B here denote numerical expressions of matching modes and A.LT.B will have the value .TRUE. precisely when A is truly less than B.

The remaining relation operations have similar meanings, the following brief summary perhaps being adequate.

| .LT. | less than | .EQ. | equal to | .GE. | greater than or equal to |
| .LE. | less than or equal to | .NE. | not equal to | .GT. | greater than |

Example 13.4.

The expression

$$A**2 + B**2.LE.1.$$

has the value .TRUE. provided that $A^2 + B^2$ does not exceed 1. More complicated mixes are clearly possible, the expression

$$A**2 + B**2.LE.1..AND.(A.GE.0..OR.B.GE.0.)$$

being true if both $A^2 + B^2$ does not exceed 1 and if A, B are not simultaneously negative. Parentheses are used here in the usual way to identify operations which are to take priority. In the absence of parentheses the compiler will assign priorities as follows.

1. Numerical operations

2. .LT., .LE., .EQ., .NE., .GE., .GT.

3. .NOT.

4. .AND.

5. .OR.

Input and output of logical data is achieved by means of the L specification in a FORMAT statement. This has the form

$$Lw$$

where w as usual gives the width of the data field being used. For input, if the leftmost character in the specified field is a T the value .TRUE. is assigned to the variable involved, other characters having no significance. If the leftmost character is an F the variable is given the value .FALSE.; a blank field also is taken to mean false. In any other case an error message may be printed, or the value .FALSE. may be assigned, depending upon the compiler. A common method represents .FALSE. as integer zero and .TRUE. as something other than zero, though this may vary with the computer being used. The programmer really does not need to know how these values are represented physically in the memory unit. For output, the single character T or F will be printed, right-justified in the specified field.

Logical statements are written in essentially the same way as numerical statements, the form again being

$$variable = expression$$

when values are to be assigned. Both sides of the statement now have logical type. Execution involves computing the expression and then storing its value, .TRUE. or .FALSE., in the memory location of the variable named. These may be combined with input-output, control and specifications statements to form programs just as in numerical computing.

A useful new control statement may now be added to our repertoire.

The logical IF statement. This has the form

$$IF (L) S$$

where L is a logical expression and S is any Fortran statement other than a DO, a specifications statement, or another logical IF. At the time of execution L is evaluated. If it has the value .FALSE. then S is ignored and computation proceeds to the next statement. If L has the value .TRUE. statement S is taken next.

Many programmers prefer to use this instead of the numerical IF, because of the freedom which is available in the choice of L among other things. If L is relatively complex this IF may be the equivalent of several IFs of the earlier sort.

Example 13.5.

The statement

$$\text{IF (X.LT.100.) GO TO 1}$$

transfers control to statement number 1 if X is less than 100 at the time of execution; otherwise normal sequencing continues. The slightly more involved

$$\text{IF (A.AND.B.AND.X.NE.Y) Z = 1./(X - Y)}$$

will bring the computation of Z as indicated provided that A is true, B is true, and X.NE.Y is true. In any other case the computation of Z will be omitted.

Applications of logical computing naturally include determining when a given expression is true and when false, whether or not one expression is equivalent to another in the sense that both always have the same value, and similar questions of what has come to be known as logical character. But as was pointed out in considerable detail in Chapter 3, certain problems of electrical machines are merely reinterpretations of the same questions. Thus logical computing can investigate the behavior of circuits, check to see if one circuit is equivalent to another, suggest circuit simplifications or design circuits to given specifications. All this is a part of current efforts to produce more sophisticated computers. Certain problems involving subsets of a master set, again as pointed out in Chapter 3, are also reinterpretations of the same questions and so can be approached by logical computing. In brief, the field of Boolean algebra and its applications is the birthplace of logical computing.

The logical IF statement, however, proves to be very helpful in programs dealing with strictly numerical affairs. It serves as a very flexible means of control, both logical and relation operations being available for the expression within parentheses. The solved problems will include a number of our earlier programs rewritten in terms of logical IFs. They also include several new applications, among which special mention must be given to those which illustrate the following method.

The Monte Carlo Method. This is a set of procedures for solving certain types of problems through the use of *random numbers*. As the term is normally used, random numbers are not numbers generated by a random process such as the flip of a coin. Instead they are numbers generated by a fully determined arithmetical process, the resulting set having various statistical properties which together are called randomness. To illustrate at a very elementary level, suppose we begin with the number 01 and multiply by 13; the result is, of course, 13. Now multiply again by 13 and *discard the 100*; this brings 69. Continuing in this way, multiplying by 13 and discarding all 100s, the following sequence of two-digit numbers is generated.

$$01, 13, 69, 97, 61, 93, 09, 17, 21, 73, 49, 37, 81, 53, 89, 57, 41, 33, 29, 77$$

After 77 the sequence would begin again at 01. There is nothing random about the way these numbers have been generated, and yet they are typical of what are called random, or sometimes *pseudorandom*, numbers. If we plot them on a scale from 00 to 99 they show a rather uniform distribution, no obvious preference for any part of the scale. This is perhaps the most fundamental feature of randomness. Our short list should not be expected to stand up to statistical tests of any spohistication, but the method used to produce it, called modular multiplication, is probably the best method available. On a larger scale it has been found to produce numbers having many features of "randomness". (See Reference 1, Chapter 30, for further details.) We shall use such numbers to *simulate* the arrival of customers for a service and the *random walk* of a dog through a maze.

Solved Problems

13.1. What is achieved by this midget program?

```
            LOGICAL A, B, C, D
            A = .TRUE.
            B = .TRUE.
            C = .FALSE.
            D = A.AND.(B.OR.C)
            WRITE (6, 1) D
          1 FORMAT (L3)
            STOP
            END
```

The values of logical variables A, B, C are assigned and that of D is then computed, proving to be .TRUE. The character T is then printed in position three of the print line.

13.2. What is achieved by this partial program?

```
            LOGICAL INPUT
            DIMENSION INPUT(10)
            READ (5, 1) (INPUT(I), I = 1, 10)
          1 FORMAT (10L1)
```

Ten values making up the logical array INPUT will be read from a single data card. If the first ten columns of that card contain TTTTTFFFFF, then the first five elements will be given the value .TRUE. and the last five the value .FALSE.

13.3. Write a program to sum the integers from 1 to 100, using a logical IF for control.

Here is one possibility.

```
            I = 1
            INTSUM = 0
          1 INTSUM = INTSUM + I
            I = I + 1
            IF (I.LE.100) GO TO 1
            STOP
            END
```

Output has been ignored but can easily be requested. This program may be compared with those given in Chapter 7.

13.4. Write a program to compute the output of the simple circuit shown in Fig. 13-1 for all possible input combinations. This amounts to *simulating* the actual behavior of such an electrical machine and corresponds to certain Boolean computations made in Chapter 2. The boxes labeled × and + are to be taken as performing the logical operations of .AND. and .OR.

Each of the three input terminals may be either electrically hot or cold, making eight input combinations possible. The values .TRUE. and .FALSE. will represent hot and cold respectively.

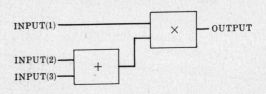

Fig. 13-1

```
        LOGICAL INPUT, OUTPUT
        DIMENSION INPUT(3)
        WRITE (6, 1)
   1    FORMAT (16H IN1 IN2 IN3 OUT)
        DO 2 I = 1, 3
   2    INPUT(I) = .FALSE.
        DO 6 I = 1, 2
        DO 5 J = 1, 2
        DO 4 K = 1, 2
        OUTPUT = INPUT(1).AND.(INPUT(2).OR.INPUT(3))
        WRITE (6, 3) (INPUT(L), L = 1, 3), OUTPUT
   3    FORMAT (L3, 3L4)
   4    INPUT(3) = .NOT.INPUT(3)
   5    INPUT(2) = .NOT.INPUT(2)
   6    INPUT(1) = .NOT.INPUT(1)
        STOP
        END
```

Both INPUT and OUTPUT are identified as of logical type and the first is dimensioned for three input contacts. A heading for the table of results to be computed is then printed. All inputs are initialized at the value .FALSE. and the three DOs arrange for all other combinations to be taken in turn. The required output value is computed by a single statement, the final product being Table 13.1. This same table was obtained in Chapter 2 by manual computation. The point of this problem is that the performance of any such Boolean machine may be simulated, and since computers themselves are built of Boolean components the present generation of machines is thus able to play a role in the design of the computers of tomorrow.

IN1	IN2	IN3	OUT
F	F	F	F
F	F	T	F
F	T	F	F
F	T	T	F
T	F	F	F
T	F	T	T
T	T	F	T
T	T	T	T

Table 13.1

13.5. The further logical operation of *implication* may be defined in terms of the operations we already have, in the form

$$A \to B = .NOT.A.OR.B$$

the .NOT. having priority over the .OR. The classical interpretation of this operation is "Statement A implies statement B". Write a program to prove that

$$(((A \to B) \to A) \to A) = .TRUE.$$

for all possible values of A and B.

Since A and B can be only true or false, there are only four combinations to be checked. To obtain them it is slightly convenient to replace A and B by S(1) and S(2) at certain points in the program.

```
        LOGICAL IMPLIC, S, A, B, VALUE
        DIMENSION S(2)
        IMPLIC(A, B) = .NOT.A.OR.B
        DO 1 I = 1, 2
```

```
        1  S(I) = .FALSE.
           WRITE (6, 2)
        2  FORMAT (10H A B VALUE)
           DO 5 I = 1, 2
           DO 4 J = 1, 2
           VALUE = IMPLIC(IMPLIC(IMPLIC(S(1), S(2)), S(1)), S(1))
           WRITE (6, 3) (S(N), N = 1, 2), VALUE
        3  FORMAT (L2, L2, L4)
        4  S(2) = .NOT.S(2)
        5  S(1) = .NOT.S(1)
           STOP
           END
```

The above is very similar to the program of the preceding problem, a new feature being the definition of a logical statement function in the third line. This is done just as for numerical statement functions, and though not entirely necessary here it is somewhat convenient. The output of this program takes the form shown as Table 13.2 which does confirm what was to be proved.

A	B	VALUE
F	F	T
F	T	T
T	F	T
T	T	T

Table 13.2

13.6. Write a program to either prove or disprove that

$$(A.OR.B).AND.(C.OR.D) = A.AND.C.OR.A.AND.D.OR.B.AND.C.OR.B.AND.D$$

for all combinations of A, B, C, D values.

The experienced eye may detect that this is the Boolean theorem $(A + B)(C + D) = AC + AD + BC + BD$ of Chapter 2 translated into the Fortran language so that a proof is anticipated.

```
           LOGICAL IN, OUT1, OUT2
           DIMENSION IN(4)
           DO 1 I = 1, 4
        1  IN(I) = .FALSE.
           DO 5 I = 1, 2
           DO 4 J = 1, 2
           DO 3 K = 1, 2
           DO 2 L = 1, 2
           OUT1 = (IN(1).OR.IN(2)).AND.(IN(3).OR.IN(4))
           OUT2 = IN(1).AND.IN(3).OR.IN(1).AND.IN(4).OR.
        1        IN(2).AND.IN(3).OR.IN(2).AND.IN(4)
           IF (OUT1.AND..NOT.OUT2.OR..NOT.OUT1.AND.OUT2) GO TO 7
        2  IN(4) = .NOT.IN(4)
        3  IN(3) = .NOT.IN(3)
        4  IN(2) = .NOT.IN(2)
        5  IN(1) = .NOT.IN(1)
           WRITE (6, 6)
        6  FORMAT (16H THEOREM IS TRUE)
           STOP
        7  WRITE (6, 8)
```

```
        8  FORMAT (17H THEOREM IS FALSE)
           STOP
           END
```

Again the details are similar to those of the preceding problems. The array IN replaces A, B, C, D since this permits the use of nested DO loops to control the main computation, four of these now being needed since there are four variables in the theorem. As a variation the output of true and false values for OUT1 and OUT2 has not been requested, though this could easily be done. Instead the computer is left to determine whether or not these always have the same logical value. The IF statement involves what was called in Example 13.2 the *exclusive or* of OUT1 and OUT2. This will take the value .TRUE. whenever OUT1 and OUT2 disagree in value; control at once passes to statement 7 and the computer declares the theorem false. Otherwise all 16 input combinations will be checked and the theorem will be declared true. Notice finally that the statement which computes OUT2 is too long to be punched on one card so that a continuation line, identified by the 1 in column six, has been used. This has not happened very often in our examples.

13.7. **Rewrite** the subprogram of Problem 12.9 for determining prime numbers, using logical IF statements in place of numerical.

The program becomes slightly simpler.

```
           FUNCTION IPRIME(N)
           I = 2
        1  IF ((N/I)*I.NE.N) GO TO 2
           IPRIME = 0
           GO TO 3
        2  I = I + 1
           IF (I.NE.N) GO TO 1
           IPRIME = 1
        3  RETURN
           END
```

13.8. **Use** a logical IF in a program to determine the smallest of N numbers.

This may be compared with the program of Problem 9.2 which uses an arithmetical IF in finding the largest number.

```
           DIMENSION A(1000)
           READ (5, 1) N, (A(I), I = 1, N)
        1  FORMAT (I5/(4E20.7))
           SMST = A(1)
           DO 2 I = 2, N
           IF (SMST.GT.A(I)) SMST = A(I)
        2  CONTINUE
           WRITE (6, 3) SMST
        3  FORMAT (23H THE SMALLEST NUMBER ISE20.7)
           STOP
           END
```

13.9. The subprogram of Problem 12.13 for solving linear systems by Gaussian elimination uses seven numerical IF statements. Modify it as necessary to use logical IFs instead.

Replace the first IF by

$$IF (N.NE.1) GO TO 4$$

and delete the number 1 of the next statement. Replace the second IF by

$$IF (A(1, 1).EQ.0.) GO TO 3$$

and delete the number 2.   Similarly the remaining IFs are replaced by

IF (ABS(A(J, I)).LE.BIG) GO TO 6

IF (BIG.NE.0.) GO TO 8

8 IF (L.EQ.I) GO TO 11

IF (A(N, N).NE.0.) GO TO 15

IF (I.GT.0) GO TO 16

numbers 5, 7, 9, 14, 18 being deleted.   It is not, of course, necessary to make the deletions just suggested, it doing no harm if the corresponding statements continue to bear these numbers.   The deletions have been mentioned largely to point out that it is because of the numerical IFs that such statement numbers were required.

13.10. Customers arrive irregularly at a service area for a service which takes ten minutes to complete.   How does the average waiting time per customer depend upon the rate at which they arrive?   To answer this question write a program for simulating the process of random arrivals.

The idea is that customers arrive irregularly and if a previous customer is being served they form a waiting line, or queue.   Our problem therefore belongs to a class of modern applications known as queuing problems.   To solve it we must discover how a generous supply of random numbers can be generated, since this is to be the basis of our simulation of random arrival. Modular multiplication turns out to be very well suited to this purpose.   In the integer mode of operation the equivalent of discarding 100s, as described in the introduction, is achieved by *overflow*.   The details vary somewhat from one machine to another and we consider first the IBM 7090/94 in which they are particularly simple.   For this machine the word length is 36 binary digits, of which one is a sign if a number is being represented.   Integer arithmetic thus proceeds with numbers of 35 binary digits.   If an arithmetic operation results in a number too large to be expressed with 35 digits the excess, those having highest place value will be lost.   This is the overflow as discussed in Chapter 4.   In general computing this loss would be tragic and the idea of real or floating-point mode was developed to avoid it.   For our present purposes, however, it is perfect.   Instead of discarding 100s we decide to swim with the tide and discard 2s to power 35. And what should we use in place of the multiplier 13 of the introductory example?   Several nominations have been made in mathematical literature, more or less equally qualified: a large number of the form $8T - 3$, an odd power of 5, and so on.   We shall choose 5^{15} since this has had wide and apparently successful use.   Our random number generator is thus the single Fortran statement

$$NUM = MUL*NUM$$

where MUL is 5^{15}.   The initial value $NUM = 1$ serves to get the generator going.   The appearance of these unusual numbers may be slightly disconcerting at first but the proof of their effectiveness, to quote from Monte Carlo philosophy, is in the results that they produce.

With this important preliminary settled, the general plan of our solution effort can be outlined.   Suppose that on the average N customers arrive every 100 minutes.   To simulate this a random number is generated.   It will fall somewhere between 0 and $2^{35} - 1$, which is the largest integer the 7090/94 can store in one word.   If it falls in the lower (N/100)th of this range we interpret this to mean that a customer has arrived, otherwise not.   In 100 such tries we can expect N successes, so making one try each minute does simulate the specified arrival rate.   (In actual computation many such trials will be made each minute but the basic idea remains the same.) As each customer arrives we must record how long he is going to have to wait for service, which depends upon how long the queue is at that moment, and when our simulation has run a reasonable length of time, say 10,000 minutes, the total waiting time must be divided by the number of customers to obtain the required average.   The following program, in which comments once again play the role of a flow-chart, converts this outline into the necessary detail.

```
C     SIMULATION OF A QUEUE
C     PRINT HEADINGS
      WRITE (6, 1)
    1 FORMAT (1X, 10H N AVERAGE)
C     CERTAIN CONSTANTS
      MUL = 5**15
      I100TH = 343597384
      NLEVEL = 0
```

```
C   SET UP FOR NEXT VALUE OF N
        DO 6 N = 1, 10
        NUM = 1
        NLEVEL = NLEVEL + I100TH
        LQUEUE = 0
        LMIN = 0
        LTOTAL = 0
        ITOTAL = 0
C   MAKE 10000 MINUTE SIMULATION
        DO 4 J = 1, 10000
        IF (LQUEUE.EQ.0) GO TO 2
        LMIN = LMIN − 1
        IF (LMIN.NE.0) GO TO 2
        LQUEUE = LQUEUE − 1
        IF (LQUEUE.EQ.0) GO TO 2
        LMIN = 10
    2   NUM = MUL*NUM
        IF (NUM.GT.NLEVEL) GO TO 4
        ITOTAL = ITOTAL + 1
        IF (LQUEUE.EQ.0) GO TO 3
        LTOTAL = LTOTAL + 10*(LQUEUE − 1) + LMIN
    3   LQUEUE = LQUEUE + 1
        IF (LQUEUE.EQ.1) LMIN = 10
    4   CONTINUE
C   COMPUTE AVERAGE AND PRINT
        AVER = FLOAT(LTOTAL)/FLOAT(ITOTAL)
        WRITE (6, 5) N, AVER
    5   FORMAT (1X, I2, F7.2)
    6   CONTINUE
        STOP
        END
```

The best way to understand this program is probably to imitate execution. Apart from initial steps, the action begins at statement 2 with the first random number. If this exceeds NLEVEL, which corresponds to (N/100) of the largest machine integer, no customer has arrived and another random number is tried. If this one does not exceed NLEVEL the first customer is counted into ITOTAL, the queue length becomes one, and LMIN is set to 10 to indicate that ten minutes will be needed to serve this customer. These ten minutes are not counted as part of his waiting time. Control then returns to the inner DO which governs the 10,000 minute simulation. LMIN is reduced by one to suggest another minute elapsed and it is again the turn of the random number generator. If a second customer has arrived he is counted into ITOTAL and the statement for computing LTOTAL then sees its first action. This statement should be examined carefully in spite of its simplicity, noting especially the dependence upon LQUEUE. Continue to imitate execution until all parts of the program have been involved. When 10,000 minutes have been simulated the average waiting time is computed, the subprogram FLOAT being used to convert to real mode; this result is printed and the outer DO passes to the next value of N. The first few lines of output will be the following.

N	AVERAGE
1	0.60
2	0.99
3	1.73
..	....

As suggested above, different computers may use different variations of the random number generator just presented. This need not upset the average user since most manufacturers provide appropriate subroutines as part of normal service. When random numbers are needed one simply calls the random number subroutine.

To further illustrate the overflow method, however, we may note briefly how it is modified for the IBM 360. Here the standard word length is 32 binary digits, of which one is again the sign. The largest storable integer is thus $2^{31} - 1$, anything larger producing overflow. The design of the 360 allows such overflow to alter the *sign* digit, an event which was not possible with the 7090/94. To prevent the occurrence of negative integers this brief program may be used.

```
        NUM = MUL*NUM
        IF (NUM) 1, 2, 2
    1   NUM = NUM + 2147483647 + 1
    2   (continuation of main program)
```

The multiplier MUL = 65539 is suggested but often something larger may be more suitable. If the NUM generated by the first statement turns out to be negative the next two statements will change its sign by adding $2^{31} = 2147483648$.

13.11. A dog is lost in the square maze of corridors shown in Fig. 13-2. At each intersection he chooses a direction at random and proceeds to the next intersection, where he again chooses at random and so on. What is the probability that a dog starting at corner (I, J) will eventually emerge on the south side? Prepare a program to answer this question by simulating many such "random walks".

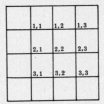

Fig. 13-2

Let P(I, J) be the probability that a dog starting at (I, J) will eventually come out on the south side. We assume that having reached any exit his walk is over. Probability theory then offers the following equation which makes each P(I, J) the average of its four neighbors.

$$P(I, J) = \tfrac{1}{4}[P(I+1, J) + P(I-1, J) + P(I, J+1) + P(I, J-1)]$$

Writing such an equation for each of the nine interior points would bring us back to the system of equations already treated by the elimination method in Problem 12.14, the notation being slightly different. Our present problem is thus equivalent to the Dirichlet problem as approximated there. Our present intention, however, is to avoid these equations entirely. Choosing one of the interior points of the maze as the starting point, a random number is to determine which direction is taken. The new position of the dog must then be recorded, after which similar steps follow until a boundary position is reached. The walk just finished is then counted as either a success or a failure and another walk is begun. After a number of such trials the ratio of successes to total trials may be taken as an approximation to P(I, J). A different starting point may then be chosen and the whole process repeated. The following program carries out the procedure just sketched.

```
C   A RANDOM WALK PROBLEM
        DIMENSION P(3, 3)
        MUL = 5**15
C   THESE DOS CONTROL THE INITIAL POINT
        DO 9 INITI = 1, 3
        DO 9 INITJ = 1, 3
C   INITIALIZE FOR A RANDOM WALK
        NUM = 1
        NUMSUC = 0
C   THIS DO PROVIDES FOR 10000 WALKS
        DO 7 K = 1, 10000
        I = INITI
        J = INITJ
C   GENERATING 1, 2, 3, 4 AT RANDOM
    1   NUM = MUL*NUM
        IRAND = NUM/8589934592 + 1
```

```
C     TAKE APPROPRIATE STEP, SEE IF WALK IS OVER
            GO TO (2, 3, 4, 5), IRAND
        2  I = I − 1
            IF (I) 1, 7, 1
        3  J = J + 1
            IF (J − 4) 1, 7, 1
        4  I = I + 1
            IF (I − 4) 1, 6, 1
        5  J = J − 1
            IF (J) 1, 7, 1
        6  NUMSUC = NUMSUC + 1
        7  CONTINUE
            P(INITI, INITJ) = FLOAT(NUMSUC)/FLOAT(10000)
            WRITE (6, 8) P(INITI, INITJ)
        8  FORMAT (1X, F6.4)
        9  CONTINUE
            STOP
            END
```

Certain comments may be helpful even though those inserted in the program do chart the course of events. The variables I, J provide a continuing record of the dog's progress, starting from the initial point INITI, INITJ. To choose a direction the random number NUM is generated just as in the preceding problem. This is then divided by 8589934592 which is one-fourth the largest machine integer. Since integer division discards all remainders, the quotient will be 0, 1, 2 or 3 depending upon which quarter of the total range includes NUM. Addition of 1 then converts the quotient into one of the integers 1, 2, 3, 4 "at random". We interpret these as directions N, E, S, W respectively. The computed GO TO then arranges for I or J to be increased or decreased to record the dog's new position, and for a test to see whether or not a boundary of the maze has been reached. If not, the action returns to statement 1 for another random number and another step. If a boundary has been reached the walk is over. In case it was the south boundary the number of successes NUMSUC is raised by one. In any case control returns to the third DO to finish the 10,000 walks. When this has been done the required probability is computed and printed. A change to a new initial point is then in order and simulation begins again.

Note that no logical IFs have been included in the program. A computed GO TO seems very effective in determining which of the four directions is to be taken at each step, and the numerical IFs function smoothly in testing for the end of a walk. By comparing the roles of the various control statements in this and the preceding problem one may decide for himself the conditions under which each is most suitable.

13.12. Write a program which outputs 100 random digits of the sort generated in the preceding problem. How "random" do they appear to be?

Here is one suitable program for the 7090/94.

```
            DIMENSION IRAND(100)
            MUL = 5**15
            NUM = 1
            DO 1 I = 1, 100
            NUM = NUM*MUL
            IRAND(I) = NUM/8589934592 + 1
        1  CONTINUE
            WRITE (6, 2) (IRAND(I), I = 1, 100)
        2  FORMAT (1X, 10I1)
            STOP
            END
```

The output of this program appears as Table 13.3 in which the four digits are found to occur with about equal frequency and no noticeable pattern.

4121322432

3444143111

2442234134

1322412422

3442333433

4313421222

2122113213

2431434124

2331241234

4332311142

Table 13.3

13.13. Table 13.4 presents a matrix M(I, J) of true and false values. Each row indicates which of five symptoms should be present for a certain disease. Thus for the first disease (row 1), symptoms 1 to 4 should occur but not symptom 5. In this miniature example only ten diseases and five symptoms are involved, but the suggestion that computers may be able to assist in medical diagnosis is evident. Suppose that a particular patient exhibits symptoms 2, 4 and 5. Prepare a program to search this table and discover which diseases are indicated.

Disease	Symptoms				
1	T	T	T	T	F
2	F	T	F	T	T
3	T	F	T	T	F
4	F	T	F	F	F
5	F	F	T	F	F
6	F	T	F	T	T
7	F	T	T	T	T
8	T	T	T	F	T
9	T	T	T	T	F
10	F	T	F	T	T

Table 13.4

Since the case in question corresponds to the pattern F T F T T, it is clear that diseases 2, 6 and 10 are the desired output. One program which achieves this is as follows.

```
C     READING THE MATRIX
      LOGICAL M(10, 5), B(10), A(5), CASE(5)
      READ (5, 1) ((M(I, J), J = 1, 5), I = 1, 10)
    1 FORMAT (5L1)
C     READING THE CURRENT CASE
      READ (5, 1) (CASE(J), J = 1, 5)
C     THE SEARCH
      DO 4 I = 1, 10
      B(I) = .TRUE.
      DO 2 J = 1, 5
      A(J) = CASE(J).AND.M(I, J).OR..NOT.CASE(J).AND..NOT.M(I, J)
      B(I) = B(I).AND.A(J)
    2 IF (.NOT.B(I)) GO TO 4
      WRITE (6, 3) I
    3 FORMAT (8H DISEASE, I5)
    4 CONTINUE
      STOP
      END
```

The logical variable B(I) is given the initial value true. For each row I of the matrix M(I, J) the variable A(J) then notes whether or not CASE(J) agrees with M(I, J). Only if agreement occurs across the entire row does B(I) remain true, in which case disease I is output as a possible diagnosis.

The program is easy to generalize to handle more diseases or symptoms. It may also be modified if less than perfect agreement is acceptable, certain symptoms perhaps not having been checked for the current case. In this event the computer may be asked to suggest which additional tests would be most useful.

There is another point which should be mentioned here. Notice that statement number 2 is the last statement in the range of the second DO and that it is also a LOGICAL IF. It was remarked earlier that transfer of control statements are not allowed in such a position. The LOGICAL IF is the only exception to this rule. It will either transfer control as indicated (in this case GO TO 4) or else initiate another cycle through the DO loop.

13.14. Suppose that hole by hole scores are available for twenty rounds of golf played by each of two golfers on the same course. If one is a better player than the other, it is the custom for him to give the weaker player strokes, meaning that the other fellow is allowed to reduce his score on the more difficult holes. This is intended to improve the chances of a good match, to give each player a fair chance to win. Write a program to test the efficiency of giving various numbers of strokes in "match play".

For the uninitiated, match play is scored by counting the individual holes won or lost. For example, let one round of scores for each golfer be as follows.

| A | 4 5 4 5 4 4 4 5 4 6 3 5 6 5 4 3 5 6 4 |
| B | 5 6 4 5 6 4 5 3 7 4 6 6 5 5 3 6 5 4 |

Suppose A gives B five strokes and that the course in question awards these strokes on holes 4, 9, 11, 12, 17 as shown by underlines. Then A wins the first hole and goes "one up". He also wins the second hole, which makes him two up. The third hole is "halved", leaving A still two up. On hole 4 player B gets his first stroke, which reduces his total of five to a "net four". He thus wins this hole and cuts A's lead to one up. But the fifth hole is again won by A and he goes two up once again. Note that it makes no difference by how much a hole is won. In match play it is the difference in *holes* won and lost that determines the ultimate winner. The present match will be won by A, two holes up.

The following program will compare in a similar way each of the twenty rounds shot by MAN1 against each of the twenty shot by MAN2. It assumes the first is the better golfer and offers the second four, five, six, and seven strokes in turn. Each time the results of the 400 matches are output.

```
C     GOLF HANDICAPPING
C     READING THE DATA
      DIMENSION MAN1(20,18), MAN2(20,18)
      READ (5,21) ((MAN1(I,J), J = 1,18), I = 1,20)
   21 FORMAT (4(2X, 18I1))
      READ (5,21) ((MAN2(I,J), J = 1,18), I = 1,20)
C     GIVE FOUR STROKES
      DO 11 I = 1,20
      MAN2(I,4) = MAN2(I,4) - 1
      MAN2(I,9) = MAN2(I,9) - 1
      MAN2(I,11) = MAN2(I,11) - 1
   11 MAN2(I,12) = MAN2(I,12) - 1
C     PRINT HEADINGS
      WRITE (6,25)
   25 FORMAT (18H STROKES MAN1 MAN2)
C     PREPARE FOR 400 MATCHES
      NEXT = 0
   19 K1 = 0
      K2 = 0
      DO 6 I = 1,20
      DO 6 K = 1,20
```

```
        C     PLAY A MATCH
                    KOUNT = 0
                    DO 3 J = 1, 18
                    IF (MAN1(I, J) − MAN2(K, J)) 1, 3, 2
              1     KOUNT = KOUNT + 1
                    GO TO 3
              2     KOUNT = KOUNT − 1
              3 CONTINUE
                    IF (KOUNT) 5, 9, 4
              9     DO 10 J = 1, 18
                    IF (MAN1(I, J) − MAN2(K, J)) 4, 10, 5
             10 CONTINUE
        C     COUNT THE VICTORIES
                    GO TO 6
              4  K1 = K1 + 1
                    GO TO 6
              5  K2 = K2 + 1
              6 CONTINUE
        C     PRINT THE RESULTS
                    NEXPL4 = NEXT + 4
                    WRITE (6, 26) NEXPL4, K1, K2
             26  FORMAT (I5, I8, I5)
        C      GIVE ONE MORE STROKE AND REPEAT
                    NEXT = NEXT + 1
                    GO TO (12, 13, 14, 15), NEXT
             12  DO 16 I = 1, 20
             16  MAN2(I, 17) = MAN2(I, 17) − 1
                    GO TO 19
             13  DO 17 I = 1, 20
             17  MAN2(I, 2) = MAN2(I, 2) − 1
                    GO TO 19
             14  DO 18 I = 1, 20
             18  MAN2(I, 14) = MAN2(I, 14) − 1
                    GO TO 19
             15  STOP
                    END
```

Here for contrast the arithmetical IF has been used in place of the logical. Making the minor changes needed to convert to the latter will provide another chance to compare the advantages of each.

A few further comments may be added. Each round shot by the golfers appears as a row of MAN1 or MAN2. Strokes are first given on the four most difficult holes. After printing headings, the program introduces certain useful variables: NEXT will be used when more strokes are to be given; K1 counts the victories of MAN1 while K2 does the same for MAN2; KOUNT keeps track of who is "up" and how many. The section labeled PLAY A MATCH then determines the winner of one match just as illustrated a moment ago. When this has been done 400 times the results are printed, another stroke is offered to MAN2 and the process is repeated. After four repetitions execution will stop.

A typical output runs as follows:

STROKES	MAN1	MAN2
4	352	48
5	319	81
6	223	177
7	129	271

Apparently six strokes should be given for a fairly even match, perhaps occasionally seven. These particular results were produced using scores for which the handicapping system prescribed by the United States Golf Association would allow only four or five strokes to be given.

Supplementary Problems

13.15. Write a program to prove that .NOT.(A.OR.B) and (.NOT.A).AND.(.NOT.B) take the same value for all combinations of A, B values. This is Theorem 2.11, page 13.

13.16. Write a program to compute and output the values of

A.AND.B   A.AND..NOT.B   .NOT.A.AND.B   .NOT.A.AND..NOT.B

for all combinations of A, B values. These are the four "basic products" of Chapter 2.

13.17. Let A, B, C stand for the statements

> A: My aunt has fleas.
> B: My brother has fleas.
> C: My cat has fleas.

Consider these more complicated statements:

> S1: My aunt has fleas and my brother does not, or else he does while the cat does not, or maybe the cat does and my aunt does not.

> S2: My aunt does not have fleas and my brother does, or else he does not while the cat does, or maybe the cat does not and my aunt does.

They can be symbolized as follows:

(A.AND..NOT.B).OR.(B.AND..NOT.C).OR.(C.AND..NOT.A)
(.NOT.A.AND.B).OR.(.NOT.B.AND.C).OR.(.NOT.C.AND.A)

Write a program to prove that these two expressions always take matching values, so that the statements S1 and S2 are always both true or both false. (See also Problem 3.7.)

13.18. Will this program correctly compute the sum of the integers from 1 to 100?

```
      I = 1
      INTSUM = 0
    1 INTSUM = INTSUM + I
      IF (I.GE.100) GO TO 2
      I = I + 1
      GO TO 1
    2 STOP
      END
```

13.19. What will be output by this program fragment?

```
      LOGICAL A, B, C
      READ (5, 1) A, B, C
    1 FORMAT (3L2)
      WRITE (6, 1) A, B, C
```

Assume the input data card punched as follows.

TssTF

13.20. The circuit called a half-adder in Chapter 4 is shown once again in Fig. 13-3 below. Its two outputs may be represented in Fortran symbols as follows.

RECORD = (A.OR.B).AND..NOT.(A.AND.B)
CARRY = A.AND.B

Prepare a program to compute these outputs for all A, B input combinations.

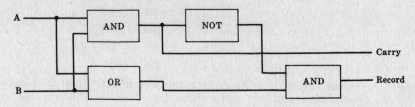

Fig. 13-3

13.21. The two outputs of a full-adder circuit as described in Chapter 4 may be expressed in Fortran as follows:

$$X = (A.OR.B).AND..NOT.(A.AND.B)$$
$$RECORD = (X.OR.C).AND..NOT.(X.AND.C)$$
$$CARRY = A.AND.B.OR.X.AND.C$$

Program the computation of these outputs for all A, B, C input combinations.

13.22. Replace the dots in this program fragment by a logical IF such that BIG proves to be the maximum of the numbers $X(I)$.

$$BIG = X(1)$$
$$DO\ 1\ I = 2, N$$
$$............$$
$$1\ CONTINUE$$

13.23. Use a logical IF to send control to statement number 10 provided that I is not zero, X does not equal Y, and Z exceeds 1. Accomplish the same thing with numerical IFs.

13.24. A baseball batter with average .300 comes to bat four times in a game. What are his chances of getting 0, 1, 2, 3, 4 hits respectively? Program a simulation to answer this question.

13.25. Fig. 13-4 shows a cross section of the lead shielding wall of a nuclear reactor. A neutron enters the wall at point E and then follows a random path of the same sort taken by the dog of Problem 13.11, a change of direction now being interpreted as a collision with an atom of lead. Suppose that after ten such collisions the neutron has lost its energy and stops. What percentage will reach the outside of the shield? Program a simulation to answer this question. Assume the wall endless to left and right.

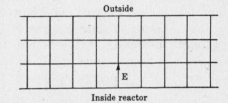

Fig. 13-4

13.26. If the two-digit random numbers of the introduction are interpreted as random directions, 00 meaning north, 25 east, 50 south and 75 west, they may be used to simulate random walks. The first four, for instance, could produce a neutron trajectory such as the solid path in Fig. 13-5 and the next ten could produce the dotted path. The first neutron thus penetrates the wall (see preceding problem) while the second is worn down by ten collisions and stops. Program a more sophisticated simulation of this process. Assume that all directions are equally likely after each collision and that the distance traveled by the neutron between collisions is always D, the width of the wall being 3D.

13.27. Program the simulation suggested in Problem 30.14 of Reference 1.

13.28. Program the simulation suggested in Problem 30.16 of Reference 1.

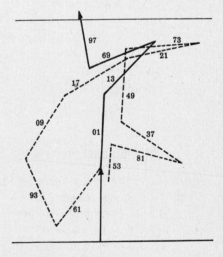

Fig. 13-5

13.29. Modify the golf program of Problem 13.14 to give from zero to eighteen strokes, the order of difficulty of the holes being 12, 4, 11, 9, 17, 2, 14, 7, 18, 5, 16, 1, 13, 3, 10, 6, 15, 8.

Chapter 14

Thinking, Learning and Intelligence

Do machines think? The difference of opinion on this question is substantial. On the one hand we hear the term "giant brain" being applied in efforts to provide a picturesque image of computers for popular consumption. In the same general spirit the term "biological computer" has crept into the vocabulary of computer science as synonymous with the human or animal brain. This sort of linking of the words computer and brain amounts to recognition that there are at least certain *similarities* between the two. It also represents a partial concession that computers do think, since thinking is, after all, a brain's principal function. But then on the other hand computers have been called "giant morons", machines which stupidly follow directions, sometimes long after any thinking device would realize that the directions are faulty. Machines are accused of having no originality, no creativity or talent for abstraction. In this case the critics are eager to point out the *differences* between computers and brains and perhaps to minimize the similarities. To them thinking is something more sacred. Both sides will, however, freely admit that the thought processes of the human brain are not very well understood so that there is no reason to become excessively dogmatic.

Similarities between computers and the brain are conspicuous and important. They are also intentional, since the human brain has designed the computer somewhat after its own image. More than one hundred years ago George Boole was studying "the laws of thought" (see Reference 15) and laying the foundations of Boolean Algebra. This mathematical structure, inspired in part by his interest in human brain activity, was shown in Chapter 4 to be central in the design of computer circuits. Many such circuits, adders for instance, imitate closely the way humans perform the same function. In overall organization there is also a strong similarity, and again it is intentional because machines have been created to solve problems formerly done by human beings. Thus the brain

(1) receives information

(2) remembers it

(3) operates on it

(4) outputs information

and so does the computer. In fact, this amounts to a compact description of the principal purpose of each. The use of the word memory for the storage unit of a computer is almost universal and amounts to general recognition that this particular machine capability is "brain-like". The use of the word thinking to describe a computer's arithmetical circuitry is not very common and this suggests both an awareness of substantial differences between machine and brain as well as, perhaps, a modest measure of human snobbishness.

Differences between computers and the brain are also both conspicuous and important. To begin, the nature of the materials from which the two are constructed is different. A computer is largely metallic, its simplest components being the OR, AND, NOT boxes discussed in Chapter 1. The brain, however, is made of biological material; its basic building block is the nerve cell or neuron which hardly at all resembles the black-box machine counterpart. With only a millionth or a billionth the size and requiring proportionately less energy to operate, it still outperforms in many ways its synthetic rivals. This small size allows the human skull to enclose a memory unit capable of storing billions of billions of binary digits or their equivalent. The comparable figure for the largest machine in existence is less than one billion.

There is a big difference in the way that information is stored in this neural memory. While the memory registers of a computer are arranged in neat geometrical units, each having a number by which it may be designated, those of the brain seem quite disorderly, perhaps because they are at the moment so little understood. One thing seems clear. The brain's method of storing information is associative; ideas which are related to each other in some way are linked together, sometimes rather loosely, so that in thinking of one it is likely that the others will be recalled. The address method does not include this capability. Turning from memory to operating, or thinking, units it seems clear that again there are major differences. In spite of the fact that very little is known about the brain's "circuitry" and essentially nothing at all about its natural "machine language", certain superficial observations have been made. For one thing there is evidence that the brain is not entirely "pre-wired" but that only the major organization features are built in. Considering the number of neurons involved, this may not be totally surprising. It would mean, however, that the brain is in part *a self-organizing device,* creating connections between component units on the basis of information received.

There is also a big difference in reliability. Though machine components rarely break down, in the sense that billions of operations may be carried out by a component before it fails, any breakdown is likely to spell catastrophe for the computation underway. A jump may occur to an unintended location or the most important digits of a number may be in error, any output becoming totally useless. Biological components, on the other hand, tend to make more individual errors and yet, because of an organization which involves substantial self-checking, the brain has an almost unbelievable overall reliability.

In summary, the important computer-brain differences include:

    (1) the nature of the basic construction materials,

    (2) the memory capacity,

    (3) associative versus numerical access,

    (4) self-organizing feature of the brain,

    (5) self-checking.

The fact that these formidable differences tend to emphasize the superiority of the brain must now be softened somewhat, because it is perfectly clear that for the purposes for which it was designed the machine takes the honors, and by a wide margin. At following detailed instructions it has no equal, due to the fact that each memory location is accessible at once by its address and to the way in which internal circuitry has been pre-wired, permitting very rapid flow of information along paths which can more or less be predicted in advance. As everyone knows, human beings often follow directions very badly. Associative storage and self-organization of internal circuitry no doubt contribute to the explanation. The differences listed above must not therefore be taken as totally prejudiced in either direction.

Can machines learn? Here we have another word with a slightly imprecise meaning. In one sense the answer is a clear yes. Machines do take in information, which is surely a sort of learning. They have been taught, which suggests that they have learned, to sort, classify, schedule, simulate and do both logical and arithmetical computations, among other things. Every program we have written amounts to a sort of teaching on our part and learning on the part of the machine. But in another sense the answer is more doubtful; some would say it is a definite no. Machines, it is argued, may very well pile up memories but they do not "understand" them. They are unable to generalize, to apply what has been memorized to a parallel situation which differs by more than a trivial amount from the one in memory. This response indicates that both the words learning and thinking are being reserved for a higher level of intellectual performance. Whether or not a machine can attain such a level remains to be seen, the questions of larger memory capacity and associative storage perhaps being relevant.

Backing down a ways on the intellectual ladder some different examples of machine learning may be mentioned, examples in which to a certain extent the machine learns by its own experience rather than being spoon-fed by the programmer. In a game such as chess, playing skill involves learning first the basic rules, how the pieces move and what is the object of the game, and then which moves and positions are good or bad for each player. A beginner usually accumulates a stock of such information from instruction books and then learns by actual play, remembering which patterns turned out well and which did not. There is no reason, apart from memory capacity, why a computer could not learn by the same process. The human player also generalizes upon his experience, developing rules by which the relative merits of various moves open to him in a situation never encountered before may be judged. The machine can be taught these rules. It is possible that because of its superiority at following specific rules and instructions a machine so-taught might manage to beat its human teacher, though this point has not yet been reached. The deeper question of whether or not a machine could learn to develop general rules of play all by itself is still more remote. One might wonder why a machine, with its facility for high speed processing of information, could not simply play through all the possible games of chess and separate the successful efforts from the others. A brief pencil-and-paper computation shows that millions of years would be needed for the feat, the number of possible games being astronomical. Even for far simpler games, checkers for example, this method of exhausting all possibilities proves to be beyond reach. Somewhat different, but again illustrating learning by experience, are programs in which a machine is taught to play a matrix game (or mathematical game) and to choose the best strategy. A miniature example is included among the solved problems.

Are machines intelligent? Here we have the third key word of the chapter. Along with thinking and learning, intelligence surely merits a precise definition, and in all three cases the definition should be broad enough to stretch beyond strictly human boundaries. But a familiar obstacle again appears: our understanding of the terrain is insufficient. Only tentative definitions can be given, and clearly they will be interdependent. We could say that thinking is information processing, learning is the accumulation of information, and intelligence is the ability to do both. This would be quick, reasonably clear, and fuzzy enough to conform to the present state of the art. Needless to say, acceptance of these definitions is not universal. Notice that the word information appears in a fundamental role. It was pointed out in Chapter 1 that this represents another idea we need to see more clearly. Add to all this the word processing (including both Boolean and biological circuitry) and the word accumulation (perhaps both numerical address and associative memory) and our thought-provoking threesome of troublesome words has grown to a serious sixsome.

The caution against becoming excessively dogmatic in this area may well be repeated. One thing in favor of the above definitions is that they do leave room for different levels of performance. The three questions of this chapter may thus be answered yes: machines do think and learn, though perhaps at a rudimentary level, and so they are intelligent, in their own way. The intelligence of biological organisms has been described as an ability to recognize, in the flood of input information received through their senses, patterns which can be useful to the organism, an ability to organize this information by bringing together bits which are natural associates even though currently scattered apparently at random in the flood. Once recognized a pattern may help the organism to survive, reproduce, progress, enjoy life, and so on. Now it is true that machines have also scored some successes at pattern recognition. They have been taught to distinguish geometrical shapes, to write poetry (word patterns such as

A dog can always fly today,

What house depends so softly)

to compose music (note patterns such as the Illiac Suite), and to discover theorems (logical patterns) among other things. The phrase which seems to distinguish biological from machine intelligence is, however, the "useful to the organism" part of the above description. Even a mosquito appears to know what is useful to him. He is aware or conscious of certain goals or ambitions. He may even be aware of his own existence, though perhaps not capable of the Cartesian "I think; therefore, I am". The present generation of computers apparently cannot match this performance. They do not know what is useful to them; they have no consciousness of their own existence. Future generations may have a form of awareness; they may be made of materials more closely resembling biological matter, primitive "artificial neutrons" being already in existence.

It is hard to really believe, standing where we are, that the human brain will eventually create machines with a free will, a sense for survival, the ability to propagate their kind, or in brief almost-human capabilities, but this has long since been within the realm of science fiction. Though by the above measure our present machines must be judged less intelligent than mosquitoes, in other respects more fully explored in the preceding chapters they are infinitely superior. They are early achievements in the creation of *artificial intelligence*. Achievements to come are visible just barely through the fog that usually obscures mankind's future.

Solved Problems

14.1. The payoff matrix

$$\begin{pmatrix} 1 & -2 \\ 0 & 1 \end{pmatrix}$$

provides a simple example of a mathematical game. Player R chooses a row at random: player C chooses a column. They announce their choices simultaneously. The number which is the intersection of this row and column then becomes the amount which C must pay to R. This completes one play of the game and another follows. For example, if row 1 and column 1 are chosen, then C pays R one dollar. If row 1 and column 2 are chosen, then R pays C two dollars, because of the minus. Write a program in which the machine plays the role of player R.

　　　We shall also arrange for the machine to keep its human opponent informed of the course of events. Note that the first statement of the program is being left incomplete temporarily.

```
      C    PLAYING A MATHEMATICAL GAME
              LEVELR =
              IWON = 0
              NUMR = 1
              MUL = 5**15
              WRITE (6, 6)
        6   FORMAT (19H I AM READY TO PLAY)
        7   NUMR = MUL*NUMR
              WRITE (6, 8)
        8   FORMAT (10H YOUR TURN)
              READ (5, 9) NUMCOL
        9   FORMAT (I1)
              IF (NUMR.LE.LEVELR) GO TO 15
              IF (NUMCOL.EQ.1) GO TO 13
              IWON = IWON + 1
              WRITE (6, 10)
       10   FORMAT (24H I CHOSE ROW 2 YOU PAY 1)
       11   WRITE (6, 12) IWON
       12   FORMAT (15H I HAVE NOW WON, I10)
              GO TO 7
       13   WRITE (6, 14)
       14   FORMAT (25H I CHOSE ROW 2 NO PAYMENT)
              GO TO 7
       15   IF (NUMCOL.EQ.1) GO TO 17
              IWON = IWON - 2
              WRITE (6, 16)
       16   FORMAT (22H I CHOSE ROW 1 I PAY 2)
              GO TO 11
       17   IWON = IWON + 1
              WRITE (6, 18)
       18   FORMAT (24H I CHOSE ROW 1 YOU PAY 1)
              GO TO 11
              END
```

After certain initial preparations the machine announces its readiness to play. It then chooses a random number NUMR and requests another from its opponent, NUMCOL, to be input by card. The computer then figures out the proper payment. If NUMR does not exceed the (not yet selected) number LEVELR, then row 1 is its choice, otherwise row 2. The opponents choice is punched simply 1 or 2. The logical IFs, three of them, lead to appropriate modification of IWON, the total current winnings of the computer, and to corresponding output information. Action then returns to statement 7 for the next play, which continues as long as the human opponent provides column selections. All this is familiar routine. The question remains, how is LEVELR to be determined? How often should the computer select row 1 and how often row 2? In other words, what should be its strategy? Faced with the same and similar problems the human brain has developed a theory of games, a logical structure which identifies the best strategy for a given situation. For the present miniature game this theory would advise the human player to choose column 1 three times as often as column 2, in spite of the attractive -2. The fact that this is the best strategy is learned by experience and thought, that is, by accumulating information and processing it. But what about the machine? Should we give it the benefit of our efforts and teach it the best strategy, putting the correct LEVELR onto an input card? This would be the fastest way for the computer to learn. An alternate way will, however, be adopted. The machine will be allowed to learn by its own experience. The following problem provides the details.

14.2. Write a program which leads the computer in Problem 14.1 to try various strategies and to select the one which gives best results.

One such possibility is the following. The integer 8589934592 is one-fourth of the largest integer the computer can store.

```
C     LEARNING BY EXPERIENCE
C     INITIAL PREPARATIONS
      DIMENSION IWIN(5)
      MUL = 5**15
      NUMC = 1
      LEVELC = 3*8589934592
      DO  1 J = 1, 5
    1 IWIN(J) = 0
C     THIS DO CONTROLS THE VARIOUS STRATEGIES
      DO 4 J = 1, 5
      LEVELR = (J − 1)*8589934592
C     THIS DO CONTROLS 10000 PLAYS
      DO 4 I = 1, 10000
      NUMR = MUL*NUMC
      NUMC = MUL*NUMR
      IF (NUMR.LE.LEVELR) GO TO 3
      IF (NUMC.LE.LEVELC) GO TO 4
    2 IWIN(J) = IWIN(J) + 1
      GO TO 4
    3 IF (NUMC.LE.LEVELC) GO TO 2
      IWIN(J) = IWIN(J) − 2
    4 CONTINUE
C     WHICH STRATEGY WAS BEST
      M = 1
      DO 5 K = 2, 5
      IF (IWIN(M).GE.IWIN(K)) GO TO 5
      M = K
    5 CONTINUE
C     SET LEVELR AT ITS BEST VALUE
      LEVELR = (M − 1)*8589934592
```

The pattern is similar to that of the preceding problem, there being a little more bookkeeping and less output. Instead of using a human opponent, and slowing down the action, column choices have also been determined by random numbers, the value of LEVELC being set for the best strategy. The machine thus provides its own competition. Five strategies are tried, row 1 being selected with probabilities $0, 1/4, 2/4, 3/4, 1$ in turn. More could be accommodated with no difficulty. In each case 10,000 plays are made and IWIN(J) keeps track of the machine's current winnings. The maximum winnings IWIN(M) is then found and LEVELR is set for what appears to be optimum play. The last statement of this partial program thus becomes the first statement of the one in the preceding problem.

Refinements are clearly possible, such as searching the immediate neighborhood of the final LEVELR in the hope that a still better level can be found. For the present matrix, game theory suggests taking row 2 three times as often as row 1, and we have done the computer the favor of including this option among the five tested. Presumably it will find $M = 2$ and so agree with us. The deeper question of whether a computer can be taught to examine the results of many experiments of this sort and ultimately think its way through to an abstraction such as mathematical game theory is futuristic.

14.3. A trivial version of the game of checkers may serve to illustrate other aspects of machine learning. Fig. 14-1 shows a one-dimensional checkerboard of six squares. Checkers have been placed on the left three squares and are to be moved to the right three. The usual kinds

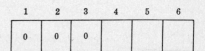

Fig. 14-1

of moves are permitted, a simple move advancing a checker one square, a jump advancing it two squares, and a double-jump four. Only one player is involved, his challenge being to complete the advance with a minimum number of moves. What does this minimum appear to be?

After a small amount of experimenting it is easy to convince yourself that the minimum is five moves. One such advance begins by moving the leading checker to square 4. A double-jump then carries the trailing checker all the way to square 5. The last three moves may then be made in various ways. But is five moves really the minimum? Even for this midget board there are many possible ways to complete the advance. Is it not possible that one of them does the job in four moves? Clearly one way to answer this question is to examine every possibility, after which there can be no further doubt. This ideal method of proof is known as "the method of exhaustion" and we now proceed to program a computer to apply it to the present problem. The computer will thus be the first to learn what is actually the quickest advance. As will be seen, however, for a problem of any size, such as a slightly larger checkerboard, exhausting all the possibilities may very well exhaust the computer also.

14.4. A systematic study of our checkerboard problem (Problem 14.3), and of its generalization to larger boards and more checkers, may begin with a listing of all positions the checkers could possibly occupy. For a still smaller version, involving just two checkers and a board of four squares, such a list is quickly found. (T denotes an occupied square.)

TTFF   TFTF   TFFT   FTTF   FTFT   FFTT

Devise a routine for preparing such a list.

There are no doubt several routines available. A reasonably natural choice is illustrated in Table 14.1 for the case of three checkers and five squares.

1	TTTFF
2	TTFTF
3	TTFFT
4	TFTTF
5	TFTFT
6	TFFTT
7	FTTTF
8	FTTFT
9	FTFTT
10	FFTTT

Table 14.1

The leading checker is steadily advanced to the end of the board, generating a new position at each step. Upon reaching the end it is returned to the square next to its starting position, which has meanwhile been filled by the second checker. The advance of the leading checker is then repeated. When two or more checkers form a block at the right end of the board all are returned together to join the next checker, which has meanwhile been advanced one square. In this way all possible positions are eventually reached. The brief list above for a board of only four squares was produced by the same routine. Notice that what are really being generated here are the possible *combinations* of occupied positions.

14.5. Write a program to list all possible positions of K checkers on a board of N squares. This amounts to listing all combinations of K things in a set of N.

The following program implements the routine described in Problem 14.4.

```
C     FINDING ALL POSITIONS
          LOGICAL POSIT(252, 10)
      1   READ (5, 100) N, K
    100   FORMAT (2I2)
          WRITE (6, 101) N, K
    101   FORMAT (25H POSITION MATRIX FOR N =  , I2, 5H, K =  , I2)

C     SET UP AND PRINT STARTING POSITION
          I = 1
          DO 2 J = 1, K
      2   POSIT(I, J) = .TRUE.
          KPLUS1 = K + 1
          DO 3 J = KPLUS1, N
      3   POSIT(I, J) = .FALSE.
          WRITE (6, 102) I, (POSIT(I, J), J = 1, N)
    102   FORMAT (I5, 2X, 10L1)
          K1 = K

C     ROUTINE WHEN LAST SQUARE IS EMPTY

C     CONTINUALLY ADVANCE LEADING CHECKER
      4   DO 5 J = 1, N
      5   POSIT(I+1, J) = POSIT(I, J)
          POSIT(I+1, K1) = .FALSE.
          POSIT(I+1, K1+1) = .TRUE.
          I = I + 1
          WRITE (6, 102) I, (POSIT(I, J), J = 1, N)
          IF (K1.EQ.(N − 1)) GO TO 6
          K1 = K1 + 1
          GO TO 4

C     ROUTINE WHEN LAST SQUARE IS OCCUPIED
      6   K2 = 1
      7   NLESK2 = N − K2
          IF (.NOT.POSIT(I, NLESK2)) GO TO 8
          K2 = K2 + 1
          IF (K2.EQ.K) GO TO 15
          GO TO 7
      8   K1 = N − (K2 + 1)
      9   IF (POSIT(I, K1)) GO TO 10
          K1 = K1 − 1
          GO TO 9
     10   DO 11 J = 1, K1
     11   POSIT(I+1, J) = POSIT(I, J)
          POSIT(I+1, K1) = .FALSE.
          KIPL1 = K1 + 1
          KIPL2 = KIPL1 + K2
          DO 12 J = KIPL1, KIPL2
     12   POSIT(I+1, J) = .TRUE.
          IF (KIPL2.EQ.N) GO TO 14
          KIPL3 = KIPL2 + 1
          DO 13 J = KIPL3, N
     13   POSIT(I+1, J) = .FALSE.
          I = I + 1
          WRITE (6, 102) I, (POSIT(I, J), J = 1, N)

C     MARK NEW POSITION OF LEADING CHECKER

C     RETURN TO ROUTINE FOR LAST SQUARE EMPTY
```

```
          K1 = KIPL2
          GO TO 4
C     IF ROUTINE FOR LAST SQUARE OCCUPIED LEAVES LAST
C     SQUARE STILL OCCUPIED REPEAT IT
     14 I = I + 1
          WRITE (6, 102) I, (POSIT(I, J), J = 1, N)
          GO TO 6
C     WHEN FINISHED RECORD NUMBER OF POSITIONS
     15 KOUNT = I
```

The output of this program appears as Table 14.2, for the case N = 6, K = 3 of our original example. No STOP or END appears in the program since it is now to be extended to seek the method of advance requiring fewest moves. Notice that the very first statement dimensions the array POSIT for checkerboards of size up to ten squares.

POSITION MATRIX FOR N = 6, K = 3

```
 1   TTTFFF
 2   TTFTFF
 3   TTFFTF
 4   TTFFFT
 5   TFTTFF
 6   TFTFTF
 7   TFTFFT
 8   TFFTTF
 9   TFFTFT
10   TFFFTT
11   FTTTFF
12   FTTFTF
13   FTTFFT
14   FTFTTF
15   FTFTFT
16   FTFFTT
17   FFTTTF
18   FFTTFT
19   FFTFTT
20   FFFTTT
```

Table 14.2

14.6. In the preceding problem devise a method of discovering and recording all possible transitions from one position to another.

For each position I = 1, KOUNT we shall determine whether or not a move can be initiated in square J = 1, N. For example, looking again at Table 14.2 we see that in position 1 (TTTFFF) a jump may be made from square 2, converting the board to position 5, or a simple move may be made from square 3, converting to position 2. No move may be initiated from the remaining squares, the checker on the first being blocked and the last three squares being empty. This set of results may be recorded as follows.

```
1      0    5    2    0    0    0
```

The 1 indicates that these are transitions from position 1. The zeros show that no transition is possible from the corresponding squares. Repeating this process for each position I leads to what will be called the transition matrix.

14.7. Program the routine described in the preceding problem.

```
C     FINDING ALL TRANSITIONS
      LOGICAL TEMP(10), A(252), B(252)
```

```
             DIMENSION ITRANS(252, 10)
             WRITE (6, 103)
      103    FORMAT (9X, 18H TRANSITION MATRIX)
C     SET ALL MATRIX VALUES INITIALLY TO ZERO
             DO 20 I = 1, KOUNT
             DO 20 J = 1, N
       20    ITRANS(I, J) = 0
C     FINDING A TRANSITION
C     IS IT A SIMPLE MOVE OR A JUMP
             DO 30 I = 1, KOUNT
             NLESS1 = N − 1
             DO 29 J = 1, NLESS1
             IF (.NOT.POSIT(I, J)) GO TO 29
             IF (.NOT.POSIT(I, J+1)) GO TO 22
             IF (J.GE.(N−1)) GO TO 29
             IF (POSIT(I, J+2)) GO TO 29
             JUMP = 2
       21    JPJUMP = J + JUMP
             IF (J.GE.(N − (JUMP + 1))) GO TO 23
             IF (.NOT.POSIT(I, JPJUMP+1).OR.POSIT(I, JPJUMP+2)) GO TO 23
             JUMP = JUMP + 2
             GO TO 21
C     MAKE A SIMPLE MOVE
       22    DO 24 J1 = 1, N
       24    TEMP(J1) = POSIT(I, J1)
             TEMP(J) = .FALSE.
             TEMP(J + 1) = .TRUE.
             GO TO 26
C     MAKE A JUMP OF CORRECT SIZE
       23    DO 25 J1 = 1, N
       25    TEMP(J1) = POSIT(I, J1)
             TEMP(J) = .FALSE.
             TEMP(JPJUMP) = .TRUE.
C     WHICH POSITION HAS BEEN REACHED
C     RECORD IT AND CONTINUE TO NEXT SQUARE
       26    DO 28 I1 = 1, KOUNT
             B(I1) = .TRUE.
             DO 27 J1 = 1, N
             A(J1) = TEMP(J1).AND.POSIT(I1, J1).OR..NOT.TEMP(J1).AND..NOT.
            1 POSIT(I1, J1)
             B(I1) = B(I1).AND.A(J1)
             IF (.NOT.B(I1)) GO TO 28
       27    CONTINUE
             ITRANS(I, J) = I1
             GO TO 29
       28    CONTINUE
       29    CONTINUE
C     PRINT ROW I OF ITRANS
C     CONTINUE TO COMPUTATION OF NEXT ROW
             WRITE (6, 104) I, (ITRANS(I, J), J = 1, N)
      104    FORMAT (I5, 2X, 10(I3, 2X))
       30    CONTINUE
```

The transition matrix produced by this program when N = 6 and K = 3 appears as Table 14.3 below.

TRANSITION MATRIX

1	0	5	2	0	0	0
2	14	5	0	3	0	0
3	12	6	0	0	4	0
4	13	7	0	0	0	0
5	11	0	8	6	0	0
6	12	0	8	0	7	0
7	13	0	9	0	0	0
8	14	0	0	10	9	0
9	15	0	0	10	0	0
10	16	0	0	0	0	0
11	0	0	14	12	0	0
12	0	19	14	0	13	0
13	0	18	15	0	0	0
14	0	17	0	16	15	0
15	0	18	0	16	0	0
16	0	19	0	0	0	0
17	0	0	0	19	18	0
18	0	0	20	19	0	0
19	0	0	20	0	0	0
20	0	0	0	0	0	0

Table 14.3

14.8. How may all possible paths from position 1 to position 20 above be discovered by use of the transition matrix?

We note first from row 1 of the matrix that a transition from position 1 to position 5 can be made. Shifting to row 5 we then see that a second move can achieve position 11. From there successive moves produce positions 14, 17, 19 and 20. This path requires six moves and was found by taking the first possible choice from each active row of the transition matrix. A second path may now be found by altering the first. We adopt the policy of making such alterations as late as possible. Thus since no options exist from position 19, we see what else could have been done from position 17. As the matrix shows, the transition 17-19 can be replaced by 17-18. In making such replacements we adopt the further policy of always taking the next option available in the row, omitting none. In this way all possible paths will ultimately be found. The first few, in the order discovered, are the following.

$$1\text{-}5\text{-}11\text{-}14\text{-}17\text{-}19\text{-}20$$
$$1\text{-}5\text{-}11\text{-}14\text{-}17\text{-}18\text{-}20$$
$$1\text{-}5\text{-}11\text{-}14\text{-}17\text{-}18\text{-}19\text{-}20$$
$$1\text{-}5\text{-}11\text{-}14\text{-}16\text{-}19\text{-}20$$
$$1\text{-}5\text{-}11\text{-}14\text{-}15\text{-}18\text{-}20$$
$$1\text{-}5\text{-}11\text{-}14\text{-}15\text{-}18\text{-}19\text{-}20$$

Notice that once a new selection has been made in any row of the matrix, we must begin again with the first choice in all later rows. Otherwise some possibilities would be lost. If the number of moves for each path is computed, the minimum length can be determined. The problem of minimizing the number of moves will thus have been solved by a method of exhaustion, the generation and testing of every available path.

14.9. Program the computation suggested in the preceding problem.

Here is one possibility.

```
C     FINDING THE SHORTEST PATH BY TESTING ALL PATHS
      DIMENSION IPATH(25), MINPA(300, 25), KT(252)
      MOVES = 25
      I2 = 0
      K3 = 0
      DO 31 I = 1, KOUNT
```

```
         31  KT(I) = 1
             NOW = 1
             N1 = 2
             IPATH(1) = 1

C     FIND A PATH
         32  KTNOW = KT(NOW)
             IF (ITRANS(NOW, KTNOW).NE.0) GO TO 33
             KT(NOW) = KT(NOW) + 1
             GO TO 32
         33  IPATH(N1) = ITRANS(NOW, KTNOW)
             IF (IPATH(N1).EQ.KOUNT) GO TO 34
             N1 = N1 + 1
             NOW = IPATH(N1 − 1)
             GO TO 32

C     WHEN PATH IS FINISHED
         34  K3 = K3 + 1
             IF ((N1 − 1).GT.MOVES) GO TO 37
             IF ((N1 − 1).EQ.MOVES) GO TO 35
             MOVES = N1 − 1
             I2 = 0
         35  I2 = I2 + 1
             DO 36 J3 = 1, N1
         36  MINPA(I2, J3) = IPATH(J3)

C     HOW IS NEXT PATH TO BE FOUND
         37  IF (KT(NOW).EQ.(N − 1)) GO TO 38
             KT(NOW) = KT(NOW) + 1
             KTNOW = KT(NOW)
             IF (ITRANS(NOW, KTNOW).NE.0) GO TO 39
             GO TO 37
         38  IF (NOW.EQ.1) GO TO 41
             N1 = N1 − 1
             NOW = IPATH(N1 − 1)
             GO TO 37
         39  NOWPL1 = NOW + 1
             DO 40 I1 = NOWPL1, KOUNT
         40  KT(I1) = 1
             GO TO 33

C     OUTPUT AND STOP
         41  WRITE (6, 105) K3
        105  FORMAT (19H NUMBER OF PATHS IS, I6)
             WRITE (6, 106) I2
        106  FORMAT (28H NUMBER OF SHORTEST PATHS IS, I6)
             WRITE (6, 107) MOVES
        107  FORMAT (25H SHORTEST PATH HAS LENGTH, I6)
             WRITE (6, 108)
        108  FORMAT (19H THE SHORTEST PATHS)
             MOVPL1 = MOVES + 1
             DO 42 I3 = 1, I2
         42  WRITE (6, 109) (MINPA(I3, J3), J3 = 1, MOVPL1)
        109  FORMAT (10(I4))
             STOP
             END
```

The output from this program appears as Table 14.4. Having proved these paths to be the shortest, the computer will be unbeatable at this miniature checkers game.

NUMBER OF PATHS IS   200
NUMBER OF SHORTEST PATHS IS   7
SHORTEST PATH HAS LENGTH   5
THE SHORTEST PATHS

1	5	11	12	19	20
1	5	6	12	19	20
1	2	14	17	19	20
1	2	14	17	18	20
1	2	14	16	19	20
1	2	14	15	18	20
1	2	3	12	19	20

Table 14.4

The basic idea of this program is suitable for any size checkerboard. However, in the various dimensioning statements the size has been limited to at most N = 10. At most 252 positions are thus possible. The number of paths to be tested for a board of even this modest size proves to be many thousands. It is pointless to apply the method of exhaustive search to larger boards because of the excessive amount of computer time which would be required. Having become used to the very great computing speed of modern machines, it comes as something of a surprise to learn that many problems of apparently small size demand speeds even faster; but problems of combinatorial character, in which all the combinations of certain elements must be used, definitely make such demands. The prospect of exploiting computer speed to establish results by testing all possible alternatives turns out to be illusory in such cases. Our little checkerboard problem is of this type.

Supplementary Problems

14.10. Write a program which permits a computer to learn from experience the best way to choose rows in the following matrix game.

$$\begin{pmatrix} 0 & 1 & 2 \\ 1 & 0 & 1 \\ 1 & 2 & 0 \end{pmatrix}$$

14.11. Modify the program of the preceding problem so that two computers play against each other, each trying to learn the best strategy by experience.

14.12. How many chess queens are needed to "cover" a chessboard? (A board is called covered when every square is either occupied or threatened.) Fig. 14-2, for example, shows four queens covering a 6 × 6 board. Write a program to determine by exhaustive search whether or not three queens could do the same job.

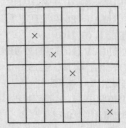

Fig. 14-2

14.13. Continuing Problem 14.12, it is known that five queens can cover the regular 8×8 chessboard. Is it feasible to test by exhaustive search whether or not four queens could also cover?

14.14. Teach a computer to read by first developing a standard set of characters somewhat as illustrated in Fig. 14-3 and then writing a program by which the machine may recognize such patterns.

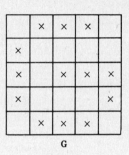 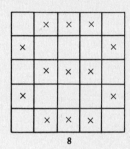

Fig. 14-3

14.15. Fig. 14-4 presents an ancient puzzle. Without turning the pieces, simply sliding them up and down or sideways, the square is to be moved to the lower left corner. Could a computer be taught to think its own way through to a solution?

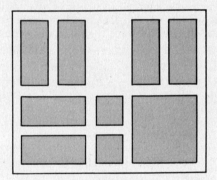

Fig. 14-4

Further Fortran

Double precision arithmetic provides a means for improving the accuracy of a computation. It can be used, for example, if unusual accuracy is a requirement in a given problem, or if the length of the computation in question is so great that round-off errors may accumulate to the point where they obscure the actual result. A double-precision value is stored in two memory locations. The programmer, however, refers to it by a single Fortran name, the arrangements necessary for proper treatment of the combined locations being made by the compiler. Variables which are to take double-precision values in a program must be identified as such. A type-declaration statement of the form

DOUBLE PRECISION A, B, C

makes A, B, C double-precision variables. Only real variables may be so declared, not integers. The values assumed by such variables are called double-precision numbers and may be written by the programmer as one to seventeen decimal digits plus decimal point. A minus sign must be used if the number is negative; a plus sign is optional. An exponential form is also available as for single-precision variables, the letter D replacing the E, in which case the decimal point may be omitted and will be assumed at the end. If fewer than ten digits are given, the exponent is necessary. Here are a few examples of double-precision constants as they might appear in a program:

1492.D0   −1620.14921066   1492D2

Arithmetic expressions including double-precision variables and constants are formed by our earlier rules, single-precision variables being included if desired. The expression will be computed in double-precision if even one such variable is included. The result will be stored in the mode indicated by the left side of the statement being executed. Suppose, for instance, that A, B, C are double-precision variables. Then

A = B + C**2 − (1./X)

will be computed and stored in double-precision, even though X is a single-precision variable. However

X = A + B*C

will be computed in double-precision and stored in single.

Subprograms may be prepared in double-precision mode, the heading indicating this as in the example

DOUBLE PRECISION FUNCTION NAME(A, B, C)

where NAME is the function name and A, B, C the arguments. This name must also be listed in the type-declaration statement of the master program. Library routines include many of this type, such as DSIN which gives the double-precision sine of a double-precision argument, or DSQRT which gives a double-precision square root.

Input and output of double-precision values is achieved by a FORMAT statement using the D specification

Dw.d

in which as usual w is an integer giving the total field width (including sign, decimal point, at least one place to the left of the decimal point, and a four place exponent) and d designates the number of places to the right of the decimal point. In general, apart from the points just mentioned, double-precision arithmetic is handled by the same rules as single-precision.

Complex arithmetic is also provided for in the Fortran language. A complex value, like a double-precision value, is stored in two memory locations but once again the programmer refers to it by a single Fortran name, the arrangements necessary for proper treatment of the combined locations being made by the compiler. Variables which are to take complex values must be identified in a type-declaration statement of the form

$$\text{COMPLEX A, B, C}$$

which makes A, B, C complex. The values assumed by such variables are called complex numbers and are written by the programmer as (X, Y) where X and Y are single-precision real constants. X and Y are known as the real and imaginary parts of the complex number, even though both as just indicated are in real mode. This double use of the word real is not usually troublesome. The statement

$$A = (2., 3.)$$

thus assigns A the value shown, otherwise represented by the symbol $2 + 3i$, though not in Fortran.

Complex expressions may combine both real and complex quantities by the usual arithmetic operation symbols. Integers may also appear, but only as subscripts or exponents. Exponents of complex expressions are restricted to integer mode. Other than this, complex expressions are formed in the same way as real expressions.

Arithmetical statements such as

$$\text{complex variable} = \text{complex expression}$$

$$\text{complex variable} = \text{real expression}$$

will lead to storage of the variable in complex mode. An integer expression may not, however, appear on the right side. Further, if the expression on the right side is complex the variable on the left must also be complex. Thus

$$A = B**2 + C**2$$

is permissible, as is $$A = X*Y$$

for X and Y real. But we are not allowed to write

$$A = I + J$$

for I, J integers, while $$X = B**2 + C**2$$

is also forbidden. Since complex numbers do not have an order relationship, they cannot appear as the expression in an arithmetic IF statement. Nor may they be used with the operations .LT., .LE., and so on.

Complex subprograms may be prepared much as real subprograms, identification in the form $$\text{COMPLEX FUNCTION NAME(A, B, C)}$$

then being appropriate. Numerous library routines of this sort exist.

Input and output of complex numbers amounts to the transferral of real number pairs, the F and E specifications being appropriate. Thus

$$\text{READ (5, 1) A}$$
$$\text{1 FORMAT (2F10.6)}$$

will read the single complex number A. It is not necessary that the two parts of A have the same specifications, though ordinarily one would expect this to be the case.

The input-output capability of the Fortran language includes several features not already mentioned.

1. **The A specification.** This is used for reading and writing alphabetic information that is to be processed. This processing may involve sorting the data into alphabetical order, classifying it, or simply rearranging it for a specified purpose. The H specification for such data is already familiar, but information read under it cannot be processed. It is used largely for printing headings and other identification.

The general form of the A specification is

$$\text{Aw}$$

where w is a positive integer designating the number of characters to be processed. In the code usually used, six binary digits are required to represent one character. A memory location of 36 binary digits can thus hold six characters. If w exceeds six, only the six rightmost characters in the field are stored; if w is less than six, the w characters are stored left justified in the storage register. For example, suppose a card punched NOW IS THE TIME. Then

$$\text{READ (5, 1) A, B}$$
$$\text{1 FORMAT (2A6)}$$

would cause the characters NOWsIS to be stored in the memory location of the variable A while sTHEsT would be stored for B. For output the w leftmost characters of the storage register designated are written. If w exceeds six, these characters are preceded by blanks. Two examples of processing alphabetical information will be given.

Example A.1.

Suppose the variables I, J, K represent registers containing alphabetic data and consider this brief program fragment.

```
      IF (I.LT.J) GO TO 2
      IF (J.LT.K) GO TO 1
      GO TO 3
    1 L = J
      GO TO 5
    2 IF (I.LT.K) GO TO 4
    3 L = K
      GO TO 5
    4 L = I
    5 ...
```

Because of the way in which standard codes are designed, alphabetical order often conforms with numerical order, making the relation symbols such as .LT. available for alphabetizing. Here we may interpret .LT. to mean "comes before" in the alphabetical order. A modest inspection will show that the above fragment finds out which of the three elements I, J, K comes before the others, and then assigns this element to the name L. Statement 5 continues the program.

Example A.2.

A warehouse stocks N different items. Each item is identified by a name such as XT1492 or BH1620 consisting of six characters. These names are stored as NAME(I) along with a second array INV(I) which records the current inventory of each item. As orders are placed they are punched onto cards, the item name in the first six columns and the number wanted in the next five. The following program fragment then keeps the inventory up to date.

```
                    DIMENSION NAME(5000), INV(5000)
              1  READ (5, 2) ITEM, NUMB
              2  FORMAT (A6, I5)
                 DO 3 I = 1, N
                 IF (ITEM.EQ.NAME(I)) GO TO 4
              3  CONTINUE
                 GO TO 1
              4  IF (NUMB.GT.INV(I)) GO TO 1
                 INV(I) = INV(I) − NUMB
                 GO TO 1
```

As each card is read, the DO loop searches for the corresponding NAME(I). If none is found, because of an error, another card is read. If the item is found the corresponding INV(I) is reduced by the amount of the order, unless the stock was insufficient. Improvements in the program may be made to output an account of the actions taken.

2. **The O specification.** Information in octal form may be input or output by using the specification

$$Ow$$

in which w again gives the field width. As suggested in Chapter 4, octal symbols provide a convenient abbreviation of binary symbols and may be helpful in the transferral of binary data. The statements

$$READ (5, 1) I$$

$$1 \ FORMAT (O12)$$

would take the digits 000000002724 (octal equivalent of decimal 000000001492) and store them in memory as

$$000000000000000000000000010111010100$$

each octal digit having been converted to three binary digits. In a machine with 36 bit registers, the rightmost 12 octal digits will be chosen if w is greater than 12; if w is less than 12 the w digits are right-justified in the register and zeros are filled in to the left. Octal format is used rarely if at all by the average programmer.

3. **The DATA statement.** This provides another way for introducing values of variables, such as initial values. It has been shown how these can be read from data cards or assigned by arithmetic statements. The form

$$DATA \ LIST/VALUES/$$

will assign values as provided to the variables named in the list. For example,

$$DATA \ A, I/1.0, 1/$$

sets the real variable A equal to 1.0 and the integer I equal to 1. Similarly

$$DATA \ ARRAY/1., 2., 3., 4./$$

provides values for an array which has already been dimensioned. Only the array name, without subscript, appears. A built-in DO loop is also possible, the statement

$$DATA \ (B(I), I = 1, 100)/100*1.0/$$

giving each element of the array B the initial value 1.0. The 100* instructs the compiler to use the 1.0 one hundred times. A suitable DIMENSION statement is again assumed. Other modes may also be handled. Thus

$$COMPLEX \ C$$

$$DOUBLE \ PRECISION \ D$$

LOGICAL L

DATA C, D, L/(1., 2.), 1492.D2, .TRUE./

accommodates the assortment C, D, L. Alphabetic information may also be input, identified by an H specification. Thus

DATA Z/6HITEM12/

gives variable Z the value ITEM12.

4. **The BLOCK DATA statement** provides a similar service for variables assigned to labeled common storage. Here the simple DATA statement is not enough since the problem of communications between subprograms using this common storage must be faced. BLOCK DATA is essentially a subprogram for effecting such communications. It can contain only DATA, COMMON, DIMENSION and type-declaration statements. The example

BLOCK DATA

COMMON/ALPHA/A, B/BETA/C, D

DIMENSION A(2)

COMPLEX C

DATA A, B/2*1., 3.14/

DATA C, D/(1.414, 1.731), 2./

suggests the pattern. Both DATA statements could have been blended into one.

5. **The NAMELIST statement** is also available for reading data. Used in combination with a READ, it makes it unnecessary for the programmer to describe his data in FORMAT statements. The statements

NAMELIST/ONE/A, B, C, D

READ (5, ONE)

would cause the card

$ONE, A = 1.4, B = 1.7, C = 2.0, D = 2.2$

to be read. The first $ sign must be in column two. **All commas are necessary.** Variables A, B, C, D will be assigned the indicated values. NAMELIST statements should be placed at the beginning of a program, before any executable statements. If they involve arrays the accompanying DIMENSION statement should come earlier, as in the example

DIMENSION X(10)

NAMELIST/TWO/X, Y, Z

READ (5, TWO)

for which the accompanying card might be this:

$TWO, X = 1, 1, 1, 1, 1, 2, 2, 2, 2, 2, Y = 3.14, Z = 2.72$

Again the first $ sign must be in column two. Here all values for list TWO have been provided at once. This is not necessary; another READ elsewhere in the program could finish the job if it were not finished here. However, when an array is referred to by name only, without subscript, all values as dimensioned should be provided. This was done here for array X. Note that no decimal point appears in the X data. The computer will make the necessary conversions to real mode. If the data are too long for one card, continuations may be made. Each card should have a comma for its last character, except the last which has the $. Only the first card should have the initial

$, the others resuming the data flow beginning in column two or beyond. The asterisk can again be used to show repeated values, 5*(1.) meaning five consecutive ones. Values in complex, double-precision or logical mode can be read more or less as usual. Alphabetic information should be punched in a form such as $THREE, E = 6HITEM12$ which reads the value ITEM12 for E, assuming this has already been identified as belonging to namelist THREE.

Arranging output information in a form convenient to a given problem is made easier by the use of H specification and slashes as described earlier. The first position of a print line is also of some use in this regard. We have been leaving this position blank, which is actually the equivalent of requesting single-spacing of the output lines. Other possibilities exist. If 0, 1 or + is designated for this position it will not be printed. Instead the following action will be taken:

0　Double spacing. One line will be skipped before the indicated line is printed.

1　A new page will be positioned before printing of the indicated line.

+　No advance. The indicated line will be printed on top of the previous line.

As an example, the statements

WRITE (6, 1)

1 FORMAT (6H1TITLE)

will cause the heading TITLE to be printed beginning in column two of a new output page. Much more versatile is

6. **The FORMAT GENERATOR** with its companion statements RESTORE, SPACE, REPEAT and END OF FORMAT. With these it becomes possible to plan outputs almost pictorially.

Example A.3.

The statements

WRITE (6, 1)

1　FORMAT GENERATOR

RESTORE

　　　SIMULATION OF RANDOM WALK

SPACE 2

　　　MAZE SIZE 4 BY 4

END OF FORMAT

lead to these developments. The RESTORE positions the printer for a new page. The heading SIMULATION OF RANDOM WALK is then printed, beginning at position 12 since this is where it begins in the program. Two lines will then be left blank and MAZE SIZE 4 BY 4 will be printed beginning in position 16. The output is thus arranged as layed out in the program itself.

Example A.4.

Numerical results may be displayed in selected patterns by using their earlier specifications slightly modified. Thus

WRITE (6, 1) (A(I), I = 1, 100)

1　FORMAT GENERATOR

'F3　　'F3　　'F3　　'F3

'F3　　'F3　　'F3

'F3　　'F3

'F3

REPEAT 4

END OF FORMAT

will generate a triangular pattern of potential interest to bowlers. Each value of A will be printed to three decimal places, the last digit appearing in the same column as the 3 shown in the program. The statement REPEAT 4 causes the preceding four lines to be imitated until all A(I) values have been accommodated. For a pattern requiring more than the 72 positions available on the coding sheet a second line may be used, with an X placed in position one.

Certain other statements not presented earlier include the following.

1. **The ASSIGNED GO TO.** This takes the form

$$\text{GO TO N, (I, J, K, } \ldots)$$

where $N, I, J, K, \ldots$ are statement numbers. Control will be transferred to statement $I, J, K, \ldots$ depending upon which of these numbers has last been assigned to the index N. Such an assignment is made by

2. **An ASSIGN statement** of the form

$$\text{ASSIGN num TO N}$$

where num denotes the desired statement number. For example, at some point in the program we may place the statement

$$\text{GO TO INDEX, (1, 2, 3, 10, 50)}$$

to effect a jump. If INDEX was last changed by

$$\text{ASSIGN 10 TO INDEX}$$

the jump will be to statement 10. The value of INDEX may later be changed, in which case the next execution of this GO TO would bring a jump to 1, 2, 3 or 50. Any name used for the index of an ASSIGN must not be used elsewhere in the same program in arithmetic activities, an ASSIGN being intended only for use with an assigned GO TO.

3. **The PAUSE statement.** This causes the computer to pause and wait. If the start button is then pushed, the computation resumes where it left off. This may offer the programmer a chance to think during execution of his program but is not popular at busy centers.

4. **The CALL EXIT statement.** This is a substitute for STOP and is required procedure at certain monitor controlled centers.

5. **The EQUIVALENCE statement.** This has the form

$$\text{EQUIVALENCE (A, B, C, } \ldots)$$

and results in variables $A, B, C, \ldots$ sharing the same memory location. This may be convenient if a programmer has written parts of a long program at different times using different names for what was intended to be the same variable. It may also be used to economize on memory space if two variables play nonconflicting roles in a program.

6. **The EXTERNAL statement.** This is used to indicate names of subprograms which appear as arguments in a CALL statement. Thus

$$\text{CALL RUTINE(A, B, PRIME)}$$

calls a subprogram named RUTINE. Suppose that PRIME is itself a subprogram. Then it should be identified as such by

$$\text{EXTERNAL PRIME}$$

which allows the compiler to distinguish this from an ordinary variable.

7. Certain statements such as BACKSPACE, END FILE, REWIND and certain modifications of READ and WRITE are available for the direct control of magnetic tape operations. The average programmer does not have much occasion to use them. Details are best found at the computing center being used.

Appendix II

Library Subprograms

The following subprograms are compiled as closed routines, the letters R, I, C, D denoting real, integer, complex and double-precision arguments respectively.

SQRT(R)	Real square roots of real numbers
CSQRT(C)	Complex square roots of complex numbers
DSQRT(D)	Double-precision square roots
SIN(R)	Sines of real numbers
CSIN(C)	Sines of complex numbers
DSIN(D)	Double-precision sines
COS(R)	Cosines of real numbers
CCOS(C)	Cosines of complex numbers
DCOS(D)	Double-precision cosines
TAN(R)	Tangents of real numbers
COTAN(R)	Cotangents of real numbers
ARSIN(R)	Arcsines of real numbers
ARCOS(R)	Arccosines of real numbers
ATAN(R)	Arctangents of real numbers
ATAN2(R1, R2)	Arctangent of R1/R2
DATAN(D)	Double-precision arctangents
DATAN(D1, D2)	Double-precision arctangent of D1/D2
EXP(R)	e to a real power
CEXP(C)	e to a complex power
DEXP(D)	Double-precision powers of e
ALOG(R)	Logarithms to base e
CLOG(C)	Complex logarithms to base e
DLOG(D)	Double-precision logarithms to base e
ALOG10(R)	Logarithms to base 10
DLOG10(D)	Double-precision logarithms to base 10
SINH(R)	Hyperbolic sines of real numbers
COSH(R)	Hyperbolic cosines of real numbers
TANH(R)	Hyperbolic tangents of real numbers
ERF(R)	The error function $(2/\sqrt{\pi}) \int_0^R e^{-t^2} dt$
GAMMA(R)	The gamma function $\int_0^\infty e^{-t} t^{R-1} dt$
ALGAMA(R)	Logarithm to base e of GAMMA(R)
CABS(C)	Absolute value of a complex number
DMOD(D1, D2)	The remainder in double-precision D1/D2

261

The following are usually compiled as open routines. The letters R, I, C, D have the same meaning as above.

IABS(I)	Integer absolute values
ABS(R)	Real absolute values
DABS(D)	Double-precision absolute values
ISIGN(I1, I2)	Absolute value of integer I1, with sign of I2
SIGN(R1, R2)	Absolute value of R1 with sign of R2
DSIGN(D1, D2)	Absolute value of D1 with sign of D2
INT(R)	Sign of R times largest integer less than R
AINT(R)	Same as INT(R) but output is in real mode
IDINT(D)	Same as INT but double-precision argument
MOD(I1, I2)	The remainder in I1/I2
AMOD(R1, R2)	The remainder in R1/R2
IFIX(R)	Converts number R to integer mode
FLOAT(I)	Converts integer I to real mode
SNGL(D)	Converts from double to single precision
DBLE(R)	Converts from single to double precision
REAL(C)	Takes real part of C
AIMAG(C)	Takes imaginary part of C
CMPLX(R1, R2)	Forms complex number (R1) + i(R2)
CONJG(C)	Forms complex conjugate of C
MAX0(I1, I2,..)	Finds maximum of integer arguments listed
MAX1(R1, R2,..)	Finds integer part of maximum argument listed
AMAX0(I1, I2,.)	Same as MAX0 but output is in real mode
AMAX1(R1, R2,.)	Finds maximum of real arguments listed
DMAX1(D1, D2,.)	Double-precision maximum
MIN0(I1, I2,..)	Same as MAX0 but finds minimum
MIN1(R1, R2,..)	Same as MAX1 but finds minimum
AMIN0(I1, I2,.)	Same as AMAX0 but finds minimum
AMIN1(R1, R2,.)	Same as AMAX1 but finds minimum
DMIN1(D1, D2,.)	Same as DMAX1 but finds minimum
IDIM(I1, I2)	I1 − MIN0(I1, I2)
DIM(R1, R2)	R1 − AMIN1(R1, R2)

Appendix III

Bibliography

Numerical Applications

1. Scheid, F.: "Theory and Problems of Numerical Analysis", Schaum's Outline Series, McGraw-Hill Book Company, New York, 1968. (A general introduction to methods available for the solution of numerical problems on computers)

Other Applications

2. Feigenbaum, E. A., and J. Feldman, editors: "Computers and Thought", McGraw-Hill Book Company, New York, 1963. (Articles on artificial intelligence including game playing, theorem proving, pattern recognition and learning)

3. Freiberger, W. F., and W. Prager, editors: "Applications of Digital Computers", Ginn and Co., 1963. (Articles on operations research, sorting, learning and other topics in science, medicine, law, etc.)

4. Gruenberger, F., and G. Jaffray: "Problems for Computer Solution", John Wiley & Sons, Inc., New York, 1965. (A collection of elementary problems to be programmed)

Programming

5. IBM 7090/7094 Programming Systems Fortran IV Language, Form C28-6274-3, IBM Corporation, 1964.

6. McCracken, D. D.: "A Guide to Algol Programming", John Wiley & Sons, Inc., 1962. (Another popular language for computers)

Historical and General

7. Arbib, M. A.: "Brains, Machines and Mathematics", McGraw-Hill Book Company, New York, 1964.

8. Bernstein, J.: "The Analytical Engine", Random House, 1963. (Nontechnical introduction)

9. Bowden, B. V.: "Faster Than Thought", Sir Isaac Pitman and Sons, 1953.

10. Morrison, P., and E. Morrison, editors: "Charles Babbage and His Calculating Engines", Dover Publications, 1961. (Selections from the writings of Babbage and others)

11. McCarthy, J.: Information; W. H. Freeman and Co., 1966. (Articles which appeared originally in the September 1966 issue of *Scientific American*)

12. Singh, J.: "Great Ideas in Information Theory, Language and Cybernetics", Dover Publications, 1966. (Introductory but up-to-date comparison of machines and the human brain)

13. Von Neumann, J.: "Collected Works", vol. 5, edited by A. H. Taub, The Macmillan Co., 1963. (The fundamental work of one of the most important pioneers)

Design of Computers

14. Bartee, T. C.: "Digital Computer Fundamentals", McGraw-Hill Book Company, New York, 1966. (Introductory, and contains a very extensive bibliography)

15. Boole, G.: "An Investigation of the Laws of Thought", London, 1854; reprinted by Dover Publications, 1954. (For its historical interest)

Answers to Supplementary Problems

CHAPTER 1

1.17.   156

1.18.   455

1.19.   20

1.20.   ACT, ATC, CAT, CTA, TAC, TCA

1.21.   (*a*) 010001   (*b*) 01010   (*c*) 0000

1.22.   (*a*) 110111   (*b*) 11111   (*c*) 1111

1.23.   (*a*) 001000   (*b*) 00000   (*c*) 0000

1.24.   (*a*) 0001   (*b*) 0010   (*c*) 0100 given   (*d*) 1000

1.25.   (*b*) and (*c*)

1.26.   1001

1.27.   Output always equals top input.

1.28.   Both output 0110.

1.30.   (*a*) One output is always hot, the other always cold.
        (*b*) The outputs duplicate the inputs.

CHAPTER 2

2.32.   01101, 01101, 11111 respectively

2.33.   100000

2.34.   011010

2.35.   5 and 6

2.36. $AB + \bar{A}\bar{B}$

2.37.   They are inverses.

2.38.   Yes

2.39.   18

2.40.   19

2.45.   37

2.46.   The left side.

2.47.   It computes $\bar{A}$.

2.48.   It computes $A + B$.

2.49.   It computes $\overline{A + B}$.

2.50.   It computes $(A + B + C)\overline{ABC}$.

CHAPTER 3

3.28. $\bar{C}D$, $\overline{C + \bar{D}}$, Theorem 2.11.

3.29.   1000100

3.30.   1*b*, 2*c*, 3*a*.

3.31.   Top to bottom: 3, 1, 2.

3.32.   (*a*) 1101111   (*b*) 0010000   (*c*) 0001010

3.33.   1*a*, 2*b*, $AB\bar{C}\bar{D} + A\bar{B}C\bar{D} + \bar{A}BC\bar{D} + A\bar{B}\bar{C}D + \bar{A}B\bar{C}D + \bar{A}\bar{B}CD$

3.34.   Exactly one: 1000000; exactly two: 0100100; exactly three: 0000001.

3.35. $A + A$, AA, $\bar{\bar{A}}$, $AB + A\bar{B}$, $A + AB$; all equal A itself.

264

3.36. $A + \bar{A} = I, \ A\bar{A} = 0.$

3.39. Number 6; $ABCD$.

3.40. 2, 3, 4, 7, 10; $A\bar{D} + \bar{A}D$.

3.41. The comparator.

3.42. 0001111001, 1000000010

3.43. Compute $(A + B)(C + D)$ and $\overline{A + B}$.

3.44. This subset equals I; all the prisoners belong.

3.48. They are equivalent; diagrams include all but the $\bar{A}B$ corner.

3.49. Compute $A + B$.

3.50. Compute $\overline{A + B}$.

3.51. They are equivalent by Theorem 2.24.

3.52. Theorem 2.34.

3.53. It computes $(A + B + C)\overline{ABC}$. See also Theorem 2.38.

3.54. $AB + AC + BC$

3.55. See Fig. 3-35 and Theorems 2.35 and 2.38.

3.56. The comparator.

3.59. Row 1: $AB\bar{C}\bar{D},\ AB\bar{C}D,\ \bar{A}B\bar{C}D,\ \bar{A}B\bar{C}\bar{D}$
Row 2: $ABC\bar{D},\ ABCD,\ \bar{A}BCD,\ \bar{A}BC\bar{D}$
Row 4: $A\bar{B}\bar{C}\bar{D},\ A\bar{B}\bar{C}D,\ \bar{A}\bar{B}\bar{C}D,\ \bar{A}\bar{B}\bar{C}\bar{D}$

3.60. Row 1: 3; none; 4, 7; 8
Row 2: none; 6; none; 5
Row 3: 10; none; none; 1
Row 4: 2; none; none; 9

3.61. Opium eaters never wear white kid gloves.

CHAPTER 4

4.68. (a) 23, (b) 30, (c) 27, (d) 51, (e) 56, (f) 35, (g) 240, (h) 204, (i) 170

4.69. (a) 7, (b) 15, (c) 31, (d) 63, (e) 127

4.70. (a) 1111, (b) 10100, (c) 11001, (d) 110010, (e) 1100100, (f) 10101001, (g) 11111111

4.71. (a) 1023, (b) 1048575, (c) $2^N - 1$

4.72. (a) 3/8, (b) 7/8, (c) 13/16, (d) 9/16, (e) 17/32, (f) 25/32

4.73. (a) .375, (b) .875, (c) .812, (d) .562, (e) .531, (f) .781

4.74. (a) .10101, (b) .00110, (c) .1111

4.75. (a) 27, (b) 36, (c) 33, (d) 63, (e) 70, (f) 43, (g) 360, (h) 314, (i) 252

4.76.

Decimal	Binary	Hexadecimal
12	1100	C
15	1111	F
187	10111011	BB
2748	101010111100	ABC
110	1101110	6E
43	101011	2B

4.77. (a) 00000001, (b) 10000001, (c) 00001111, (d) 10001111, (e) 00000000, (f) 11111111

4.78. (a) −64, (b) −42, (c) −112, (d) −76, (e) +51, (f) +85

4.79. (a) 10101111, (b) 11111111

4.80. All the sums are 1101.

4.81. All the sums are 111000.

4.82. It computes $(A + B)(\bar{A} + \bar{B})$ which equals $(A + B)\overline{AB}$ and so is a proper record, and also computes AB which is a proper carry.

4.83.   See Fig. A-1. Of each pair of values the upper one is for the present problem and the lower for Problem 4.84 which follows.

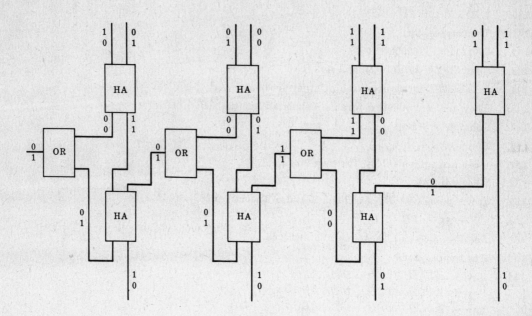

Fig. A-1

4.84.   0010

4.85.   15 decimal

4.86.   No; 10001

4.87.   31 decimal

4.88.   It computes $AB C + A \bar{B} \bar{C} + \bar{A} B \bar{C} + \bar{A} \bar{B} C$ for record and $ABC + AB\bar{C} + A\bar{B}C + \bar{A}BC$ for carry.

4.89. $AB + (A\bar{B} + \bar{A}B)C$

4.90.   Problem 3.57 on the three-way hall light.

4.91.   (a) 0110, (b) 0011, (c) 0111, (d) 0111

4.92.   (a) 110001, (b) 000101, (c) 010111

4.93.   COMP produces a correct record and $\bar{A}B$ is carry.

4.94. $(AC + \bar{A}\bar{C})B + \bar{A}C$

4.95.   Record is 01101001; borrow is 01110001.

4.96. $A\bar{C} + \bar{A}C = 01011010,\ \ AC + \bar{A}\bar{C} = 10100101,$ etc.

4.97.   It computes $ABC + A\bar{B}\bar{C} + \bar{A}B\bar{C} + \bar{A}\bar{B}C$ for record and $ABC + \bar{A}B\bar{C} + \bar{A}\bar{B}C + \bar{A}BC$ for borrow.

4.99.   Difference is 0110, with no overflow.

4.100.   Output is 1010 plus a hot overflow.

4.101.   Difference is 00111, with no overflow.

4.102.   (a) 01111, (b) 00111, (c) 10111, (d) 11111

4.103.   (a) Gate 3 yields 00001; (b) Gate 1 leads to 10001; (c) Gate 4 yields 00001; (d) Gate 1 leads to 10001.

4.104.   It produces minus zero.

4.105.   01001, Gate 1

4.106.   10011, Gate 3

4.107.   (a) +174, (b) −174

4.108.   (a) +0010, (b) −0010, (c) +001110, (d) −001110

4.109.   (a) 54, (b) 154, (c) 1702

4.111. In octal: (*a*) 120, (*b*) 1714, (*c*) 5777; in decimal: (*a*) 80, (*b*) 972, (*c*) 3071.

4.112. 0011

4.113. 1001

4.114. 1010

4.115. 1.0001

4.116. 1.0001

4.117. 11.010101...

4.118. (*a*) 0531000, (*b*) 0521000, (*c*) 0501000, (*d*) 0481000.

4.119. 0531001

4.120. 0521000

4.121. (*a*) 0 10000011 1000...   (*d*) 0 10000000 1000...
(*b*) 0 10000010 1000...   (*e*) 0 01111111 1000...
(*c*) 0 10000001 1000...

4.122. (*a*) 0 01111100 1100110..., (*b*) 0 10000000 1110111..., (*c*) 0 10000000 1110000...

4.123. 0 10000000 1110110... or 0 10000000 1110111... if rounded up.

4.124. 0 10000001 1110011... or 0 10000001 1110100... if rounded up.

4.125. 0 01111100 1011001... or round up.

4.126. 180,000

4.127. 4096×36

4.128. 64 rows, 64 columns, 000000 to 111111, 12.

4.129. 262,500

4.130. Last character should be an E.

4.132. Top to bottom: 111, 110, 101, 100, 011, 010, 001, 000.

CHAPTER 5

5.22. All the details appear in Problems 5.1 to 5.10.

5.23. The error makes instruction 7, as well as 8, a conditional jump; both are refused since the content of the accumulator is positive. The machine punches out X_1 and stops.

5.24. Instruction 7 then brings a jump to location 15. As an instruction the content of 15 means stop.

5.25. The sequence 000000001 would be copied into location 15. The machine then punches out X_1 and stops.

5.26. No effect at all.

5.27. The sum $X_1 + X_2 + \cdots + X_{16}$ would be computed and punched out. Debugging might begin by checking the actual final count, though alternatives certainly exist.

5.28. Including the final count in the output information is a useful safeguard. See Problem 5.18.

5.29. The computation would run normally and the correct sum would be punched out, followed by a mysterious second output sequence, the content of location 0.

5.30. The content of location 16 would never change. The program would run its 32 cycles and output 000000000.

5.31. The consequences are the same as in Problem 5.30 and the output is again 000000000.

5.32. There would be an overflow signal when instruction 2 was modified from 011111111 to 000000000. Computation would stop on the next execution of this instruction, after a total running time of about eight minutes.

5.33. Results similar to those in preceding problem.

5.34. Location 15; 000101101, or decimal 45.

5.35. More than one arrangement is possible, the following being an example.

51	100010011	Punch an X number	57	000000000	Stop
52	001111110		58	001110011	
53	010010010	Count	59	010010010	Modify the punch instruction
54	011111110		60	011110011	
55	111001111	Subtract 32	61	101110011	Jump to location 51
56	110111010	Jump (if) to location 58	62	000000000	Count

5.36.   Add Fig. A-2 to the chart of Fig. 5-2, after the "Punch sum" box, first deleting the stop from this box.

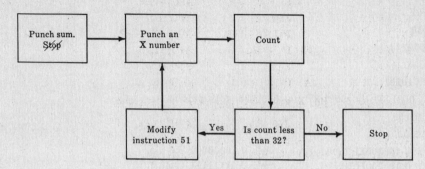

Fig. A-2

5.37. | 8 | 100010000 | 51 | 110110101 | 54 | 010010010 |
         | 9 | 111001111 | 52 | 000000000 | 55 | 011000111 |
         | 10 | 101110011 | 53 | 001000111 | 56 | 101001011 |

5.38.   See Fig. A-3.

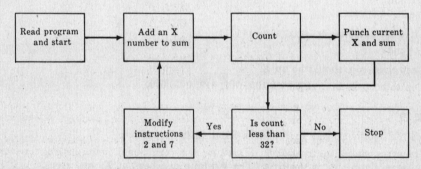

Fig. A-3

5.40. | 8 | 010010010 | 53 | 100010000 | 57 | **111001111** |
         | 9 | 011111100 | 54 | 100010001 | 58 | **110001011** |
         | 10 | 101110011 | 55 | 011111100 | 59 | 000000000 |
         | 52 | 110001011 | 56 | 001010001 | | |

5.42.

Location	Sequence	Location	Sequence
2	011111111	11	000000000
3	001000000	12	001000001
4	111111111	13	010010011
5	110001100	14	011000001
6	001111111	15	001001010
7	111000000	16	010010011
8	110001100	17	011001010
9	100111111	18	101000001
10	100101001	19	000000001

5.44.

Location	Sequence	Location	Sequence
2	010101001	11	010010101
3	011110011	12	011000001
4	001010100	13	001000010
5	010010101	14	010010101
6	011010100	15	011000010
7	111010110	16	001000011
8	110001010	17	010010101
9	000000000	18	011000011
10	001000001	19	101000001

5.46.

Location	Sequence	Location	Sequence	Location	Sequence
3	110001011	9	100010110	15	010010111
4	001010101	10	000000000	16	011000010
5	010010111	11	001100000	17	001001011
6	011010101	12	011010110	18	010010111
7	111011000	13	101000100	19	011001011
8	110001110	14	001000010	20	101000001

3.36. $A + \bar{A} = I,\ A\bar{A} = 0$.

3.39. Number 6; $ABCD$.

3.40. 2, 3, 4, 7, 10; $A\bar{D} + \bar{A}D$.

3.41. The comparator.

3.42. 0001111001, 1000000010

3.43. Compute $(A + B)(C + D)$ and $\overline{A + B}$.

3.44. This subset equals I; all the prisoners belong.

3.48. They are equivalent; diagrams include all but the $\bar{A}B$ corner.

3.49. Compute $A + B$.

3.50. Compute $\overline{A + B}$.

3.51. They are equivalent by Theorem 2.24.

3.52. Theorem 2.34.

3.53. It computes $(A + B + C)\overline{ABC}$. See also Theorem 2.38.

3.54. $AB + AC + BC$

3.55. See Fig. 3-35 and Theorems 2.35 and 2.38.

3.56. The comparator.

3.59. Row 1: $AB\bar{C}\bar{D},\ AB\bar{C}D,\ \bar{A}B\bar{C}D,\ \bar{A}B\bar{C}\bar{D}$
Row 2: $ABC\bar{D},\ ABCD,\ \bar{A}BCD,\ \bar{A}BC\bar{D}$
Row 4: $A\bar{B}\bar{C}\bar{D},\ A\bar{B}\bar{C}D,\ \bar{A}\bar{B}\bar{C}D,\ \bar{A}\bar{B}\bar{C}\bar{D}$

3.60. Row 1: 3; none; 4, 7; 8
Row 2: none; 6; none; 5
Row 3: 10; none; none; 1
Row 4: 2; none; none; 9

3.61. Opium eaters never wear white kid gloves.

CHAPTER 4

4.68. (a) 23, (b) 30, (c) 27, (d) 51, (e) 56, (f) 35, (g) 240, (h) 204, (i) 170

4.69. (a) 7, (b) 15, (c) 31, (d) 63, (e) 127

4.70. (a) 1111, (b) 10100, (c) 11001, (d) 110010, (e) 1100100, (f) 10101001, (g) 11111111

4.71. (a) 1023, (b) 1048575, (c) $2^N - 1$

4.72. (a) 3/8, (b) 7/8, (c) 13/16, (d) 9/16, (e) 17/32, (f) 25/32

4.73. (a) .375, (b) .875, (c) .812, (d) .562, (e) .531, (f) .781

4.74. (a) .10101, (b) .00110, (c) .1111

4.75. (a) 27, (b) 36, (c) 33, (d) 63, (e) 70, (f) 43, (g) 360, (h) 314, (i) 252

4.76.

Decimal	Binary	Hexadecimal
12	1100	C
15	1111	F
187	10111011	BB
2748	101010111100	ABC
110	1101110	6E
43	101011	2B

4.77. (a) 00000001, (b) 10000001, (c) 00001111, (d) 10001111, (e) 00000000, (f) 11111111

4.78. (a) −64, (b) −42, (c) −112, (d) −76, (e) +51, (f) +85

4.79. (a) 10101111, (b) 11111111

4.80. All the sums are 1101.

4.81. All the sums are 111000.

4.82. It computes $(A + B)(\bar{A} + \bar{B})$ which equals $(A + B)\overline{AB}$ and so is a proper record, and also computes AB which is a proper carry.

4.83. See Fig. A-1. Of each pair of values the upper one is for the present problem and the lower for Problem 4.84 which follows.

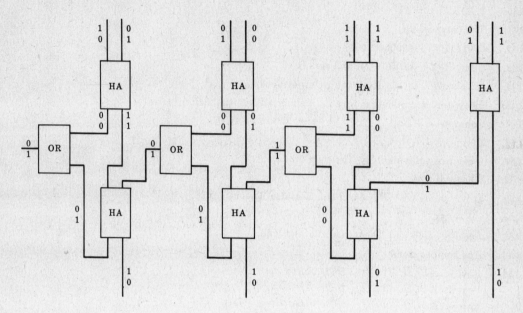

Fig. A-1

4.84. 0010

4.85. 15 decimal

4.86. No; 10001

4.87. 31 decimal

4.88. It computes $ABC + A\bar{B}\bar{C} + \bar{A}B\bar{C} + \bar{A}\bar{B}C$ for record and $ABC + AB\bar{C} + A\bar{B}C + \bar{A}BC$ for carry.

4.89. $AB + (A\bar{B} + \bar{A}B)C$

4.90. Problem 3.57 on the three-way hall light.

4.91. (a) 0110, (b) 0011, (c) 0111, (d) 0111

4.92. (a) 110001, (b) 000101, (c) 010111

4.93. COMP produces a correct record and $\bar{A}B$ is carry.

4.94. $(AC + \bar{A}\bar{C})B + \bar{A}C$

4.95. Record is 01101001; borrow is 01110001.

4.96. $A\bar{C} + \bar{A}C = 01011010, \ AC + \bar{A}\bar{C} = 10100101,$ etc.

4.97. It computes $ABC + A\bar{B}\bar{C} + \bar{A}B\bar{C} + \bar{A}\bar{B}C$ for record and $ABC + \bar{A}B\bar{C} + \bar{A}BC + \bar{A}\bar{B}C$ for borrow.

4.99. Difference is 0110, with no overflow.

4.100. Output is 1010 plus a hot overflow.

4.101. Difference is 00111, with no overflow.

4.102. (a) 01111, (b) 00111, (c) 10111, (d) 11111

4.103. (a) Gate 3 yields 00001; (b) Gate 1 leads to 10001; (c) Gate 4 yields 00001; (d) Gate 1 leads to 10001.

4.104. It produces minus zero.

4.105. 01001, Gate 1

4.106. 10011, Gate 3

4.107. (a) +174, (b) −174

4.108. (a) +0010, (b) −0010, (c) +001110, (d) −001110

4.109. (a) 54, (b) 154, (c) 1702

Chapter 14

Thinking, Learning and Intelligence

Do machines think? The difference of opinion on this question is substantial. On the one hand we hear the term "giant brain" being applied in efforts to provide a picturesque image of computers for popular consumption. In the same general spirit the term "biological computer" has crept into the vocabulary of computer science as synonymous with the human or animal brain. This sort of linking of the words computer and brain amounts to recognition that there are at least certain *similarities* between the two. It also represents a partial concession that computers do think, since thinking is, after all, a brain's principal function. But then on the other hand computers have been called "giant morons", machines which stupidly follow directions, sometimes long after any thinking device would realize that the directions are faulty. Machines are accused of having no originality, no creativity or talent for abstraction. In this case the critics are eager to point out the *differences* between computers and brains and perhaps to minimize the similarities. To them thinking is something more sacred. Both sides will, however, freely admit that the thought processes of the human brain are not very well understood so that there is no reason to become excessively dogmatic.

Similarities between computers and the brain are conspicuous and important. They are also intentional, since the human brain has designed the computer somewhat after its own image. More than one hundred years ago George Boole was studying "the laws of thought" (see Reference 15) and laying the foundations of Boolean Algebra. This mathematical structure, inspired in part by his interest in human brain activity, was shown in Chapter 4 to be central in the design of computer circuits. Many such circuits, adders for instance, imitate closely the way humans perform the same function. In overall organization there is also a strong similarity, and again it is intentional because machines have been created to solve problems formerly done by human beings. Thus the brain

(1) receives information

(2) remembers it

(3) operates on it

(4) outputs **information**

and so does the computer. In fact, this amounts to a compact description of the principal purpose of each. The use of the word memory for the storage unit of a computer is almost universal and amounts to general recognition that this particular machine capability is "brain-like". The use of the word thinking to describe a computer's arithmetical circuitry is not very common and this suggests both an awareness of substantial differences between machine and brain as well as, perhaps, a modest measure of human snobbishness.

Differences between computers and the brain are also both conspicuous and important. To begin, the nature of the materials from which the two are constructed is different. A computer is largely metallic, its simplest components being the OR, AND, NOT boxes discussed in Chapter 1. The brain, however, is made of biological material; its basic building block is the nerve cell or neuron which hardly at all resembles the black-box

13.21. The two outputs of a full-adder circuit as described in Chapter 4 may be expressed in Fortran as follows:

$$X = (A.OR.B).AND..NOT.(A.AND.B)$$
$$RECORD = (X.OR.C).AND..NOT.(X.AND.C)$$
$$CARRY = A.AND.B.OR.X.AND.C$$

Program the computation of these outputs for all A, B, C input combinations.

13.22. Replace the dots in this program fragment by a logical IF such that BIG proves to be the maximum of the numbers X(I).

$$BIG = X(1)$$
$$DO\ 1\ I = 2, N$$
$$\cdots\cdots\cdots$$
$$1\ CONTINUE$$

13.23. Use a logical IF to send control to statement number 10 provided that I is not zero, X does not equal Y, and Z exceeds 1. Accomplish the same thing with numerical IFs.

13.24. A baseball batter with average .300 comes to bat four times in a game. What are his chances of getting 0, 1, 2, 3, 4 hits respectively? Program a simulation to answer this question.

13.25. Fig. 13-4 shows a cross section of the lead shielding wall of a nuclear reactor. A neutron enters the wall at point E and then follows a random path of the same sort taken by the dog of Problem 13.11, a change of direction now being interpreted as a collision with an atom of lead. Suppose that after ten such collisions the neutron has lost its energy and stops. What percentage will reach the outside of the shield? Program a simulation to answer this question. Assume the wall endless to left and right.

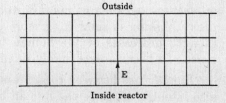

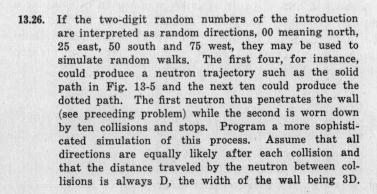

Fig. 13-4

13.26. If the two-digit random numbers of the introduction are interpreted as random directions, 00 meaning north, 25 east, 50 south and 75 west, they may be used to simulate random walks. The first four, for instance, could produce a neutron trajectory such as the solid path in Fig. 13-5 and the next ten could produce the dotted path. The first neutron thus penetrates the wall (see preceding problem) while the second is worn down by ten collisions and stops. Program a more sophisticated simulation of this process. Assume that all directions are equally likely after each collision and that the distance traveled by the neutron between collisions is always D, the width of the wall being 3D.

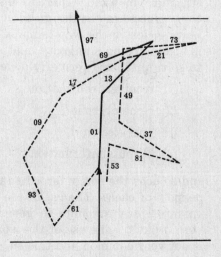

13.27. Program the simulation suggested in Problem 30.14 of Reference 1.

13.28. Program the simulation suggested in Problem 30.16 of Reference 1.

Fig. 13-5

13.29. Modify the golf program of Problem 13.14 to give from zero to eighteen strokes, the order of difficulty of the holes being 12, 4, 11, 9, 17, 2, 14, 7, 18, 5, 16, 1, 13, 3, 10, 6, 15, 8.

```
C     LEARNING BY EXPERIENCE
C     INITIAL PREPARATIONS
      DIMENSION IWIN(5)
      MUL = 5**15
      NUMC = 1
      LEVELC = 3*.85899345E92
      DO 1 J = 1,5
    1 IWIN(J) = 0
C     THIS DO CONTROLS THE VARIOUS STRATEGIES
      DO 4 J = 1,5
      LEVELR = (J − 1)*.85899345E92
C     THIS DO CONTROLS 10000 PLAYS
      DO 4 I = 1,10000
      NUMR = MUL*NUMC
      NUMC = MUL*NUMR
      IF (NUMR.LE.LEVELR) GO TO 3
      IF (NUMC.LE.LEVELC) GO TO 4
    2 IWIN(J) = IWIN(J) + 1
      GO TO 4
    3 IF (NUMC.LE.LEVELC) GO TO 2
      IWIN(J) = IWIN(J) − 2
    4 CONTINUE
C     WHICH STRATEGY WAS BEST
      M = 1
      DO 5 K = 2,5
      IF (IWIN(M).GE.IWIN(K)) GO TO 5
      M = K
    5 CONTINUE
C     SET LEVELR AT ITS BEST VALUE
      LEVELR = (M − 1)*.85899345E92
```

The pattern is similar to that of the preceding problem, there being a little more bookkeeping and less output. Instead of using a human opponent, and slowing down the action, column choices have also been determined by random numbers, the value of LEVELC being set for the best strategy. The machine thus provides its own competition. Five strategies are tried, row 1 being selected with probabilities 0, 1/4, 2/4, 3/4, 1 in turn. More could be accommodated with no difficulty. In each case 10,000 plays are made and IWIN(J) keeps track of the machine's current winnings. The maximum winnings IWIN(M) is then found and LEVELR is set for what appears to be optimum play. The last statement of this partial program thus becomes the first statement of the one in the preceding problem.

Refinements are clearly possible, such as searching the immediate neighborhood of the final LEVELR in the hope that a still better level can be found. For the present matrix, game theory suggests taking row 2 three times as often as row 1, and we have done the computer the favor of including this option among the five tested. Presumably it will find M = 2 and so agree with us. The deeper question of whether a computer can be taught to examine the results of many experiments of this sort and ultimately think its way through to an abstraction such as mathematical game theory is futuristic.

14.3. A trivial version of the game of checkers may serve to illustrate other aspects of machine learning. Fig. 14-1 shows a one-dimensional checkerboard of six squares. Checkers have been placed on the left three squares and are to be moved to the right three. The usual kinds

1	2	3	4	5	6
O	O	O			

Fig. 14-1

of moves are permitted, a simple move advancing a checker one square, a jump advancing it two squares, and a double-jump four. Only one player is involved, his challenge being to complete the advance with a minimum number of moves. What does this minimum appear to be?

After a small amount of experimenting it is easy to convince yourself that the minimum is five moves. One such advance begins by moving the leading checker to square 4. A double-jump then carries the trailing checker all the way to square 5. The last three moves may then be made in various ways. But is five moves really the minimum? Even for this midget board there are many possible ways to complete the advance. Is it not possible that one of them does the job in four moves? Clearly one way to answer this question is to examine every possibility, after which there can be no further doubt. This ideal method of proof is known as "the method of exhaustion" and we now proceed to program a computer to apply it to the present problem. The computer will thus be the first to learn what is actually the quickest advance. As will be seen, however, for a problem of any size, such as a slightly larger checkerboard, exhausting all the possibilities may very well exhaust the computer also.

14.4.   A systematic study of our checkerboard problem (Problem 14.3), and of its generalization to larger boards and more checkers, may begin with a listing of all positions the checkers could possibly occupy. For a still smaller version, involving just two checkers and a board of four squares, such a list is quickly found. ('T denotes an occupied square.)

TTFF   TFTF   TFFT   FTTF   FTFT   FFTT

Devise a routine for preparing such a list.

There are no doubt several routines available. A reasonably natural choice is illustrated in Table 14.1 for the case of three checkers and five squares.

1	TTTFF
2	TTFTF
3	TTFFT
4	TFTFT
5	TFTFT
6	TFFTT
7	FTTTF
8	FTTFT
9	FTFTT
10	FFTTT

Table 14.1

The leading checker is steadily advanced to the end of the board, generating a new position at each step. Upon reaching the end it is returned to the square next to its starting position, which has meanwhile been filled by the second checker. The advance of the leading checker is then repeated. When two or more checkers form a block at the right end of the board all are returned together to join the next checker, which has meanwhile been advanced one square. In this way all possible positions are eventually reached. The brief list above for a board of only four squares was produced by the same routine. Notice that what are really being generated here are the possible *combinations of occupied positions.*

14.5.   **Write a program to list all possible positions of K checkers on a board of N squares.** This amounts to listing all combinations of K things in a set of N.

The following program implements the routine described in Problem 14.4.

CHAPTER 6

6.6.

(B) COP An	SUB X	ADD ONE
STO ISITX	JIF (A)	STO (B)
COP X	PUN ISITX	COP (C)
SUB ISITX	(C) PUN Bn	ADD ONE
JIF (A)	STP	STO (C)
COP ISITX	(A) COP (B)	JUM (B)

The values for An, Bn, X and ONE must also be provided.

6.7.

(B) COP Xn	JIF (A)	ADD ONE
(C) ADD Yn	STP	STO (C)
(D) STO SUMn	(A) COP (B)	COP (D)
COP COUNT	ADD ONE	ADD ONE
ADD ONE	STO (B)	STO (D)
STO COUNT	COP (C)	JUM (B)
SUB TEN		

The values for Xn, Yn must be provided as well as ONE = 1, TEN = 10 and initially COUNT = 0.

6.8.

(E) COP MAX	JIF (B)	ADD ONE
(D) SUB Xn	PUN MAX	STO (D)
JIF (A)	STP	COP (A)
(C) COP COUNT	(A) COP Xn	ADD ONE
ADD ONE	STO MAX	STO (A)
STO COUNT	JUM (C)	JUM (E)
SUB NUMB	(B) COP (D)	

Initially MAX must be given the value of the number X1 and COUNT must be 0. In addition NUMB = 31, ONE = 1 and Xn must be associated with the numbers X2 to X32.

6.10. The compiler system uses a problem-oriented programming language, the assembler system a language oriented to a particular machine. In the former, instructions may thus represent more significant portions of the problem and this brings a reduction in the amount of fine detail which the programmer must consider. Compiler programs are thus shorter than assembler programs, from the user's point of view. The compiler processor is much larger than the assembler processor.

6.11. See text.

CHAPTER 7

7.30. Top row: R, R, I, R, I, R   Bottom row: All improper.

7.31. First three pairs; last pair mixes modes.

7.32. First column real; second column integers; third column improper: too long, slash, decimal point; fourth column improper: digit leads, *, +

7.33. $A + B^2$, $2AB$, A^{I+2}, $A + \dfrac{B}{C}$ or $A + (B/C)$, $2 + 3X$

7.34. Top row: 3*I + 4*J, N*(N + 1)/2, B*W/2. where a letter change is necessary to avoid mixed modes, 1./X**2, 1./(A + B)

Bottom row: 3.*A + 4.*B, 1. + 3.14*R**2, A*B + C*D, (1./A) + (1./B), X**2 + (2.*Y)**2

7.35. X**2 is real mode and 2 is integer mode; mixed modes; the parentheses do not come in pairs; (1./2.) was probably intended.

7.36. Top row: 16., 7., 121., 3.   Bottom row: 7., 12., 31., 6.5

7.37. 16. is stored as AL; 121. as BOB; 12. as CARL; and 31. as DAN.

7.38. A becomes 16., then B becomes 8., and finally AB (which is to be thought of as another variable and not as a product) becomes 16. − 16. = 0.

7.39. C = 1.2, A = 7., B = 12., C = 0., A = 12., B = 0.

7.40. The integers from 1 to 100 are again summed. Compare with Problem 7.14, noting that here the fourth and fifth statements are interchanged, so that the exits from the IF are altered and also 101 appears in place of 100.

7.41. The sum of the odd integers from 1 to 99.

7.42. Change the first statement to I = 2 and change the exits from the IF to read 1, 1, 2.

7.43. Leave the first five statements as they are. Then put

```
2 WRITE (6, 3) INTSUM
3 FORMAT (I10)
```

followed by STOP and END.

7.44. The product of the integers from 1 to 10.

7.45.
```
    J = 1
    DO 1 I = 1, 10
1   J = I*J
    WRITE (6, 3) J
3   FORMAT (I10)
    STOP
    END
```

7.46.
```
    SUM = 0.
    DO 1 I = 1, 100
    X = I
1   SUM = SUM + 1./X**2
    WRITE (6, 2) SUM
2   FORMAT (F10.6)
    STOP
    END
```

7.47.
```
    INTSUM = 0
    DO 1 I = 1, 99, 2
1   INTSUM = INTSUM + I
    WRITE (6, 2) INTSUM
2   FORMAT (I10)
    STOP
    END
```

7.48. With three separate data cards, the first being the

ssss.10sss3.00

of Fig. 7-9, the others   ssss.15sss3.00

ssss.20sss3.00

in that order. Also replace STOP by a GO TO the READ statement.

7.49. Specification 2I7 would read in the integers 123 and 45670, assuming that blank columns and zeros are considered the same for read-in purposes. I7, I6 is the correct specification. I9, I4 reads in 12300 and 4567. 2I6 reads in 12 and 300456.

7.50. Both specifications in the first column would actually be all right, because in the F specification the number may appear anywhere in the indicated field, not necessarily right-justified. This is also true for the E specification, but not for the I. The 2F7.1 would also work, blank columns being read as zeros. However, the 2F6.1 would read in 12.3 and 4., the second of these being incorrect.

7.51. All of these specifications are satisfactory except, of course, the one with the F's. In the E format the number may appear anywhere in the indicated field. Blank columns will be read as zeros.

7.52. FORMAT (I4, F10.6)

7.53. FORMAT (2I4, 2F10.5)

7.54. E14.8 is minimal. If a zero is always printed before the decimal point, making the present output

$$-0.12345678E-01$$

then specification E15.8 is needed. If several such numbers are to be printed on one line, with spaces between them to facilitate reading, then the 15 can be further increased.

7.55.

```
C FOR COMMENT
STATEMENT NUMBER | FORTRAN STATEMENT
         X = 1.
         SUM = 0.
    1    IF (10.-X) 3, 3, 2
    2    SUM = SUM + 1./X
         X = X+1.
         GO TO 1
    3    STOP
         END
```

7.56.

STATEMENT NUMBER	Cont.	FORTRAN STATEMENT
		X = 19.
1		Z = X-7.
		ROAD = SQRT (16.+Z**2) + SQRT (49.+(28./z)**2)
		WRITE (6,2) X,ROAD
2		FORMAT (2F7.2)
		IF (X-14.) 3,4,4
3		X = X+.01
		GO TO 1
4		STOP
		END

7.57.
```
      K = 1
      L = 1
      SUM = 0.
    1 A = K
      TERM = A/2.**K
      SUM = SUM + TERM
      L = L + 1
      K = K + 1
      IF (L − 5) 4, 4, 2
    4 GO TO 1
    2 WRITE (6, 3) SUM
    3 FORMAT (E15.7)
      IF (K − 30) 5, 5, 6
    5 L = 1
      GO TO 1
    6 STOP
      END
```

7.58.
```
      K = 1
      L = 1
      SUM = 0.
    1 A = K
      TERM = (−1.)**(K + 1)/(2.*A − 1.)
      SUM = SUM + 4.*TERM
      IF (L − 100) 2, 3, 3
    2 L = L + 1
      K = K + 1
      GO TO 1
    3 WRITE (6, 4) SUM
    4 FORMAT (E15.7)
      IF (K − 1000) 5, 6, 6
    5 L = 1
      K = K + 1
      GO TO 1
    6 STOP
      END
```

CHAPTER 8

8.31.   2, 8, 33

8.32.   This is one possibility:
```
      DIMENSION N(10)
      N(1) = 1
      DO 1 I = 1, 9
    1 N(I + 1) = I*N(I) + I**2
      WRITE (6, 2) (N(I), I = 1, 10)
    2 FORMAT (I10)
      STOP
      END
```

8.33.   1.2, 1.24, 1.248, 1.2496, 1.24992

8.34.   This is one possibility:
```
      DIMENSION Y(15)
      Y(1) = 1.0
      X = .2
      DO 1 I = 1, 14
    1 Y(I + 1) = Y(I) + X**I
      WRITE (6, 2) (I, Y(I), I = 1, 15)
    2 FORMAT (I3, F10.6)
      STOP
      END
```

8.35.
```
      DIMENSION Y(15)
      Y(1) = 1.0
      READ (5, 3) X
    3 FORMAT (F5.2)
      DO 1 I = 1, 14
    1 Y(I + 1) = Y(I) + X**I
      WRITE, FORMAT, STOP, END as in preceding problem
```

8.36.
```
      DIMENSION Y(15)
      Y(1) = 1.0
      X = .05
    4 DO 1 I = 1, 14
    1 Y(I + 1) = Y(I) + X**I
      WRITE (6, 2) (I, Y(I), I = 1, 15)
    2 FORMAT (I3, F10.6)
      X = X + .05
      IF (X − .5) 4, 4, 5
    5 STOP
      END
```

8.37.

0	1	1	1	1	1	1	1	0
0	1/2	1	1	1	1	1	1/2	0
0	1/2	3/4	1	1	1	3/4	1/2	0
0	3/8	3/4	7/8	1	7/8	3/4	3/8	0

8.38. The third, fifth, sixth, ninth and tenth statements were incomplete and should read as follows.

```
    1 A(1, J) = 1.
      A(I, 1) = 0.
    2 A(I, 9) = 0.
    3 A(I, J) = .5*(A(I − 1, J − 1) + A(I − 1, J + 1))
      WRITE (6, 4) ((A(I, J), J = 1, 9), I = 1, 77)
```

8.39.

0	1	1	1	1	1	1	1	0
0	5/6	1	1	1	1	1	5/6	0
0	13/18	35/36	1	1	1	35/36	13/18	0

8.40. The second, third, fourth, seventh, eighth and ninth statements were incomplete and should read as follows.

```
      DO 1 J = 1, 9
    1 A(1, J) = 1.
      DO 2 I = 2, 49
      DO 3 I = 2, 49
      DO 3 J = 2, 8
    3 A(I, J) = (A(I − 1, J − 1) + 4.*A(I − 1, J) + A(I − 1, J + 1))/6.
```

8.41.

1	5	10	10	5	1		
1	6	15	20	15	6	1	
1	7	21	35	35	21	7	1
1	8	28	56	70	56	28	8	1

8.42. (a) The four DO statements were incomplete and should read

```
      DO 1 I = 1, 20
      DO 2 I = 2, 20
      DO 2 J = 2, I
      DO 3 I = 1, 20
```

and STOP, END should be appended. The error is the I + 1 in the WRITE statement. This is an arithmetic expression, because of the +, and only constants or variables are allowed in this position. Replace it by IPLUS1, or some other integer name, and precede this statement by IPLUS1 = I + 1 to properly set the value of this new variable. (b) 20 rows. (c) Up to 12. (d) Two lines will be needed for each. (e) By making a preliminary estimate of the largest element and allowing adequate space for it.

8.43. (a) ss.123ss.456ss.789ss.012ss.345ss.678 etc.   (all ten numbers on one such card)

(b) ss.123ss.456ss.789ss.012ss.345   first card

ss.678ss.901ss.234ss.567ss.890   second card

8.44. sss75   first card
Other cards as in part 1 of preceding problem.

8.45. 100 cards for program at left, first three being

$$ss.333$$
$$ss.200$$
$$ss.143$$

10 cards for program at right, first three being

ss.333ss.200ss.143ss.111ss.099ss.077ss.067 etc.
ss.250ss.167ss.125ss.100ss.083ss.071ss.062 etc.
ss.200ss.143ss.111ss.099ss.077ss.067ss.059 etc.

the etc. meaning that the pattern continues until there are ten such values to a card.

8.46. The second, third, fifth and sixth statements are incomplete and should read

1 Y = (4. − X)*X**3/16.
WRITE (6, 2) X, Y
X = X + .01
IF (X − 2.) 1, 1, 3

8.47. Only the fifth statement needs to be changed, becoming

1 Y(I) = (4. − X(I))*X(I)**3/16.

8.48. ssss4sssssssss.1000000Es01   first card
sssssssss.4166667E−01sssssssss.1666667Es00sssssssss.5000000
(continued) Es00sssssssss.1000000Es01   second card
sssssssss.1000000Es01   third card

8.49. (a) **Degree 20.** (b) Conversion to noninteger mode. (c) **An empty card reader.** (d) By multiplying preceding term by X and dividing by A. (e) First five lines of output are

sssssss0.1000000Es01
ss1sssssss0.1000000Es 01sssssss0.2000000Es01
ss2sssssss0.5000000Es 00sssssss0.2500000Es01
ss3sssssss0.1666667Es 00sssssss0.2666667Es01
ss4sssssss0.4166667E−01sssssss0.2708334Es01

8.50. The second, fourth, fifth and sixth statements were incomplete and should read

READ (5, 11) N, (X(I), I = 1, N)
SUM = 0.
DO 1 I = 1, N
1 SUM = SUM + X(I)

8.51. Remove the number 1 from the statement SUM = SUM + X(I) and attach it to the WRITE.

8.52. Change the WRITE to   1 WRITE (6, 11) I, X(I), SUM
borrowing the number 1 as in the preceding problem.

8.53. Numbers are summed as long as they appear in the reader.

CHAPTER 9

9.10. These statements were incomplete. Also, STOP and END should be added.

READ (5, 1) N, (MAN(I), NUM(I), I = 1, N)
IF (MAXNUM − NUM(I)) 3, 2, 2
3 MAXNUM = NUM(I)
MAXMAN = MAN(I)
WRITE (6, 4) MAXMAN
4 FORMAT (21H THE BEST SALESMAN IS, I10)
5 FORMAT (14H HIS RECORD IS, I10)

9.11.   The READ, DO and all FORMATS are the same as in Problem 9.10, and STOP, END must be added.   Other incomplete statements were these:

IF (NUM(M) − NUM(I)) 3, 2, 2
2 CONTINUE
WRITE (6, 4) MAN(M)
WRITE (6, 5) NUM(M)

9.12.   The following were incomplete.   Also, STOP and END are to be added.

READ (5, 1) N, (A(I), I = 1, N)
NM1 = N − 1
DO 2 I = 1, NM1
DO 2 J = IP1, N
IF (A(I) − A(J)) 3, 2, 2
TEMP = A(I)
A(I) = A(J)
A(J) = TEMP

9.13.   Down through IP1 = I + 1 the statements are the same as in Problem 9.9.   At the finish the WRITE, FORMAT, STOP and END are also the same.   Other incomplete statements were these:

DO 2 J = IP1, N
IF (NUM(I) − NUM(J)) 3, 2, 2
3 ITEMP = NUM(I)
NUM(J) = ITEMP
MAN(I) = MAN(J)
MAN(J) = ITEMP

9.14.   Leave the **WRITE** as it is.   The **FORMAT** should read
11 FORMAT (35H ORDERED SALES RECORD FOR THE MONTH)

9.15.   WRITE (6, 11) NUM(M)
11 FORMAT (14H HIS RECORD IS, I10, 6H SALES)

9.16.   WRITE (6, 11) MAN(M), NUM(M)
11 FORMAT (15H THE TOP MAN IS, I10, 5H WITH, I10, 6H SALES)

9.17.   WINNERsISsssssss1492ssssssssssss HEsMADEssss162000sSALES

9.18.   I from columns 6 to 10; MAN(I) from columns 16 to 25; NUM(I) from columns 31 to 40.

9.19.   FORMAT (15X, E20.7)

9.20.   Two continuation lines are needed.   (Fig. A-4)

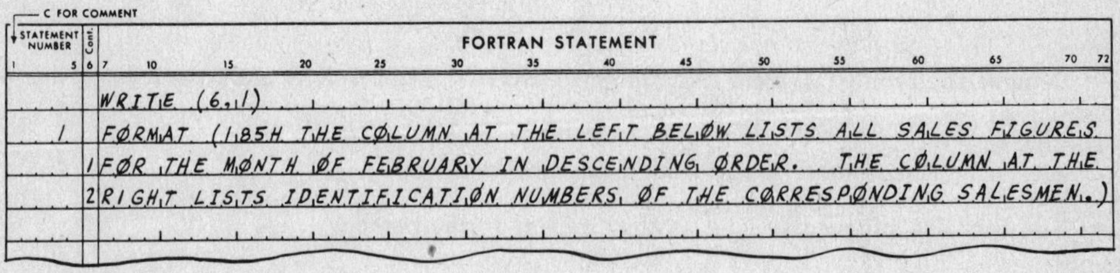

Fig. A-4

CHAPTER 10

10.8.   Delete old first, tenth and eleventh statements.

Add DO 5 I = 1, N after K = 0.

Replace statements numbered 5 and 7 by these:

5 CONTINUE
7 WRITE (6, 8) N

10.9. Change first IF to IF (MARK − 70) 5, 5, 4. Delete second IF. Change last FORMAT appropriately.

10.10. Change first IF to IF (MARK − 50) 4, 5, 5. Delete second IF. Change last FORMAT appropriately.

10.11. Replace first two statements by these.

$$\text{DIMENSION K(20)}$$
$$\text{DO 1 I = 1, 20}$$

Replace first two statements of classification loop.

$$\text{DO 11 I = 1, 20}$$
$$\text{LIM = 5*I}$$

Replace last output pair.
$$\text{WRITE (6, 8) (K(I), I = 1, 20)}$$
$$\text{8 FORMAT (20I6)}$$

10.12. The program could be left as it is, zero counts being printed for the missing candidates 4, 5, 6. Or five of the statements could be changed to eliminate these candidates: the first two, the second and third DO, and the last WRITE.

$$\text{DIMENSION K(3)}$$
$$\text{DO 1 I = 1, 3}$$
$$\text{DO 7 I = 2, 3}$$
$$\text{DO 10 I = 1, 3}$$
$$\text{WRITE (6, 13) (K(I), I = 1, 3)}$$

10.13. Replace the first and third statements.

$$\text{DIMENSION N(10, 5), M(10)}$$
$$\text{DO 1 J = 1, 5}$$

Make appropriate changes in FORMAT statements 8 and 10, and use J = 1, 5 in WRITE statement number 9.

10.14. Suppose I has just been raised to 4. These statements are then encountered, plus the unnumbered ones in between: 3, 1, 3, 1, 3, 2, 6, 6, 6, 5, 7, 1

The output takes this form:

sITOPs=ssss1ssssssIBOTs=ssss3			
ITOP =	6	IBOT =	9
ITOP =	11	IBOT =	12
ITOP =	16	IBOT =	19

10.15. (a) 7, 13, 19, 9, 11, 13, 12, 16, 18, 16, 18, 15, 9, 11, 13

(b) The output will be, using arbitrary student identification numbers and the same N = 800 of Problem 10.7,

STUDENTssssRANK	
001492	100.00
001620	99.87
001066	99.87
001969	99.87
016200	99.50

CHAPTER 11

11.15. By rows: 54902, 04, 12; 10701, 01, 07.

11.16.

I	1	2	3	4
KTOP(I)	1	2	4	9
KBOT(I)	1	3	7	9

Processing order: K1 = 1, K2 = 2, K3 = 4, K4 = 9.

Output: IDEN on one line; second line has 39701 in block 5, 10701 in block 7, 14901 in block 12 and 54901 in block 13.

11.17. For the order of processing read the following table row by row. The letter C means that a conflict is encountered at this point. The letter E means that KBOT has just been exceeded.

K1	K2	K3	K4
1	2	4F, 5F, 6F, 7	9C, 10E
		8E	
	3	4F, 5F, 6F, 7	9C, 10E
		8E	
	4E		
2E	(Here NPROC is 4 and we abandon course 4.)		
1	2	4F, 5F, 6F, 7	

11.18. The same layout used in the preceding answer is also used in the next six.

K1	K2	K3	K4
9	4F, 5F, 6F, 7C, 8E		
10E	(Here NPROC is 2 and we abandon course 2.)		
9		2	1

11.19.

K1	K2	K3	K4
4F, 5F, 6F, 7	1	9C, 10E	
	2E		
8E	(Here NPROC is 3 and we abandon course 3.)		
4F, 5F, 6F, 7	1		2

11.20.

I	1	2	3	4
KTOP(I)	4	8	2	9
KBOT(I)	7	8	3	9

K1	K2	K3	K4
4F, 5	8C, 9E		
6	8	2	9

11.21.

I	1	2	3	4
KTOP(I)	2	4	8	9
KBOT(I)	3	7	8	9

K1	K2	K3	K4
2	4F, 5	8C, 9E	
6	8		9

11.22.

I	1	2	3	4
KTOP(I)	8	4	9	2
KBOT(I)	8	7	9	3

K1	K2	K3	K4
8	4F, 5C, 6F, 7	9C, 10E	
	8E		
9E	(Here NPROC is 3 and we abandon course 3.)		
8	4F, 5C, 6F, 7		2

11.23. Only the top two choices can be registered.

K1	K2	K3	K4
9	4F, 5	1C, 2E	
	6F, 7C, 8E		
10E	(Here NPROC is 3 and we abandon course 3.)		
9	4F, 5		8C, 9E
	6F, 7C, 8E		
10E	(Here NPROC is 4 and we abandon course 4.)		
9	4F, 5		

11.24. This particular suggestion is not a good one, since reprocessing is often valuable to recover sections dismissed because of conflicts with other sections later to be abandoned. Improvements can, however, be found.

11.25. Another counter may be used, call it MASTER. Early in the program, when the KOUNT(K) are initialized at zero, we could include

$$MASTER = 0$$

to initialize this also. Then near the end, perhaps in the place of

$$GO\ TO\ 10$$

we could insert the following statements.

```
       MASTER = MASTER + 1
       IF (MASTER − 1000) 10, 511, 511
   511 MASTER = 0
       WRITE (6, 512) (NUMCOR(K), KOUNT(K), K = 1, N)
   512 FORMAT (1X, I5, I5)
       GO TO 10
```

CHAPTER 12

12.16.
```
       FUNCTION SUM(X, N)
       DIMENSION X(N)
       SUM = 0.
       DO 1 I = 1, N
       SUM = SUM + X(I)
     1 CONTINUE
       RETURN
       END
```

12.17.
```
       DIMENSION A(50)
       READ (5, 1) (A(I), I = 1, 50)
     1 FORMAT (F10.5)
       AVE = SUM(A, 50)/50.
       WRITE (6, 2) AVE
     2 FORMAT (1X, F10.5)
       STOP
       END
```

12.18. It computes the real roots of the quadratic equation $AX^2 + BX + C = 0$ and sets $I = 0$, provided that real roots exist. Otherwise it sets $I = 1$.

12.19. Since $D = -8$ the subroutine sets $I = 1$. Exit 5 of the main program then leads to the next action.

12.20. It converts K to real mode and also avoids disturbing the stored value of that integer variable.

12.21.
```
       IF (PIVOT-ABS(X(NR, I))) 2, 1, 1
     2 PIVOT = ABS(X(NR, I))
     1 CONTINUE
       RETURN
       END
```

12.22.
```
       TRAP = Y(1) + Y(N + 1)
       DO 1 I = 2, N
     1 TRAP = TRAP + 2.*Y(I)
       TRAP = TRAP*H/2.
       RETURN
       END
```

12.23. N = 8

An appropriate program is:
```
      DIMENSION Y(100), T(100)
      T(1) = .7854
      N = 2
    5 NPLUS1 = N + 1
      H = 1.5708/FLOAT(N)
      DO 1 I = 1, NPLUS1
    1 Y(I) = SIN(H*FLOAT(I − 1))
      T(N) = TRAP(Y, NPLUS1, 0., 1.5708)
      WRITE (6, 2) N, T(N)
    2 FORMAT (I4, E20.7)
      IF (ABS(T(N) − T(N − 1)) − .001) 3, 3, 4
    4 N = N + 1
      GO TO 5
    3 STOP
      END

      FUNCTION TRAP(Y, NPLUS1, A, B)
      DIMENSION Y(NPLUS1)
      N = NPLUS1 − 1
      H = (B − A)/FLOAT(N)
      TRAP = Y(1) + Y(N + 1)
      DO 1 I = 2, N
    1 TRAP = TRAP + 2.*Y(I)
      TRAP = TRAP*H/2.
      RETURN
      END
```

12.24. 57 loads

An appropriate program is:
```
      DIMENSION X(100)
      N = 1
      X(1) = 1.
    3 S = SUM(X, N)
      WRITE (6, 6) N, S
    6 FORMAT (I4, E20.7)
      IF (S − 3.0) 1, 2, 2
    1 N = N + 1
      AN = N
      X(N) = 1./(2.*AN − 1.)
      GO TO 3
    2 STOP
      END

      FUNCTION SUM(X, N)
      DIMENSION X(N)
      SUM = 0.
      DO 1 I = 1, N
      SUM = SUM + X(I)
    1 CONTINUE
      RETURN
      END
```

12.25. The dots should be replaced by these statements.
```
      T0 = T0 + Y(I)
    1 T1 = T1 + X(I)*Y(I)
      A = (S0*T1 − S1*T0)/(S0*S2 − S1**2)
      B = (S2*T0 − S1*T1)/(S0*S2 − S1**2)
```

12.26. 3.76, 3.85, 3.94, 4.03, ..., 4.57

12.27.
```
      DO 1 K = 1, N
    1 C(I, J) = C(I, J) + A(I, K)*B(K, J)
      RETURN
      END
```

12.28. Exact result would be $\begin{pmatrix} 1 & 0 & 0 \\ 0 & 1 & 0 \\ 0 & 0 & 1 \end{pmatrix}$.

12.29. The exact answer, using the matrix A of Problem 12.28, would be X(1) = 9, X(2) = −36, X(3) = 30. Using the rounded-off matrix as given, one obtains instead X(1) = 7.0, X(2) = −23, X(3) = 17 approximately. The serious errors are due to the "near-singularity" of the A matrix. (See Reference 1, Chapter 26 and page 247 for further details.)

12.30. 1.259921049 to nine places

12.31. 2.7182818 to seven places

12.32. Too many terms of the series are needed for a comfortable computation.

12.33. 3.14159264 to eight places

12.34. 2.43281×10^{18}

12.37. Variables A, B, C, I, SUM, PROD are assigned to the first six locations of common storage.

12.38. Variables I, J are assigned to the first two locations of common storage. The elements of array A are given the next 100 locations followed by 5 locations for the much smaller array B. Finally SUM is assigned the 108th location.

12.39. COMMON I, J, A(10, 10), B(5), SUM

12.40. The values of array B will be the same as A(1) to A(10) since these names refer to the same ten locations in common storage. Similarly the values of array C will be the same as A(11) to A(20).

12.41. ALPHA, BETA, GAMMA will refer to the same common storage locations as A, B, C. KOUNT1, KOUNT2, INTSUM, ISODSQ will refer to the same locations as I, J, K, L.

12.42. KOUNT1, KOUNT2 will refer to the same common storage locations as I, J. The elements of ARRAY will be in the same places as those of A.

CHAPTER 13

13.15. Follow the model of Problem 13.5, computing and outputting the values of both expressions.

13.16. Final results should be these:

A	F	F	T	T
B	F	T	F	T
A.AND.B	F	F	F	T
A.AND..NOT.B	F	F	T	F
.NOT.A.AND.B	F	T	F	F
.NOT.A.AND..NOT.B	T	F	F	F

13.17. Follow the model of Problem 13.4.

13.18. Yes

13.19. sTsTsF

13.20. Follow the model of Problem 13.5.

13.21. Follow the model of Problem 13.4.

13.22. IF (BIG.LT.X(I)) BIG = X(I)

13.23. IF (I.NE.0.AND.X.NE.Y.AND.Z.GT.1.)

13.24. The theoretical values are
$$.2401, .4116, .2646, .0756, .0081$$

13.25. Modify the program of Problem 13.11.

13.26. About 28 percent of the electrons get through. A much thicker wall would make for a more realistic problem.

INDEX